TRAGEDY IN OVID

Ovid is today best known for his grand epic, *Metamorphoses*, and elegiac works like the *Ars amatoria* and *Heroides*. Yet he also wrote a *Medea*, now unfortunately lost. This play kindled in him a lifelong interest in the genre of tragedy, which informed his later poetry and enabled him to continue his career as a tragedian – if only on the page instead of the stage. This book surveys tragic characters, motifs, and modalities in the *Heroides* and the *Metamorphoses*. In writing love letters, Ovid's heroines and heroes display their suffering in an epistolary theater. In telling transformation stories, Ovid offers an exploded view of the traditional theater, although his characters never stray too far from their dramatic origins. Both works constitute an ***intra***textual network of tragic stories that anticipate the theatrical excesses of Seneca and reflect the all-encompassing spirit of Roman *imperium*.

DAN CURLEY is Associate Professor of Classics at Skidmore College.

TRAGEDY IN OVID

Theater, Metatheater, and the Transformation of a Genre

DAN CURLEY

Skidmore College

CAMBRIDGE
UNIVERSITY PRESS

CAMBRIDGE
UNIVERSITY PRESS

University Printing House, Cambridge CB2 8BS, United Kingdom

Published in the United States of America by Cambridge University Press, New York

Cambridge University Press is part of the University of Cambridge.

It furthers the University's mission by disseminating knowledge in the pursuit of education, learning and research at the highest international levels of excellence.

www.cambridge.org
Information on this title: www.cambridge.org/9781107009530

First published 2013

Printed by CPI Group (UK) Ltd, Croydon CR0 4YY

A catalogue record for this publication is available from the British Library

Library of Congress Cataloguing in Publication data
Curley, Dan, 1966–
Tragedy in Ovid : theater, metatheater, and the transformation of a genre /
Dan Curley, Skidmore College.
pages cm
Includes bibliographical references and index.
ISBN 978-1-107-00953-0 (hardback)
1. Ovid, 43 B.C.–17 A.D. or 18 A.D. – Criticism and interpretation.
2. Tragedy – History and criticism. I. Title.
PA6537.C87 2013
871′.01–dc23 2013009509

ISBN 978-1-107-00953-0 Hardback

Additional resources for this publication at www.cambridge.org/curley

Contents

Preface

This book, a study of tragic theatricality in Ovid's *Heroides* and *Metamorphoses*, has its origins in my doctoral dissertation (University of Washington, 1999). Although the intervening period of rereading, rethinking, and revising has been long, the result is the book I wanted to write. Whether the end is justified is naturally for the reader to decide.

Ovidian studies have changed during this time, and for the better. When I began work on this topic in the mid-1990s, the reclamation of Ovid as a major Augustan poet was already well under way. This effort continued into the new millennium with major companion volumes from Cambridge, Brill, and Blackwell, the long-awaited Oxford Classical Texts edition of the *Metamorphoses* (Tarrant 2004), and that poem's new, six-volume commentary overseen by Alessandro Barchiesi (2005–). Yet for all the shoring up of Ovid's reputation, there remains room for a comprehensive treatment of his engagement with the genre of tragedy. The same scholarly industry that heralds or affirms an author as a classic also signals that it is time to move on. In the case of Ovid, it would be a shame to heed that call without a fuller appreciation of his aspirations to be a tragic poet, in addition to being a consummate poet of elegy and epic.

The seven chapters of *Tragedy in Ovid* cover different aspects of the genre, whether actual plays or poetry indebted to tragedy. Chapter 1 establishes the critical bearings for reading "the tragic." Chapter 2 focuses on the lost *Medea*, Ovid's first attempt to be a tragedian, in light of Roman dramaturgical tradition and practice. Chapter 3 posits the *Heroides* as the poet's next best alternative to writing tragedy and identifies key aspects of the genre on display both there and in the *Metamorphoses*, the main subject of the next three chapters. Chapter 4 discusses manipulation of space and time in the epic with an eye toward the tragic stage; Chapter 5, the epic's tragic monologues; Chapter 6, its comprehensive network of tragic heroes and heroines, which also incorporates the *Heroides*. Chapter 7 offers some conclusions on Ovid as a tragic poet of the imperial age, particularly his intermediary stance between Vergil and Seneca. Each chapter may be read on its own, but the book overall is cumulative, much like the poet's approach to tragedy over the course of his career.

A few words on references, editions, quotations, and translations. All references to commentaries, unless otherwise noted, are *ad locum* (or *loca*). That is, they cite an editor's comments on the passage or passages in question without numerical indicators. If, however, the comments appear elsewhere – e.g., in notes on a different passage or prefacing a new section of the text – their location is usually given in parentheses: thus "Anderson 1972 (after *Met.* 7.349)" references remarks found after his note on line 349 of *Met.* 7. The only instances in which I cite a commentary by page number are when referring to the editor's introduction or to an appendix.

In this study I regularly cite the following editions. Ovid: *Metamorphoses*, Tarrant 2004; *Heroides*, Showerman and Goold 1977; *Amores*, McKeown 1987; *Tristia*, Luck 1967. Greek tragedies: *Agamemnon*, Denniston–Page 1957; *Hecabe*, Collard 1991; *Hippolytus*, W. S. Barrett 1964; *Iphigenia at Aulis*, Murray 1913; *Medea*, Page 1938; *Trachiniae*, Davies 1991. Roman tragedies: Sen. *Medea*, Costa 1973; *Thyestes*, Tarrant 1985; fragments of the Roman tragedians, including Ovid, Klotz 1953 (*SRF*, vol. 1). Quotations from the text of these editions are so ubiquitous that I do not mention the editors by name, as I do when quoting other texts and authors. Naturally, I have made use of other editions, and textual departures from those listed above are noted as necessary.

In quotations I employ a system of underlining, developed by Clauss 1993, which facilitates the comparison of two or more allusive passages. Single underlining in one passage denotes a word or words that appear verbatim in a second passage, the citation of which follows. Double underlining denotes a word or words appearing verbatim in a third passage, which is cited after the second passage. Dashed underlining denotes a word or words that differ, however significantly or slightly, from passage to passage.

All Greek and Latin is translated or closely paraphrased; the renderings, which strive to balance the literal and the figurative, are usually mine. Subsequent quotations of a previously quoted Greek or Latin passage are typically given without translation. In such cases I direct the reader to the first, translated quotation.

I have many debts of gratitude to acknowledge. I begin by thanking above all Stephen Hinds, the director of the original dissertation and astute reader of subsequent revisions, whose support and mentoring over the years have been indispensable and unwavering. I also thank Catherine Connors and Michael Halleran, whose comments on the original dissertation guided its revision, and Alison Keith and Denis Feeney for their insights as the book developed.

Thanks to Michael Sharp, Senior Editor at Cambridge University Press, and to Gillian Dadd, Assistant Editor. Thanks also to my anonymous readers, particularly "A," whose criticism was both constructive and useful at every juncture. I am grateful to Rob Wilkinson and Annie Jackson at Out of House Publishing Solutions (on behalf of Cambridge University Press) for editorial guidance and assistance during the production phase. To say that any errors or omissions are ultimately my own responsibility is a timeless *topos*, but no less true or necessary.

I want to thank my partners in Classics at Skidmore College – Michael Arnush, Ruby Grande, Leslie Mechem, Jackie Murray, David Porter, and Jessica Westerhold – for their advice, assistance, and encouragement. I am also grateful to the Office of the Dean of the Faculty for awarding two sabbatical leaves (2004–2005, fall 2012) to work on the book and for supporting travel to conferences and ancient theatrical sites. Profuse thanks to the Interlibrary Loan Department at Lucy Scribner Library for meeting my requests time and again; teacher-scholars at small colleges know that my gratitude here is fully warranted. Thank you to Amari Boyd, my research assistant, for help in organizing secondary sources and proofing the final typescript.

It is a pleasure to thank the Loeb Classical Library Foundation for its generous financial support, which allowed me to devote a full year of leave to this project. Thank you to Special Collections, University of Vermont, especially Jeffrey Marshall, Director of Research Collections, and Sharon Thayer, Collections Specialist, for supplying the cover image of Medea (by Abraham Aubry, after Johann Wilhelm Baur). In addition, Mr. Marshall hospitably granted me access to several illustrated volumes of the *Metamorphoses*, which helped to drive home for me the visuality of Ovid's poetry. I am very grateful to Giulia Bartrum, Curator of German Prints and Drawings at the British Museum, for assistance in confirming the dates of two different Baur–Aubry editions.

I have had opportunities to present on Ovid and tragedy in professional venues since completing the dissertation. I learned much from audiences and co-presenters at the University of Nottingham (2000), Skidmore (2000), the Langford Latin Seminar (2001), the American Philological Association (2001), the Classical Association of the Atlantic States (spring 2001), the Pacific Rim Roman Literature Seminar (2001 and 2004), the

Classical Association of the Empire State (2009), and the University of Vermont (2010).

It would be remiss of me not to acknowledge my Skidmore seminars on the *Metamorphoses*, in which I shared some of my ideas with groups of interested and talented undergraduates. Let me single out two students by name, Andy Cabell (fall 2005) and Claire Saxe (fall 2010), whose own projects on Ovid buoyed my faith in this project.

Over the years friends and acquaintances have shaped my perspectives in ways great and small, although hopefully not too small for them to remember: Antonios Augoustakis, Michael Clapper, Anne Duncan, Kendra Eshleman, David Fitzpatrick, John Franklin, Laurel Fulkerson, Jenny March, Lily Panoussi, Alan Sommerstein, and Andrew Zissos. Thank you one and all.

Finally, although the book has been transformed many times over, one thing remains constant and true: my devotion to my wife, Krista Anders, and to our daughter, Kaitlin, who has grown up alongside the project. Without their love, patience, and support it would never have been completed. It is to them I dedicate the book now, *pignus amoris non mutandi.*

Abbreviations

CAF	Kock, T. (ed.) (1880–8) *Comicorum Atticorum Fragmenta*, 3 vols. Leipzig.
EGF	Davies, M. (ed.) (1988) *Epicorum Graecorum Fragmenta.* Göttingen.
LIMC	(1981–) *Lexicon Iconographicum Mythologiae Classicae.* Zurich.
LSJ	Liddell, H. G., R. Scott, H. S. Jones, and R. McKenzie (eds.) (1996) *A Greek–English Lexicon.* Oxford.
NTDAR	Richardson, L. (1992) *A New Topographical Dictionary of Ancient Rome.* Baltimore, Md.
OCD[2]	Hammond, N. G. L. and H. H. Scullard (eds.) (1970) *The Oxford Classical Dictionary.* 2nd edn. Oxford.
OED	Simpson, J. A. and E. S. C. Weiner (eds.) (1989) *The Oxford English Dictionary.* Oxford.
OLD	Glare, P. G. W. (ed.) (1982) *Oxford Latin Dictionary.* Oxford.
SRF	Klotz, A. (ed.) (1953) *Scaenicorum Romanorum Fragmenta.* 2 vols. Vol. I. *Tragicorum Fragmenta.* Munich.
TGF[2]	Nauck, A. (ed.) (1964) *Tragicorum Graecorum Fragmenta.* 2nd edn. Hildesheim.
TrGF	*Tragicorum Graecorum Fragmenta.* Göttingen. Snell, B. (ed.) (1971) Vol. I. *Poetae Minores.* Kannicht, R. and B. Snell (eds.) (1981) Vol. II. *Adespota.* Radt, S. (ed.) (1985) Vol. III. *Aeschylus.* Radt, S. (ed.) (1999) Vol. IV. *Sophocles.* 2nd edn. Kannicht, R. (ed.) (2004) Vols. V.1 and V.2. *Euripides.*

CHAPTER ONE

Mutatas dicere formas

The transformation of tragedy

At the climax of Seneca's *Medea*, the protagonist-heroine does something surprising – not for a Medea, perhaps, but surprising in comparison with her Euripidean counterpart, whom the Senecan audience would have remembered. Euripides' Medea appears atop the *skēnē*, her sons already slain within, their corpses stowed aboard the chariot of Helios (1317–22). Seneca's Medea, however, kills one child in front of her house, bears the corpse to the roof, kills the other child, and finally hurls the bodies to the stage, from where Jason has been watching (967–1027).[1]

The actions of both Medeas, so starkly different in their presentation of violence, illustrate how far the genre of tragedy had come over the course of nearly 500 years. Nevertheless, the road from Euripides to Seneca is an extremely lacunary one: from the death of the former to the *floruit* of the latter, no Greek or Latin tragedies have survived intact (with the lone and notable exception of the *Rhesus*). The extant fragments and *testimonia* are of course invaluable, but they cannot by themselves bridge the gap between fifth-century BCE Athens and first-century CE Rome.

Enter Publius Ovidius Naso. An admirer and author of tragedy, Ovid occupies a vital, if underappreciated, place in the history of the genre. *Tragedy in Ovid* offers an assessment of the poet's contributions to tragedy in the context of prior dramaturgical tradition, his own times and career, and the later principate. The premise is plain enough. However, those who consider Ovid a specialist in elegy or epic might well ask why he should be considered a tragedian, let alone an influential one, with only a single play to his name. In a sense, this question is the inverse of one that critics have asked about the career of Shakespeare, namely whether he should be considered a poet in addition to a dramatist. Nevertheless, the "Shakespearean question" implies a dichotomy between the literary and the professional – between the laureate and the "jobbing playwright" – that would have been

[1] On the logistics of staging of this scene see Hine 2000, 41–2.

rather alien to poets of Ovid's era, who were accustomed to compose in different genres.[2] To call Ovid a tragedian is both to call him a poet and to highlight an aspect of his poetic career often overlooked in the predominant elegist–epicist–elegist arc. In view of this, my first chapter introduces strategies for reading Ovid as a tragic poet.[3]

1 Theater and metatheater

Ovid, elegist and epicist, is a relatively recent invention. Patrick Cheney rightly notes that Renaissance scholars of the twentieth century have privileged this invention over that of Ovid, tragedian.[4] Yet Ovid the tragic poet has fared only marginally better among nineteenth- and twentieth-century classicists, primarily for lack of evidence. His tragedy, *Medea* (*c.* 13 BCE), and its meager remains are standard features of the Ovidian biography, and discussions of the lost play occupy a small but enduring niche in classical scholarship. All the same, the bulk of attention has been paid, understandably, to the poet's surviving epic and elegies. Lack of evidence, however, did not deter Renaissance-era scholars and authors from inventing an Ovid fully invested in dramaturgy. The fact that the *Medea* had once existed was enough to establish a stable elegist–tragedian–epicist arc for Ovid's career, which became a model for the careers of Shakespeare and Marlowe.[5] Furthermore, the reputation of the play, already favorable in antiquity, garnered further acclaim and amplified its author's own reputation. Thomas Heywood's *Apology for Actors* (1612) draws much more on Ovid in explaining the ancient theater than on Horace or Seneca.[6] That Ovid should have greater authority as a dramatist than Seneca is especially striking: not only was the former's *Medea* considered (no doubt correctly) a model for the latter's, the Senecan tragedy was actually deemed by some to be the Ovidian original.[7]

[2] Jobbing playwright: the term of Cheney 2010, 160, describing the professional Shakespeare often contrasted with the literary Shakespeare. Cheney 2004 is concerned to show the dichotomy as exaggerated, if not false. Farrell 2002 illustrates the diversity of genres in Roman poetic careers, which he distinguishes from Roman political careers; see Chapter 2, pp. 30–1.

[3] I would like to take this opportunity now, more than in any other chapter, to thank Reader "A" for his or her comments. Particularly helpful were comments on Ovid's approach to genre, which saved me much prevarication and circumlocution.

[4] Cheney 2004, 56. Cheney's first two chapters have influenced both this paragraph and the preceding one.

[5] Ovid and Marlowe: Cheney 1997.

[6] Cheney 2004, 29.

[7] Cheney 2004, 56, citing the introductory "Life of Ovid" in George Sandys' monumental translation of the *Metamorphoses* (1626).

Modern readers continue to mine Ovid's poetry for insights into the *Medea*, tragedy, and Augustan theatrical culture.[8] Nevertheless, an important development in the tragic reception of Ovid has been to appreciate the theatrical qualities of the poems themselves. This development is as much a dramatic enterprise as a scholarly one, originating with Seneca's reception of Ovid's poetry and continuing on to Shakespeare and into the present.[9] In 1687 a viewbook of 150 scenes from the *Metamorphoses*, illustrated by Johann Wilhelm Baur, was published in Nuremberg under the title *Bellissimum Ovidii Theatrum* (*Ovid's Most Delightful Theater*).[10] *Theatrum* derives from the Greek *theatron* (viewing place), in which tragedies and other dramatic works were put on public display. Its usage in the title of the Baur edition, although typical of illustrated books from this period,[11] speaks directly to the theatricality of the *Metamorphoses* – as if to appreciate Ovid's transformations is to view them as episodes on a stage. Dramatists of the twentieth century have put this principle into action. No one who has seen a production of Ted Hughes's *Tales from Ovid* (1997) or Mary Zimmerman's *Metamorphoses* (1996–8) can doubt the inherent theatricality and performability of Ovid's unorthodox epic.[12]

Recognizing the theatricality of the *Metamorphoses* (before 8 CE) involves reading the poem as a series of spectacles, especially where supernatural change and violence are concerned. The notion of the reader as spectator is somewhat contradictory, since the *Metamorphoses* is technically a work of words, intended for the page instead of the stage. Nevertheless, the narration entails an unmistakable visuality that verges on the theatrical, such that actions become staged for the reader. Moreover, the poem appeals

[8] E.g., Wiseman 2002; also Jouteur (ed.) 2009: "Mais qu'Ovide ait été spectateur de mimes, qu'il ait assisté à des représentations des pièces du répertoire classique, et qu'il les connaisse parfaitement, le présent volume en apporte la confirmation irréfutable" (16).

[9] On Ovid and Seneca see Chapter 7, section 2. The topic of Ovid's influence on Shakespeare's dramatic and non-dramatic works is too large to address here. In addition to the studies already noted, at minimum Bate 1993 and, more generally, Martindale and Taylor 2004 deserve mention.

[10] The title page of the 1687 edition and the illustrations (the engravings of Abraham Aubry based on Baur's original etchings: Henkel 1929, 131) may be viewed online at www.uvm.edu/~hag/ovid (accessed November 28, 2012). The cover illustration of this book is from Plate 65 (Special Collections, University of Vermont).

[11] E.g., Ortelius' *Theatrum Orbis Terrarum* (1570); Besson's *Theatrum Instrumentorum et Machinarum* (1571–2); Valvasor's *Theatrum Mortis Humanae Tripartitum* (1682).

[12] Some noteworthy productions: The Royal Shakespeare Company staged a version of Hughes's *Tales from Ovid* in London during its summer 2000 season; Zimmerman's *Metamorphoses* ran off-Broadway from September to December 2001, and on Broadway from March 2002 to February 2003. Both Hughes's and Zimmerman's works continue in repertory. The performability of Ovid's epic is of scholarly interest, e.g., Cahoon 1998; S. A. Brown 1999, ch. 12; Gildenhard and Zissos 2007, 4–5.

to the auditory as well as the visual. Stephen Wheeler makes a compelling case for the *Metamorphoses* as a continuous *viva voce* performance at its outermost level.[13] Within this overarching oral structure are numerous dialogues and internal speeches, most notably the monologues of characters in turmoil. The poem's visual and aural tendencies trope the act of reading as acts of seeing and hearing, the traditional sensory pathways for experiencing drama.[14]

This book privileges the *Metamorphoses* not only as a theatrical work, but also as a tragic one. "Tragic" does not merely invoke the modern vernacular sense of sad, unfortunate, or pitiful[15] – although some of Ovid's tales have these characteristics. Rather, the term refers first and foremost to tragedy as a poetic genre, which is fundamental to the interpretation and appreciation of the poem. Like epic, tragedy was a poetic enterprise appropriate to the Augustan principate, whose empire prompted reflection in grand genres. Unlike epic, however, tragedy was in need of professional poets. Rome under Augustus had no Pacuvius or Accius producing play after play. Apparently Ovid had intended to fill this void after writing the *Amores*, but he returned to elegy after writing the *Medea*. The poet nevertheless continued to harbor interest in tragedy, and when he finally turned to epic and the *Metamorphoses*, he used many stories from Greek and Roman tragedy and told them in ways that pay homage to the genre. Vergil, whose own epic was deeply rooted in tragedy, was an important antecedent for Ovid in this regard. But Ovid's deployment of the genre outstrips the *Aeneid* in both scale and scope, such that the *Metamorphoses* at times reads like a single-handed revival of Greco-Roman tragedy.[16]

Beyond its inherent visual and verbal staginess, the *Metamorphoses* deploys tragedy as an organizing principle. The genre itself, quite apart from any one play or author, furnishes layers of meaning unavailable in other generic perspectives. In particular, an awareness of how tragedies function – how, for example, they demarcate offstage and onstage action or foster comparison of character archetypes – creates new opportunities for reading the *Metamorphoses* within and across narratives. Reading tragically can even explain certain incongruities in the text, which now find resolution without conjuring a careless or cavalier poet. The transformation of

[13] Wheeler 1999.

[14] That the poetry of Ovid's era was dramatic by virtue of being read aloud for elite audiences is foundational for Jouteur (ed.) 2009: see especially p. 5 of the volume's preface.

[15] On this usage see Most 2000, 20.

[16] Compare Barchiesi 2005, cxlv: "Nel momento in cui il teatro romano affronta una complessa transizione, l'epos di Ovidio si offre come sbocco a tutta la tradizione della tragedia greca e latina."

tragedy into epic, therefore, involves a hierarchy of models, from individual plays to their unwritten rules, all of which we might collectively label "the tragic."

Tragedy also provides an organizing principle for Ovid's career, since his work in the genre was not limited to his play or to his epic. No study of Ovid as a tragedian would be complete without due consideration of the *Heroides*. Begun not long after the *Medea*, the "single" epistles (1–15, *c.* 10 BCE or later) pursued tragedy under the aegis of elegy and garnered a sequel in the "double" epistles (16–21, *c.* 1 CE). This pursuit consisted not only of borrowing characters from the tragic stage, but also of developing the epistolary mode, which resembles tragedy in constructing a space for heroines and heroes to display their suffering. The *Heroides* paved the way for the *Metamorphoses*, initiating generic and intertextual negotiations to be continued within the more expansive epic.

The transformation of tragedy into other genres is metatheatrical as well as theatrical. The term *metatheater* refers to the effect created when a drama calls attention to its own theatricality, whether through a play-within-a-play, through characters who realize they are dramatic characters, or through other related devices.[17] I use the term in this sense throughout the book, particularly when discussing Ovid's theater of epic or his theater of elegy.[18] Yet metatheater is also meant as shorthand for the poet's overall approach to transforming tragedy: the prefix *meta-* is to be construed both in its radical sense ("change"[19]) and as an allusion to the ***Meta****morphoses*, where much of the transformation occurs. This shorthand application of the term overlaps with its primary meaning in one respect. The success of any metatheatrical gesture rests with the audience, without whose participation the so-called "fourth wall" cannot be broken. Ovid's transformations require similar participation from the reader.

Even in the last decade of the twentieth century, it was still something of an oxymoron to use the words "Ovid" and "tragedy" in the same sentence, with three exceptions: his lost play; his relegation to the Black Sea in 8 CE; and his adaptations of Greek and Roman dramas – although studies of these tended to pit their ostensibly un-tragic tenor against their tragic models. The mid 1990s and beyond, however, saw increasing interest in commingling "Ovid" and "tragedy" more productively, especially in studies of the *Metamorphoses*. Alison Keith, for example, focuses on how the

[17] *OED* s.v. metatheater.

[18] Theater of epic: not to be conflated with Brechtian "epic theater," though Laird 2003 reads the *Aeneid* as a precursor to this movement.

[19] LSJ *s.v.* μετά G.VIII.

Pentheus narrative (book 3) engages with the *Bacchae* of Euripides and the lost *Pentheus* of Pacuvius.[20] Ovid, even as he derives his plot from these Dionysiac plays, also borrows their attendant themes and motifs, which he puts to work in the subsequent Pyramus and Thisbe episode (book 4), a story never dramatized on any stage. Ingo Gildenhard and Andrew Zissos likewise examine how tragic themes and motifs cohere in the disembodied figure of Oedipus and are reincorporated throughout book 3, particularly in the "narcissism" of Narcissus.[21] In a separate study Gildenhard and Zissos demonstrate that the dismemberment of tragic characters, especially ephebes such as Actaeon (*Met.* 3) and Hippolytus (15), is articulated in self-consciously theatrical ways.[22] Most expansively, Isabelle Jouteur has edited a volume devoted to theatricality – tragic, comic, and otherwise – across the Ovidian corpus.[23]

These works challenge Ovid's readers to interrogate the idea of genre. What does it mean for an epic poem to exhibit both tragic material and, more important, tragic modalities? The same question applies to Ovid's elegiac letters, which also draw upon the material and modes of the stage. The new formalist "movement" in Latin literary studies, current from the 1980s and beyond, actively seeks answers to questions such as these.[24] Sara H. Lindheim broadly defines new formalism as having "twin concerns with questions of genre and intertextuality," which are for Ovid "a corrective and far more productive method of reading."[25] Gildenhard and Zissos offer a more elaborate definition of new formalist concerns in relation to Ovid: "[T]he search for meaning in form, close attention to [his] sophisticated handling of generic demarcations, and a heightened interest in how he accessed, assimilated, and altered the poetic modalities and semantic patterns of his literary sources."[26] Note the emphasis placed on interpretation, which suggests that the "genre question" is less about arriving at an ultimate definition of a work's kind, and more about engaging in

20 Keith 2002.

21 Gildenhard and Zissos 2000.

22 Gildenhard and Zissos 1999. See also Gildenhard and Zissos 2007, an analysis of the Tereus–Procne–Philomela episode of *Met.* 6.

23 Jouteur (ed.) 2009.

24 For the *Metamorphoses* the foundational new formalist analysis is Hinds 1987b, which focuses on negotiations of elegy. For the *Heroides* see Barchiesi 1993, although Kennedy 1984 is an early entry in this putative movement.

25 Lindheim 2003.

26 Gildenhard and Zissos 1999, 163 n. 4, brackets mine. Further reflections on the new formalist agenda in Gildenhard and Zissos 2007, 13: the "movement … revolutionized conceptions of Ovid's literary artistry by exploring his sophisticated handling of, above all, genre, allusion, and narrative technique."

the process of defining. New formalism is demonstrably a reader-oriented strategy. The author, or at least the concept of an "intention-bearing authorial voice,"[27] is not dead, nor are his (or her) intentions irrelevant. But the search for meaning, though begun by the author, ends with the reader.

By the standards of new formalism, career criticism, and even source criticism, the study of Ovid and tragedy requires further attention. The contributions of Gildenhard and Zissos, Keith, and others provide insightful individual studies, but a full and systematic examination is in order. *Tragedy in Ovid* attempts to address this need, and it borrows many tools from the critical kits mentioned above. Nevertheless, as the *Cambridge Companion to Ovid* has shown, interest in literary discourse – allusion, genre-formation, and intertextuality – can and should take stock of cultural discourse in its many forms: social, political, ideological, historical, and material.[28] Philip Hardie, the *Companion*'s editor, points in his introduction to the erosion of the "sharp division between text and history" by new historicist and cultural materialist criticism, and sets the tone both for the volume and for future Ovidians by declaring that the poet "cannot escape from the discursive universe out of which emerges the 'reality' of the Augustan order."[29] I have tried to keep this reality in view, even during the closest of tragic readings.

2 Sources and genres

To judge solely on the basis of both extant and well-known fragmentary tragedies, Ovid's poetry is indebted to the material of the genre. The *Heroides* present the letters of women famous from the tragic stage: Phaedra (*Her.* 4), Deianira (9), and Medea (12), to name only three. The *Metamorphoses*, in turn, features a panoply of tragic heroes and heroines, sometimes devoting almost entire books to their exploits: Phaëthon

[27] Hinds 1998, 49.

[28] Thus Lindheim 2003, 136, though the tentative list of cultural discourses is mine. In fairness to Gildenhard and Zissos, their 1999 essay by no means attempts to read Ovid in a literary vacuum; see, e.g., 181: "Ovid contrasts the cultural ideologies of Greece and Rome that traverse the tragic body in pain." Also Gildenhard and Zissos 2007, 14: "[A]n episode can be laced with programmatic, intertextual, or generic gestures and still offer a meditation on human experience." The work of Keith is likewise broadly engaged: her book, *Engendering Rome* (2000), places the construction of Roman epic in dialogue with (to borrow, for the purposes of making this point, the assessment of Hinds 2000, 235) "the construction of elite male education and homosocial discourse." Feldherr 2010 offers a most conscientious reading of the *Metamorphoses* in terms of literary and cultural discursiveness, with due emphasis on spectacle in its many forms – including, at times, the tragic.

[29] Hardie (ed.) 2002, 9.

(book 2); the Theban History (3–4, including Actaeon and Pentheus); Niobe and Tereus–Procne–Philomela (6); Medea (7); Meleager (8); Deianira–Hercules (9); Iphigenia (12); the Contest of the Arms, Ajax, the Trojan Women, Polyxena, Hecabe (13); Phaedra–Hippolytus (15). And this is just scratching the surface.

Whoever would make a comprehensive study of Ovid and tragedy has two choices: to address all texts with tragic subject matter, or to select from them in a more illustrative manner. Faced with the daunting task of the former, critics have opted for the latter. Strategies for selection vary, but a typical one for the *Metamorphoses* is to choose thematic clusters – hence the ample coverage of the Theban narratives in the scholarship, for example.[30] My strategy is to focus on four characters and the texts in which they appear: Hecabe, Medea, Deianira, and Hercules. Although others, such as Phaedra, Polyxena, and Laodamia, will enter the picture, these four will generate most of my case studies. The selection is narrow enough to foster cohesion, yet broad enough to span the poet's career: Hecabe appears in the *Metamorphoses* alone, but both Deianira and Medea appear there as well as in the *Heroides*, and Medea was also the subject of the lost tragedy;[31] Hercules also appears in the epic and, as Deianira's husband, is the ideal reader of her epistle. Recurring characters will demonstrate how Ovid continued to play the tragedian long after the *Medea*, even within different works and genres.

Another criterion for selecting these characters is that all of them appear in at least one surviving Greek tragedy: Medea in Euripides' *Medea*; Hecabe, Euripides' *Hecabe*; Deianira and Hercules (or Heracles), Sophocles' *Women of Trachis*. Whereas studies of Ovidian tragic characters from fragmentary plays must necessarily be conditional and speculative, my study (however speculative in other areas) at least has the luxury of making comparisons with extant sources. Naturally, I do not imply that the plays listed above are the only extant models, tragic or otherwise. Nor do I mean to neglect lost plays, particularly on the Roman side, where we would expect to find considerable influence on Ovid. I do, however, assert the canonicity of the *Medea*, the *Hecabe*, and the *Women of Trachis* in Ovid's poems. The Athenian stage was an incubator for lasting transformations of myth, and the tragedies under discussion are outstanding examples of poetic innovation. The *Women of Trachis* is both the only known play to treat Heracles' death and, it seems, the earliest instance of Deianira's misguided desire.[32] The *Hecabe* originally combined the deaths

30 Hardie 1990. Gildenhard and Zissos 2000. Keith 2002. Janan 2009.

31 Arcellaschi 1990, 231–47, discusses "le personnage gigantesque" of Medea in Ovid's works and life.

32 March 1987, 48–77; see Chapter 6, pp. 203–6.

of Polydorus and Polyxena,[33] while the *Medea*, if not the first tragedy to cast the heroine as the murderer of her children, was doubtless the best known.[34] Though Ovid invokes other texts in adapting these plays, the prospect of his transforming the transformers is intuitively right.

The most self-conscious poet of his generation, Ovid constantly encourages his readers to weigh his work against the literary tradition. This is especially true for the *Metamorphoses*, which is concerned as much with transformation stories as with the transformation *of* stories. A metamorphosis, especially the "metamorphosis of literature,"[35] involves a comparison of the past and the present. If something or someone passes from one state to another, the current state cannot be appreciated without reference to the old. This principle informs every transformation in the poem, especially that of the tyrant Lycaon, the first human character to be given new shape:

> territus ipse fugit nactusque silentia ruris
> exululat frustraque loqui conatur. ab ipso
> colligit os rabiem solitaeque cupidine caedis
> vertitur in pecudes et nunc quoque sanguine gaudet.
> in villos abeunt vestes, in crura lacerti:
> fit lupus et veteris servat vestigia formae.
> canities eadem est, eadem violentia vultus,
> idem oculi lucent, eadem feritatis imago est.

> He runs away in terror and when he reaches the quiet of the country he howls, his efforts to speak all in vain. His mouth foaming, he turns his usual lust for killing against the flocks, and delights again in spilling blood. His clothes vanish in place of fur, his arms in place of legs. He becomes a wolf, and yet bears traces of his prior form. There is the same gray hair, the same violent looks, the same glimmering eyes, the same savage appearance. (*Met.* 1.232–9)

Critics have rightly warned against deriving universal theories of metamorphosis from a "deceptive paradigm" like Lycaon.[36] Nevertheless, a

[33] Collard 1991, 32–4; see Chapter 4, p. 102.

[34] On Euripides' putative debt to Neophron regarding the murder of Medea's children see Michelini 1989 – although Boedeker 1997 argues for the canonical status of Euripides' heroine regardless of the infanticide's origins.

[35] Kirby 1989, 237: "Ovid ... truly conjures with the very forms of literature themselves, turning them inside-out and back-to-front ... The *Metamorphoses* represents nothing less than the metamorphosis of literature."

[36] Deceptive paradigm: from the title of Anderson 1989. Both Anderson and Feldherr 2002, 171–2, demonstrate that Lycaon's transformation is far less tidy than it would seem. Feldherr 2010, in a thorough rehearsal of contemporary scholarship on Ovidian metamorphosis (26–37), asserts that

quantifiable transformation occurs at the very least: clothes turn into fur, arms into legs, man into wolf. Yet the wolf retains traces of his former self (*veteris servat vestigia formae*, 237), such as his grizzled mane and gleaming eyes. Nor are these traces limited to his physical form. Although he victimizes sheep instead of people, he has retained his bloodthirsty nature (*nunc quoque sanguine gaudet*, 235).

This passage implies much about literary Ovid's program, even a program of transforming tragedy. Taking Lycaon's metamorphosis as analogous to the adaptation of a play, we have at least two avenues of appreciation and interpretation at our disposal. One is to interrogate the details. Of what do Lycaon's eyes remind us? Was his appearance always so savage? Such inquiries are similar to ones we might make when reading Ovid's tragic texts. Why does Deianira send Hercules a poisoned robe? Did Euripides' Medea ever write a letter to Jason? Questions like these are the essence of source criticism or *Quellenforschung*. In terms of tragedy, this approach manifests itself in cataloguing model plays and detecting references to them in any given text. All well and good, though the net effect is often to reduce Ovid to a set of influences. Just as a transformation from man into wolf invites further consideration, *Quellenforschung* is not the end of reading tragically, but rather the point from which reading must proceed.

A second avenue of interpretation leverages details toward interrogating purpose. Why do Lycaon's eyes gleam in wolf form? Why is Polyxena's death so visceral? These are questions of a different order, reflecting concerns not only with Ovid's program, but also with the very forms of his poetry. The notion of an element continuing from form to form or genre to genre is much more dynamic and unsettled than it might seem. In the case of Lycaon's eyes, perhaps their gleam is distinctly human, a holdover from his original shape. Yet the metamorphosis might also have clarified that they were lupine from the start.[37] Similarly, Polyxena's sacrifice, when "staged" within epic, provides a semblance of tragic theatricality appropriate to her original genre. Furthermore, her death in Euripides' *Hecabe* occurs offstage, reported after the fact by a messenger. Because messenger speeches uphold the traditions of epic narrative and because Ovid, too, is narrating, Polyxena's demise is much as it always was. Lycaon suggests by

the process is fundamentally ambiguous: "[T]he poem offers no clear prescription for understanding the phenomenon of metamorphosis" (35).

37 On metamorphosis as clarification and continuation in general see Solodow 1988, 174–88. Feldherr 2002 subscribes to such a reading of Lycaon: his "metamorphosis is above all a clarification of who he really is" (170).

example that the metamorphosis of literature is subject to interpretation and negotiation. Far from a cut-and-dried process, with old elements residing static and inert in a new form, we have instead forms in flux arising from forms which themselves are in flux. Where does the wolf end? Where does tragedy begin?

3 Tension and synergy

The concept of genres in flux has been a mainstay of Ovidian criticism for nearly a century. In 1924 Wilhelm Kroll set the bar for subsequent interpretations of the *Metamorphoses*, describing its hybridization of epic and elegy as *die Kreuzung der Gattungen* (the crossing of genres).[38] A hybridized approach also has room for tragedy, as Brooks Otis has shown. Though primarily concerned with epic-elegiac blending, Otis elucidates tragic devices like pathos and irony, particularly in narratives based on tragedy.[39] Underlying these approaches is generic impurity, a sense of genre arising less in the observance of convention than in the breach. Stephen Hinds, in the most influential reading of the *Metamorphoses* to date, demonstrates that genre, especially in Ovidian hands, is not only an impure but also an elusive construct. Its very constructedness, in turn, thematizes and exposes its own negotiability.[40] In these broader critical frameworks, readers embrace productive tension by interrogating the play of differences.

The appeal to tension is obvious, since it suggests interpretive mobility rather than inertia.[41] The *Heroides* in particular are susceptible to readings that highlight tension between elegy and tragedy. Alessandro Barchiesi, working from the proposition that "[d]rama and elegy have different and conflicting codes," takes the end of *Her.* 12 as exemplary.[42] Medea concludes her epistle to Jason with a warning: *nescio quid certe mens mea maius agit* (To be sure, my mind is contriving some greater act, 12.212). The reader, of course, knows that in her chronological future, which is also her tragic literary past, she will eventually kill Creon, his daughter, and her own children. But Medea does not yet know this: she is still writing elegy,

[38] Kroll 1924, ch. 9. Hinds 2000 and Keith 2002 offer annotated histories of epic and elegiac (and in the latter, tragic) readings of the *Met.* See also S. J. Harrison 2002, a survey of Ovid's entire career from the perspective of elegy.

[39] Otis 1970. [40] Hinds 1987b.

[41] The generic "dialogue" of Gildenhard and Zissos 2007, 14, strikes me as a useful alternative to "tension."

[42] Barchiesi 1993 (quotation, 345).

in which such dire acts cannot be inscribed.[43] Furthermore, the appearance of tragic irony in her last line signals an imminent return to the genre in which irony flourishes.[44] Medea, in admitting limits to her knowledge, negotiates her own place in different poetic forms.

Equally enabling, and no less open to negotiability, is generic synergy. By "synergy" I mean the capacity of different genres, or elements thereof, to work together to create something greater than their mere sum. This is, I suppose, a kind of hybridization, but the result is often less important than the synergy itself, which is legible to the reader. To put it in terms of Lycaon, the wolf he becomes is less important than the fact of becoming a wolf, in which Ovid invests considerable poetic industry. Synergy stems from similarities between genres, a truth recognized in antiquity. Aeschylus, for example, reportedly claimed that the works of playwrights are "slices from the banquet of Homer" (Ath. 8.347e). This remark posits Homeric poetry, first and foremost, as a source of tragic material.[45] Aristotle goes a little further, noting near the beginning of the *Poetics* that tragedy has everything epic has, although not everything tragic is available in epic (ἃ μὲν γὰρ ἐποποιία ἔχει, ὑπάρχει τῇ τραγῳδίᾳ, ἃ δὲ αὐτῇ, οὐ πάντα ἐν τῇ ἐποποιίᾳ, *Poet.* 5.1449b). Aristotle is referring to the constituent parts (μέρη) of both genres, of which plot and character are but two – the other four being diction, thought, spectacle, and song (6.1450a). Aristotle's point, whatever we make of his taxonomy, is teleological. As a descendant of epic, tragedy possesses the intrinsic qualities of the parent genre.

A synergistic reading of the *Heroides* proceeds from the notion that the letters are elegiac spaces with boundaries resembling those of the stage, regardless of the genre in which their writers originate. The letter of Penelope, an epic heroine, emulates the form of tragedy as much as the letters of Medea, Phaedra, and Deianira. That said, the emulation is more palpable in the texts of tragic characters. In Medea's case, the many deaths she causes in Euripides occur offstage. Hence her inability to consider them in *Her.* 12 renders them "offstage" in the epistle as well.[46] A similar demarcation occurs in Ovid's epic version of the Medea myth (*Met.* 7), which at face value might be surprising. Epic theatricality, as I have suggested, often blurs the distinction between offstage and onstage where

[43] So Barchiesi 1993, 343–5. Compare Hinds 1993, 41–2, and Spoth 1992, 202–5.

[44] I return to this line in Chapter 3, p. 82.

[45] For a recent assessment of the debt of Aeschylus, Sophocles, and Euripides to Homeric epic see Scodel 2005.

[46] Compare Jouteur 2009, who situates *Her.* 12 in the wings ("dans les coulisses") of tragedy.

tragic action is concerned: witness Polyxena. Hence we might approach Ovid's narrative expecting the mayhem of Medea to be the climax. In reality it is an anticlimax, occupying only four verses (7.394–7). It is "onstage," but barely so. In both cases, generic synergy obtains when the epistle or narrative of a tragic heroine conforms to standards of presentation in her original genre.

Why might events like infanticide have been barred from the tragic stage in the first place? Conventional thinking suggests limitations imposed by technology and decorum, but these are questionable. Although the ancient theater was spare by modern standards, stage devices like the *ekkyklēma* and the *mēchanē* attest that it was by no means primitive. In fact, these technological refinements might easily have inspired other refinements to facilitate direct and sequential presentation. As for matters of taste, particularly regarding violent or fantastic events, the standard must have shifted constantly across generations, audiences, playwrights' careers, and even plays. The ultra-violent climax of Seneca's *Medea* is proof enough. Moreover, the effect of vivid *ex post facto* narratives is often to highlight, rather than to suppress, ostensibly indecorous acts. Were tragedians unable or unwilling to stage certain acts, or were they simply uninterested?

Or, as a corollary, we might ask what did interest the tragedians. Here is Oliver Taplin's response:

> [A]ctions which take place off-stage and outside the play, although they are generally larger and more violent, are comparatively unimportant. A Greek tragedy concentrates on a certain short sequence of events set at a particular place and within a certain brief space of time; and every action outside that time and place, however huge and horrendous, only matters in so far as it is brought to bear on the focus of the play on stage. It has only as much prominence as the attention it is given. The actions on the stage, on the other hand, although usually rather slight and lacking in violence, become the object of concentrated attention and bear the visible burden of the tragedy.[47]

In other words, a play with a violent act is less about the act itself and more about its impact on the play's characters. Taplin theorizes a process that, instead of removing certain elements from the stage, keeps others firmly in view, with room for more as needed. This latter arrangement suggests different associations for actions inside and outside the *theatron*. Offstage is a world of super- and sub-human experience, while onstage is human experience, the world most familiar to the tragic audience. Ovid's

[47] Taplin 1977, 25–6.

elegiac and epic Medeas, as far as we can see, are not yet so removed from this world as to be monsters.

4 Decoding tragedy

In speaking of genres, it is important to offer specific examples, lest we seem to hypostasize the genre – to give it, as Glenn Most writes, "a substantial existence independent of ... poets, works, and readers."[48] Even the *Poetics* and Horace's *Ars poetica*, the two most prescriptive ancient treatises on tragedy, support their claims with examples from actual plays or stage practices. That said, the aim of their examples is to permit some degree of generalization – to glimpse the genre itself at work. Let me offer a case in point, which also takes stock of the discussion thus far.

In the extant *Hippolytus* (*Stephanias, HS*) of Euripides, Phaedra makes a famous speech about the pleasures of life, one of which is *aidos* or modesty:[49]

> εἰσὶ δ' ἡδοναὶ πολλαὶ βίου,
> μακραί τε λέσχαι καὶ σχολή, τερπνὸν κακόν,
> αἰδώς τε· δισσαὶ δ' εἰσίν, ἡ μὲν οὐ κακή,
> ἡ δ' ἄχθος οἴκων. εἰ δ' ὁ καιρὸς ἦν σαφής,
> οὐκ ἂν δύ' ἤστην ταὔτ' ἔχοντε γράμματα.

> Life holds many delights: long conversations and leisure, a wicked pleasure, and modesty. But there are two kinds of modesty, one not bad, the other a burden on houses. If what is proper were clear, two notions would not share the same spelling. (Eur. *HS* 383–7)

This passage is notorious, but it is widely agreed that the good *aidos* (or, at least, the "not bad") has enabled Phaedra to repress her desire for Hippolytus out of concern for her reputation. Yet *aidos* has also proven burdensome, since repression has devastated the heroine in mind and body. In another sense, also negative, *aidos* has precipitated Phaedra's revelation of her love in yielding to the Nurse's entreaties in verse 335: σέβας γὰρ χειρὸς αἰδοῦμαι τὸ σόν (I cannot for reverence turn away your hand, tr. Barrett 1964). The opinions of others, which had encouraged her silence, have moved her to speak out.[50]

From the perspective of *Quellenforschung*, the passage is a model for Ovid's *Her.* 4, the letter of Phaedra to Hippolytus:

[48] Most 2000, 17.

[49] Modesty: my expedient and traditional, but not entirely satisfactory, rendering of *aidos* and (below) the Latin *pudor*.

[50] On *aidos* in the *Hippolytus* see Halleran 1995, an excellent summary of the major interpretations.

> qua licet et sequitur, pudor est miscendus amori;
> dicere quae puduit, scribere iussit amor.[51]

> Modesty and love must mingle, where it is proper and sensible. What I was too modest to say, love has commanded me to write. (*Her.* 4.9–10)

Like her Euripidean counterpart, the Ovidian Phaedra is caught between two opposing forces: *pudor*, which corresponds to the good *aidos*, and *amor*, which assimilates to the bad *aidos* in its secondary sense, the motivating factor in the disclosure of her desire (*dicere quae puduit, scribere iussit amor*, 10).[52] The allusion to the *Hippolytus* offers the source-critic much to discuss, if only for its lexical brilliance, which goes well beyond mere translation. Applying the Roman predilection for antithesis, the epistolary Phaedra transcends the typical Greek duality that the tragic Phaedra disparages (οὐκ ἂν δύ’ ἤστην ταὔτ’ ἔχοντε γράμματα, 387). Ovid's heroine can, and does, employ different words for different ideas.

It is one thing to appreciate the allusion on its own terms, another to construe it in the context of Phaedra's letter. A potentially fruitful approach is to consider how Ovid recapitulates a key Euripidean theme – a woman's anxiety over her reputation – and adapts it to the seductive aims of the erotic epistle.[53] In particular, we might note how Phaedra rewrites the bad *aidos* as *amor*, the strongest elegiac signifier of all, and does so at the precise moment at which (she claims) *amor* has compelled her to write. So doing, we would begin to take stock of the generic tensions and synergies at work in this letter: tension, perhaps, in Phaedra communicating directly with Hippolytus through an erotic epistle; synergy in the external forces that compel Phaedra to express herself in both tragedy and elegy.

Yet another approach is to read *pudor–amor* as not only adapted from the extant *Hippolytus*, but also mobilized as a dilemma representative of the genre to which the play belongs. To recognize a tragic dilemma is to recognize a parameter of the "code" of tragedy: one of many devices, modes, themes, motifs, character types – in sum, the unwritten rules that prescribe this or any other genre. At the same time, the parameter is refracted through a particular model. To put it in terms familiar from the work of Gian Biagio Conte, Euripides' double *aidos* is a specific *locus*, or the local model (*modello-esemplare*), that Ovid emulates with *pudor–amor*.

[51] In some texts *amor* is capitalized, perhaps on analogy with *Am.* 1.1: Love the deity, or Cupid, inspires Phaedra to write, just as he did Ovid. For now, however, I am interested only in the dichotomy between *pudor* and *amor* as concepts.

[52] The best overall discussion of *pudor–amor* and its relationship to *aidos* is Verducci 1985, 192.

[53] So Davis 1995.

It is also Ovid's code model (*modello-codice*), which affords Phaedra and her readers access to the tragic.[54]

When individual parameters of tragic code can be isolated, it is convenient to organize them into distinct yet fluid categories. One category involves the format of tragedy, from its characteristic modulation between speech and song, to its depiction of onstage and offstage events. Also under this category is the first-person perspective of tragic characters, who are both participants and narrators in their dramas. A second category is concerned with the material of tragedy, not merely its reliance on traditional myths and legends, but also the shaping of plot through conventional story patterns, such as the so-called "revenge pattern."[55] A third category encompasses the devices, actions, and attitudes characteristic of tragedy. Many Aristotelian concepts like reversal (*peripeteia*) and recognition (*anagnorisis*) reside here;[56] in fact, it is legitimate to think of Aristotle as one of the first decoders of tragedy.

The dilemma of *pudor–amor* belongs in this third category as well. The dilemma both reminds us of Phaedra's original genre and drives her written discourse, just as the double *aidos* prompted the speech of her Euripidean counterpart. In this sense, her letter is no less tragic than the original play, with synergy between elegy and tragedy occurring at the level of code. Note that, while the terms *pudor* and *amor* are stable, the actual dilemma might encode a story in any number of ways. A Phaedra will experience the struggle differently from a Medea, who will experience it differently from another heroine. When it befalls a heroine with no prior tragic history, as sometimes happens, it is nevertheless appropriate to say that her story has been encoded as a tragedy.[57]

Although tragic parameters can be isolated for purposes of discussion, in actual dramatic practice they tend to combine with other parameters. Recognition, for instance, is a device around which an entire story may be constructed. Pathos, in turn, intensifies in the first-person: "I suffer" is

[54] Conte 1986, 31, a discussion of Vergil's relationship to Homer with obvious implications for other Latin poets. I use the term "local model" in place of Conte's "exemplary model," which, although a literal translation of the Italian *modello-esemplare* in Conte 1985, 121, sounds too much like the notion of a generic exemplar particular to "code model." Thus Hinds 1998, 42 n. 46.

[55] Burian 1997 traces out several tragic plot patterns including revenge, returns, and recognition, the last of which recalls the Aristotelian device.

[56] On reversal and recognition in Ovidian poetry see Jolivet 2009. See also Casanova-Robin 2009, who finds several Aristotelian codifications in *Her.* 11, the letter of Canace to Macareus.

[57] I explore the *pudor–amor* dilemma in subsequent chapters. On the Byblis narrative see Chapter 3, pp. 92–3. On the Medea narrative, Chapter 5, pp. 145–7.

often more powerful and immediate than "she suffers." Just as no genre or text thereof operates in a total vacuum, no generic parameter is truly independent of any other. The interconnectivity of tragic parameters becomes almost tangible when we regard characters not only as trademarks of certain poets or plays, but also as tragic paradigms in their own right. Ovid is particularly fond of juxtaposing tragic heroines, sometimes violently so, forcing the reader to confront their underlying codes. How does Phaedra, the embodiment of *aidos*, repression, and suicide, compare to Medea, who in many ways embodies the opposite? Seeing characters as tragic paradigms allows us to put a face to what might otherwise be an abstract, disembodied genre.

No attempt to define a genre's code will be complete. Three categories of parameters, no matter how clear or closely intertwined, cannot do justice to the tragic code as a whole. For example, metapoetic parameters involving the ritual, social, and political aspects of tragedy have influenced the composition, production, viewing, and reading of individual plays. Moreover, no definition of the tragic code can encompass the evolution of the genre as developed by generations of playwrights and received by generations of audiences. The meager remains of Aeschylus, Sophocles, and Euripides by themselves illustrate the complexity of tragedy in fifth-century Athens; the survival of the fourth-century *Rhesus* complicates, for better or for worse, our view of the genre even more. How much more complicated would it be if there survived even one tragic play from another Greek state, or from early Rome? And, as we have seen, the road from Athens to Seneca affords the most complex vista yet. None of this is to dissuade the reader from reading; in fact, the effect is quite the opposite. Here we are in good company with the tragedians themselves, who were the original mobilizers and interpreters of their genre's code.

Reading tragedy in Ovid is an active enterprise, one necessarily involving texts that, at least formally, are not tragedies. The Ovidian reader naturally seeks out traces of tragic models (language, plot, characters), yet also expects to find them transformed – not into static genres but into dynamic new forms. Whether their dynamism comes from tension or synergy is really not so important. What matters more is recognizing the play of genres and accepting the poet's invitation to negotiate a text's construction and meaning. Before we embark on a fuller exploration of tragedy in the *Heroides* and the *Metamorphoses*, we must first consider Ovid's lost *Medea*, itself a reflection of five centuries' worth of tragic coding. As we will see, the play was intended to transform Ovid from an elegist into a tragedian. So it did, but not in the manner he had anticipated: it was his second turn as an elegist, followed by a turn as an epicist, that created his tragic career. In a paradox worthy of Lycaon, these later poetic guises would clarify Ovid as the tragedian he already was … and otherwise never would have become.

CHAPTER TWO

Nunc habeam per te Romana Tragoedia nomen
Ovid's Medea *and Roman tragedy*

Around 13 BCE, Ovid composed his first and only tragedy, *Medea*. The play made good on his resolution at the end of *Amores* edition one to become a tragic playwright (3.15.17–20). Although the *Medea* garnered a favorable reputation beyond the poet's lifetime, he wrote no subsequent plays. Nevertheless, his foray into tragedy had a profound impact on his later work, especially the *Heroides* and the *Metamorphoses*.[1]

This chapter has two goals. First, to situate Ovid's lost tragedy within the context of its times. Second, to situate the play within the context of the poet's career. The first goal entails a survey of tragic authors and texts from the middle and late republic to the early principate. Given a renascence of interest in Roman drama in recent decades, my survey will be selective, approaching the fragments and testimonials in terms of the issues most relevant to the *Medea*.[2] Above all, I will address certain key

[1] I will expand upon this premise in section 3. However, some remarks on the tangle of thorns that is Ovidian chronology are in order. The relative sequence of Ovid's major early works – *Amores* (first edition), then the *Medea*, the single *Heroides*, *Ars amatoria* 1 and 2, and *Amores* (second edition) – is widely accepted. But absolute dates are beyond recovery. 13 BCE, the date I propose for the *Medea*, is more or less the middle of the time-frame between the editions of the *Amores*, and it meshes with other proposals: Jouteur (ed.) 2009, 5, suggests the years 15–12. The most insightful study of early Ovidian chronology is McKeown 1987, 74–89. I accept McKeown's premise that the poet "began writing *Amores*-poems *c.* 26–25 [BCE], [and] a large number of those now extant were written after 20" (84, brackets mine). The dating of *Amores* edition two is more complicated. McKeown, 84, advocates for a date as early as 7 BCE. T. Heinze 1997, 21–4, pushes the date back to 5 BCE, while Farrell 2004, 45–6, cogently argues for a date not much earlier than 1 BCE. Other discussions of the chronology include Cameron 1968; Booth 1991, 1–4; Conte 1994b, 340–1; and (more spaciously) White 2002 and Tarrant 2002. I disagree with Cameron (332) and Conte (341), who suggest the *Heroides* were composed before the *Medea*. My thanks to Jessica Westerhold for reading and commenting on an earlier draft of this chapter.

[2] Recent works helpful in seeing the larger picture are Goldberg 1996 on "The fall and rise of Roman tragedy," which makes good sense of the post-Accian period; Manuwald 2003 on Pacuvius; Erasmo 2004, a study of Roman tragedy from a metatheatrical perspective; and Boyle 2006, a broad survey of the genre from Andronicus to Seneca. Among older works Ribbeck 1875 remains foundational, while Beare 1965 and Beacham 1992 incorporate other forms (such as mime and pantomime) into their surveys.

questions. How did the genre of tragedy develop in the centuries before Ovid? What did it mean to be a tragedian in Ovid's era? What would the expectations of a Roman audience have been?

These questions will also support my second goal. As components of a larger tragic project, the *Heroides* and *Metamorphoses* ought to share in the literary and cultural concerns of the lost play. Nevertheless, this goal entails a different survey: reading the poet's own views on the *Medea* and its impact on the trajectory of his career. Distinct from poetry as a profession, a poetic career refers both to progress within a poet's oeuvre (in the sense of moving along a *cursus* or course[3]), and to his or her fashioning of that progress. Careerist self-fashioning is usually legible across a range of works and sometimes within a work. Remarks on a career may be consistent or may contradict one another in the flux of lived experience, historical reality, and poetic sensibilities.[4] Moreover, subsequent readers and authors, who fashion their own careers in light of their predecessors, often reify these contradictions even as they reveal new areas of consistency.[5] Such is the case with Ovid and Vergil. The *Medea* represents an ascent to a higher genre, much like Vergil's own ascent from the *Eclogues* to the *Georgics*. Tracking the generic oscillation of Ovid's works, not to mention the oscillation in "Ovid's construction of his literary career," requires caution.[6] Where Vergil next graduates to epic, our poet seems to backslide to elegy. However, the encoding of the *Aeneid* as a tragic text

[3] Though the English word "career" ultimately derives from the Latinized Gallic *carrus* (wagon), its sense of "course of action" or "full swing of a person's activity" (*OED* 4) is a sixteenth-century association with the etymologically distinct *cursus*, which encapsulated the Roman notion of the career (*OLD* 9). See Ernout *et al.* 2001 s.v. *curro* and Cheney 2002, 8.

[4] See the introduction of Hardie and Moore 2010: Career criticism "is to be distinguished from the older fashion for a life-and-works approach … [It] takes as its starting point the totality of an author's textual output and asks how that oeuvre as a whole shapes itself, both in its intratextual relationships … and in the claims it makes to reflect or mould extratextual conditions of production" (1). Classicists, or at least specialists in late republican and early imperial literature, have traditionally been alive to these concerns, though not necessarily with career criticism as a theoretical impetus. Meanwhile, the foundational studies, Lipking 1981 and especially Helgerson 1983, emerged with a focus on English Renaissance poets who followed the career models of Vergil and Ovid (among others). Cheney 2002 and Lipking 2010 offer annotated histories of the movement several decades removed. For Ovid's career Farrell 2002 and 2004 have become seminal studies; see also Barchiesi and Hardie 2010.

[5] Cheney 1997, for example, posits Ovid as a stable career model (albeit an anti-Vergilian, non-progressive, and non-typological one) for the career of Marlowe; likewise Cheney 2004, which posits a similar relationship between Ovid and Shakespeare. Kilgour 2010, taking stock of Cheney's work, offers an assessment of Vergil and Ovid vis-à-vis Milton.

[6] Barchiesi and Hardie 2010, 60, rightly ascribing "oscillation" to Cheney 1997. The authors summarize Ovid's complicated relationship with Vergil's career, which Farrell 2004 illustrates in greater detail.

inspired Ovid to further progress as a tragedian, even while working in other genres.

In introducing these goals, I should also identify what is *not* a goal of this chapter, namely to attempt an exhaustive reconstruction of the *Medea*. That work has been done, and done well.[7] Naturally, I will pay due attention to the surviving fragments, verdicts from antiquity, and Medea's appearances in other Ovidian works – all of which will furnish a clear picture of the play's content and scope. Yet in the end I am concerned less with what the *Medea* said and more with what it meant. Why did the poet choose tragedy for the second phase of his career? And how did he carry on in the aftermath? Just as Ovid made a point of moving beyond the *Medea*, so this chapter offers some strategies for doing the same.

I Repetition and innovation

Understanding the work of the Roman tragedians means seeing it not in isolation, but as following closely on, and even coexisting with, the work of the Greek tragedians. The guiding principles for composing tragedy in antiquity were repetition and innovation.[8] Greek and Roman tragedians trafficked in paradox: traditional stories, themes, and motifs combined with new plots, emphases, and interests. These principles are by no means exclusive to tragedy. They pervade all Greco-Roman literature, particularly on the Roman side, such that Latin literary studies are often couched in oxymoronic terms like "tradition and originality" or "creative imitation."[9] Nevertheless, repetition and innovation aptly describe the creative dynamic of tragedy, which extended as a kind of *agon* or contest from fifth-century Athens to republican Rome.

Who were the best known Roman tragedians before Ovid? Lucius Livius Andronicus (born *c.* 292 BCE), Gnaeus Naevius (*c.* 280–201), Quintus Ennius (239–*c.* 169), Marcus Pacuvius (nephew of Ennius, 220–*c.* 130), and Lucius Accius (170–*c.* 86). Although practiced in other literary forms,[10] each produced a substantial and sizeable tragic corpus over many years, sometimes decades. To Andronicus are ascribed the titles of some

[7] E.g., Arcellaschi 1990, 231–67; T. Heinze 1997, 221–52.

[8] The terms are those of Burian 1997, deployed in discussing how the Greek playwrights shaped their plots. Sommerstein 2005 shares many of Burian's points.

[9] Tradition and originality: G. W. Williams 1968. Creative imitation: West and Woodman 1979.

[10] Most notably, Andronicus, Naevius, and Ennius wrote epic poetry: Andronicus, a rendering of Homer's *Odyssey* in Saturnians; Naevius, the *Bellum Punicum*, also in Saturnians; Ennius, the *Annales*, an overview of Roman history in dactylic hexameter. See section 2, pp. 30–1.

ten tragedies; to Naevius, six; Ennius, twenty; Pacuvius, twelve; Accius, almost fifty. The surviving fragments exemplify repetition and innovation under four distinct rubrics: Hellenism, or the perpetuation of a Greek dramatic form; material, or the mythic subject matter of the plays; theatricality, which includes the sounds and sights of the stage; and socio-political awareness, which was strong from the very beginning. These rubrics will guide our survey of Roman tragedy from the time of Andronicus down to Ovid's own era.

First, Hellenism. Roman tragedy was always indebted to Greek tragedy. Andronicus, the founder of the genre in Rome, was, like Ennius, a native of Magna Graecia and had never known anything other than Greek drama. Both tragedy and comedy were popular throughout the Hellenic world, including southern Italy, where traveling troupes performed older Greek plays at local festivals and other theatrical groups were established.[11] Moreover, new tragedies still premiered at the Athenian Dionysia when Andronicus staged his first tragedy in 240.[12] Arriving in Rome a slave in the retinue of Andronicus Salinator, later freed and teaching as a *grammaticus*, Livius Andronicus was well qualified to bring versions of Greek tragedy and comedy to a Roman audience. "Version" is a better term than "translation" to describe the efforts of Andronicus and his peers. Although the titles clearly emulate those of known Greek plays,[13] side-by-side comparison of Greek "originals" with their so-called Latin "translations" reveals correspondence in thought and sentiment to be more frequent than correspondence in word.[14] The challenge seems to have been how to render Greek tragedy for a different culture.[15]

[11] Established theatrical groups included actors' guilds like the Artists of Dionysus and poetic colleges like the Alexandrian Pleiad. On the history of later Greek tragedy see Gentili 1979, 15–41; Csapo and Slater 1995, 186–206; and Easterling 1997.

[12] Schiesaro 2005, 269.

[13] E.g., Liv. Andron.: *Tereus* (Soph.), *Andromeda* (Eur.); Naev.: *Iphigenia*; Enn.: *Aiax*, *Andromacha*, *Eumenides*, *Hecuba*, *Medea exul*; Pacuv.: *Armorum iudicium* (Aesch.), *Dulorestes*; Acc.: *Alcestis*, *Antigona*, *Bacchae*, *Meleager* (Eur.), *Prometheus*, *Philocteta*, *Troades*, *Telephus* (Eur.).

[14] Thus Conte 1994b, 41: "[The Romans] were, at most, adapters, but not translators." Note the oft-quoted judgment of Cicero, that Ennius translated the Greek word for word (*ad verbum e Graecis expressas*, *Fin.* 1.4 Schiche); but Boyle 2006, 86, cites Cicero against Cicero: the Roman tragedians captured the force of the Greek, not the words (*non verba sed vim*, *Acad.* 1.10 Plasberg).

[15] If Andronicus' canny substitution of *Camena* for the Homeric Μοῦσα in the *incipit* of his *Odusia* is any indication, he was equal to the task. Compare Hinds 1998: Andronicus "quite evidently chose to invoke the [Italic water goddess] *Camena* not out of some twilit ignorance of the Muse, but out of a different view of how the Muse should be translated from Greece to Rome" (60, brackets mine).

Our best opportunity to weigh a Latin tragedy against its Greek original comes in the *incipit* of Ennius' *Medea exul*, whose remains are far more extensive than those of Ovid's play:

Utinam ne in nemore Pelio securibus
caesa accidisset abiegna ad terram trabes,
neve inde navis inchoandi exordium
cepisset, quae nunc nominatur nomine
Argo, quia Argivi in ea delecti viri
vecti petebant pellem inauratam arietis
Colchis, imperio regis Peliae, per dolum.
nam numquam era errans mea domo efferret pedem
Medea animo aegro amore saevo saucia.

How I wish that in Pelion's grove the beam of fir had never fallen to the ground, cut by axes! And how I wish that the ship had never found a point of departure, the ship now named with the name *Argo*, because the Argives, the chosen men, were carried on it and tried to obtain by guile the golden ram's fleece, by order of king Pelias! For then my mistress would never have wandered from home, Medea, sick at heart, wounded by a fierce desire. (Enn. *M. exul* fr. 103 Jocelyn)

Εἴθ' ὤφελ' Ἀργοῦς μὴ διαπτάσθαι σκάφος
Κόλχων ἐς αἶαν κυανέας Συμπληγάδας,
μηδ' ἐν νάπαισι Πηλίου πεσεῖν ποτε
τμηθεῖσα πεύκη, μηδ' ἐρετμῶσαι χέρας
ἀνδρῶν ἀρίστων, οἳ τὸ πάγχρυσον δέρας
Πελίᾳ μετῆλθον. οὐ γὰρ ἂν δέσποιν' ἐμὴ
Μήδεια πύργους γῆς ἔπλευσ' Ἰωλκίας
ἔρωτι θυμὸν ἐκπλαγεῖσ' Ἰάσονος.

How I wish that the Argo had never flown to the land of Colchis through the dark-blue Symplegades! And how I wish that that the pine trees had never fallen, cut down in the groves of Mount Pelion, and had never become oars for the hands of the heroes, who by order of Pelias set out for the golden fleece! For then my mistress, Medea, would not have sailed to the towers of Iolcus, her heart stricken with desire for Jason. (Eur. *Med.* 1–8)

H. D. Jocelyn notes how the Ennian prologue keeps the "bones of Euripides' grammatical arrangement," including "the series of negative wishes, the relative clause, [and] the independent apodotic sentences." These similarities demonstrate Ennius' familiarity with the original Greek and suggest his play as a close approximation. But Ennius adapts as well. He does not mention the passage through the Symplegades, as Euripides does (2). He etymologizes the name *Argo* (*quia Argivi in ea vecti*, 212–13).

He renders the Greek pine (πεύκη, 4) as the more familiar Roman fir (*abiegna*, 209).[16] Most important, his aristocratic Argonauts are carried by the ship (*vecti*, 213); they do not row it themselves.[17] The *incipit* is evidence both of Ennius' reputation as *dicti studiosus*,[18] and of a Roman audience able to appreciate his erudition. The play went on to achieve canonical status, to judge from the reception of this passage in Catullus 64.

Second, material. The Latin tragedians quickly found innovative ways to repackage traditional myths. With Naevius is associated tragic *contaminatio*, the "contamination" or creative fusion of Greek models within plays.[19] Although actual instances of *contaminatio* in Naevius' tragic fragments are difficult to find, critics have embraced the principle as his *modus operandi*. As A. J. Boyle notes, this "thoroughly Roman practice ... signal[s] the city's predilection for merging diverse items of cultural plunder into single tokens of power."[20] Such a practice is also emblematic of a living theatrical tradition, of which Naevius and Andronicus are continuators as much as founders. Furthermore, *contaminatio* would become a means of participating in that tradition, with later poets like Ovid using creative fusion to position themselves as tragedians.

Pacuvius and Accius were the great mythographers of the Roman theater. Particularly arresting are the remains of Pacuvius' *Iliona*, which dramatized an innovative version of the Polydorus myth.[21] In Hyginus' summary, Priam and Hecuba send Polydorus to Iliona, their daughter and the wife of the Thracian Polymestor. Iliona raises her brother as Deipylus, her son by Polymestor, and Deipylus as Polydorus. When Troy falls, the Achaeans bribe Polymestor to slay "Polydorus," while "Deipylus" learns from Apollo that his fatherland is destroyed, his father dead, and his mother enslaved. After revealing her brother's true identity, Iliona blinds and kills Polymestor.[22] Some fragments seem reminiscent of Euripides'

16 Jocelyn 1967, a groundbreaking discussion. Further thoughts on Ennian "imitation" in Cowan 2010, including the phrase *per dolum* (fr. 103.214), which had special resonance in the wake of the Second Punic War. See also Arcellaschi 1990, 69–74.

17 Erasmo 2004, 23; Boyle 2006, 72; Cowan 2010, 43.

18 *Ann.* fr. 209 in Skutsch 1985, a rendering of φιλόλογος.

19 So Terence in the prologue of the *Andria*, citing Naevius, Plautus, and Ennius as his forebears (*qui quom hunc accusant, Naevium, Plautum, Ennium | accusant*, 18–19 Kauer–Lindsay–Skutsch). While Naevius could have been Rome's first practitioner, he was surely not the inventor of *contaminatio*, as critics sometimes imply. Schiesaro 2005, 272, notes that the practice is demonstrable in post-classical Greek theater before its emergence as "a trademark of Roman authors." Schiesaro further suggests that Andronicus was also a practitioner of *contaminatio* in his *Tereus*. As we will see in Chapter 6, the practice is also demonstrable among the classical Greek tragedians.

20 Boyle 2006, 37.

21 Pacuv. *Iliona*: *SRF* I.191–217. Discussion in Manuwald 2000.

22 Hyg. 109.

Hecabe to the point of *contaminatio*. Particularly evocative are Deipylus' ghostly appearance to the sleeping Iliona (Pacuv. fr. 196–201; Eur. *Hec.* 55–9), Iliona's outrage (fr. 206–7; *Hec.* 864–75), and her revenge (fr. 208–9, 215; *Hec.* 1035–108).

While Pacuvius' strategy was to steep individual plays in recherché myth, Accius seems to have specialized in multi-generational sagas for which he adapted Homer and other non-dramatic authors.[23] His *Medea/Argonautae*, which treated the murder of Apsyrtus, apparently drew from *Argonautica* 4.[24] A sizeable fragment survives, the speech of a Colchian shepherd commenting on his sighting of the *Argo*, which as the very first ship defies description. An excerpt:

> tanta moles labitur
> fremibunda ex alto ingenti sonitu et spiritu.
> prae se undas volvit, vortices vi suscitat:
> ruit prolapsa, pelagus respergit, reflat. 394
>
> What a huge mass glides, howling out of the sea with a loud crash and hiss. It rolls the waves before it, it raises eddies with its force: it falls forward, it splashes, it blows back the sea. (Acc. *Medea sive Argonautae* fr. 391–4)

This is an intensely metatheatrical moment, in which a character speaks at length about his inability to speak.[25] If his speech belonged to the prologue, it continued the Euripidean and Ennian traditions of having a minor character begin with the voyage of the *Argo*. Only now the voyage is not a matter of the distant past, but the contemporary present, and Accius' work becomes the originator of the "first ship" motif, now seemingly echoed in the Ennian and Euripidean prologues.[26]

Third, theatricality. Andronicus seems to have followed the trend, already under way in the fourth century in Middle and New Comedy, of restricting the singing and dancing of the chorus.[27] In place of choral odes the poet favored solo songs – *cantica* or monodies – by his actors.[28] Livy's anecdote about a boy singing the *canticum* in the poet's stead, while the poet himself mimed the part, reveals that the solo songs were popular

[23] Boyle 2006, 112.

[24] Erasmo 2004, 45. Acc. *Medea*: *SRF* 1.391–423.

[25] Erasmo 2004, 46.

[26] Likewise Cowan 2010, 48–9, who also postulates in Accius' play an almost Ovidian or Senecan self-consciousness, in which Medea was set on the path to becoming the legendary Medea.

[27] Wigodsky 1972, 18–20, whose view Erasmo 2004, 11, and Schiesaro 2005, 272, share. Boyle 2006, 29 and 247 n. 15, cites evidence to the contrary in Andronicus' disputed *Ino*, which "is reported to have contained a chorus who sing a hymn to Diana."

[28] Boyle 2006, 29, speculates that the increased monodic element in Andronicus' plays was probably less the poet's own innovation and more a reflection of the "existing musical emphasis."

with his audiences, who did not seem to mind the patent artificiality of this arrangement.[29] Naevius shared his contemporary's partiality for *cantica* and helped make them conventional.[30] Ennius seems to have had a high, if not higher, musical quota in his plays. Boyle reports an impressive figure: more than 70 percent of the poet's surviving tragic verses would have been sung, or at least recited, to musical accompaniment.[31] In addition to preserving the monodies of Greek drama, *cantica* were also powerful moments of self-expression akin to monologues.

Roman tragedy was known for featuring rhetoric, more so than Greek tragedy, and the speeches of Latin tragic poets fared rather well in the judgment of later critics. Cicero is fond of quoting the tragedians as oratorical *exempla*, although he condemns Andronicus as not worth reading twice.[32] Accius visited Pergamum and became acquainted with the Asianic style of oratory, which he put to ornamental and emotional use in his plays – though, as Mario Erasmo notices, Accian rhetoric tends to thematize the negative and insidious effects of rhetoric itself.[33] Of Pacuvius, Boyle singles out a fragment of the *Periboea*, which seems to constitute a piece of stagecraft familiar to postclassical theatergoers, but infrequent on the classical Greek stage: the "first extant undeniable soliloquy of Roman tragedy."[34] Here is Diomedes, appealing to his *animus* and his *mens* (Latin approximations for the Greek *thumos*):

> consternare, anime, ex pectore aude ecvolvere[35]
> consilium subito, mens, quod enatumst modo,
> qui pacto inimicis mortem et huic vitam offeras.
>
> Awake, my spirit, dare to unroll from my breast the plan, O mind, that was just now conceived, by which you might deal death to my enemies and life to this man here. (Pacuv. *Periboea* fr. 284–6)

29 Livy 7.2.8–9. Andronicus had lost his voice after one too many encores, and this temporary solution became an established practice. Erasmo 2004, 11, presses the point of artificiality further: "The effect of having the lead actor(s) gesticulating onstage while someone else sang offstage was to make an already unrealistic depiction of human interaction onstage even further removed from the audience's experience outside of the theater."

30 Erasmo 2004, 14; Boyle 2006, 37.

31 Boyle 2006, 61, citing similar proportions in Plautus, which show this figure to be consonant with practices of the period.

32 *Livianae fabulae non satis dignae quae iterum legantur* (Cic. *Brut.* 71 Malcovati). On Cicero's affinity for Roman tragedy see Goldberg 1996, 274, citing Cic. *De or.* 3.217–19; also (more expansively) Wright 1931 and Fantham 2004.

33 Erasmo 2004, 43, following La Penna 1979, 63–71. On Accian Asianism see Boyle 2006, 113–15.

34 Boyle 2006, 99.

35 Boyle 2006, 255 n. 115, accepts Ribbeck's *aude ecvolvere* for Klotz' obelized *hac et volvere* in *SRF* I.

Although we cannot know whether Diomedes is literally alone onstage, there is no denying the compelling interiority of this fragment.

Spectacle seems to have been a hallmark of Pacuvian and Accian theater. Gesine Manuwald suggests that the *Orestes* of Pacuvius showed the protagonist pursued by the Furies, and that this confrontation formed the basis for the famous stage simile in *Aen.* 4 (to be examined later).[36] Equally memorable was the appearance of the ghost of "Polydorus" to his mother Iliona: *mater, te apello, tu quae curam somno suspensam levas* (I call on you, mother, you, alleviating with sleep your suspended anxiety, fr. 196), which recalls not only Polydorus in the *Hecabe* of Euripides but also the ghost of Achilles in the lost *Polyxena* of Sophocles.[37] Accian spectacles were both verbal, as the virtuoso description of the *Argo* has already shown,[38] and visual, especially in departures from model plays. In the *Antigona*, for example, the heroine is captured onstage (fr. 138–41), visible proof of her struggle against authority, whereas her capture is reported after the fact in Sophocles.[39]

Finally, politics and society. Roman tragedy from the beginning was political. Andronicus' first production at the *ludi Romani* of 240 was commissioned by the Senate, which wanted something extraordinary to celebrate victory in the First Punic War.[40] Under Naevius (unusual among Roman poets for being of plebeian status[41]) politics enters the genre through his invention of the *fabula praetexta*, or Roman historical drama. This tragic sub-genre seems to have been formally and modally no different from the *cothurnata*, even to the point of employing a chorus.[42] Naevius' *praetextae* treated both older Roman history and contemporary events, such as the founding of Rome (*Romulus*) and the victory of M. Claudius Marcellus over the Insubrian Gauls (222 BCE, *Clastidium*).[43] The latter, with a barb aimed at the powerful Metelli, the political rivals of the Marcelli, might have cost Naevius dearly: *fato Metelli Romae fiunt consules*

36 Manuwald 2003, 115, following Serv. *Aen.* 4.473.

37 Boyle 2006, 94, cites other instances of spectacle in Pacuvius, including the *Medus*, which might have featured Medea on her dragon-drawn chariot (Cic. *Rep.* 3.14).

38 So Boyle 2006, 117: "Linguistic spectacle anticipates, in part constitutes, dramatic spectacle."

39 Boyle 2006, 119–20.

40 Gruen 1996, 87–8. Cicero records the date and the occasion, but not the title of the play (*Brut.* 72).

41 Accius, however, was the son of a freedman father.

42 Thus Gratwick 1982, 128; also Boyle 2006, 49.

43 In *SRF* I see Naev. *Romulus* (fr. 3–4, distinguished from *Lupus*, fr. 5–8, though perhaps unnecessarily) and *Clastidium* (fr. 1–2). Ennius and Pacuvius followed suit in their respective *Ambracia* (fr. 1–4), celebrating the military victory of M. Fulvius Nobilior (189 BCE), and *Paullus* (fr. 1–5), perhaps a dramatization of L. Aemilius Paullus' victory at Pydna (in 168: Schiesaro 2005, 273–4). Ennius also composed a *Sabinae* (fr. 5–6), while Accius' two known *praetextae* were *Aeneadae/Decius* (fr. 1–16) and *Brutus* (fr. 17–41).

(the Metelli are made consuls at Rome through fate).[44] The public slight led at least to his imprisonment, and perhaps even to his exile in African Utica.[45]

Unlike Naevius, Ennius is remembered as a friend of the aristocracy.[46] Oscan by birth, he was brought to Rome in 204 or 203 BCE by M. Porcius Cato. He became the client of M. Fulvius Nobilior, whom he accompanied to Ambracia in 189, and who was doubtless instrumental in Ennius' becoming a Roman citizen in 184. His tragedies are steeped in aristocratic ideals, such as *pietas*, *pudor*, *imperium*, and *concordia*, which reflect the influence of the city's elite.[47] This influence was literally dramatized at the *ludi Romani* of 194 BCE, not on the stage, but in the audience, after Scipio Africanus arranged exclusive seating for senators in the orchestra.[48] Pacuvius seems the least politically invested, perhaps owing to his putative equestrian status, which is suggested by his lack of patronage, as well as his nebulous affiliations with the Scipios.[49] His fragments, however, do reflect the theme of power and its abuses: *Iliona* fr. 206–7 show the titular heroine plotting revenge against her husband.[50] The great Roman stage tyrants are to be found in the fragments of Accius, who lived through one of the most tumultuous periods in Roman history.[51] Two plays in particular, *Atreus* and *Tereus*, dramatize the dangers of autocracy and the corruption of power.[52] A fragment of the latter describes Tereus' uncontrollable lust for Philomela:

[44] As Erasmo 2004, 15, explains, the line implies that "the Metelli owed their political power to chance rather than intelligence." Both Erasmo and Boyle 2006, 54, quote the famous rejoinder from the Metelli themselves (preserved in ps.-Asconius and elsewhere): *dabunt malum Metelli Naevio poetae* (the Metelli will give the poet Naevius trouble). Boyle, 54, follows Mattingly 1960 and Jocelyn 1969 in assigning the line to the *Clastidium* rather than a Naevian comedy. The date of the performance of the *Clastidium* is usually given as 208, at the funeral games for Marcellus, or 205, the dedication of the temple of *Virtus*, two very public occasions.

[45] See, e.g., Gell. 3.3.15 (imprisonment), Jer. *Chron.* 201a (exile). Naevius is probably the imprisoned *poeta barbarus* mentioned at Plaut. *Mil.* 211.

[46] On Ennius' life, works, and patronage see Jocelyn 1967, 43–7; also Boyle 2006, 58–9, who rightly emphasizes the aristocratic element. Farrell 2002, 37–40, links Ennius' career to that of his patron: see section 2, pp. 30–1.

[47] Thus Boyle 2006, 61, an exhaustive list keyed to the fragments; see also, more generally, Schiesaro 2005, 274. On the "celebration of aristocratic *virtus*" in the *Annales* see Conte 1994b, 83.

[48] Thus, e.g., Livy 34.44.5; Val. Max. 2.4.3.

[49] So Boyle 2006, 88. Erasmo 2004, 35, following Bilinski 1957, alleges Pacuvius' sympathy for the *plebs* in the *Dulorestes*.

[50] So Boyle 2006, 97–8.

[51] Boyle 2006, 110, offers a thoughtful summary of what Accius would have seen and experienced during the period from the destruction of Carthage to the Marian proscriptions. See also Conte 1994b, 307. Hardie 1997, 325, following La Penna 1980, notes that Mezentius in the *Aeneid* is a close analogue to an Accian stage tyrant.

[52] Acc. *Atreus*: *SRF* I.197–235b; *Tereus*: Chapter 3, n. 33.

> Tereus indomito more atque animo barbaro
> conspexit in eam, amore vecors flammeo,
> depositus facinus pessimum ex dementia
> confingit. 639

> Tereus, with indomitable character and barbarian mind, caught sight of her. Driven mad by love's flames, desperate, he conceived in his madness the worst of all crimes. (Acc. *Tereus* fr. 636–9)

These lines were famous enough for Ovid to recall them in his depiction of Tereus' *innata libido* (*Met.* 6.455–60).[53]

Our four rubrics reveal the Roman tragic poets as creators of and participants in a vibrant theatrical tradition. Deeply engaged with Greek models, inventive in their use of myth, assured in their stagecraft, and alive to the concerns of their audiences, they sustained their genre for nearly two centuries. Ovid clearly understood what was at stake both in joining the ranks of the Roman playwrights and in fashioning a tragedy about so famous a heroine:[54]

> Ennius arte carens animosique Accius oris
> casurum nullo tempore nomen habent.
> Varronem primamque ratem quae nesciet aetas
> aureaque Aesonio terga petita duci?

> Ennius, though lacking polish, and Accius with his bold rhetoric have immortal names. What era will not know of Varro and that first ship, and of the golden hide sought by Aeson's heroic son? (*Am.* 1.15.19–22)

In order to live up to the standards of his predecessors, Ovid needed his *Medea* to be cognizant of prior versions, innovative enough to be distinctive, steeped in rhetoric and spectacle, and connected to its times. To judge from the *Heroides* and the *Metamorphoses*, Ovid was ready for the challenge. Both works take the canons of Greco-Roman myth head-on, and both are highly rhetorical – a reflection of the robust forensic training among members of Ovid's class.[55] Furthermore, the *Metamorphoses* is celebrated for its visuality, which not only embellishes the world of which the poet wrote, but also exemplifies the world in which he wrote (*ad mea tempora*, *Met.* 1.4).

[53] So Currie 1981, 2725: "The whole picture in Ovid is one of blazing, uncontrollable passion, and this is doubtless what he found in large measure in the original Accian context."

[54] Arcellaschi 1990, 236–7.

[55] On Ovid's rhetorical education, attested by the elder Seneca (*Controv.* 2.2) and by Ovid himself (*Tr.* 4.10), see Auhagen 2007, 415, following Auhagen 1999, 20–2. See also Barchiesi 2005, cl–cli ("Rhetorica poetica"), and Schiesaro 2002, 70–4.

2 Careerism and gentrification

The seven or so decades that separate Ovid from Accius brought lasting changes to the genre, in terms of both who wrote tragedy and how plays began to look and sound. On the one hand, there seems to have been a decline in professional tragedians, accompanied by a rise in amateurs from the ranks of the aristocracy. Sander Goldberg explains, "The first thing to understand about Roman tragedy after Accius is that it underwent the same process of gentrification common to all Roman poetry."[56] On the other hand, tragedy apparently became bifurcated in its modes of presentation, with an even greater reliance on spectacle in the theaters and on rhetoric in the recital halls, where the genre found a second lease on life. Understanding these developments is critical to understanding why a successful elegist like Ovid would have contemplated a career change.

To speak of a socio-political dimension to early Roman tragedy is also to speak of careerism, both the literary careers of the poets themselves and the political careers of their aristocratic patrons. The two are not easily disentangled. Joseph Farrell singles out Andronicus and Ennius as early examples of a poetic career paradigm that might be called the *cursus litterarum*, a literary reflection of the political *cursus honorum*.[57] That dramatic productions should have been vital to both *cursus* is plain when we consider the reciprocal relationship between the patron, who relied on theatrical entertainments to further his career, and the poet-client, who provided them and shared in his patron's success.[58] Not only did Andronicus, Ennius, and their peers compose for public occasions, but the many genres in which they worked also illustrate the variety essential for a poetic career. In the case of Ennius, we find variety as well as a sense of progression worthy of a true *cursus*. Although he wrote tragedies until his death (his last, the *Thyestes*, premiered in 169 BCE[59]), his masterpiece was the *Annales*, an epic narrative of Roman history – in effect Rome's national epic until the *Aeneid*.

[56] Goldberg 1996, 270, following Beare 1965, 125–7. See also Beacham 1992, 125–6.

[57] Farrell 2002, 34–40, though the term *cursus litterarum* is that of Barchiesi and Hardie 2010, 65. Farrell focuses on Andronicus and Ennius because the evidence for their careers is clearest, particularly for Ennius'. Many of Farrell's remarks, however, can also apply to the careers of Naevius, Pacuvius, and Accius. Naevius, of course, is an example of a *cursus litterarum* clashing with the *cursus honorum* of the Metelli.

[58] Farrell 2002, 36.

[59] Conte 1994b, 76. Enn. *Thyestes*: *SRF* 1.295–312.

Even in fragments the *Annales* is unmistakably a career highlight, in which Ennius ascended to epic and made his reputation as Homer reincarnated. This was a significant achievement, but more significant still for the poet and his successors was the addition of three books to the poem, from fifteen to eighteen.[60] Like Ennius' earlier *praetexta*,[61] book 15 celebrated the victory of Fulvius Nobilior at Ambracia (189 BCE) and linked the culmination of the epic with the culmination of a political career. Expanding the *Annales* moved the work past Fulvius Nobilior's career into Ennius' own present. As Farrell observes, "[T]he original, patron-centered climax of the epic was later trumped by a plan that identified the end of the poem with that of the poet's life."[62] The arc of Ennius' career – its beginnings in dramatic poetry, its ascent to epic, and its terminus independent of a patron – was perhaps the best example of a self-sustaining *cursus litterarum* before Vergil.

The death of Accius (between 90 and 80 BCE) marks the end of an epoch. Although revivals of both Greek and Roman tragedies were common at the *ludi*,[63] and although new tragedies continued to be written, professional interest in the genre seems to have declined. We hear of tragic poets like Santra, Pompilius, and Pupius, but we know very little about them. Only four verses of Santra's *Nuptials of Bacchus* (*Nuptiae Bacchi*) survive.[64] A single verse of Pompilius survives as well as a two-line epitaph in elegiacs, in which he claims fame as a student of Pacuvius, who learned from Ennius, who learned from the Muses.[65] Of Pupius, a contemporary of Horace, there remains nothing, though in an extant lampoon he is made to say that his friends will lament his death, since audiences lamented him in life (*nam populus in me vivo lacrimavit satis*).[66] The latter two poets might have approached tragedy with careerist aspirations: Pompilius' epitaph vaunts his mastery of the genre by tracing his discipleship to Ennius and beyond, while Pupius' teary-eyed public suggests sustained, if unsuccessful, efforts.

[60] Farrell 2002, 37–40. On Ennius' dream, in which he was visited by Homer's ghost and revealed to be his reincarnation see sections ii–x (incorporating fr. 2–11) in Skutsch 1985.

[61] Enn. *Ambracia*: n. 43, above.

[62] Farrell 2002, 39.

[63] Beare 1965, 126. Boyle 2006, 145 and 260 n. 7–8, cites Wright 1931, 31–61, a study of performance citations in Cicero, to whom we owe much of our information about revivals of old plays.

[64] Santra: *SRF* I *s.v.* "*Nuptiae Bacchae*." I accept, along with Boyle 2006, Ribbeck's emendation of the title. See also Beare 1965, 126.

[65] Pompilius: epitaph and fr. 1 in *SRF* I; discussion in Courtney 1993, 51.

[66] Pupius: *SRF* I and Courtney 1993, 307.

Granted, a decline in professional tragedians is conjectural for lack of direct evidence. Nevertheless, the same period saw rising interest in tragedy among the aristocracy, such that the genre seems to have become a gentrified "prestige business."[67] Exemplary of tragedy's gentrification are figures like C. Titius and Julius Caesar Strabo, both contemporaries of Accius, as well as Cicero's brother, Q. Tullius.[68] Titius, a member of the equestrian order, won Cicero's praise for Attic liveliness in his plays.[69] Caesar Strabo, aedile in 90 BCE and murdered in 87 by supporters of Marius, was the author of at least three tragedies: *Adrastus*, *Tecmessa*, and *Teuthras*.[70] Quintus Cicero once wrote four tragedies in sixteen days, presumably for his own amusement.[71] In Goldberg's opinion, such plays were "amateur efforts of little significance. They were not produced, and most never even circulated."[72] Such an assessment might be overly categorical:[73] Caesar Strabo's activity, for instance, was serious enough to admit him into the *Collegium Poetarum*.[74] All the same, writing tragedy in the late to mid first century BCE apparently became a pastime for Rome's elite: a test of literary mettle, but nothing on which to base a poetic career.

A story involving Caesar Strabo and Accius at the *Collegium* speaks to this trend. Valerius Maximus recounts how Accius never stood up to acknowledge the approach of Caesar Strabo, who, although his social superior, was in Accius' view an inferior tragedian (*se superiorem esse confideret*, 3.7.11 Kempf).[75] Especially telling is how this slight was perceived: Valerius notes that Accius' behavior was not criminally arrogant (*insolentiae crimine caruit*), since rivalries within the *Collegium* were a matter of artistry,

[67] Prestige business: Boyle 2006, 143, with specific reference to the poetic *auctoritas* of Accius, but an apt description of the genre until Seneca.

[68] Goldberg 1996, 271, adding the sons of Piso, as well as Julius Caesar and Octavian (on whom see below); also Pomponius Secundus, 272. Boyle 2006, 143–4, cites Caesar Strabo, C. Titius, Q. Tullius Cicero, Julius Caesar, and Octavian, as well as Cornelius Balbus, Asinius Pollio, and Cassius of Parma (on the latter two see below). See also Farrell 2002, 40–1.

[69] C. Titius: *SRF* I cites Cic. *Brut.* 167: *huius orationes tantum argutiarum, tantum exemplorum, tantum urbanitatis habent ut paene Attico stilo scriptae esse videantur* (Malcovati). See also Beare 1965, 126.

[70] Caesar Strabo: *SRF* I.1–2 (*Adrastus*), 3 (*Tecmessa*, title only), 4 (*Teuthras*). See also Beare 1965, 125–6.

[71] Q. Tullius Cicero: *SRF* I, *test.* III.

[72] Goldberg 1996, 271.

[73] Boyle 2006, 260 n. 6, finds Goldberg "more than a little prejudicial," especially where Caesar Strabo is concerned.

[74] On the *Collegium Poetarum* see Horsfall 1976. On Caesar Strabo's admission see Beacham 1992, 125. We should also remember that Caesar Strabo was relatively young (only thirty-four) at the time of his death. Who knows what his literary achievements would have been had he survived the factionalism of the early first century?

[75] On this story see Beare 1965, 126; Goldberg 1996, 270–1; Boyle 2006, 143.

not of ancestry (*ibi voluminum, non imaginum certamina exercebantur*). The distinction between literary and political careers, first glimpsed with Ennius, seems to have become institutionalized. Even though the Roman elite were writing tragedy, an author more advanced in the *cursus honorum* could have lesser status than one more advanced in his *cursus litterarum*. The distinction held into the early principate: the juvenile *Oedipus* of Julius Caesar, and its abortive sequel in the *Ajax* of Augustus, never saw the light of day.[76] Rome had not yet reached the point where both rulers and ruled consistently comported themselves in theatrical terms.[77]

Nevertheless, there were exceptions. The political and the theatrical merged spectacularly in 55 BCE at the dedication of the Theater of Pompey, Rome's first permanent theater. According to Cicero, who was an eye-witness, two old tragedies were revived for the ceremonies: the *Clytemnestra* of Accius and the *Equos Troianus* of (probably) Naevius, both chosen to celebrate the conquests of Pompey by way of depicting Agamemnon's conquests. In a letter to M. Marius (*Fam.* 7.1), Cicero describes the lavish productions, noting that the *Clytemnestra* featured 600 mules, possibly for Agamemnon's grand entrance, while the *Equos Troianus* involved 3,000 bronze bowls, perhaps as the plunder of Troy.[78] Both tragedies, along with the other spectacles surrounding the dedication of the theater, tried to "recapture and transcend" Pompey's own lavish triple triumph of 61 BCE.[79] Even the very theater made a political statement with the Temple of Venus Victrix (Bringer of Victory) at the top center of the *cavea*, a monument to Pompey's military success.[80]

Pompey's mule-and-bowl pageantry, although consonant with his political ambition and appropriate to the occasion, indicates that staged tragedies were becoming visually unwieldy. Writing to Augustus over

[76] Suetonius describes the fate of both plays. Augustus forbade the *Oedipus* and Julius Caesar's other juvenilia to be published (*Iul.* 56.7), and said that his own *Ajax* had fallen on his eraser (i.e., was deleted for good: *in spongiam incubuisse, Aug.* 85.2 Ihm).

[77] Bartsch 1994 explores theatricality in the relationship between the emperor and his subjects from Nero onward, a relationship that may be back-projected onto Augustan Rome within the more general terms of spectacle: see Beacham 1999, ch. 1 (especially 11–44), Boyle 2006, 160–76, and more generally Hardie 2002, 38–42, and Feldherr 2010 *passim.*

[78] Cic. *Fam* 7.1.2: *quid enim delectationis habent sescenti muli in Clytaemestra aut in Equo Troiano creterrarum tria milia aut armatura varia peditatus et equitatus in aliqua pugna?* (Shackleton Bailey). On these productions see Beacham 1992, 167; Goldberg 1996, 265–7; and Boyle 2006, 155–6. Rudd 1989 notes that the bowls were "presumably part of Pompey's Asian loot" (Hor. *Epist.* 2.1.193).

[79] Boyle 2006, 155; Beacham 1992, 158.

[80] Boyle 2006, 150–2, offers a detailed description of the theater and its grounds. See also Beacham 1999, 61–72, and *NTDAR s.v. Theatrum Pompeii.*

three decades later, Horace would lament that high production values had become all too common:

> verum equitis quoque iam migravit ab aure voluptas
> omnis ad incertos oculos et gaudia vana.
> quattuor aut plures aulaea premuntur in horas,
> dum fugiunt equitum turmae peditumque catervae;
> mox trahitur manibus regum fortuna retortis,
> esseda festinant, pilenta, petorrita, naves,
> captivum portatur ebur, captiva Corinthus.

> But now all pleasure has wandered from the knight's ear to his shifting gaze and to empty delights. The curtain is drawn four hours or more, while squads of cavalry and companies of infantry are routed; soon kings, the victims of fortune, are dragged onstage, their hands bound behind them; chariots of war, coaches, carts, ships all hasten past. Ivory is carried on as a spoil of war, and Corinthian bronze as well. (Hor. *Epist.* 2.1.187–93 Rudd)

Horace describes an ungainly hybrid of tragic plot (*regum fortuna*, 191) and triumphal procession.[81] His account, couched in the generalizing present tense, suggests that the elaborate revivals in the Theater of Pompey some thirty years prior had become more the rule than the exception.

What ostensibly kept these tragic spectaculars in production was their mass appeal, and not just at the level of the *plebs*. Although Cicero carefully distinguishes between his and Marius' distaste for Pompey's revivals and popular acclaim for them (*quae popularem admirationem habuerunt, delectationem tibi nullam attulissent*, *Fam.* 7.1.2 Shackleton Bailey), Horace claims that admiration for spectacle, if not outright pleasure in it, has spread even to the equestrian class (*equitis quoque iam migravit ab aure voluptas | omnis ad incertos oculos*, 2.1.187–8). Moreover, the scale of the Theater of Pompey and, later, the Theater of Marcellus accommodated ever grander productions, which probably whetted the public's appetite for more. Likewise the Theater of Curio, a unique wooden structure erected in 52 BCE: an enclosed amphitheater that became two hemi-theaters, its halves pivoting along a hinge, Curio's theater was opened in the morning for simultaneous performances of dramas, and closed in the afternoon for

81 The phrase *regum fortuna* suggests a kind of plot that, according to Aristotle, might inspire pity or fear – but only if executed properly, since a good man passing from prosperity to misfortune inspires only revulsion (*Poet.* 13.1452b). Perhaps Horace is arguing for the bankruptcy of tragic productions in terms of both plot and spectacle. Goldberg 1996, 272, maintains that the poet's confusion of tragedy and pageantry is "precisely the point."

gladiatorial combat.[82] The structure seems emblematic of the increasingly blurred boundaries between drama and spectacle, at least in spatial terms.

The last great Roman tragedy before Ovid's *Medea* attended the triple triumph of Octavian and the celebration of his victory at Actium (29 BCE).[83] L. Varius Rufus, a poet in Maecenas' circle and future publisher of the *Aeneid*, was commissioned to write a *Thyestes* for the occasion. Two partial lines survive:[84]

> iam fero infandissima,
> iam facere cogor.

> Now I endure the unspeakable, now I am compelled to do it. (Varius *Thy.* fr. 1–2)

Given Pompey's political theatrics, a grand tragic production would have been a fitting, and perhaps expected, tribute to the emerging principate. However, a play about fraternal strife, adultery, and infanticide seems at first blush an odd choice for the future Augustus. Thyestes himself had become a paradigm of abusive autocracy in the *Atreus* of Accius and the *Thyestes* of Cassius of Parma, one of Julius Caesar's assassins.[85] Octavian's sponsorship of a Thyestean tragedy could have become a political disaster (much like plays about Agamemnon, triumphant but doomed, could have been for Pompey), particularly with the reversion of *imperium* to a single ruler. Nevertheless, the soon-to-be emperor might also have acknowledged the danger of autocracy by embracing this risky play, converting it into a "negative paradigm which his own hegemony disavowed."[86]

Varius' *Thyestes* feels like the start of a new era in Roman tragedy, a work in a high and venerable genre that reflected the neo-classicism of the Augustan age.[87] Certainly it was a career highlight for Varius, to judge from the one million sesterces he was paid and from the verdicts of later

[82] Plin. *HN* 36.117. Both Goldberg 1996, 268 (who dates the theater to 53), and Boyle 2006, 21–2, note that Curio's theater was less temporary than others, since (according to Cic. *Fam.* 8.2.1) it was still being used for dramatic productions in 51 BCE. Beacham 1992, 251 n. 57, claims that the structure was Rome's first elliptical amphitheater.

[83] Goldberg 1996, 272, offers a second possible date: the *ludi Apollinares* of 28 BCE, another high-profile Augustan event.

[84] Varius Rufus: *SRF* I.1–9 (1–2, *Thyestes*). See Courtney 1993, 271–5, on Varius' other poetry.

[85] Acc. *Atreus*: n. 52, above. Cass. Parm.: *SRF* I, *test.*; also Boyle 2006, 143, who notes that Cassius also wrote an *Oresteia* and a *Brutus*.

[86] Boyle 2006, 161–2 (and 156–7 on the negative political overtones of the tragedies inaugurating Pompey's theater).

[87] Compare Hardie 1997: "Pollio [on whom see below, pp. 36–7] and Varius may have aspired to create a new, 'classic,' stage in the development of Roman tragedy, challenging directly the great tragedians of fifth-century Athens" (324, brackets mine).

critics.[88] Yet as a standalone play, the *Thyestes* represents one endpoint in the gentrification of tragedy. With fewer professional tragedians to set the standards, the genre seems to have lost its familiar footing in the theater. Tragic performances, whether revivals of old plays or new ones composed for special occasions, became isolated and aggrandized. Old or new, these tragedies were more for the eye than the ear, and the *Thyestes* was probably no exception.[89] Meanwhile, other dramatic forms like mime and pantomime, the first of which had long had a place on the Roman stage, became ever more popular and began to fill the gaps in between lavish tragic spectaculars – perhaps because producing them was less complicated.[90]

A second endpoint of gentrification was the relocation of tragedy from grand productions in public theaters to smaller venues, "the more intimate (and more aristocratic) confines of … roofed halls and private houses," where it flourished in recitation.[91] A renowned practitioner of this trend was C. Asinius Pollio (76 or 75 BCE–4 or 5 CE), arguably the most successful politician-turned-tragedian of the late republic.[92] Though none of his plays survive, Pollio apparently went well beyond the recreational plays of his fellow gentry, embarking on a true *cursus litterarum* upon retiring from political life sometime after 39 BCE. Horace, for example, found his tragedies worthy of the Attic stage: *grande munus* | *Cecropio repetes coturno* (*Carm.* 2.1.11–12 Klingner).[93] According to Seneca the Elder, Pollio was the first to recite his works before select audiences (*primus enim omnium Romanorum advocatis hominibus scripta sua recitavit, Controv.* 4.*pr*.2) – works that should have included his tragedies.[94] Plays like these were more for the ear than the eye, and their authors, writing with such spaces

88 On the amount see Jocelyn 1980. For the verdicts of later critics see below, pp. 43–4.

89 Goldberg 1996 warns against seeing the million sesterces paid to Varius as an indicator of lavish production values: "[T]he [sum] may have been … [a] reward for long service, rather like Horace's Sabine farm" (272 n. 10, brackets mine). Furthermore, Horace's description of theatrical excess implies a production of the *Thyestes* with some degree of moderation (and more moderate than Pompey's revivals of Accius and Naevius in Cicero's account), since in writing to Augustus Horace would not have impugned the *Thyestes* by implication. Then again, the notion of moderation is perhaps relative: the lavishness of Octavian's triple triumph overall suggests a similar kind of tragic production (Cass. Dio 51.21.5–8).

90 On the origins of mime and pantomime, and their popularity in the late republic and early empire, see Beacham 1992, 129–53. On Ovid's use of mime in the *Fasti* and elsewhere see Wiseman 2002.

91 Goldberg 1996, 273, with bibliography at n. 11.

92 Asinius Pollio: Courtney 1993, 254–6 (with a summary of Pollio's unfortunate affiliation with Antony); Conte 1994b, 260 and 377–8; Beacham 1999, 136–8. *SRF* I, *test.*, affirms Pollio's success as a tragedian, but without clear indications of the plays he wrote.

93 Likewise Verg. *Ecl.* 8.10: *sola Sophocleo tua carmina digna coturno* (Mynors).

94 So Tarrant 1978, 260, noting that Horace's reference to Pollio's *theatris* in *Carm.* 2.1.10 could imply formal theaters or recital halls.

and audiences in mind, doubtless put their forensic educations to work. Particularly useful would have been training in declamation, specifically the arts of argumentation (*controversiae*), deliberation-persuasion (*suasoriae*), and speeches in character (*ethopoeiae*).[95] Tragedy had always been rhetorical, Roman tragedy especially so. Composing for recital halls and suppressing the visual dimension must have induced the genre to even greater rhetorical heights.[96]

3 The *Medea* of Ovid

This was the gentrified, bifurcated state of tragedy that greeted Ovid in the wake of *Amores* edition one. That collection, we will see, had already broadcast the poet's intent to move on from elegy – although it was less a matter of moving on than of moving *up*, of marking progress within his career. The concept of career progress had taken shape in Ennius' ascent from tragedy to epic. Yet the career of Vergil, with its ascending, tripartite structure, was for Ovid a clearer and more contemporary model.[97] Farrell traces Ovid's Vergilian self-fashioning in *Amores* 1.1, whose *recusatio* of epic *arma* (1) emulates the *recusatio* of *reges et proelia* at *Eclogue* 6.3;[98] and in the closing *sphragis* of *Ars amatoria* 2, where *arma* (741) quotes the first word of *Am.* 1.1, just as the closing *sphragis* of *Georgics* 4 (566) quotes the first line of *Ecl.* 1.[99] Farrell reads these patterns as careerist gestures, with which Ovid follows Vergil in assigning his initial poetry to a lower genre, and then in looking back – or down – on that work from the higher ground of didactic. The *Ars* ultimately represented a poetic advance like the *Georgics*. The key word in this scenario is "ultimately," because

[95] The indispensable work on Roman declamation is still Bonner 1949.

[96] Goldberg 1996, 275–84 discusses how previous generations of critics, beginning with Leo 1878 and his typology of *tragoedia rhetorica*, faulted the rhetorical nature of recitation drama, especially as (ostensibly) represented and epitomized by Seneca's plays. Against their objections Goldberg asserts that rhetoric exerted an incubatory influence over the genre, allowing it to survive and even flourish when other dramatic forms like comedy were eventually lost: "Declamatory rhetoric may … be the scholar's despair, but it was certainly the salvation of tragedy" (284). On the gradual rhetoricization of literature at large from the Augustan principate to the Second Sophistic, see G. W. Williams 1978, 303–6.

[97] Theodorakopoulos 1997, 155–6, and Cheney 2002, 7–8, discuss the tidy medieval trope of the *rota* or wheel as a symbol for Vergil's career, "quite literally a vehicle for tracking later poets" (Cheney, 7). Barchiesi and Hardie 2010 suggest that the Vergilian career pattern was established early enough for Ovid to emulate: "[T]he Vergilian model is always present, whether through affirmation or negation, and the Ovidian career is the first episode in the long history of the reception of the Vergilian career" (60).

[98] Farrell 2004, 42–3. [99] Farrell 2004, 44–6.

Ovid's first project after the *Amores* was not a loftier strain of elegy, but a loftier genre altogether.

The *Medea*, therefore, was Ovid's first attempt at "generic escalation"[100] in the manner of Vergil, even as it emulated tragedies by Ennius, Euripides, and others. As the preceding survey has shown, there would have been room for an ambitious poet to work within the genre, to produce a series of plays or even just one of note. Furthermore, this seems to have been the attitude of Ovid himself, to judge from his own testimonials in *Amores* 3 – which now belong to the collection's second edition (*c.* 1 BCE), but which had been part of the original, five-book edition (after 20 BCE). In *Am.* 3.1 the very personification of tragedy, contesting with elegy for Ovid's loyalty, issues a call for a professional poet:

> "tempus erat thryso pulsum graviore moveri;
> cessatum satis est – incipe maius opus! 24
> ... nunc habeam per te Romana Tragoedia nomen!
> implebit leges spiritus iste meas." 30

> "It is high time you moved to the beat of a heavier thyrsus; enough with your indolent ways – begin a greater work! ... Now let me have through you the name Roman Tragedy! That spirit of yours will carry out my precepts." (*Am.* 3.1.23–4, 29–30)

A chance to restore the name of Roman tragedy suggests the dawning of a new age in the genre (*nunc habeam per te Romana Tragoedia nomen*, 29). This is a bold formulation. Even while it supports the theory that tragedy was no longer what it had been, it suggests that the age will begin with Ovid, despite the efforts of poets like Varius and Pollio. Note, too, the emphasis on tragedy as a *maius opus* (24), a phrase that not only heralds generic escalation, but also couches it in distinctly Vergilian terms. In the famous *proemio al mezzo* ("proem in the middle") of *Aeneid* 7, Vergil signals a higher register within his emerging epic career: *maius opus moveo* (45). Tragedy imposes a similar register on Ovid's putative tragic career.[101]

At the end of *Am.* 3.1, the poet elects to remain an elegist for the time being (*exiguum vati concede, Tragoedia, tempus*, 67). His formal farewell to

[100] Generic escalation: I borrow the term from Hinds 1993, 42, who discusses the escalation from elegy to tragedy at the end of *Her.* 12 (*nescio quid certe mens mea maius agit*, 212); see Chapter 3, p. 82. Compare the equally efficient "generic ascent" of S. J. Harrison 2002, 82.

[101] I return to this passage in section 4, pp. 56–7. On Ovid's programmatic usage of *maius opus* throughout his career, see Hardie 2004, 162–4 and n. 36; also Barchiesi and Hardie 2010, 62.

the genre comes in *Am.* 3.15, the last poem of edition two, and probably of edition one as well:

> corniger increpuit thyrso graviore Lyaeus:
> pulsanda est magnis area maior equis.
> imbelles elegi, genialis Musa, valete,
> post mea mansurum fata superstes opus!

> Horned Bacchus has brandished a heavier thyrsus. Grand horses must tread a grander arena. Farewell, passive elegies, congenial Muse. May you, my labor, be destined to stand beyond my doom! (*Am.* 3.15.17–20)

Again quantifiable ascendancy as Ovid transitions to the *area maior* (18) of tragedy. In addition, he activates fully the career metaphor of the race-course: *pulsanda est magnis area maior equis.*[102] This new, tragic phase of his *cursus litterarum* will require large horses to progress within its larger boundaries.[103]

An *area maior* resonates not only with Ovid's career progress and the classicism of the emerging principate, but also with the ostensible realities of theatrical space in Rome. We have already noted that tragic performances were given on grand occasions and in theaters grand enough to accommodate the spectacles implied by Horace. In 32 BCE Octavian completed costly restorations on the Theater of Pompey (11,000 spectators), and by 17 work on the even larger Theater of Marcellus (13,000 spectators) was advanced enough for the structure to be used for the *ludi Saeculares*. The Marcellus was formally dedicated in 13, the same year in which L. Cornelius Balbus dedicated a smaller theater (still impressive at 7,700 spectators).[104] Exactly how often these structures hosted tragic performances is uncertain. Nevertheless, the extensive refurbishing of an existing theater and the allocation of urban space for two new ones demonstrate the importance of the dramatic arts in Augustus' cultural vision of the new Rome.

Ovid's reinvention of himself as a tragedian, then, appears to coincide not only with a shortage of professional playwrights, but also with the addition of new theaters to the Roman cityscape.[105] Hence my tentative

[102] So Cheney 2002, 8, noting the "final turn" metaphor of verse 2: *raditur haec elegis ultima meta meis.* Cheney also notes a similar careerist metaphor from Vergil at *G.* 3.18: *centum quadriiugos agitabo ad flumina currus* (Mynors).

[103] So Barchiesi and Hardie 2010, 62.

[104] *NTDAR s.v. Theatrum Balbi, Theatrum Marcelli,* and *Theatrum Pompeii.* An alternative date for the dedication of the Marcellus: 11 BCE (Pliny *HN* 8.65).

[105] So Boyle 2006, 167, who suggests that the *Medea* "may well have been written in conjunction with, and inspired by, the opening of two new stone theaters [i.e., those of Balbus and Marcellus] in Rome in the period 13–11 BCE" (brackets mine).

date for the composition of the *Medea*, 13 BCE, is a rough middle ground between the two editions of the *Amores* as well as the year in which the structures were dedicated, and therefore the apex of this building phase. It is not difficult to imagine the poet witnessing over a period of years the renovation and creation of permanent theatrical spaces in Rome and being inspired to write for the stage. Beyond this, matters become very hazy, very quickly. Did Ovid intend to write more than one play, or did he plan to stop with the *Medea*? Ovid's description of tragedy as a labor for the ages (*tu labor aeternus*, *Am.* 3.1.68), as well as the grandiose expressions considered earlier, strike me as preludes to a sustained run within the genre. Add to them Ovid's *recusatio* of tragedy in *Am.* 2.18 (to be examined shortly), which seems more poignant as a dismissal of additional plays. But this is only guesswork.

Another burning question about the composition of the *Medea* is whether Ovid intended it for performance. And, if so, whether he envisioned a stage spectacular like Pompey's revivals and (presumably) Varius' *Thyestes*, or recitation dramas like those of Pollio. A new age of Roman tragedy would seem to require full theatrical treatment, but Ovid himself gives evidence to the contrary. In *Tristia* 5.7, the poet, now relegated to Tomis, reacts to news that his songs have been performed in the theaters:

> carmina quod pleno saltari nostra theatro,
>   versibus et plaudi scribis, amice, meis,
> nil equidem feci – tu scis hoc ipse – theatris,
>   Musa nec in plausus ambitiosa mea est.

> As to what you, my friend, write about my poems, that they are danced in a crowded theater and that my verses are applauded: I have composed nothing for the theaters – you know this fact yourself – nor is my Muse eager for applause. (*Tr.* 5.7.25–8)

At face value, *nil equidem feci theatris* (27) confirms that Ovid intended the *Medea* only for reading and/or recitation.[106] We should nonetheless remember that a good twenty years and many other volumes of poetry separate Ovid the exile from Ovid the tragedian. The present perfective sense of *feci* might apply only to his more recent works. Likewise the present tense of *Musa nec in plausus ambitiosa mea est* (28): maybe Ovid's muse once sought applause, but not now. Furthermore, the *Medea* is an unlikely referent of the plural *carmina* and an unlikely subject of *saltari*

[106] So Nikolaidis 1985, 384 n. 12: "That Ovid's *Medea* was not intended for the stage, but was a piece of rhetorical closet-drama like those of Seneca, we learn from the poet himself." Likewise Arcellaschi 1990, 246, and T. Heinze 1997, 229.

(25), which indicates pantomime more than tragedy.[107] Thus H. MacL. Currie: "[P]erhaps the poet is implying that the theatrical representations of his work at Rome (with dance and music) have taken place without his collaboration and prior knowledge or permission, the *Medea* belonging to quite a separate category."[108] Or perhaps Ovid, in the interest of salvaging his shattered career, is simply downplaying any work that might expose him to public scrutiny.[109]

Even less is known about the contents of the *Medea* than about its origins, although some informed speculation is possible. To judge from the length of Senecan tragedies, the *Medea* had at least 1,000 verses, and perhaps more. Only two have survived, both as quotations in the works of other authors. Quintilian quotes a line in his *Institutio oratoria*:

> servare potui – perdere an possim rogas?
>
> I was able to help – now you ask if I can harm? (Quintilian *Inst.* 8.5.6 = Ovid *Medea* fr. 1)

The context is a larger discussion on variation within *sententiae*, in which the line succeeds as a forceful variation on the old saw, "It is easy to harm, but difficult to help": *cum sit rectum, "nocere facile est, prodesse difficile," vehementius apud Ovidium Medea dicit.*[110] Thus we also learn from Quintilian that Medea is the speaker of this fragment. Because the meter of the verse is iambic senarius, Medea is likely involved in a dialogue, which the second person singular *rogas* corroborates. To whom she speaks is unknown, but a faithless Jason seems the most likely addressee. An echo of the fragment in *Her.* 12, the letter of Medea to Jason, upholds this assumption:

> "perdere posse sat est, siquem iuvet ipsa potestas;
> sed tibi servatus gloria maior ero."

[107] Cunningham 1949, 101; Spoth 1992, 208 n. 18; T. Heinze 1997, 229–30.

[108] Currie 1981, 2702. Also Cunningham 1949, 101–2; Spoth 1992, 208 and n. 18; Sargent 1997, 128 and 143 n. 45; T. Heinze 1997, 230. Note that underlying Cunningham's and Sargent's support for this reading is the belief that the *Heroides* were (or became) *libretti* for pantomime: see Chapter 3, p. 61 and n. 5. Cunningham suggests that the *saltata poemata* mentioned at *Tr.* 2.519 are the same as the *carmina* of *Tr.* 5.7.25, and would have been selections either from the *Amores* or, as he thinks more likely, the *Heroides*. Jouteur 2009, 74, theorizes that the *carmina* of 5.7.25 refer to the *Medea* as well as other poems.

[109] Likewise Arcellaschi 1990, 246: "Ovide peut très bien faire ici mine de renier une oeuvre qui a contribué à la décision de son exil."

[110] Boyle 2006 draws attention to the alliteration of /p/ and /r/, which makes for "a forceful and speakable line reflective of Medea's contempt and strength of will" (168).

> "To have the power to destroy is sufficient, if anyone should be pleased with power itself; but if you save me, I will be a greater glory for you." (*Her.* 12.75–6)

Here Medea quotes what Jason had said to her when seeking her assistance in winning the fleece. Written by Ovid after his tragedy, these verses recall and expand upon the heroine's sentiment in that work. Yet within the overall chronology of the Ovidian myth, Medea first expresses the sentiment in her epistle as a reminiscence of Jason's request, and she will refashion it as a taunt to Jason in her subsequent tragedy.[111]

Seneca the Elder quotes the *Medea* on the topic of poetic borrowings:[112]

> feror huc illuc ut plena deo.
>
> I am borne here and there as if overcome by a god. (Seneca *Suas.* 3.7 = Ovid *Medea* fr. 2)

This fragment, spoken by a woman (*plena*), suggests a Medea pulled in different directions. Boyle, noting the line's anapestic rhythms, assigns it to a *canticum* sung by the heroine, a "deliberative aria just before she kills her children."[113] This is probably a recollection of Medea's "great monologue"[114] in Euripides' play (1021–80), in which she is torn between shame at becoming a laughing stock and remorse at ending her sons' lives. Boyle also posits an allusion to this fragment in the *Medea* of Seneca the Younger, whose heroine contemplates infanticide in similar terms:[115]

> ora quid lacrimae rigant
> variamque nunc huc ira, nunc illuc amor
> diducit? 939
>
> Why do tears wet my cheeks, and why do anger and love pull me in two, one here, the other there? (Sen. *Med.* 937–9)

Even if Ovid's Medea is caught up in some other dilemma, her situation is nevertheless consonant with the long tragic tradition of the heroine grappling with impossible situations.[116]

[111] Thus Hinds 1993, 37–8, a rebuttal of P. E. Knox 1986a, 211, who cites the correspondence between *Med.* fr. 1 and *Her.* 12.75–6 as evidence that the latter poem is not of Ovidian authorship.

[112] Seneca alleges that Ovid's *plena deo* was borrowed from Vergil, although the phrase is not Vergilian: see Hinds 1998, 22–5.

[113] Boyle 2006, 168. [114] So called by Kovacs 1986.

[115] Boyle 2006, 265 n. 28.

[116] For Medeaesque dilemmas that do not involve the murder of her sons see Chapter 5, pp. 144–50.

Where else beyond these two fragments?[117] That the *Medea* was a rhetorical masterpiece is a given,[118] and it might have had powerful visuals to match. Consider this passage from the Medea narrative of *Met.* 7:

> sed postquam Colchis arsit nova nupta venenis
> flagrantemque domum regis mare vidit utrumque,
> sanguine natorum perfunditur impius ensis,
> ultaque se male mater Iasonis effugit arma.

> But after the new bride was burned with the Colchian poisons, and the two seas saw the king's palace burning, her impious sword is stained with the blood of her sons, and the mother flees Jason's sword after seeking revenge in this evil fashion. (*Met.* 7.394–7)

Currie suspects that Ovid abbreviated for epic what he had treated fully in the *Medea*.[119] Sparing though the narrative is, one detail stands out: the burning of Creon's house (*flagrantemque domum regis*, 395), unknown in any prior version of the story. Flames engulf the bodies of Creon's daughter in Euripides' play (1186–94), and setting fire to the king's house (or at least the bridal chamber: ὑφάψω δῶμα νυμφικὸν πυρί, 378) is among the reprisals Medea initially considers. The burning palace of *Met.* 7 perhaps derives from Ovid's lost tragedy, and its appearance there – even if only narrated and not shown onstage – would have suited the theatrical culture of the late republic and early empire.[120]

The most reliable information we have about the *Medea* pertains to its reception. Tacitus' *Dialogus de oratoribus* places its reputation on equal footing with Varius' *Thyestes*:

> "nec ullus Asinii aut Messallae liber tam inlustris est quam Medea Ovidii aut Varii Thyestes."

> "No other work of Pollio or Messalla is as famous as Ovid's *Medea* or Varius' *Thyestes*." (Tacitus *Dial.* 12.6 Furneaux)

The speaker, the poet Curiatus Maternus, does not say why the plays were famous, only that they were. Perhaps the alleged notoriety of the *Thyestes* stems from its association with the emerging principate. Perhaps the *Medea* found a comparable venue for public viewing or listening.

[117] T. Heinze 1997, 251–2, discusses the possibility (first raised by Faider 1922) of a third fragment, *magnasque irae minas agens*, in Sen. *De ira* 1.1.4.

[118] Nikolaidis 1985, 385; Arcellaschi 1990, 247–53; Auhagen 2007, 416.

[119] Currie 1981, 2704. See also Bömer 1976b, following Haupt and Ehwald 1916, and T. Heinze 1997, 226.

[120] The conflagration in Sen. *Med.* (*avidus per omnem regiae partem furit | ut iussus ignis*, 885–6) might be another detail inspired by Ovid. Costa 1973 is perhaps too confident in his assessment: "[T]his detail is found in Ovid … and was no doubt a spectacular feature of his *Medea*."

However Ovid's play achieved fame, its mention here implies that it was remembered well in later generations.[121]

Apart from preserving our fr. 1, Quintilian seems to praise the *Medea* for its moderation. Among noteworthy Roman tragedians Accius and Pacuvius rank first due to their *gravitas*, or seriousness.[122] Quintilian next mentions Varius and the *Thyestes*, which compares favorably with Greek tragedy, and then Ovid:

> Ovidi Medea videtur mihi ostendere quantum ille vir praestare potuerit, si ingenio suo imperare quam indulgere maluisset.
>
> I think Ovid's *Medea* shows his potential for excellence, had he preferred to control rather than indulge his innate genius. (Quintilian *Inst.* 10.1.98 Winterbottom)

The past contrafactual *maluisset* indicates that, in Quintilian's view, Ovid was not accustomed to reining in his *ingenium*, his "innate genius."[123] Among the poet's many ingenious qualities, A. G. Nikolaidis lists several that Quintilian might have deemed inappropriate for tragedy: his "unrivalled dexterity in handling amorous themes, his ... bold imagination, his light and polished verse, his facile and neat language, and his smooth and vivid narrative."[124]

In this case it is unclear whether Quintilian's *maluisset* refers to Ovid's entire career apart from the play (i.e., the *Medea* was the exception to a

[121] Granted, the context of the *Dialogus* and Maternus' speech is quasi-fictional. Curiatus Maternus was himself an author of *praetextae*: *SRF* I, titles and *test.* It is appropriate to his character to use tragedians as *exempla* (he cites Euripides and Sophocles in the same manner as Ovid and Varius, *Dial.* 12.6). His alleged familiarity with the *Medea* and the *Thyestes* may have more to do with establishing himself as an authority on the genre than the actual fame of either work. Furthermore, the internal audience is a small gathering of Roman literati *c.* 75–77 CE, who presumably were comfortable with a passing mention of the *Medea.* All the same, unless Tacitus was trying to paint Maternus and his companions as antiquarian collectors of forgotten literature, the Tacitean readership *c.* 100 CE should have known the *Medea*, at least by reputation. As Goldberg 1996 notes, "The literary climate evoked by the *Dialogus* ... must at least have been congruent with the expectations of [its] audience" (273 n. 13, brackets mine).

[122] Quint. *Inst.* 10.1.97: *Tragoediae scriptores veterum Accius atque Pacuvius clarissimi gravitate sententiarum, verborum pondere, auctoritate personarum* (Winterbottom).

[123] Quintilian frequently employs *ingenium* (*OLD* definitions 2 and 6) in this way. Select examples from *Inst.* 1: *Getae tuo, cuius prima aetas manifestum iam ingenii lumen ostendit* (1.*pr.*6 Winterbottom); *ea vero destituta infirmioribus ingeniis velut praedae fuit* (1.*pr.*14); *sed pueris quae maxime ingenium alant atque animum augeant praelegenda* (1.8.8). On Ovid's *ingenium* see also *Inst.* 10.1.88 (*Ovidius ... nimium amator ingenii sui*) and Nikolaidis 1985, 383 n. 5.

[124] Nikolaidis 1985, 385, listing the "positive aspects" of Ovid's poetry at odds with tragedy's "rigid form and solemn contents." Compare the Elder Seneca's assessment of Ovid as a young student of declamation: the poet, who even then was of the highest talent, lacked not judgment as much as willpower in checking his impetuousness (*adparet summi ingenii viro non iudicium defuisse ad compescendam licentiam carminum suorum sed animum, Controv.* 2.2.12 Winterbottom). Nikolaidis, 383, cites a slightly earlier passage to similar effect: *non ignoravit vitia sua sed amavit.*

body of work fraught with impetuous ingenuity) or includes the play as well (i.e., it had moments of moderation but, like Ovid's other works, was also too impetuous). Nikolaidis endorses the latter view: the *Medea* "must have been fraught to a greater extent with … rhetorical style and diction, excessive mannerism, artificial sentimentality, undue sophistication and diffuseness."[125] The former view, however, seems entirely possible: Quintilian praises Ovid for controlling his ingenuity in the play rather than indulging it (*ingenio suo imperare quam indulgere*). The *Medea* was a more restrained work, sharing the quality found in the tragedies of Accius and Pacuvius (and presumably Varius): seriousness or *gravitas*.[126]

I press this point because *gravitas* is also the quality for which Ovid had aimed. In his epistle to Augustus, the relegated poet notes that tragedy outstrips all other genres in seriousness: *omne genus scripti gravitate tragoedia vincit* (*Tr.* 2.381). Ovid goes on to mention a work he gave "to the buskins":

> et dedimus tragicis scriptum regale cothurnis,[127]
> quaeque gravis debet verba cothurnus habet. 554

> To the tragic actors' shoes I gave a kingly work, and with the weighty shoes went weighty words. (*Tr.* 2.553–4)

This work is clearly a tragedy. Furthermore, it must be the *Medea*, both because this was the poet's only known play, and because it was a play with a royal protagonist: the daughter of king Aeëtes is an appropriate heroine of a *scriptum regale*.[128] Ovid explicitly links his tragedy with the genre's *gravitas*: *quaeque gravis debet verba cothurnus habet* (554). Of course, he is also making a polemical point, citing the play in order to erase the stigma of the *Ars amatoria*.[129]

It is easy to see why Ovid, reflecting on his *cursus litterarum*, would claim as much *gravitas* as possible. Yet his statements in *Tristia* 2 are consistent with the programmatics of his earliest elegiac work. The *Amores* are replete with lightheartedness in tone, style, and subject matter – with

[125] Nikolaidis 1985, 384, calling these characteristics "the faults we" – and presumably Quintilian – "usually find with [Ovid's] poetry" (brackets and ellipsis mine). Auhagen 2007, 415, also deems the *Medea* the rule rather than the exception.

[126] *OLD s.v. gravitas* 6.

[127] I prefer the MSS reading, *scriptum regale cot(h)urnis*, to Housman's emendation, *sceptrum regale tyrannis*.

[128] I thank Reader "A" for this observation.

[129] Several verses earlier, Ovid had claimed that not all his works were trifling (*ne tamen omne meum credas opus esse remissum*, *Tr.* 2.547). Following the *Fasti* (549–52) and the *Metamorphoses* (555–60), the *Medea* is actually the third point in a career arc based on *gravitas*.

levitas, in other words – such that the collection at times recalls comic situations and themes.[130] The *Amores* would brand Ovid as a *tenerorum lusor amorum* (a player of tender love, *Tr.* 4.10.1). A poet so branded, contemplating a career change to tragedy, needed to account for the aesthetic shift. Hence Ovid expressly acknowledges tragic *gravitas* in *Amores* 3:[131]

> "tempus erat thryso pulsum graviore moveri;
> cessatum satis est – incipe maius opus!" 24
> (*Am.* 3.1.23–4)

> corniger increpuit thyrso graviore Lyaeus:
> pulsanda est magnis area maior equis. 18
> (*Am.* 3.15.17–18)

In addition to depicting tragedy as a genre of greater size, Ovid ascribes to it greater seriousness through the *thyrso graviore* of both *Am.* 3.1 and 3.15. The image of a heavier thyrsus matches the weighty words and buskins of *Tr.* 2.554, and together these references show Ovid portraying the *Medea* as a project with *gravitas* throughout his career. In the oscillating oeuvre of a mercurial poet, such consistency is nothing short of remarkable.

To sum up: Ovid wrote the *Medea* during a boom in the construction of theaters at Rome and with an eye toward advancing his career, if not a new age in Roman tragedy. The play, which likely treated the same myth as those of Euripides and Ennius, no doubt took stock of these versions, as well as the conventions in which they had participated. Certainly, it was a triumph of rhetoric, especially if it had been intended only for recitation, and perhaps also a triumph of visual spectacle, if it depicted Creon's palace in flames. The *Medea* achieved a certain measure of fame and garnered praise for its seriousness and restraint, in which Ovid himself was demonstrably invested. This is more or less everything that can be said with confidence. But a question remains, arguably the most important for relating the *Medea* to the rest of the poet's career. If Ovid meant to restore the name of Roman tragedy, and if his first play was successful, why did he stop after only one?

[130] So Currie 1981, introducing Plautus' and Terence's influence on Ovid: "The vein of *levitas* or frivolity runs through the whole of Ovid's work. If there was any feature of his output to which the authorities might take exception it was certainly this" (2729). On Ovid's lightheartedness in the *Amores* see McKeown 1987, 11–31, and the introduction of Barsby 1973, 14–18. On the collection's comic traditions see Barsby 1996.

[131] See Karakasis 2010 on the *agon* of aesthetics in *Am.* 3.1; also Dangel 2009, 30.

The answer seems to lie with *Amores* 2.18, which belongs to the collection's second edition and "in which Ovid reviews his career to date."[132] In poem 2.18 his friend, Macer, is engaged in the task of writing epic, while Ovid himself continues to write elegy under the watchful eye of his *puella* (1–12). Nevertheless, there was a time when he wrote something else:

> sceptra tamen sumpsi curaque tragoedia nostra
> crevit, et huic operi quamlibet aptus eram.

> I nevertheless took up the scepter and under my care a tragedy grew, and I was as suited for this task as for anything else. (*Am.* 2.18.13–14)

If this poem was written after the *Medea*, Ovid would seem to be reflecting on his prior experience as a tragedian. Yet Stephen Hinds advises against reading too literally: "In the end, [*Am.* 2.18, along with 3.1, and 3.15] do more to develop a programmatic attitude towards tragedy than to give interpretable information about the progress of actual compositional activity."[133] Hence some read *Tragoedia*, capitalized like the personified genre of 3.1, in order to distinguish it from the actual *Medea*.[134]

The principal reason for reading *tragoedia* only generally and programmatically comes with Cupid's reaction to Ovid's tragic costume:

> risit Amor pallamque meam pictosque cothurnos
> sceptraque privata tam cito sumpta manu;
> hinc quoque me dominae numen deduxit iniquae,
> deque cothurnato vate triumphat Amor.

> Cupid laughed at my tragic cloak and shoes, and at the scepter taken up in my free hand so soon; from here also the power of my unjust mistress led me, and Cupid triumphs over the tragically shod poet. (*Am.* 2.18.15–18)

Readers of the *Amores* have been down this road of *recusatio* twice before, first when Cupid ceased Ovid's preparations for composing an epic (*Am.* 1.1.1–4), next when Ovid's mistress disturbed his nascent gigantomachy (2.1.11–17). Not only were these projects interrupted, but they were

[132] Farrell 2004, 45. On the poem's date I agree with the preface of McKeown 1998: certain verses "seem inconsistent with a chronological reading of the *Amores*, for there is no hint in 3.1 that Ovid had ever before attempted tragedy. It is therefore probable that 2.18, or at least [verses 13–18], will have appeared for the first time in the second edition" (brackets mine); I discuss verses 13–18 below. Tarrant 2002, 16, suggests a similar scenario: "[T]he progression toward tragedy seen in the extant *Amores* could be a product of Ovid's revision, designed to update the collection by making it 'predict' the turn taken by Ovid's career in the intervening years."

[133] Hinds 1993, 31 n. 49 (brackets mine).

[134] So Hollis 1977, 150: "Some older scholars, (rightly, I think) gave a capital to *Tragoedia*" (author's parentheses). McKeown 1987 prints *Tragoedia*, despite his view that *Am.* 2.18 refers to the *Medea*.

probably never real to begin with.[135] Their only purpose was to serve the conceit of the *recusatio*. The problem, then, is that the tragedy mentioned in 2.18, which prompts Cupid's derision and the intervention of Ovid's *domina*, might also be an effigy – not the *Medea*, but an unspecified play conjured in order to be rejected.

Perhaps, perhaps not. Although the poet's recusal of a fictitious work is the norm, the recusal of a known and attested work is conceivable. Thus Joan Booth: "The unwritten rules of the *recusatio* did not demand that the grand poetry abandoned must be fictitious, but only that it must *be* abandoned, and then not necessarily for good."[136] Furthermore, Ovid could be recusing himself not from writing one play, but from writing new plays beyond the finished *Medea*. A recusal based on an existing work suits the biographical context of 2.18, which goes on to mention poems that the poet did in fact write. Verses 19–26 refer to the *Ars amatoria* and the single *Heroides* and continue in the vein, begun by recalling the *Medea*, of updating Ovid's readers.[137] James McKeown asserts, "Ovid is ... unspecific about his attempt at tragedy (13–18), but this claim probably has more substance. To invent a further work as a foil ... to his own amatory poetry would lack purpose."[138]

I believe that Ovid is referring to the *Medea* in *Am.* 2.18, and that he is doing so both to acknowledge the absence of sequels and to launch a new elegiac phase of his career. The portrayal of his tragic project is consistent with what we have seen before. The kingly *sceptra* (13) preserve the idea that tragedy is a grander form, while *crevit* (14) denotes generic escalation and therefore progress within the poetic *cursus*.[139] Furthermore, Ovid declares his own aptitude as a tragedian: *quamlibet aptus eram* (14) suggests that he was able to adjust his style as necessary. In fact, he threw himself into the part: the scepter, cloak, and boots (*pallam*, *cothurnos*, 15) are the very costume of Tragedy in *Am.* 3.1:[140]

> venit et ingenti violenta Tragoedia passu:
> fronte comae torva, palla iacebat humi;
> laeva manus sceptrum late regale movebat,
> Lydius alta pedum vincla cothurnus erat. 14

[135] On the gigantomachy as a fiction see Wilkinson 1955, 48 n., *OCD*² *s.v.* "Ovid" §11, and McKeown 1998 on *Am.* 2.1.11–16.

[136] Booth 1991, 86 (author's emphasis), arguing for a "substantially advanced, but temporarily interrupted" *Medea*.

[137] I discuss *Am.* 2.18.19–26 at greater length in Chapter 3, pp. 59–60.

[138] McKeown 1998, preface to commentary on *Am.* 2.18 (ellipses mine).

[139] For *crevit* as marking such an escalation in many senses see McKeown 1998, following Hollis 1977, 150–1.

[140] Booth 1991 also notes the correspondences.

> Mighty Tragedy came also in gigantic strides, her hair covering her grim brow, her cloak trailing along the ground; her left hand brandished the regal scepter, the Lydian boot tied high around her feet. (*Am.* 3.1.11–14)

McKeown notes that depicting poets as being "personally involved" in their genres is typical of Ovid.[141] His friend Macer dresses his soldiers in armor (*iuratis induis arma viris*, 2.18.2), and Ovid claims to have held the clouds and thunderbolt when composing his putative gigantomachy (*in manibus nimbos et … fulmen habebam*, 2.1.15). By donning Tragedy's costume, the poet conveys genuine seriousness, *gravitas*, in undertaking the new genre.

Ovid's metapoetic commentary on his career is also metatheatrical, since putting on a costume is appropriate for a genre predicated on role-play. The derision of Cupid (15) should be considered in the same light. The god's laughter is a comic reaction, and it brings to a halt the poet's tragic performance/career. It does not mean that the *Medea* was a failure. The favorable opinions of Tacitus and Quintilian are evidence enough of the play's worthiness, as is Ovid's own recollection in *Tr.* 2, where there would be no point in reminding Augustus of a botched job. Instead, Cupid is calling attention to the inherent artificiality of role-playing, which requires the suspension of disbelief. He sees not a tragedian, but an elegist playing one, and he laughs in response. All of this is Ovid's way of saying that additional tragic efforts, at least in the form of actual plays, were not right for him, his ambition and aptitude notwithstanding. If I were to hazard a guess, I would propose that the genre's intrinsic *gravitas* – the quality that heralded career progress, that would be leveraged toward winning the emperor's pardon, and that won Quintilian's approval – was too restrictive for Ovid's *ingenium*. Or, to put it in the terms with which this chapter began, tragedy's *gravitas* required too much repetition, and not enough innovation.

4 Textualization and transformation

By dramatizing a return to *Amor* and elegy in poem 2.18, Ovid would seem to have taken a backward step in his *cursus litterarum*. But did he? His next two elegiac works, the *Heroides* and the *Ars amatoria*, are hardly the *Amores* all over again. Indeed, in the career arc that Farrell traces, the

[141] McKeown 1998, also noting, "We may perhaps think of [Ovid] as adopting the role of one of his characters" – in which case Ovid might very well resemble Creon. McKeown offers additional examples, both from Ovid and other elegists, of poets "doing what [they describe] being done" (*Am.* 2.18.1–2, brackets mine).

Ars represents progress of a distinctly Vergilian kind in combining the erotic and the didactic. However, if we accept the premise that the *Medea* also represented progress, perhaps we should speak of the *Ars* as less of a forward move than a lateral one – a resumption of the elegiac "track" but without necessarily stepping down from the career heights tragedy had afforded.

A similar case can be made for the *Heroides*. Here also Ovid remains on an elegiac track, but he marks progress by incorporating both the material and the modalities of tragedy. Making this case will be the agenda of Chapter 3, which will revisit *Am.* 2.18 and its depiction of the *Medea*'s aftermath. To pave the way, I will recount a third development in the history of Roman tragedy, whereby the genre found currency not only as stage spectaculars or as recitation dramas, but also as texts. This development is crucial for Ovid's later tragic career, which requires the medium of the text both "to comment on the theatrical experience and to reproduce it."[142] A project of such a scale is scarcely conceivable in other media, and it avails itself of the long process by which tragedy itself became textualized. The process is not merely one of publishing Greek and Roman plays, though this is the starting point. Written publication liberated tragedies from the confines of the theater and the recital hall and inspired new modes of reception.[143] I will discuss some of these below, but the most important for Ovid was Vergil's reception of tragedy in the *Aeneid.*

The textualization of tragedy has its roots in the revivals of older Athenian tragedy in the fourth century BCE, which not only required written versions of the plays, but also resulted in official state copies under Lycurgus. The formation of a tragic repertoire, in turn, encouraged the anthologizing of tragedy in the third century, a process that explains the long-term survival of the genre apart from performance alone.[144] As P. E. Easterling observes, to preserve a play in writing is not only to record the libretto of a performance, but also to provide a new way of experiencing it: "[O]ut of the thousands of … plays produced from the fifth century onwards, a (fluctuating) selection became classics with a book life of their own."[145] Aristotle's *Poetics* is a testament to the book lives of Aeschylus, Sophocles, and Euripides in the century after their deaths. Although

[142] Feldherr 2010, 199.

[143] So the preface of Jouteur (ed.) 2009: "L'implantation de formes dramatiques dans un espace qui n'est pas celui du théâtre mais celui, extensible et plus intellectuel, de la littérature, conduit à un mouvement de la scène vers le texte, qui inverse celui que connaît habituellement le texte dramatique, passant d'un support écrit aux feux de la rampe" (7).

[144] On the textual transmission of Greek tragedy see Kovacs 2005.

[145] Easterling 1997, 225 (author's parentheses).

Aristotle is cognizant of tragedy in performance, he notes that plays are effective even when read (*Poet.* 26.1462a). Furthermore, reading tragedy makes the philosopher's treatise possible, for his analysis of the genre through the rigorous comparison of tragedy, comedy, and epic involves access to the plays in textual form.[146]

The anthologizing of Greek tragedy involved not only selecting and preserving whole examples of the genre, but also breaking plays into exemplary fragments. Bruno Gentili demonstrates the striking and varied results of this process with a survey of Hellenistic anthologies on papyri, among them a portion of Euripides' *Hipp.* (*Stephanias* = *HS*) without choral parts (*P.Sorb.* 2252); a collection of Euripidean prologues only (*P.Hamb.* 118–19); a collection of lyric odes from Euripides and Astydmas (*P.Strassb. W.G.*); and a compilation of Euripidean aphorisms in trimeters (*PSI* XV).[147] These examples, apart from attesting to the postclassical popularity of Euripides, all show how reading tragedy, in itself a refinement of watching tragedy, became further refined through the anthology trade. It was not enough to make bouquets or garlands of whole plays. Now portions were culled and assembled into new texts, each designed for a different reading constituency and offering an even more selective experience of the genre and its authors.

Roman tragedy was also susceptible to anthologizing. Grammarians, for example, quoted the plays out of context in the service of collecting words. Even Cicero's quotations of Latin playwrights are anthological: his catalogue of quotations from Ennius and Accius at *De or.* 3.217–19 explores the principle of effective delivery. These quotations, although divorced from their plays, are still recalled in a performative context and thus remain connected to the living stage. At other times, however, Cicero quotes from Roman tragedy as grammarians do, citing examples of text rather than performance. Goldberg illustrates this point with the orator's quotations from the *Andromacha* of Ennius (*Tusc.* 3.44–5), which sound "much more like the product of a literary than a stage memory. Cicero praises [the heroine's] song … for its content, diction, and rhythm – no mention of its choreography or setting."[148]

[146] Compare Taplin 1977, 25: "During the fourth century it had become possible to regard the text of a Greek tragedy as the tragedy itself and not as the libretto of a performance … Once tragedy is treated as a text then it is all too easy to lose sight of its visual meaning. That Aristotle did, and critics ever since have turned their backs in the same direction."

[147] Gentili 1979, 19–20.

[148] Goldberg 2005, 126–7, with additional examples (quotation on 126).

A bifurcated take on Roman tragedy, therefore, needs a third prong, one that considers tragedy experienced as text, in addition to rhetoric and spectacle. Tragedy in textual form not only removes a play from the *theatron*, but also turns it to purposes unforeseen by its author. The "repurposing" of the genre goes beyond anthologies and philosophical or technical treatises. It occurs in narrative texts as well: the histories of Livy and the biographies of Plutarch are noted for their dramatic arcs, in which tragic storytelling imposes itself on the historical record.[149] Yet tragic patterning is perhaps nowhere more conspicuous than in Roman epic poetry. Vergil's *Aeneid* is the most celebrated example of tragic epic, though the longer works of Catullus, especially poems 64 (Ariadne) and 63 (Attis, in galliambics), also deserve to be singled out. Poem 64, for instance, pays homage to the *Medea exul* both by refashioning the Ennian *incipit* as a new prologue, and by "contaminating" Ariadne's plight with that of Medea.[150] Catullus, with all the zeal and attentiveness of a grammarian, anthologizes and repurposes the text of Ennius within his own.

These and other gestures will be familiar to readers of the *Aeneid*, which though an epic is as invested in the concerns of Roman tragedy as any play. Although the tragic reception of the poem begins with Ovid, it is Martial who twice endows the poet with the epithet *cothurnatus* (5.5.8, 7.63.5; compare *Am.* 2.18.18),[151] which tropes the epic as worthy of the tragic stage and Vergil himself as a buskined actor.[152] The process of cataloguing Vergil's debts to tragedy began under later commentators, most notably Servius and Macrobius, who trace out verbal and material parallels between the *Aeneid* and Greco-Roman plays. These parallels are important for our understanding of the Latin tragedians, since the commentators quote from and sometimes even summarize the lost plays. But most important is that, without Vergil's demonstrable interest in the genre, there would have been nothing on which to comment in the first place.

Vergilian metamorphoses of tragedy have a long and varied critical history.[153] Hence only a few examples are needed, both to demonstrate the

149 Tragic Livy: M. D. Thomas 1991; Mader 1993; and (more generally) Conte 1994b, 372–3. Tragic Plutarch: Braund 1993; Zadorojnyi 1997; Mossman 1998.

150 On Catullus as a tragic poet, with emphasis on poems 63 and 64, see Panoussi 2003. On Catullus' adaptations of the Ennian prologue see R. E. Thomas 1982 and Zetzel 1983.

151 Hardie 1997, 312; also Panoussi 2002, 95 and n. 1.

152 In fact, in Martial's era the term *tragoedus* or tragedian meant less "tragic poet" than "tragic singer" (or actor): Csapo and Slater 1995, 369.

153 Recent milestones in that history include Hardie 1997, Panoussi 2002, Galinsky 2003, and Panoussi 2009, who places the scope and the significance of Vergil's tragic program on a new footing, well beyond the traditional focus on Dido and Aeneas.

eminence of the *Aeneid* in the canon of tragic Roman texts, and to suggest how high the bar was set for Vergil's successors. Tragic readings of the *Aeneid* have historically clustered around books 1–4, which tell the story of Dido. Richard Heinze founded an epoch in Vergilian criticism by describing Dido's madness in terms of Aristotelian *peripeteia* (reversal of fortune, *Poet.* 11.1452a).[154] Writing at a time when Vergil had largely been deemed a mere imitator of Homer and others,[155] Heinze appealed to the *Poetics* in order to liberate the *Aeneid* from the constraints of *Quellenforschung* and to invest it with a sense of its own legitimacy.[156] On occasion Heinze goes so far to suggest that Aristotle's treatise served as a "how-to" manual.[157] Whichever way this suggestion might seem to undermine the poet's originality, the efforts of Heinze and later critics[158] posit a Vergil engaged with the tragedy at the level of code – a level that the Aristotelian text had made accessible.

Another enduring critical approach has been to identify Vergil's *contaminatio* of Dido with characters from the tragic stage.[159] Although an era more dubious of the poet's achievements might have read Dido's correspondences with Medea (her best known analogue)[160] as further evidence of artistic bankruptcy, later generations have productively mobilized this and other parallels. Philip Hardie, for example, discusses the various ways

154 R. Heinze 1903/1993, 96: "At the beginning of [book 4] we find [Dido] caught in the toils of love. She attains her heart's desire; then comes the *peripeteia* of the drama, leading to a rapid plunge from the heights of happiness and to the fatal conclusion." Furthermore, Heinze maintains that Vergil's use of reversal is "borrowed from the dramatist's box of tricks." Its aim, he declares, is to rouse in the reader pity and fear (particularly the former), the two emotions Aristotle singles out (*Poet.* 6.1449b, 13.1452b) as *sine quibus non* for tragedy (370–1, quotation on 370).

155 "In the eyes of [nineteenth-century] critics, the *Aeneid* lacked everything that prevailing opinion considered essential for true poetry: originality of poetic creation, spontaneity of emotion, liveliness, and a vivid and graphic representation of events" (Wlosok in R. Heinze 1903/1993, x).

156 So Hardie 1995, 274, a review of the translated third edition, which does the historicizing and contextualizing work that Wlosok's "factual and laudatory" preface (so Barchiesi 1996, 230) by and large has neglected.

157 R. Heinze 1903/1993: "[Aristotle] taught that the best kind [of drama] was a combination: Vergil probably believed he had achieved this in his epic" (364); "Vergil has sought to follow Aristotle's rules, and has learnt from Apollonius' mistake" (348); "If we look at the composition of the *Aeneid* in this light, it is clear that Vergil was attempting to follow Aristotle's rules" (349); "It would not be surprising if Vergil had used analyses of [Aristotle's] kind" (276 n. 30).

158 E.g., Moles 1984, a study of Dido's *culpa* (*Aen.* 4.172) as Aristotelian *hamartia* (*Poet.* 13.1453a).

159 Muecke 1983, 144, offers a comprehensive list of tragic and epic analogues, with bibliography: "Dido is Helen, Calypso, Circe, Penelope, Hypsipyle, Medea, Ariadne ... not to mention Ajax and Hector." Panoussi 2002 demonstrates how, in the case of Ajax, associations with epic can highlight and enhance associations with tragedy. On Dido as an Alcestis figure, see Panoussi 2005.

160 On the similarities between Dido and Medea see Collard 1975, as well as Austin 1955 *passim* on *Aen.* 4.

in which Dido recalls the Phaedra of Euripides, particularly in her desire for Aeneas, which runs counter to her widowly devotion to Sychaeus. Notes Hardie, "Dido is the victim of transgressions thoroughly at home in Attic tragedy."[161] Furthermore, Vassiliki Panoussi has identified parallels between Dido and Ajax, whom Vergil recalls as an embodiment of marginalized heroic ideals.[162]

Apart from recalling specific tragic heroes and heroines, Dido also comports herself in dramatic terms. For example, a famous simile portrays her as an actor wandering through a theatrical dreamscape:

> semper longam incomitata videtur
> ire viam et Tyrios deserta quaerere terra,
> Eumenidum veluti demens videt agmina Pentheus,
> et solem geminum et duplices se ostendere Thebas;
> aut Agamemnonius scaenis agitatus Orestes,
> armatam facibus matrem et serpentibus atris
> cum fugit ultricesque sedent in limine Dirae.

> Ever alone, unaccompanied, she seems to take a long journey, seeking her Tyrians in the lonely countryside, just as Pentheus, utterly senseless, sees a throng of Furies, and a double sun, and a double Thebes revealing itself, or just as Agamemnon's son, Orestes, pursued across the stage, when he flees his mother, who brandishes torches and black snakes, and the dire Avengers sit on the threshold. (Verg. *Aen.* 4.467–73 Mynors)

The queen is likened not only to tragic characters such as Pentheus and Orestes, but also to versions of these characters on the Pacuvian stage.[163] Indeed, within about sixty verses of this simile, the heroine delivers the first of three monologues (534–52), in which she articulates her abject misery and despair.[164] These speeches, like that of Ariadne in Catullus 64 (132–201), constitute metatheatrical engagements with the very form of tragedy, and present Dido as the protagonist within her own drama.

161 Hardie 1997, 322. 162 Panoussi 2009, 182–98.

163 Hardie 1997, 322, calls these lines "a jarring pointer to the theatricality of the story." Goldberg 2005, 115–18 and 138–40, follows Leo 1913 and Steiner 1952 in tracing Dido's dream back to the dream of Ilia in book 1 of Ennius' *Annales*: "The dream as it unfolds certainly moves from epic to tragedy, but then it moves back again. And it clings throughout to the world of books, where tragic examples commonly share the page with epic ones" (140).

164 Compare R. Heinze 1903/1993, 328–9: "The only other monologues which [Vergil] gives are those of Dido when she is alone: here … Vergil has moved … closer to the dramatic monologue."

Even as the *Aeneid* becomes a stage for the rhetoric of despair, that stage is initially set through the rhetoric of exposition. In book 1 Venus tells Aeneas and his men about Carthage, visible off in the distance:

> "Punica regna vides, Tyrios et Agenoris urbem;
> sed fines Libyci, genus intractabile bello.
> imperium Dido Tyria regit urbe profecta,
> germanum fugiens. longa est iniuria, longae
> ambages, sed summa sequar fastigia rerum.
> huic coniunx Sychaeus erat, ditissimus auri
> Phoenicum, et magno miserae dilectus amore,
> cui pater intactam dederat primisque iugarat
> ominibus."

> "You see this Punic kingdom: the citadel and its people, the Tyrians, are descended from Agenor. Bordering it are the Libyans, a race undefeated in battle. Dido rules it, after journeying from her Tyrian city, fleeing from her brother. Long were her hardship and her wanderings – But let me follow the main points of the matter. Her husband was Sychaeus, richest of all the Phoenicians, and possessed of a powerful love for the poor woman. Her father betrothed her, still a maiden, to Sychaeus, and joined her to him in marriage." (Verg. *Aen.* 1.338–46 Mynors)

Between the surviving *incipit* of Ennius' *Medea exul* and the tragedies of Seneca, this passage is our closest approximation of a Latin tragic prologue – and a divine prologue at that. Venus recalls not the initial words of any one play, but the expository conventions of drama at large, establishing who, what, when, and where in systematic fashion. Furthermore, she is aware of setting the scene for an audience: *Punica regna vides* (338) implies a demonstrative gesture, singling out Carthage for the Trojans, while *summa sequar fastigia rerum* (342) annotates her own words as exposition. Capping this metatheatrical display is Venus' costume, with which she plays the role of Diana's acolyte. The crucial accessory is her *cothurnus* (337), ostensibly a kind of hunting boot, but in this context the notorious tragic buskin as well, in which Martial dresses Vergil himself.[165]

The tragedy of Dido in the first half of the *Aeneid* gives way to more persistent manifestations of the genre in the poem's second half:[166] a series

[165] On the metatheatrics of this passage see E. L. Harrison 1972–3; Barchiesi 1993, 353; and Hardie 1997, 321–2, who finds in Venus' resemblance to Diana further support for reading Dido as a Phaedra.

[166] I use "half" advisedly after Horsfall 2000: "[I]t is improper, and dangerous, to talk about 'halves' of the *Aeneid*" (7.37–45).

of ephebes, young men like Nisus and Euryalus (book 9) and Pallas (10), whose early deaths prevent their reaching manhood; the liminal figure of Camilla (11), trapped like Dido between opposing forces; the wrath of Turnus, a second Ajax, whose outmoded brand of heroism precipitates his death at Aeneas' hands (12).[167] In addition to validating Aristotle's correlation of epic and tragedy (*Poet.* 5.1449b), the encoding of the *Aeneid* as a tragic text reveals the genre as essential to the story of Roman nationhood. Rome's founding cannot be told without the words, devices, narrative patterns, and characterizations of tragedy. Whereas tragedy arises in passing in books 1–4, with Aeneas forced to move on from Carthage to Latium, books 7–12 suggest the genre as an inevitable destination in both literary and ideological terms.[168]

Inevitable, too, in terms of Vergil's career, which intersects the literary and the ideological. The poet continued in the tradition, exemplified by Andronicus, Naevius, and especially Ennius, of writing both tragedy and epic – albeit he did so under the auspices of a single work, as opposed to maintaining separate tragic and epic careers.[169] Vergil presents the second half of the *Aeneid* as a career highlight in the *proemio al mezzo* glimpsed earlier in this chapter:

> dicam horrida bella,
> dicam acies actosque animis in funera reges,
> Tyrrhenamque manum totamque sub arma coactam
> Hesperiam. maior rerum mihi nascitur ordo,
> maius opus moveo.

> I will sing of frightening wars, of battle lines, of kings driven to death by bravery, of the Tyrrhenian band, and the whole of Hesperia forced into arms. A greater order of matters is being born in me, I am setting in motion a greater work. (Verg. *Aen.* 7.41–5 Mynors)

Here the poet takes up the theme of *reges et proelia* first recused at *Ecl.* 6.3, elevating his already elevated genre.[170] No one would deny that, as he embarks on the Iliadic half of his poem, it is appropriate for Vergil to

[167] Ephebes (including Marcellus, book 6) and "liminal" Camilla: Hardie 1997, 320–1; see also Chapter 4, p. 99 and n. 13. Turnus and Ajax: Panoussi 2009, 198–217. Tragedy and the end of the *Aeneid*: Galinsky 2003, 284–90.

[168] See Chapter 7, pp. 223–4.

[169] So Hardie 1997, 323, also including Varius and Ovid in the tragic-epic tradition. Hardie suggests that Ennius' *Annales* contained some tragic notes, such as in the sack of Alba Longa in book 2.

[170] Here, too, Vergil repeats the *horrida bella* that the Sibyl prophesied at *Aen.* 6.86.

chart his progress. I would only add that the proem leaves room for tragedy in the midst of epic warfare. In particular, *actosque animis in funera reges* (42) evokes tragic mourning and excessive pride as much as martial courage and bloodshed.[171]

According to Hardie, the "pervasiveness of tragic patterns in the *Aeneid*" illustrates "how Vergil managed to reinvigorate the flagging tradition of Greco-Roman epic and thus produce *the* Roman classic text."[172] Did Ovid read Vergil this way? I believe so, and I would go so far as to claim that each edition of the *Amores* contained its own response to Vergil's tragic epic, a response reflecting the state of Ovid's career at the time. In edition one's final book, what we call poem 3.1 placed Ovid on the path to a Vergilian *maius opus* (24) in the form of the *Medea*, and perhaps other plays, with which he meant to revive the "flagging tradition" of tragedy on its own terms. Poem 3.15, in turn, officially launched this new phase of his career. Edition two, issued after the *Medea*, contains *Am.* 2.18, which offers Ovid's second thoughts on tragedy and maps a new path to the genre in the form of the *Heroides*.[173] Yet Ovid allowed poems 3.1 and 3.15 to follow 2.18, leaving them as before in the final book of the collection. Now 3.1 imagines a *maius opus* more like the *Aeneid* itself, a tragic text worthy of the name *Romana Tragoedia*, but not a tragic play. The *Heroides* are a step in this direction, and Tragedy's injunction to sing the deeds of men (*cane facta virorum*, 25) might even look ahead to the tragic-epic synergy of the *Metamorphoses*. *Am.* 3.15, then, launches Ovid onto the textual phase of his tragic career, where he is in good company. References to Vergil and Catullus (*Mantua Vergilio gaudet, Verona Catullo*, 7) perhaps celebrate them for their part in the textualization of tragedy.

Unlike other lost works from antiquity, it is impossible to know exactly when the *Medea* ceased to be an extant text. Evidently it happened well before the Renaissance, whose scholars knew only the same two fragments known to us.[174] For all of modernity the play has been lost, a seeming

[171] Compare Horsfall 2000: "The whole expression seems created out of simple, common words and quite *ad hoc* ... for this grim context of tragic anticipation."

[172] Hardie 1997, 322.

[173] McKeown 1987, 90–102, discusses the often confusing arrangement, which most critics assume to be Ovidian, of *Amores* edition two. Cameron 1968, 330, argues plausibly that "it would not have been an easy task" to scale down five books of poetry into three and to devise "a thoroughgoing new arrangement." Hence the premise that 3.1 and 3.15 stand more or less in the new edition where they stood in the old – which is not to say that they do not take on new meaning.

[174] Cheney 2004, 57.

casualty of a prior age's vicissitudes. Yet within the literary vicissitudes of the early principate and those of Ovid's *cursus litterarum*, the *Medea* was already something of a lost work – a throwback to an earlier era, too grave for the poet's *ingenium*. In the ongoing arc of his career, however, the *Heroides* and the *Metamorphoses* would demonstrate that tragedy was hardly a lost cause.

CHAPTER THREE

Lacrimas finge videre meas
Epistolary theater

When last we saw Ovid, in *Amores* 2.18, he was costumed as a tragic poet – wearing a cloak, with a scepter in his hand and buskins on his feet (*pallam, cothurnos*, 15; *sceptra*, 16). He was dressed for success as a playwright (*huic operi quamlibet aptus eram*, 14), but ultimately he inspired Cupid's derision (*risit Amor*, 15). Because of this reaction, Ovid's tragic efforts ended in defeat for himself, and in victory for elegy: *deque cothurnato vate triumphat Amor* (18).[1]

What was a love poet with an aptitude and an appreciation for tragedy to do? Although his avowed genre was elegy, Ovid did not consign himself to a *cursus litterarum* of repeating the *Amores*. On the contrary, the next section of poem 2.18 demonstrates ample opportunity for innovation within the genre, and hence within Ovid's career:

> quod licet, aut artes teneri profitemur Amoris
> (ei mihi, praeceptis urgeor ipse meis!) ...

> Doing what I can, I either profess the arts of tender Love (and how I am constrained by my own teachings!) ... (*Am.* 2.18.19–20)

The phrase *artes Amoris* (19) refers to the *Ars amatoria*,[2] which by the second edition of the *Amores* would have been well under way, if not already published. Although the *Ars* was a return to love poetry, it still marked career progress in combining the erotic and the didactic.

The next three couplets of 2.18 mark further progress with a catalogue of writers and addressees from the *Heroides*:

> ... aut quod Penelopes verbis reddatur Vlixi
> scribimus et lacrimas, Phylli relicta, tuas,
> quod Paris et Macareus et quod male gratus Iason
> Hippolytique parens Hippolytusque legant,

[1] Chapter 2, pp. 47–9.

[2] As McKeown 1998 notes, some take *artes Amoris* as a reference to the *Amores*.

quodque tenens strictum Dido miserabilis ensem
dicat et Aoniam Lesbis amica lyram.

> ... or I write what Penelope writes to Ulysses, and your laments after you were abandoned, O Phyllis; I write what Paris and Macareus and ungrateful Jason read, and what Hippolytus' father and Hippolytus himself read; I write what poor Dido says while holding the sword or what the Lesbian girlfriend says while holding the Aonian lyre. (*Am.* 2.18.21–6)

As many as ten of the fifteen extant single letters are mentioned: *Her.* 1, Penelope to Ulysses (21); 2, Phyllis to Demophoön (22); 4, Phaedra to Hippolytus (24); 5, Oenone to Paris (23); 6, Hypsipyle to Jason, or 12, Medea to Jason, or even both (23); 7, Dido to Aeneas (25); 10, Ariadne to Theseus (24); 11, Canace to Macareus (23); and, if the text is sound, 15, Sappho to Phaon (26). The catalogue has generated enormous interest and has been put to many different uses, including discussions about the chronology of Ovid's early career and the authenticity of certain epistles.[3]

In the ensuing discussion the catalogue suggests the *Heroides* as elegiac ventures into epic and especially tragedy, the two genres that once provoked Cupid's laughter (*Am.* 1.1.3–4, 2.18.15). The catalogue is rich in tragic myth. The mention of Jason (23) at the heart of the catalogue is striking in the wake of the poet's recusal of tragedy, for *Her.* 6 and 12 constitute a new approach to the characters and situations of the *Medea*. Flanking Jason are Macareus (23) and Hippolytus (24), heroes bearing strong associations with the Euripidean stage. Ovid also joins ranks with Catullus and Vergil, whose epic poetry provided exemplars for transforming tragedy, by mentioning Ariadne and Dido (24 and 25, respectively). Yet while they appropriate the material of tragedy, the *Heroides* also engage with tragic modalities, regardless of the genres in which their correspondents originate. Each letter serves as an epistolary *theatron*, wherein heroines and heroes give themselves over to displays of emotion, as they open their innermost feelings to scrutiny, or displays of exposition, as they contextualize the moment of writing by setting the scene. I propose, then, that the *Heroides* allowed Ovid to continue the career in Roman tragedy begun with the *Medea*, even as he continued his illustrious career in elegy.

Seeking out instances of tragic theatricality in the *Heroides* is an enterprise not without scholarly baggage. Some regard the poems, for better or

[3] P. E. Knox 1995, 5–14, Kenney 1996, 20–6, and P. E. Knox 2002, 118–21, offer useful summaries of the controversies surrounding the letters' authenticity and transmission. For purposes of discussion, I regard the entire collection, including poem 15 (Sappho) and the double letters, as genuine. Even if it could be proven conclusively that one or more letters are spurious, they could still be mined for examples of the tragic theatricality I intend to elucidate.

for worse, as monologues in letter form.[4] Others suppose them to have been written for the theaters, whether to be danced as pantomime or recited.[5] Although it is important to acknowledge the critical history, both approaches place too much emphasis on the stage (that is, confining the letters to particular venues, occasions, or practices) at the expense of the page (the textualization of tragedy in Latin poetry). Given the *Heroides* as a kind of Roman tragedy, which was rhetorical in the extreme, it would be foolish to deny rhetoric a place in the collection. Two rhetorical traditions, *ethopoeiae* (speeches in character) and *suasoriae* (deliberation) are especially relevant to the personae and aims of Ovid's correspondents.[6] Nevertheless, we can consider the letters rhetorical without classifying them as pure rhetoric, and they can be dramatic even if Ovid never intended them for performance.[7]

My approach to reading the *Heroides* proceeds from the standpoint of code, the unwritten rules that govern (epistolary) elegy. Surveying both the single letters (*Her.* 1–15), as well as the so-called double letters (16–21) later added to the collection, I will identify and describe five theatrical

[4] Kennedy 2002, 219, offers a primer on the reception of the *Heroides* as rhetoric in the nineteenth and twentieth centuries, and the damage done to their (and Ovid's) reputation as a result. Auhagen 2007, making a major effort toward rehabilitation, interrogates the term "rhetorical." Following Fränkel 1945, Auhagen distinguishes between rhetorical as (1) referring to the ancient art of effective speaking and writing; and (2) connoting artifice and insincerity – these latter qualities being, for some, "incompatible with poetry" (413). Recent advocates for reading the single *Heroides* as monologues include Auhagen 1999 ("Die *Heroides* sind Monologe par excellence – wenigstens gilt das uneingeschränkt für die Einzelbriefe," 12) and Steinmetz 1987 ("Als solche Monodramen können diese Gedichte gelesen, rezitiert, aber auch aufgeführt, wie man es ja auch getan hat," 140). See further Auhagen 1999, 45–53, a comprehensive bibliographic survey.

[5] The *locus classicus* for the performance theory is Cunningham 1949: "The novelty of the *Heroides* lies in the fact that they present Latin erotic elegy in a form adapted to a new type of theatrical performance [pantomime] which was first introduced at Rome when Ovid was a young man" (100, brackets mine). Compare Sargent 1997, who reads the letters as *libretti* for pantomime. As discussed in Chapter 2, pp. 40–1 and n. 108, the performance theory focuses on two passages from the *Tristia* (2.515–20 and 5.7.25–8), in which Ovid claims his poems have been danced in public. Also relevant is *Ars am.* 3.345, with its injunction that the *Heroides* be performed by singing or by recitation (*vel tibi composita cantetur epistula voce*, Kenney): Cunningham 1949, 101–2 (singing); Jouteur 2009, 73–4 (recitation). Although the *Heroides* were part of Ovid's tragic program, and although they might have been adapted – and easily so – for pantomime while Ovid was in exile, I do not insist that they were intended for any kind of theatrical performance.

[6] On these traditions, subcategories of Roman *declamatio*, see Chapter 2, pp. 36–7. Barsby 1978, while generally skeptical about the influence of declamatory practices on the collection, nevertheless finds no detriment in their impact on the poet: "[I]t is no discredit to a writer to have had some formal training in the techniques of his art" (13).

[7] Auhagen 2007, 416–24, demonstrates the importance of rhetoric throughout the Ovidian *corpus*: the *Heroides* are more the rule than the exception. In her preface Jouteur (ed.) 2009 reminds us that the poetry of Ovid's era was written to be read aloud, hence "performed" by a reader: "[L]a poésie de l'âge d'or comporte nécessairement des accents dramatiques – indépendamment des genres littéraires de rattachement – en ce qu'elle est écrite pour être lue à haute voix" (5).

parameters shared between the codes of elegy and tragedy. My discussion will include formal similarities, shared devices, and the system of myth underlying both genres.[8] Although some critics have emphasized tensions between the codes of elegy and tragedy,[9] I concentrate on their synergy, and on the synergistic cooperation among parameters that allows the letters to be read as tragic texts.[10] It is not simply a matter of isolating a single parameter like irony in the collection at large, nor even of enumerating several parameters like myth or pathos. Rather, I insist on the interdependence of the parameters: irony flourishing in a mythical context, for example, or myth magnifying pathos. These and other synergies not only enabled Ovid to continue playing both elegist and tragedian, but also validated his famous claim that the *Heroides* were a new form previously unknown (*ignotum hoc aliis ille novavit opus*, *Ars am.* 3.346 Kenney).

1 Writing within margins

Let me begin with the epistolary format, the single most important parameter for reading the *Heroides* in light of tragedy. Other parameters might by themselves be equally well represented in epic or other genres. The epistolary format, however, not only configures the letters as theatrical displays, but also focuses other parameters toward interpretations that privilege the tragic. Just as the physical confines of the *theatron* restrict the setting of a tragic play to a certain place and time and foster Aristotelian semblances of unity (*Poet.* 5–6.1449b),[11] so in ancient epistolography the

[8] Rhetoric might well have been one of these parameters, but it will remain in the background for now. Nevertheless three of my parameters – the boundaried here-and-now, first-person perspective, and the pathos of love – can also be read as essential rhetorical parameters. Chapter 5, a survey of monologues in the *Metamorphoses*, takes fuller stock of Ovidian rhetoric. With its emphasis on the *topoi* of tragic speeches (some of which are drawn from the letters), the discussion could double, *mutatis mutandis*, for a discussion of rhetoric in the *Heroides*.

[9] E.g., Hinds 1993, 39: "[Medea's] tragic identity is not suppressed, but rather is set in productive tension with her new epistolary environment" (brackets mine); Barchiesi 1993, 345 (previously cited in Chapter 1): "Drama and elegy have different and conflicting codes." Compare Casali 1995a, whose title is "Strategies of tension."

[10] Jouteur 2009 offers a synergistic reading of *Her.* 12 (Medea to Jason), situating the poem on the threshold (*seuil*) between elegy and tragedy. Jouteur explores some of the shared modalities I present below: a heroine's subjective narration (77–80), the dramatization of pathos (81–2), and dramatic irony (82–3). Likewise Casanova-Robin 2009, who reads the letter of Canace in Aristotelian terms. As I hope to make clear, we are perhaps more alive to elegiac–tragic synergies in poems like 11 and 12 because their heroines are synonymous with the stage. Yet such synergies operate in the letters of all heroines and heroes, even those on loan from other genres.

[11] Semblance of unity: at least as far as time is concerned. The so-called unity of place, implicit in the *Poetics*, is a late Renaissance addendum. Of course, space and time in tragedy and epistolography are not absolute. The scene of a tragedy sometimes changes (as in *Aj.* and *Eum.*), and the time-frame is somewhat elastic (so *Trach.*).

media of composition, the tablet and the papyrus, restrict the reach of letters. Ovid's correspondents sometimes call attention to their letters (*epistulae* or *litterae*) in physical terms, making references to the *charta* (page) and the *calamus* (pen).[12] The *Heroides* are "object[s] which can be moved, transmitted and, on occasion, hidden away."[13] Cydippe's attempts to write in secret, concealing the document when receiving visitors (21.17–28), both objectify her letter and suggest a world beyond its margins.

Both tragedy and epistolary elegy, therefore, occur within specific spatial and temporal boundaries: Argos before the return of Agamemnon, Ithaca before the return of Odysseus. Regardless of the specifics, from the perspective of the actor or the writer the place is always here; the time, always now. The events of other places and times lie outside this frame of reference and belong, generally, to the there and the then. In the same way that Naxos in Catullus 64, doubly framed by the ocean and by the coverlet of Peleus' and Thetis' marriage bed, becomes an ekphrastic theater for Ariadne's performance, the letters of the *Heroides* create epistolary theaters for Ovid's correspondents.[14] The often confined spaces in which they write find analogues in the limited media of the letters themselves. Efrossini Spentzou, for example, likens compartmentalization in the single *Heroides* to the Kristevan-Platonic concept of the *chora*: the texts become feminine spaces of subversive creativity.[15] M. Catherine Bolton, in turn, connects the self-described isolation of certain heroines, which often contrasts with their prior and future mobility, with their efforts to transcend isolation by writing.[16] I would go further and say that the here-and-now within a letter's margins renders its author the focus of the reader's attention, effectively placing him or her center stage. Phaedra, in asking Hippolytus to pretend that he sees her tears (*lacrimas finge videre meas*, 4.176), tropes her letter as viewing place, and her reader as a spectator.[17] In a sense, Phaedra's request is made on behalf of all the writers in the collection, who are just as much on display as she.[18]

[12] Examples of *charta* in the *Heroides*: 1.62, 11.4, 18.20, 21.244; *calamus*: 11.3, 21.245.

[13] Kyriakidis 2010, 8, following Farrell 1998, 316.

[14] On the resemblance between Ariadne's epistolary context in *Her.* 11 and her ekphrastic context in Cat. 64 see Barchiesi 1993, 346–7.

[15] Spentzou 2003, ch. 3.

[16] Bolton 2009. Compare Auhagen 2007 (following Auhagen 1999, 63–77), who calls the desolate Naxian landscape of *Her.* 10 "a mirror of Ariadne's soul" (417).

[17] So Barchiesi 1993, 338: "If Hippolytus ... follows her suggestion literally, ... he will find himself sharing the exact viewpoint (*finge videre*) of a spectator in the Euripidean tragedy" (author's parentheses).

[18] *Pace* Dangel 2009, who finds such displays of pathos dramatic, but just shy of theatrical: "L'espace d'écriture qu'offre l'épistolaire permet de développer un pathétique, sinon de théâtralité, tout au moins de théâtralisation" (24).

A second formal parameter involves the perspectives of the characters, who inhabit the boundaried worlds of tragedy and epistolography. Like tragic characters, the authors of the *Heroides* are internal narrators, commentators on the stories in which they are participating. As Oliver Taplin has shown, tragic internal narrative manifests itself in embedded stage directions, with which characters mark entrances and exits, as well as refer to scenery and stage props.[19] A famous example of the latter are Ajax's preparations for his suicide, when he describes the sword embedded in the ground: ὁ μὲν σφαγεὺς ἕστηκεν ᾗ τομώτατος | γένοιτ᾽ ἄν (815–16 Lloyd-Jones and Wilson). Although the settings of the *Heroides* are rather nondescript, one can glean the immediate circumstances from the writers' accounts of the recent past. Ariadne's description of her frantic meandering is a case in point (10.13–50), as is Leander's account of the recent storms that divide him and Hero (18.25–36).

A letter's beginning or ending often yields scenic references. Thus the *incipits* of Hypermestra, Canace, and Leander:

> clausa domo teneor gravibusque coercita vinclis;
> est mihi supplicii causa fuisse piam.

> I am held captive within the palace and bound with heavy chains; that I was faithful to you is the reason for my punishment. (*Her.* 14.3–4)

> dextra tenet calamum, strictum tenet altera ferrum,
> et iacet in gremio charta soluta meo.

> My right hand has a reed; my left, a drawn sword; a scroll lies unfurled in my lap. (*Her.* 11.3–4)

> talibus exiguo dictis mihi murmure verbis,
> cetera cum charta dextra locuta mea est.
> at quanto mallem, quam scriberet, illa nataret,
> meque per adsuetas sedula ferret aquas!

> After uttering such words in a mere murmur, my right hand has said the rest on paper. But how much I would rather my hand swim than write, and bear me in earnest through the water I know so well! (*Her.* 18.19–22)

These early references are reminiscent of tragic prologues, in which internal narrators set the stage through exposition. Later references can provide a certain closure. Helen, for example, anticipates an end to her letters and to Paris' advances by noting that the Trojans are making ready to sail from

[19] Taplin 1977, a study of Aeschylean stagecraft with broad implications for tragedy as a genre.

Sparta (*expediunt iam tua vela Phryges*, 17.200). Dido, meanwhile, makes a terminal revelation near the end of her epistle:

> scribimus, et gremio Troicus ensis adest,
> perque genas lacrimae strictum labuntur in ensem,
> qui iam pro lacrimis sanguine tinctus erit.

> As I write the Trojan sword lies in my lap, and tears stream down my cheeks onto the drawn blade, soon to be stained with blood instead. (*Her.* 7.184–6)

This is a bold gesture in itself, although it is not entirely unexpected: readers of the *Aeneid* know the heroine will die in the manner of Ajax. Yet by acknowledging the blade, Dido is already emulating the Sophoclean hero, not only as suicide but also as internal narrator.[20]

The boldest gesture of all comes toward the close of Deianira's letter, after her recollection of Nessus:

> sed quid ego haec refero? scribenti nuntia venit
> fama, virum tunicae tabe perire meae. 144

> But why rehearse the past like this? While I write word has come that my husband is dying from the poison I placed on the cloak. (*Her.* 9.143–4)

This is a rare moment in the collection when an outside event intrudes upon the writer. Cydippe, as we have observed, marks the intervals of composition (21.17–28); she also seems to repeat the Delphic oracle as it reaches her ears for the first time (231–6).[21] Yet Deianira's acknowledgement of the *nuntia* (143) is the most explicit marking of an event that occurs during a letter's writing. Note that even a letter without references to its setting is still implicitly theatrical. The perception of the epistle as a product of a certain time and place (even if unspecified) creates a stable here-and-now, which gains additional stability from a writer's self-portrait "in the moment."

Although tragic and epistolary narrators exist in here-and-nows of their own making, they can look beyond the boundaries of their respective genres by narrating events from other places and times, or there-and-thens. Such narratives, typically couched as personal observations and recollections, provide a more remote context for the here-and-now. They also enable readers to determine at what point in the story a letter is written.

[20] In *Aeneid* 4 Dido vows to die by the sword (547), but all other references to the blade are the province of the external narrator. For general comparisons between Dido and Ajax see R. D. Williams 1972 (introduction to book 4), as well as Chapter 2, p. 54 and n. 162.

[21] So Kenney 1979, 426–7, and Rosati 2005, 174.

Likewise, tragic prologues situate plays within a larger body of myth, while messenger speeches bring recent offstage events onstage. Oedipus' account of meeting a stranger at the crossroads (*OT* 774–813) and the messenger's description of Jocasta's suicide (1237–85), for example, both follow similar narrative principles.[22] With few concurrent or even recent events, Ovid's correspondents usually look to the more distant past.

A sampling of memories from Phyllis, Sappho, Dido, Cydippe, and Paris:

> ausus es amplecti colloque infusus amantis
> oscula per longas iungere pressa moras
> cumque tuis lacrimis lacrimas confundere nostras,
> quodque foret velis aura secunda, queri
> et mihi discedens suprema dicere voce:
> "Phylli, fac exspectes Demophoönta tuum!"

You dared to embrace me and to caress my neck, lingering over our kisses, and to mingle our tears, mine with yours, and to lament because the wind favored your sails, and to say to me as you finally left, "Phyllis, be sure to look out for your Demophoön!" (*Her.* 2.93–8)

> at mea cum legerem, sat iam formosa videbar;
> unam iurabas usque decere loqui.
> cantabam, memini – meminerunt omnia amantes –
> oscula cantanti tu mihi rapta dabas.
> haec quoque laudabas, omnique a parte placebam –
> sed tum praecipue, cum fit amoris opus.

But when I read my songs, I seemed beautiful enough already; you would swear that speech suited me alone. When I would sing, I recall – lovers recall everything – you would steal kisses from me as I sang. You would praise my kisses, too, and in every way I would please you – but especially when we made love. (*Her.* 15.41–6)

> occidit internas coniunx mactatus ad aras,
> et sceleris tanti praemia frater habet;
> exul agor cineresque viri patriamque relinquo,
> et feror in dubias hoste sequente vias.
> adplicor his oris fratrique elapsa fretoque
> quod tibi donavi, perfide, litus emo.

My husband falls, bleeding before the altars, and my brother reaps the rewards of a horrible crime; I am driven into exile and abandon my fatherland and my husband's ashes, borne on an uncertain path, my enemy

[22] See J. Barrett 2002, a study of the dynamics of messenger speeches in tragedy.

pursuing me. I make landfall here and, safe from my brother and the waves, purchase the shore I gave to you, faithless man. (*Her.* 7.113–18)

forsitan haec spectans a te spectabar, Aconti,
visaque simplicitas est mea posse capi.
in templum redeo gradibus sublime Dianae –
tutior hoc ecquis debuit esse locus?

Perhaps while I gazed at these wonders, Acontius, I was gazed at in turn by you, and my naiveté seemed apt for the taking. I returned to Diana's temple, its steps on high – should any place have been safer than this? (*Her.* 21.103–6)

dulce Venus risit. "Nec te, Pari, munera tangant
utraque suspensi plena timoris!" ait;
"nos dabimus, quod ames, et pulchrae filia Ledae
ibit in amplexus pulchrior illa tuos!"

Venus gave a sweet laugh. She said, "Do not let [Minerva's and Juno's] gifts affect you, Paris, each one full of doubt and fear. I will give you something worthy of love, and the daughter of beautiful Leda, more beautiful still, will enter your embrace." (*Her.* 16.83–6)

Both Phyllis and Sappho recall their lovers' devotion in order to expose their betrayals. The troubles Dido has overcome seem less onerous in comparison to her doomed affair with Aeneas, while Cydippe's former good health and mobility, which permitted a voyage to Delos, contrast sharply with her current illness. Paris attempts to seduce Helen by the authority of Venus. Whatever the underlying motivation, the writers of the *Heroides*, when not describing the here-and-now, contextualize it by rehearsing the past.[23]

Emerging from this discussion is a sense not only of where tragic and epistolary narrative intersect, but also of how the latter is a more intensive, and therefore intensifying, project. Although the setting of tragedy is fixed, the genre itself is somewhat spacious: despite a limited number of actors, it has room for an array of characters over the course of a single drama. It also allows movement in the entrances and exits of characters, who demarcate the alternation between episode and stasimon. The *Heroides*, in contrast, have one narrator and little formal structure apart from the occasional salutation. When a heroine or hero tells a story, the past, which is usually more populous and dynamic than the present, is momentarily on display. But only momentarily. Whereas a tragic narrative can become a

[23] Ovid's correspondents sometimes look to the future as well, usually with ironic results. See section 4, below.

catalyst for further action, an epistolary narrative leads back to the narrator, whose present solitary state becomes magnified when contrasted with a past featuring other characters. Narrative acts in Ovid's letters tend to shore up as much as transcend the boundaries of the here-and-now.

2 The pathos of love

Turning aside from formal issues, I come to a third tragic parameter in the *Heroides*: the device of suffering or pathos. When Ovidian correspondents are not recalling the past, they are proclaiming the pathos of love[24] in the present. The letters document, as if in real time, the abject misery of the writers, who find meaning in the act of documentation. The expression of pathos is doubly appropriate for elegy. On the one hand, the suffering of any given heroine or hero is predicated upon love. On the other hand, their suffering often finds expression as lamentation, which recalls the genre's original funereal traditions. Either way, elegy is a most appropriate genre for the pathos of Ovid's correspondents. Yet pathos is also a fixture of tragedy – Aristotle calls it a third component of tragic plotting, behind recognition and reversal (*Poet.* 11.1452b) – which brings the anguish of heroes and heroines into public view. At first glance, there might seem to be little overlap between elegiac and tragic pathos, since the latter can involve any kind of physical or mental suffering, while the former is almost exclusively erotic. Digging deeper, however, we can find considerable common ground. Here Ovid situates his letters.

A test. There would seem to be a world of difference between the pathos of Phaedra in the *Hippolytus* and in poem 4:

> τὸ γὰρ παρ' ἡμῖν πάθος
> πέραν δυσεκπέρατον ἔρχεται βίου.
> κακοτυχεστάτα γυναικῶν ἐγώ. 679

My inextricable suffering exceeds my life. I am the most unfortunate woman of all. (Eur. *HS* 677–9)

> addimus his precibus lacrimas quoque; verba precantis 175
> qui legis, et lacrimas finge videre meas.

I also add tears to my supplications. You, who read the words of a suppliant, imagine you can see my tears as well. (*Her.* 4.175–6)

[24] Pathos of love: Otis 1970, 166, a term that applies to the *Heroides* as well as the *Metamorphoses*.

After suffering in silence and in sickness, Euripides' Phaedra proclaims her misery, which is connected to her concern for her reputation. Although she loves Hippolytus, she would rather die than approach him; in fact, at no point in the drama do the two characters interact onstage. For Ovid's Phaedra, love has removed the barriers of modesty (*pudor sua signa reliquit*, 155), allowing her to leverage her woes toward seducing Hippolytus. Tragic pathos appears to have been recodifed as elegiac pathos.[25]

But has it? We default to the *Hippolytus* as the primary model because it is extant. Yet what if the intertextual range were expanded to encompass another tragedy about Hippolytus and Phaedra, even a fragmentary one? Sergio Casali has advocated for multiple models in *Her.* 4, placing two lost plays – the *Hippolytus Kalyptomenos* (*HK*) of Euripides and the *Phaedra* of Sophocles – alongside the extant play.[26] Both reputedly featured Phaedras who were more proactive, if not outright seductresses: in particular, the Sophoclean Phaedra might have disclosed her desire for Hippolytus in a letter.[27] Against a broader tragic background, Ovid's heroine does what her counterparts appear to have done in two other tragedies; three, if we also include the desperate supplication of Seneca's Phaedra. The virtuous heroine of Euripides' extant play now seems more the exception than the rule, and *Her.* 4 now seems to elaborate and enlarge upon a tragic pathos of love instead of recodifying it. Sophocles' *Women of Trachis*, which like his lost *Phaedra* is an apposite reminder that not all lovelorn heroines are Euripidean,[28] offers a similar lesson. *Her.* 9 does not simply eroticize Deianira's tragedy. Rather, it begins with problems of desire already present in the Sophoclean play.

When we consider *eros* as a motivator of tragic action, we begin to align tragedy with elegy in distinctly Ovidian ways. At *Tristia* 2.381–408 the poet offers a comprehensive catalogue of tragedies indebted to *amor*.[29] Some excerpts:

> omne genus scripti gravitate tragoedia vincit:
>   haec quoque materiam semper amoris habet.
> numquid in Hippolyto, nisi caeca est flamma novercae?
>   nobilis est Canace fratris amore sui. 384

[25] Compare Casali 1995a, 4: "The means of communication in the second *Hippolytus*, the nurse, is absorbed by Phaedra herself as a function of her new elegiac competence."

[26] Casali 1995a, 1–4. Eur. *HK*: *TrGF* V.428–47; discussion in Halleran 1995, 25–37. Soph. *Phaedra*: *TrGF* IV.677–93; see also Lloyd-Jones 1996.

[27] I explore this notion below in section 5, pp. 90–1 and n. 89.

[28] The fragmentary evidence generally demonstrates more affinities between Sophocles and Euripides than critics have been prepared to admit. This is a foundational point for Sommerstein 2003.

[29] On the catalogue in general see Luck 1977.

fecit amor subitas volucres cum paelice regem,
quaeque suum luget nunc quoque mater Ityn. 390

qui legis Electran et egentem mentis Oresten, 395
Aegisthi crimen Tyndaridosque legis.

quid Danaën Danaësque nurum matremque Lyaei
Haemonaque et noctes cui coiere duae?
quid Peliae generum, quid Thesea, quique Pelasgum
Iliacam tetigit de rate primus humum? 404

tempore deficiar, tragicos si persequar ignes, 407
vixque meus capiet nomina nuda liber.

Tragedy outstrips every genre of writing in seriousness; yet it, too, always has love as its subject matter. Does Hippolytus concern anything other than a stepmother's blind passion? Canace is renowned for loving her own brother ... Without warning love changed the king and his mistress into birds, as well as the mother, who now mourns her poor Itys ... The reader of Electra and Orestes driven mad reads the adulterous crime of Aegisthus and the daughter of Tyndareus ... Why mention Danaë and her daughter-in-law, and the mother of Bacchus, and Haemon, and her, for whom two nights became one? Why mention the son-in-law of Pelias, why Theseus, why he who was the first of the Pelasgians to go ashore and touch Trojan soil? ... I will run out of time if I trace the fires of passion in tragedy; my book will barely hold the names by themselves. (*Tr.* 2.381–4, 389–90, 395–6, 401–4, 407–8)

Although this catalogue is a gambit – Ovid is writing to Augustus in an attempt to destigmatize the *Ars amatoria* – some of his choices are canny. The poet does well to begin with Phaedra and to continue with Canace (383–4), whose forbidden love for her brother Macareus was the subject of Euripides' *Aeolus*.[30] Furthermore, Ovid had already displayed the erotic pathos of both heroines in *Her.* 4 and 11, respectively. The tragic Phaedra and Canace would make fitting elegiac heroines because they have already done so. In fact, Ovid's catalogue reads in part as a retrospective on the single *Heroides*, for it overlaps with the collection in five other instances: Medea (387), Hermione (399), Ariadne (via Theseus, 403), Laodamia (via Protesilaus, 403–4), and Deianira (405).

At the same time, the catalogue affords a glimpse of the poetic road not taken. If seven of the heroines were featured in Ovid's epistolary

[30] Eur. *Aeolus*: *TrGF* V.13a–41, with reconstructions in Jäkel 1979 and G. D. Williams 1992. Williams also traces the relationship of *Her.* 11 to the lost play.

collection, what might the poet have done with the rest? Whereas some of his tragic *exempla* are patently erotic, others seem less susceptible to this interpretation, such as Clytemnestra (396). The saga of the house of Atreus was many times the subject of Greek and Roman tragedy, from the fraternal strife of Atreus and Thyestes, to the murder of Agamemnon, to the dementia of Orestes. But to place his madness on equal footing with his mother's adultery seems like perverse erotic revisionism – or so a traditional approach to the extant Aeschylean tragedy would suggest.[31] Likewise conventional thinking about Antigone (402), who in Sophocles' extant play has no time for *eros*.[32] Like Phaedra and Hippolytus in the *Hippolytus*, she and Haemon never share the stage, despite his professed devotion to her.

Most arresting is Ovid's characterization of Philomela as the mistress rather than the victim of Tereus (*cum paelice regem*, 389). This is not to say that the story need be devoid of *eros*: a fragment of Accius' tragedy, which depicts Tereus as aflame with desire (*amore vecors flammeo*), clearly shows this force at work in the drama.[33] Love is also at work in Ovid's own Tereus narrative in the *Metamorphoses*, with the king portrayed as a stereotypically elegiac *amator* after meeting Philomela (6.455–85), and Philomela labeling herself as his mistress following her rape (*paelex ego facta sororis*, 537).[34] Nevertheless, it is one thing to recognize the presence of *eros* in a tragedy, or even in one of the poet's tragic narratives. It is quite another to discover that tragedy repackaged as something akin to Ceyx and Alcyone in *Met.* 11, where the love between husband and wife persists even after their transformation into kingfishers.[35] Ovid's claim that desire precipitated the metamorphosis of Tereus and the sisters (*fecit amor subitas volucres*, 389) seems especially tendentious. Readers of *Met.* 6 know that, regardless of the role *amor* plays toward the beginning of the narrative, the predominant emotions in its dénouement are fear and anger – the sisters' fear at the anger of Tereus, who seeks retaliation for the slaughter of Itys.

[31] Of Accius' *Clytaemnestra* not enough survives to indicate whether or not the play had an erotic dimension: *SRF* 1.30–41 (which might be the same play as Acc. *Aegisthus*, fr. 22–7).

[32] In Euripides' lost *Antigone*, however, the heroine married Haemon and bore his child (*Hyp.* Soph. *Ant.* 1). Accius also wrote an *Antigona*, but its remains are too meager to assess the heroine's relationship with Haemon: *SRF* 1.135–44.

[33] Acc. *Tereus*: *SRF* 1.634–50 (quotation, fr. 637). Other plays by this title: Liv. Andron., *SRF* 1.24–9; Soph., *TrGF* IV.581–95b. For more on the influence of Accius' play on Ovid see Chapter 2, pp. 28–9.

[34] Gildenhard and Zissos 2007, 14–16, discuss the Tereus–Procne–Philomela narrative not only in terms of its "robust heterogeneity of generic elements and narrative energies," but also as a "negative dialectics in which epic and elegiac elements distort and pervert one other" (14).

[35] Compare *Met.* 11.743–4: *tum quoque mansit amor, nec coniugiale solutum est | foedus in alitibus.*

But before we conclude that Ovid is hurting his case before the emperor with a reckless or perverse view of tragedy, let us note that modern critics of the genre have found eroticism in unlikely plays, some of which overlap with the catalogue of *Tristia* 2. Nancy Sorkin Rabinowitz has demonstrated that female suffering is eroticized in the most Aristotelian and orthodox of plays, *Oedipus Tyrannos*. Jocasta, she notes, hangs herself within her bridal chamber, her corpse violated by Oedipus, her son and husband, as he rips the brooches from her gown (1265–70). Rabinowitz also finds Antigone sexualized in her suicide. Sealed within a cavern, a so-called bridal chamber of Hades (νυμφεῖον Ἅιδου, 1205 Lloyd-Jones and Wilson), the maiden hangs herself with her veil, her skin stained with Haemon's blood (1219–43): "The veil evokes the virgin about to be married, the blood the blood of defloration."[36] Rabinowitz demonstrates that tragedy systematically conflates *eros* with the pathos of female characters. This conflation, we might say, is encoded within the genre, and can apply even to Aeschylus – this contrary to Aristophanes' famous (and polemical) claim that the tragedian never wrote "whores" like Euripides' Phaedra and Stheneboea (ἀλλ' οὐ μὰ Δί' οὐ Φαίδρας ἐποίουν πόρνας οὐδὲ Σθενεβοίας, *Ran.* 1043 Hall and Geldart). The *Agamemnon* ultimately portrays Clytemnestra as lascivious in her jealousy of Cassandra and her almost orgasmic delight in murdering her husband (*Ag.* 1380–92). Rabinowitz observes, "If in the rhetoric of the *Antigone* death is made marriage, in the rhetoric of Clytemnestra murder is made erotic."[37]

Our reconsideration of Ovid's tragic catalogue opens up new possibilities for the *Heroides*. What if Antigone had written to Haemon from the cave moments before her suicide, as Canace writes to Macareus? What if Clytemnestra, ironically fashioning herself as a Penelope, had written to Agamemnon, lamenting his absence and welcoming his return? What if the men had written first? Even Philomela might find a place in Ovid's collection due to her reputation as a weaver of narrative texts. A letter to Tereus could justifiably be called a *carmen miserabile*, which is also Ovid's description of her tapestry at *Met.* 6.582. Furthermore, such an epistle, with its likely rhetorical flourishes, would stand in stark

[36] Rabinowitz 1992: Jocasta, 43–4; Antigone, 39–41 (quotation on 40). Rabinowitz contends that erotic pathos is essential to tragedy's function as pornography. Whether or not the *Heroides* share this function lies outside my focus, but the letters' subordination of women to men and the alignment of the reader with the male addressee/viewer might be provocative starting points. On hanging as a female death in tragedy see Loraux 1987, ch. 1, "The rope and the sword" (1–30).

[37] Rabinowitz 1992, 41–3, quotation on 42.

contrast to Philomela's literal voicelessness as an elegiac version of the κερκίδος φωνή, the "voice of the shuttle," from Sophocles' play (*TrGF* IV.595).[38] The fact that epistles by these and perhaps other heroines and heroes are within the realm of the imagination says as much about parallel constructions of desire in tragedy and elegy as about the poet's own ingenuity.

If in the *Tristia* Ovid posits erotic pathos as a fixture of tragedy, perhaps it is because his epistolary version of elegy aspires to tragic pathos. In the end, would the miseries of the *Heroides* have been out of place on the tragic stage? Especially an Ovidian stage, which we know featured Medea decrying some kind of dilemma (*feror huc illuc ut plena deo*, fr. 2)?[39] Consider Briseis:

> at lacrimas sine fine dedi rupique capillos –
> infelix iterum sum mihi visa capi!

> I have cried endless tears and torn out my hair – wretched me, I seem to be taken captive once again. (*Her.* 3.15–16)

Or Hermione:

> flere licet certe; flendo defundimus iram,
> perque sinum lacrimae fluminis instar eunt.
> has solas habeo semper semperque profundo;
> ument incultae fonte perenne genae.

> I can certainly weep, at least. I pour out my wrath by weeping, and tears flow like a river over my breast. Only these tears remain, and they spill forth unceasingly, drenching and spoiling my cheeks with their eternal stream. (*Her.* 8.61–4)

Or Phyllis:

> ah, laceras etiam puppes furiosa refeci –
> ut, qua desererer, firma carina foret! –
> remigiumque dedi, quod me fugiturus haberes.
> heu! patior telis vulnera facta meis!

> How mad I was to refit your battered ships – all so that the keel by which I would be abandoned might be strong! – and to supply the oar, which you would hold as you fled from me. Alas, I suffer wounds from my own weapons! (*Her.* 2.45–8)

[38] For another Ovidian attempt – actual, not imaginary – to give voice to Philomela, see Chapter 5, pp. 134–6.

[39] On this fragment and its interpretation see Chapter 2, p. 42.

Or Paris:

> quid faciam, dubito. dolor est meus illa videre,
> sed dolor a facie maior abesse tua.
> qua licet et possum, luctor celare furorem;
> sed tamen apparet dissimulatus amor.

> As to what to do, I hesitate. To look upon these things is painful, but to be away from your gaze is even more painful. As I can and may, I strive to conceal this madness, but my concealed desire is apparent all the same. (*Her.* 16.235–8)

Or Cydippe, whose illness is not metaphorical, but real:

> languor enim causis non apparentibus haeret.
> adiuvor et nulla fessa medentis ope.
> quam tibi nunc gracilem vix haec rescribere quamque
> pallida vix cubito membra levare puta![40]

> Weakness with no apparent cause takes hold. In my weariness I am helped by no doctor's remedy. Consider how feeble she is who can scarcely reply to you, and how weak her limbs which can scarcely support her! (*Her.* 21.13–16)

To my ear, at least, the answer is no. These and other displays are consonant with those of tragic characters, whose woes, even when not directly influenced by *eros*, often become eroticized. Even an interjection as banal as *me miseram!*, heard throughout the collection, might be heard as a conflation of elegy and tragedy. On the one hand, this is for Ovid the perennial cry of the elegist, which he utters in *Am.* 1.1 when dramatizing his initial conversion to elegy (*me miserum! certas habuit puer ille sagittas*, 25). His correspondents use the phrase less programmatically, perhaps, but no less emphatically when underscoring their status as elegiac authors. On the other hand, *me miserum/miseram!* finds a resounding antecedent in the perennial tragic cry, ὦ τάλας/τάλαιν' ἐγώ![41]

[40] I prefer the imperative *puta!* endorsed by Kenney 1996 over the interrogative *putas?*

[41] On *me miserum!* as a programmatic interjection in elegy see Hinds 1998, 29–31. *me miserum/miseram!* (and close variations) in the *Heroides*: 3.59, 3.61, 3.82, 4.161–2, 5.33, 5.123, 5.149, 7.7, 7.98, 8.88, 15.185, 15.204, 17.182, 19.65, 19.121, 19.187, 20.133 and 135 (rare masculine examples), 21.169. ὦ τάλας/τάλαιν' ἐγώ! (and variants) in extant tragedy: Aesch. *Cho.* 743, *Sept.* 808, *Pers.* 445, 1014, *PV* 158; Soph. *Aj.* 340, 981, 983, *Ant.* 1211, 1295, 1299, *El.* 807 and 1209, *OC* 753, 847, 876, 963, 1338, 1401, 1438, *OT* 744, *Phil.* 311, 416, 622, 744, 789, 934, 1187, *Trach.* 997, 1013, 1081, 1143; Eur. *Andr.* 514, 534, 1200, *Bacch.* 1282, *Hec.* 233, 1035, 1075, 1255, *Hel.* 833, 1621, *HF* 1131, 1363, *HS* 817, 875, 1090, 1350, *IA* 404, 506, 880, *IT* 549, *Med.* 511, 1400, *Or.* 768, 1048, 1073, *Phoen.* 1335, 1337, 1346, 1599, *Supp.* 570, 774.

3 Myth

My fourth parameter concerns the use of myth in both genres. Tragedy as a whole is devoted to Greco-Roman myths and legends, while individual plays treat individual myths, or portions thereof. The notion that myth is a code unto itself helps us understand why the tragedians returned to it again and again. Charles Segal notes that myth "functions as a complex network of interrelated symbols, patterns, and structures which encode the values of the culture into an extensive and comprehensive system."[42] Tragedy allowed poets and their audiences to examine shared values exemplified by their myths, in the context of both civic festivals and (as often) civil unrest. Add to this the capacity of myth to be reinvented – whether to suit changing values or the mythographer's sensibilities – which was fully realized within the agonistic context of tragedy. Here the contest or games of any given year matters less than the larger contest across generations, in which a tragedian might compete against any number of prior mythographers, tragedians and other poets alike. Furthermore, their entries in this generational contest, although we sometimes regard them as definitive, were open to revision by later poets.[43] Finally, let us note that myth has a certain magnitude (so *Poet.* 6.1449b), which both suited the tenor of the public festival, Greek or Roman, and lent itself to the scrutiny of thousands of spectators.

Myth is by and large a material parameter, and therefore widely available in epic and other genres. Yet a collection of epistles by mythical heroines and heroes elevates the genre of elegy beyond earlier practice. Much of surviving Roman elegy employs the convention of the *amator* and the pursuit of his *puella*, a convention Ovid, in the wake of Catullus, Gallus, Propertius, and Tibullus, cultivated in the *Amores*. Of course, this type of urban(e) elegy does not want for myth: the *amator* often adduces mythological *exempla* in support of his theme. In *Am.* 3.6, for instance, a flooded stream separating the lovers prompts, among other references to famous rivers and heroes in transit, an extended vignette featuring Ilia and the Anio, each speaking in character (45–82). Nevertheless, myth in this and other instances is ancillary, a metaphor for the relationship at hand. There is a gulf between the legendary world and the contemporary world of the poet and his mistress.[44]

[42] Segal 1983, 176: Greek myth coalesces into a "megatext," which includes not only the "total corpus" of Greek myth, verbal and visual, but also its unifying "deep structures."

[43] On the balance between repetition and innovation in tragedy see Chapter 2.

[44] This is not to say that tragedy lacks an exemplary use of myth. Legendary heroes and heroines must have provided their audiences with both positive and negative *exempla*.

Although the *amator–puella* relationship remained a dominant strain of elegy, other strains with different applications of myth appeared in Ovid's own time. A noteworthy example is Propertius' fourth book of elegies (*c.* 16 BCE), which marks a departure from his prior work. Whereas books 1–3 depicted the poet's affair with Cynthia against the backdrop of Rome, the focus of the new book is Rome itself.[45] This focus requires a close engagement with Roman myths and legends, through which Propertius narrows the gulf between the legendary and the contemporary. Elegy takes on an etiological function, and the poet becomes the Roman equivalent of Callimachus (4.1.64), whose *Aetia* were likewise composed in elegiac couplets. Under a Callimachean precedent, Propertius' use of myth helped to expand the genre's horizons in Augustan Rome. Ovid's predicament after the *Amores* was similar. His games with Corinna played out, Ovid uses myth in the *Heroides* to revitalize elegy. Granted, his program remains erotic (his attempt at etiological elegy, the *Fasti*, would come later), but his focus on mythical and legendary characters is a step toward something grander.[46] Moreover, it is a step taken once before in his lost *Medea*.

As a parameter with magnitude, myth bolsters other parameters within the codes of tragedy and epistolary elegy. As the next section will show, the potential for irony increases when an audience is familiar with the myth in question. Erotic pathos also becomes magnified within the context of myth, and thus encourages its assimilation to tragic pathos. The passions of mythical heroes and heroines operate at higher registers, usually with profound and devastating consequences. The passions of everyday mortals, however profound and devastating on their own terms, often fail to measure up. We can gauge the amplifying effects of myth in the *Heroides* by comparing one of Ovid's letters to that of an "ordinary" woman:[47] Propertius 4.3, a poetic epistle from one Arethusa to her husband Lycotas, who is conducting a military campaign in the East. The poem accords with Propertius' redefinition of elegy in book 4, both in portraying the domestic ramifications of imperial warfare, and in its epistolary format,

[45] Five of the eleven poems in Propertius 4 are wholly devoted to myth and mythicized history: Vertumnus (2), Tarpeia (4), Hercules (9), and the triumvirate of Romulus, Cossus, and M. Claudius Marcellus (10); poem 6, meanwhile, celebrates Augustus' victory at Actium through the eyes of Apollo and the deified Julius Caesar. Granted, Propertius' new focus was heralded in earlier books: although poem 2.1 is a *recusatio* of more elevated genres such as epic and panegyric, poem 2.10 nevertheless praises the military victories of Augustus; and poem 3.9, with its catalogue of Roman historical subjects (47–56), promises that the poet will one day produce a civic strain of elegy.

[46] On Ovid's use of myth throughout his career see Graf 2002.

[47] Letter of an "ordinary" woman: *Her.* 15 might seem a likely candidate, but the legendary aspects of Sappho's biography make her a quasi-mythical figure, hence larger than life: Lefkowitz 1973, Parker 1993.

which would have been novel even if the *Heroides* had been published first. My purpose, however, is not to continue the debate over the priority of Ovid versus Propertius, but to take advantage of the opportunity afforded by the survival of poem 4.3, which resembles the *Heroides* in all essential parameters but one.[48]

Arethusa's *incipit* illustrates the impact of myth through its absence:

> Haec Arethusa suo mittit mandata Lycotae,
>   cum totiens absis, si potes esse meus.
> si qua tamen tibi lecturo pars oblita derit,
>   haec erit e lacrimis facta litura meis:
> aut si qua incerto fallet te littera tractu,
>   signa meae dextrae iam morientis erunt.

> These mandates Arethusa sends to her Lycotas, if you can be mine when you are so often away. If any part is smudged and difficult to read, my tears will have smudged it: or if the trace of any letter seems uncertain, it signifies my hand is failing. (Prop. 4.3.1–6 Camps)

Although the name Arethusa contains the fleeting promise of a mythical epistle, as might the Hellenizing Lycotas, the poem is grounded in contemporary Roman reality. Arethusa's letter cannot be situated within a larger tradition, because no such tradition exists, as far as anyone knows. This is not to deny Arethusa's letter poignancy. The page contains not only her words, which describe her daily life without Lycotas, but also her tears, whose blots on the page – *liturae* among the *litterae* (4–5) – send the same message. The writers of the *Heroides* likewise use tears as visual signifiers of pathos. In addition to Phaedra, who as we recall claims to mingle weeping with her entreaties (4.175), Briseis weeps over the page upon which she writes (*quascumque adspicies, lacrimae fecere lituras*, 3.3), as does Sappho (*scribimus, et lacrimis oculi rorantur obortis*, 15.97). Leander, in turn, conjures the image of himself almost weeping while swimming to Sestos (*heu, lacrimas hoc mihi paene movet*, 18.180). By this standard the sufferings of epistolary heroes and heroines, Propertian or Ovidian, are equal. If anything, the image of a mythical character weeping makes his or her pathos more realistic.

[48] Zimmermann 2000 sees myth in the *Heroides* as a deliberate response to Propertius: "Das Novum der *Heroides* im Verhältnis zu Properz' Arethusa-Brief besteht also … darin, daß er Brief-Form, die Properz in seiner Elegie eingeführt hatte, in die Welt der Mythologie versetzt" (135). Likewise Anderson 1973, who notes the amplifying effect of myth on epistolary pathos: "Ovid then devised a new 'heroic' setting for his letters and a situation that stirs more pathos" (67). Arethusa does make mythical references in her letter (most notably to Hippolyte at 43–4), but like similar references in the *Amores*, these belong to a world far removed from Arethusa's day-to-day experience.

Nevertheless, the passions of Ovid's correspondents tend toward the grandiose. Canace, too, will stain her letter, but with blood instead of tears (*oblitus a dominae caede libellus erit*, 11.2). Grander passions in the *Heroides* are also rhetorical. Exaggerated utterances like *me miseram!* and *ei mihi!*, which feel at home in the epistles of mythical heroines, might be excessive coming from Arethusa, who eschews interjection in favor of illustration. But what truly sets Ovidian writers apart are the pernicious effects of erotic pathos, which are proportional to their larger-than-life status. Desire is routinely portrayed as an affliction, whether madness (Phyllis, 2.45; Hermione, 8.111–12; Paris, 16.237), a wound (Phaedra, 4.19–20; Dido, 7.190; Paris, 16.39–40; Acontius, 20.229–32), or a disease (Briseis, 3.141–2; Oenone, 5.149–50; Canace, 11.27–30; Medea, 12.164–6; Laodamia, 13.21–8; and, as we have seen, Cydippe, 21.13–16). Such hardships often require the drastic remedy of suicide – after the letter is written.

For Arethusa the absence of her husband, although painful, is tolerable. She mentions death only once: the "dying" of her hand as it struggles to write (*meae dextrae iam morientis*, 6).[49] Not surprisingly, her epistle concludes on an optimistic note:

armaque cum tulero portae votiva Capenae,
  subscribam SALVO GRATA PVELLA VIRO. 72

I will inscribe the weapons I offer as votives to the Porta Capena: "A girl thankful for her husband's safe return." (Prop. 4.3.71–2 Camps)

Arethusa imagines a day of thanksgiving when Lycotas will return safe and sound. That day will also bring a final act of writing – a dedicatory inscription marking the end of her husband's campaigning, just as it now marks the end of her own letter. Concluding epigraphs are common in the *Heroides*, as the letters of Phyllis, Dido, and Hypermestra demonstrate. But they are more properly epitaphs, couplets to be inscribed on the heroines' tombs. Unlike Arethusa's inscription, their final act as writers, the monumentalizing of pathos, is also the last of their lives.[50]

49 Those looking for the destructive consequences of *eros* in Propertius 4.3 will find it in the next poem, 4.4 (Tarpeia), in which desire drives a legendary heroine to madness (*nescia se furiis accubuisse novis*, 68 Camps).

50 Toward the end of her letter (15.183–4) Sappho promises an inscription that will adorn a lyre dedicated to Apollo. In this instance, epigraph and epitaph are one and the same, since Sappho will perish in the leap from the Leucadian cliff, from which she expects to emerge unscathed and purged of her desire for Phaon. Acontius, however, closes with a rare optimistic epigraph, much like Arethusa's: an *ex voto* celebrating his marriage to Cydippe, and inscribed on an image of the very apple whose inscription originally bound her to him (20.239–40).

4 Irony

Whereas Propertius 4.3 approximates some of the Ovidian theatrics – the static here-and-now, the display of pathos – the poet's use of non-mythical characters results in a more restrained letter. Furthermore, the absence of myth makes it impossible to know how Arethusa's story will end. Will her husband return home? Or will he die in battle? What will Arethusa do then? If Lycotas were an Odysseus or a Protesilaus, readers would know. Contrary to the dynamic of the *Heroides*, in which the reader can see beyond the margins of any given letter, our state of knowledge is no different from Arethusa's:

> sive in finitimo gemuit stans noctua tigno,
>   seu voluit tangi parca lucerna mero,
> illa dies hornis caedem denuntiat agnis,
>   succinctique calent ad nova lucra popae.

> Whether the night-owl hoots, perching nearby on a roof-beam, or the stingy lamp wants tending with wine, that day warrants the slaughter of this year's lambs, and the celebrants, robes tucked up, are eager for their share. (Prop. 4.3.59–62 Camps)

Are these omens good or bad? A sacrificial offering is an appropriate response either way.[51] Lacking an external context, it is impossible to say whether Arethusa will become a Penelope or a Laodamia.

Accordingly, my fifth and final tragic parameter in the *Heroides*, perhaps the most immediately evocative of tragedy, is irony. Irony obtains when the audience of a work is better informed than its characters, and the familiar qualifiers "dramatic" or "tragic" commemorate drama and specifically tragedy as the genre in which ironic situations flourish.[52] Writing at a particular place and time, Ovid's correspondents contextualize the present not only by looking to the past, but also by imagining the future. Thus Phaedra:

> aequora bina suis obpugnant fluctibus isthmon,
>   et tenuis tellus audit utrumque mare.
> hic tecum Troezena colam, Pittheia regna;
>   iam nunc est patria carior illa mea.

> Two seas batter the isthmus with their waves and the narrow strip of land hears the sea on both sides. There, in Troezen, I will dwell with you, in the

[51] Camps 1965, after Shackleton Bailey 1956.

[52] Feldherr 2010, 207, also correlates irony and tragic drama: "[I]ts very presence helps to frame the characters in the story as distanced from the audience's perception of things, as if on stage."

domain of Pittheus. That place means more to me than my native land. (*Her.* 4.105–8)

And Paris:

> quid valeam nescis, et te mea robora fallunt.
>   ignoras, cui sis nupta futura viro.
> aut igitur nullo belli repetere tumultu,
>   aut cedent Marti Dorica castra meo.

You do not know my power, and you do not notice my strength. You have no idea whose wife you will be. Either they will demand you back without the tumult of war, or the Spartan camp will yield to my prowess in battle. (*Her.* 16.369–72)

And Hero:

> sternuit en lumen! – posito nam scribimus illo –
>   sternuit et nobis prospera signa dedit.
> ecce, merum nutrix faustos instillat in ignes,
>   "cras"que "erimus plures," inquit et ipsa bibit.

Behold, the lamp has sputtered – for it is next to me while I write – it has sputtered and given a favorable omen. See, my nurse drips wine into the propitious flame, and she says, "Tomorrow our ranks will increase," taking a drink herself. (*Her.* 19.151–4)

In spite of such optimism, we readers, who know the full stories, know also the disasters that will follow.[53]

Although it is now accepted that the *Heroides* are ironic texts, it was not always so. Even as recently as 1974, Howard Jacobson claimed that the device is more the exception than the rule.[54] When irony was admitted, it was often treated as evidence of inferiority, much like rhetoric: a trite and obvious move in a collection to match. L. P. Wilkinson, for one, found virtue in the irony of *Her.* 13, but only by virtue of finding little else to praise.[55] Scholarship of past decades has since redeemed irony as a

[53] *Her.* 4: Hippolytus will surely give the lie to Phaedra's Troezenian fantasy. *Her.* 16: An Achaean army (not just a Spartan one) will descend on Troy, and Menelaus will best Paris in combat. *Her.* 19: Hero's flickering lamp, like that of Arethusa in Propertius 4.3, can be taken as a good omen, but it will be blown out and, lacking a beacon, Leander will drown. His body will wash ashore, increasing their number. Kenney 1996 notes that *erimus plures* (154) can also mean, "We shall be dead," that is, among "the majority."

[54] Jacobson 1974, 200–1: "[O]ne would be justified in saying that *grosso modo* Ovid deliberately avoids the irony which is so easily available in this genre."

[55] Wilkinson 1955: "[Ovid] can portray [Laodamia's] wifely devotion, but with regard to the unique parts of the story the best he can manage is elaborate tragic irony" (88, brackets mine).

productive force within the *Heroides*. Laurel Fulkerson captures the reader's ironic perspective: "Because these heroines exist prior to the *Heroides* in various textual incarnations, it is impossible to avoid comparing the characters in the poems to their predecessors, even when those predecessors exist only in fragments."[56] Appreciating irony in the letters is not an outcome of reading; it is a prerequisite. When considered along with the other tragic parameters under discussion, irony becomes evocative of tragedy itself, and the qualifiers "dramatic" and "tragic" are more literal than figurative.[57]

Duncan Kennedy, in the first comprehensive account of how the *Heroides* typically handle irony, draws attention to the place of poem 1 within the time-frame of the *Odyssey*. Penelope writes on the eve of her reunion with her husband, though she does not know it. Telemachus has returned from Pylos and Sparta, and if the mysterious Cretan beggar (Odysseus/Ulysses in disguise) is present as well, it would seem that Penelope intends to entrust her letter to him, as she has allegedly entrusted others to prior visitors (59–62).[58] Gareth Williams offers a similar analysis of *Her.* 11. Canace, in keeping with what might be the Euripidean version of the myth, writes to her brother and illicit lover, Macareus, following the birth of their son and moments before her suicide. But she does not realize that Macareus will soon win the pardon of their father, Aeolus, and rush to his sister's chamber, only to find her letter completed and the heroine herself dead.[59] In both analyses, irony arises when the reader locates *Her.* 1 or 11 in an external "dramatic context" (Kennedy's term). Each letter becomes an episode within a larger myth, and the resulting irony functions exactly as it does in tragedy, no matter what the original genre.

That said, instances of irony in the letters of Sophoclean and Euripidean heroines seem more palpably tragic and metatheatrical. An influential reading by Alessandro Barchiesi shows tragic irony at work in *Her.* 9 and 12 with a full measure of self-consciousness. Here is Deianira near the end of her letter:

[56] Fulkerson 2005, 14.

[57] Nevertheless, some critics object to the labels because their association with drama (in the radical sense of "action") seems at odds with the inner stasis of the letters. Thus Spoth 1992, 186: "Die Heroides sind als Elegien wesentlich durch ihre Handlungsfremdheit gekennzeichnet. Die sich daraus ergebende ‚dramatsiche' Ironie ist ironische Enthüllung der elegischen Schieflage zur Realität."

[58] Kennedy 1984, 416–18.

[59] G. D. Williams 1992. Casali 1995b, 510, adds that if Aeolus consented to spare Canace, he must have agreed to spare the child as well.

semivir occubuit in letifero[60] Eueno
  Nessus, et infecit sanguis equinus aquas.

The half-man, Nessus, sank down in the deadly Evenus, dyeing the waters with his horse-blood. (*Her.* 9.141–2).

She recalls how Nessus met his death at the river, felled by one of Hercules' poisoned arrows. We know, however, that the same poison will prove deadly to her husband. The verb *infecit* (142) is particularly apt, the centaur's blood tainting the waters just as it has tainted Hercules' robe (*inlita texta veneno*, 163).[61] Barchiesi reads the final verse of Medea's letter in much the same way:

nescio quid certe mens mea maius agit.

To be sure, my mind is contriving some greater act. (*Her.* 12.212)

The reader foresees in her inchoate plans (*nescio quid*) the murders of Creon, his daughter, and Medea's own children.[62] As before, locating *Her.* 9 and 12 within external contexts creates irony. Yet the fact that these contexts are tragic plays brings tragedy itself into full view. "This is," remarks Barchiesi, "not only tragic irony: this is tragic irony laid bare, a self-conscious exaggeration."[63]

Exaggerated though they are, both instances of irony deserve further consideration. The final, ironic flourish of *Her.* 12 signals a transition, an exit from Ovid's elegy and a re-entry into Euripidean (or Ennian or even Ovidian) tragedy. As Barchiesi observes, generic transition in this case means generic escalation, implicit in the coupling of *nescio quid* with *maius*: "Medea is suggesting that a new poetic kind is called for: she could not write a letter about her 'greater' actions, and this material, unspeakable for elegiacs, is reserved [for] the heights of a *cothurnata*."[64] Irony in *Her.* 9 likewise marks a return to tragedy, for Deianira soon receives word that she has unwittingly caused Hercules' demise (143–4). At this moment the heroine abandons elegiac discourse for tragic, as exemplified

[60] *letifero*: see the next note.

[61] Barchiesi 1993, 340–1, and 345 n. 19; likewise Casali 1995b, 508–9. Barchiesi notes that the Heinsian conjecture *letifero* (141, instead of *lotifero*) is justified as a matter of irony: the incident at the Evenus brought death to Nessus, but it will ultimately bring death to Hercules as well.

[62] Barchiesi 1993, 343–5.

[63] Barchiesi 1993, 341, referring specifically to *Her* 9, but with *Her.* 12 in view.

[64] Barchiesi 1993, 345. Hinds 1993, linking *maius* with *agit*, a verb suggestive of dramatic role-playing, adds, "[A] greater role awaits – … on the tragic stage" (41). See also Spoth 1992, 202–5. Note, too, how *maius* resonates with Ovid's grandiose characterizations of tragedy in *Am.* 2.18, 3.1, and 3.15 (a point also made by Hinds 1993, 42). See Chapter 2, pp. 38–9.

by the ephymnionic refrain, *inpia quid dubitas Deianira mori?* (146, 152, 158, 164): "Her repeated lament," writes Barchiesi, "identifies Deianira as a character born for the tragic scene, opens a play of difference with the elegiac medium, and finally sends her back to a kind of intertextual order of things."[65] A tension between the genres, therefore, accompanies tragic irony when used as a strategy of closure.[66]

At the same time, self-conscious irony may also foster generic synergy and constitute a strategy of continuation. The epistle of Laodamia (13), whom Ovid probably borrowed from Euripides,[67] is in many ways the mirror image of Penelope's. For example, she writes to Protesilaus upon learning the Greeks have reached Aulis, whereas ten years have elapsed for Penelope since the fall of Troy. Although both husbands have joined the Greek expedition, only Ulysses will return. Poem 13 deploys tragic irony at almost every turn, from sinister omens, such as Protesilaus' stumbling over the threshold (85–92) or his appearance in a dream (105–10), to Laodamia's ubiquitous concerns for her husband's safety:

> Hectora, quisquis is est, si sum tibi cura, caveto:
> signatum memori pectore nomen habe!

> If I matter to you at all, beware Hector, whoever he is. Keep his name stamped upon your memory! (*Her.* 13.65–6)

In stressing the memory of Hector's name, Laodamia seems to have forgotten the name of her addressee, or at least what it means. Protesilaus, "first of the host," will be the first to set foot on the Troad and the first slain.

Her ironic misidentifications soon become more pronounced:

> sors quoque nescio quem fato designat iniquo,
> qui primus Danaum Troada tangat humum.
> infelix, quae prima virum lugebit ademptum!
> di faciant, ne tu strenuus esse velis!
> inter mille rates tua sit millensima puppis,
> iamque fatigatas ultima verset aquas!
> hoc quoque praemoneo: de nave novissimus exi;
> non est, quo properas, terra paterna tibi.

65 Barchiesi 1993, 341–2.

66 Nevertheless, I have already suggested that laments like Deianira's are not out of place in a collection predicated on elegiac pathos. Furthermore, Deianira's suicide, kept offstage in Sophocles, is also "offstage" in *Her.* 9, a kind of synergy reminiscent of Medea's *nescio quid maius* at the end of *Her.* 12. See Chapter 1, section 3.

67 On the possible sources for *Her.* 13, and the prominent place of Eur. *Protesilaus* among them, see Jacobson 1974, 195–8, and Fulkerson 2002, 62–5. Fragments of the *Protesilaus*: *TrGF* V.646a–57.

> An oracle, too, determines an unjust fate for whichever Greek first touches the Troad's soil. Wretched, she who first mourns her fallen husband. May the gods ensure you will not be too eager! Among the thousand ships may yours be the thousandth, and the last to beat the already beaten waves! I warn you also of this: be the very last to disembark; you are not rushing to your fatherland. (*Her.* 13.93–100)

Problems of identity attend not only the husband – *nescio quem* (93), with *primus Danaum* (94) glossing Protesilaus[68] – but also the wife, to whom *infelix, quae prima lugebit* (95) will soon apply. Grappling with the implications of being first to die and first to mourn, Laodamia issues what are best described as ultimatums: Protesilaus' ship should be the thousandth and last (*millensima*, 97; *ultima*, 98), and he himself the very last man ashore (*novissimus*, 99). These passages are together enough to expose the mechanism of tragic irony. But readers of *Her.* 12 will find two indefinite clauses, *quisquis is est* (65) and *nescio quem fato designat* (93), particularly self-conscious. Like Medea's *nescio quid maius*, they are at once disclaimers on the heroine's part, through which she asserts her own ignorance, as well as patent appeals to the reader's knowledge. All the same, *quisquis* and *nescio quem* offer not ironic closure but prolongation. Laodamia's blindness to the facts of her myth allows her to keep writing for another sixty verses. Tragic irony sustains and promotes her elegiac text.[69]

5 *Heroides* "22" and the theater of epic

In these five interwoven parameters – a self-contained here-and-now, first-person perspective, the pathos of love, mythical subject matter, and irony – the *Heroides* incorporated enough of the form, material, and function of tragedy to gratify the erstwhile playwright in Ovid. Not only did the letters enable the poet to continue the career in Roman tragedy begun with his *Medea*, they paved the way for an even more ambitious tragic program in the *Metamorphoses*. In what remains of this chapter, I want to mark a transition from the theater of the epistle to the theater of epic, the primary subject of Chapters 4, 5, and 6. Bearing in mind the generic synergies discussed above, as well as the Roman tragic rubrics from Chapter 2, I will demonstrate how reading tragically in the *Heroides* can find a more expansive sequel in the *Metamorphoses*. For my case study, I will turn to

[68] Thus Jacobson 1974, 201.

[69] Fulkerson 2002 explores the poem's magical imagery and formulae, which suggest that Laodamia understands her myth better than critics have previously allowed.

the narrative of Byblis (*Met.* 9.450–665), who writes what might be considered Ovid's twenty-second erotic epistle.[70]

Some general principles to begin with. The *Metamorphoses* succeeds the *Heroides* – just as the letters succeeded the *Medea*, and that play succeeded Accius and his forebears – as mythography.[71] Ovid's use of myth works in concert with pathos and irony, the one elevated to a tragic register, the other activated through the reader's erudition. Moreover, as mythography the *Heroides* and the *Metamorphoses* constitute sustained projects not unlike a tragic career, with recurring themes, motifs, and characters. Ovid's heroines and heroes become associated by *contaminatio* – a seminal practice in Roman tragedy,[72] but legible in Greek tragedy as well. Clytemnestra, for instance, may be compared to Deianira, the former an intentional murderer, the latter an unintentional one. Likewise Iphigenia and Polyxena, one an unwilling sacrificial victim, the other willing. We have already seen this comparative dynamic in the letters of Penelope (1) and Laodamia (13), each awaiting her husband's return from Troy, and we will see it many times over in the *Metamorphoses*. In tragedy, associations like these normally result from generations of repetition and innovation. In Ovid they abide within works, and sometimes between works, with a matrix of tragic heroines and heroes unifying the poet's corpus.

Tragedy is a more spacious genre than epistolary elegy, whose format mandates a highly prescribed here-and-now. Epic is more spacious still, with no places and times off-limits, at least in theory. The reader need not always conjure an external context or rely on an internal narrator in order to learn what happens next: the poet himself will often say.[73] Furthermore, the poet now has the capacity to incorporate great and grandiose events directly into his narratives – everything from violent acts normally recounted after the fact, to the transformations of his characters. So doing, Ovid aligns the *Metamorphoses* with the spectacular tendencies of Roman tragedy. That said, he leaves room for different personae and perspectives, especially those of characters in turmoil, who launch out onto dramatic monologues. These speeches continue the rhetorical traditions of Roman drama already perpetuated in the *Heroides*, particularly *ethopoeiae*

[70] *Heroides* 22: a conceit found also in Kenney 2011 (before *Met.* 9.517). Perhaps a better label is *Heroides* 21.5, since the letter is by far shorter than any letter in the collection (thirty-four verses), and since it is written in pure hexameters and lacks the pentameter half of the elegiac couplet.

[71] So Barsby 1978: "[T]he *Heroides* represent Ovid's first attempt to revitalize mythology, and thus look forward to the *Metamorphoses*" (17).

[72] Chapter 2, pp. 24–5.

[73] Thus Auhagen 1999: "Die Eingebundenheit in einen größeren Kontext hat zur Folge, daß nicht alle Details von den Protagonisten selbst geliefert werden müssen" (160).

and *suasoriae*. In addition, they preserve the letters' first-person expression of pathos as a feminine mode of discourse. Just as women write the majority of the epistles, so they deliver most of the epic's monologues.

These principles apply, in one way or another, to the Byblis narrative of *Met.* 9. Why Byblis? Her story is not found in tragedy,[74] but its themes of forbidden desire and erotic pathos meet Ovid's criteria for tragic material. The narrative begins in Miletus, where Byblis gradually conceives a more-than-sisterly love for her twin, Caunus. After rationalizing her feelings, she reveals them in a letter, in which she urges her brother to reciprocate. Caunus, naturally, is disgusted by her message. Upon further reflection, Byblis renews her advances in person, eventually forcing Caunus into exile. The sister gives over to madness, roving far and wide in search of her brother, and collapsing in a torrent of weeping. The Naiads take pity and provide an endless supply of tears, which facilitate the transformation of Byblis into a spring.

Obvious, even in summary, is the sheer spaciousness of the epic narrative. Ovid treats in order everything from the first flames of Byblis' desire (457–60), to her demented wanderings through Asia Minor (638–51), to her final metamorphosis (659–65). This spaciousness becomes even more apparent through the incorporation of her letter's text (530–63), whose vivid here-and-now contrasts with the narrative's other there-and-thens. Byblis makes a display of her suffering, singling out her paleness, her gauntness, and her tearful expression (*et color et macies et vultus et umida saepe | lumina*, 536–7). She also offers a history of her struggles (539–45), and she predicts her own death from a broken heart, imagining Caunus' name on her tomb (*neve merere meo subscribi causa sepulcro*, 563).[75] Although Byblis' fashions an epistolary *theatron* in the style of the *Heroides*, hers is a less crowded structure. The narrator, in addition to presenting events well outside the letter's margins, also extracts much of the pathos we would expect the letter to document. He identifies, for example, incestuous desire long before the girl herself does (*correpta cupidine fratris ... illa quidem primo nullos intellegit ignes*, 455–7), and he describes her madness and the harm done to her person (*planxitque suos furibunda lacertos*, 637).[76] It

[74] On pre- and post-Ovidian variants of the Byblis myth see Bömer 1977 and Kenney 2011 (both after *Met.* 9.449); also Otis 1970, 415–17, who concludes that Ovid's closest source was Parthenius.

[75] On Byblis' plans for her tomb as a recollection of the *Heroides* see Kenney 2011.

[76] Kenney 2011 remarks that the inclusion of Byblis' text "riesce ad aprire una nuova dimensione drammatica" in the narrative (*Met.* 9.517–63). Kenney also points to the vividness with which the external narrator presents Byblis' inner tumult, as opposed to how a writer of the *Heroides* proper, like Canace, must do from within her own letter.

is as if Ovid has taken one of the *Heroides* – or a play entitled *Byblis* – and unpacked it for the larger environs of epic.

In two instances epic narrative opens an entirely new window on epistolary theater. Here is Byblis as she begins to write her letter:

> dextra tenet ferrum; vacuam tenet altera ceram.
> incipit et dubitat. scribit damnatque tabellas.
> et notat et delet. mutat culpatque probatque,
> inque vicem sumptas ponit positasque resumit.
>
> Her right hand holds the stylus; her left, the empty wax tablet. She starts and stops. She writes something and despises it. She makes a mark and erases it. She edits, she finds fault, and then approves. Now she picks up the tablet, and then puts it down, and then picks it up again. (*Met.* 9.522–5)

The writers of the *Heroides* often comment on their writing. Thus Canace: *dextra tenet calamum, strictum tenet altera ferrum* (11.3). In *Met.* 9 the narrator portrays Byblis imitating the stance of Canace, though her *ferrum* (522) is a stylus, not a drawn sword.[77] Nevertheless, the image of the writer at work can be incorporated into the text, if he or she wishes. What comes next, however, is something only an external narrator can provide: a glimpse over Byblis' shoulder[78] as she struggles to write. A writer of the *Heroides* might note that she has been interrupted, but such notes would be part of the finished epistle. Nowhere do we find prevarications as extreme as those in the *Metamorphoses*, where we see the letter written, unwritten, rewritten, abandoned, and reclaimed. We learn that Byblis had originally begun with the word *soror*, but then erased it (528). In allowing us to read what she never intended to be read, Ovid reveals not only the writer's tortuous process, but also the letter in palimpsest.

Just as we witness the stages of the letter's composition, so we are present for its reception:

> apta minister
> tempora nactus adit traditque latentia verba.
> attonitus subita iuvenis Maeandrius ira
> proicit acceptas lecta sibi parte tabellas.
>
> Her servant chose the appropriate moment and went to Caunus, handing over the tablet and the message it contained. Maeander's young grandson

[77] So Kenney 2011.

[78] Over the shoulder: the phraseology of Anderson 1973, describing the ironic, privileged position of someone reading the *Heroides*: "[W]e are peeking over the woman's shoulder as she is writing" (66). See also Rosati 2005, 161 ("sopra le spalle").

> took it and, after reading only part way, was immediately stricken with anger and cast it to the ground. (*Met.* 9.572–5)

Outside of the double *Heroides*, this is the only occasion in which readers of Ovidian epistles can know with certainty whether a letter has been sent and received, and how its addressee has responded. Sometimes these matters are in doubt. How, for example, does Ariadne (10) expect to get her epistle delivered from the desolate shore? If Penelope has sent other letters to Ulysses (1.59–62), but they have failed to reach him, why should the current one fare differently?[79] At other times the outcome, though unstated, is clearer. It seems probable that Protesilaus (13) will never receive Laodamia's letter. Conversely, Hippolytus will receive Phaedra's, and we may be rather sure of his reaction. Nevertheless, we never witness any of the single or double *Heroides* actually reaching the addressee and being read. The epic narrative provides an exploded view of the entire correspondence, from the moment the sister decides to write to the moment the brother throws the tablet aside. This expansion of the epistolary theater suggests the possibilities for enlarging tragic theater in the *Metamorphoses*.

In presenting what the *Heroides* – and, by extension, tragedy – cannot, Ovid sanctions the Byblis narrative as a series of spectacles and the reader as a viewer. The scale of the spectacles varies, from the small wonder of a letter's delivery to the larger miracle of the heroine's metamorphosis far from home. The poet asserts the visibility of the latter with a three-fold simile: Byblis liquefies slowly, like the flow of pitch or bitumen, or like snow melted on the breeze (659–64). Essential to the spectacularity of these events is the concept of the *locus*, or place. While epistolary and tragic theaters usually represent a single *locus*, epic presents a sequence of often disparate *loci*. Yet each there-and-then can become a theatrical here-and-now to accommodate a spectacle. The sylvan landscape of Byblis' transformation is one such *locus*. Another is the *thalamus*, or bed-chamber, where she writes her letter and also delivers her initial monologue. This is a setting virtually unthinkable in tragedy, which can offer interior views of the *skēnē* with the *ekkyklēma*,[80] but cannot allow the audience to enter as readers of epic may. Epic narrative transcends, or rather transgresses, the conventions of stagecraft and presents a setting suitable for transgressive *eros*. The bedroom becomes an intimate *theatron*, a venue for Byblis to put her pathos on display, talking to herself first and then writing to Caunus.

[79] Kennedy 1984, 416–18, following Anderson 1973, 66, considers these and other problems.

[80] One example from extant tragedy: Eur. *Alc.* 244–392 (Alcestis on her deathbed).

Her epistle has two frames: the margins of the tablet and the chamber in which she writes.

Byblis' monologues (474–516 and 585–629) exemplify the multivocal enterprise of epic poetry. The voice of the external narrator dominates, but at the right moments gives way to other voices: hence even Caunus has a brief but decisive speech in rejecting the letter (577–9). The heroine's extended speeches give her ample opportunity not only to express her innermost feelings but also to plot a course of action.[81] In her first monologue, which begins with a pathetic *me miseram!* (474), Byblis rationalizes her incestuous desire and talks herself into writing to Caunus. In her second, she re-evaluates her epistolary tactics and elects to approach her brother directly. In both, Byblis "relies heavily on conditional and hypothetical arguments" steeped in the subjunctive: the potential in the former, as she explores the possibility of taking Caunus as a lover; the contrary-to-fact in the latter, following the failure of her letter.[82] Her speeches serve the general functions of stage rhetoric, deliberation and (self-)persuasion, in addition to being displays of erotic pathos in themselves. Even as the narrative elides reading with viewing, reading now becomes listening as Byblis makes herself heard.

The placement of the monologues both before and after her letter underscores Byblis' seeming audibility and invites comparisons between "spoken" and written discourse. Those who prize the *Heroides* as rhetorical texts will find validation in the similarities between her words on the page and those delivered from the stage of her *thalamus*. After the failure of her letter, Byblis second-guesses the power of writing:

> "et tamen ipsa loqui, nec me committere cerae
> debueram praesensque meos aperire furores.
> vidisset lacrimas, vultum vidisset amantis.
> plura loqui poteram, quam quae cepere tabellae."

> "All the same, I should have spoken to him myself, and not entrusted myself to wax. I should have displayed my passions in person. He would have seen my tears, he would have seen the face of his lover. I could have said more things than a tablet can hold." (*Met.* 9.601–4)

Speech is more persuasive, since it not only permits more words, but also involves direct visual contact: *vidisset lacrimas, vultum vidisset* (603). Whereas heroines like Phaedra use writing to inspire spectacles of pathos

[81] Kenney 2011 offers some general but useful comments on Byblis' command of rhetoric in each monologue (after *Met.* 9.469–71 and on 9.585). See Auhagen 1999, 144–52.

[82] Tarrant 2005, 78.

(*lacrimas finge videre meas*, 4.176), Byblis criticizes the epistolary mode as not spectacular enough. These, of course, are her second thoughts on the genre, and to judge from Caunus' immediate reaction, the images conjured in the letter were plenty powerful. Byblis is destined to be wrong about the persuasiveness of direct speech (and about any other tool at her disposal: *committit saepe repelli*, 632). In the end there is little difference between her spoken and written performances, in terms of both their content and their intended effect.

Byblis' performances constitute a type of role-playing, whereby she does and says what we might expect her character to do and say, depending on our prior knowledge of her myth. Byblis plays the part of a woman in love, as well as the roles of specific women.[83] We have already seen, for example, how she adopts the writing posture of Canace. The same heroine becomes a positive exemplar of incest in her first monologue:

> "at non Aeolidae thalamos timuere sororum.
> unde sed hos novi? cur haec exempla paravi?" 508

> "And yet the sons of Aeolus did not shrink from their sisters' chambers. But from what source do I know this? Why have I furnished these examples?" (*Met.* 9.507–8)

Byblis might know Canace from reading the *Odyssey*, in which Aeolus is said to have allowed the intermarriage of his children (10.7). Yet an equally likely source is *Her.* 11, as if she were familiar with Ovid's earlier collection.[84]

Byblis most consistently takes the part of Phaedra, the seductress known from the lost Euripidean and Sophoclean plays and from *Her.* 4. Consider the *incipits* both of Byblis and of Ovid's Phaedra:

> "Quam, nisi tu dederis, non est habitura salutem,
> hanc tibi mittit amans; pudet, a, pudet edere nomen!"

> "A lover sends you greetings, wishes for the good health she will not have, unless you return them. She is ashamed, so ashamed, to name herself!" (*Met.* 9.530–1)

[83] Raval 2001, especially 298–300. Raval, in a sharp analysis that heralded a brilliant career, reads Byblis' monologues and letter as enacting a Barthesian lover's discourse, "a script that has been played out by many before" her (286). Compare Kenney 2011, who finds Byblis not ready to play the part: "Le sue domande sono piene di ironia intertestuale, da cui il lettore deduce che la preparazione letteraria di Biblide per il ruolo di eroina, specie se messa a confronto con quella di Medea (una sopravvissuta), è inadeguata" (*Met.* 9.507–8).

[84] Compare Raval 2001, 298: "While Byblis follows the prescriptives of the *Ars amatoria* in her decision to write a letter, in the composition of it, she 'reads' the *Heroides*."

> Quam, nisi tu dederis, caritura est ipsa, salutem
> mittit Amazonio Cressa puella viro 2
>
> The girl from Crete sends to the Amazon-born man greetings, wishes for the good health that she herself will lack, unless you return them. (*Her.* 4.1–2)

If Byblis has read the *Heroides*, she seems to understand Phaedra's opening gambit, namely to suppress the awkward familial ties that a conventional salutation might invoke.[85] Instead of using terms like *noverca* or *privignus* (stepmother, stepson), Phaedra employs the ethnic signifiers *Amazonio* and *Cressa* (2) in an effort to distance herself socially and geographically from Hippolytus. Byblis follows suit, calling herself merely *amans* (531), an improvement over the *soror* with which she would have begun.[86] In addition to Phaedra's stratagem, Byblis has followed her language quite closely, selecting Phaedra as the best paradigm for a seductive enterprise, and implicating Caunus as her Hippolytus.[87]

However, Byblis seems to have forgotten that Phaedra's efforts were in vain; or perhaps she hopes to do better.[88] The failure of her letter, accordingly, confirms Byblis' failure either to choose a good exemplar or to transcend it. Although the heroine cannot see beyond the scenario she has enacted, the narrator can. As narrated, Caunus' outburst is appropriate to a Phaedraesque letter, and not merely for rejecting unwanted overtures. Hurling the tablets to the ground (*proicit ... tabellas*, 575), he recalls depictions of the Phaedra–Hippolytus myth on Roman sarcophagi and in murals. In such representations Phaedra typically stands to one side, turning her head in shame, while on the other side Hippolytus has dropped a pair of tablets; often between them is a nurse, who supplicates the youth.[89] Caunus enacts the visual tradition and "plays the part of

85 So Raval 2001, 300: "In addition to appropriating Phaedra's opening line, Byblis deploys some of the same arguments in favor of incest that the former makes in her letter to Hippolytus."

86 At the same time, Byblis' declaration that she is ashamed to name herself (*pudet, a, pudet edere nomen*, 531) betrays any subtlety in the term *amans*. Her attempt to smooth over the anxieties of an incestuous relationship might unwittingly magnify them. Yet even these problems might have an origin in *Her.* 4. Casali 1995a, 2–3, notes the difficulties inherent in Phaedra's use of *Cressa* (Cretans are liars) and *Amazonio* (Amazons deny their sexuality), and in *puella* and *viro* (Phaedra is no longer a maiden; Hippolytus, not yet a man).

87 Kenney 2011 observes the parallels with *Her.* 4 and also considers the *incipit* of *Her.* 16 as a model.

88 Compare Liveley 2011, 97: "Byblis also demonstrates a perverse faith in the power of words, the power of letters and names to shape and reshape reality according to her own desires."

89 See *LIMC* 5.456. The source of the motif is uncertain, though most critics attribute it to tragedy. W. S. Barrett 1964, 37 n. 2, dismisses the motif as a "garbling" of the nurse's intervention in Eur. *HS*, which as an oral exchange does not lend itself to visual representations as readily as a written message. Radt in *TrGF* IV prefaces the fragments of Soph. *Phaedra* with less skepticism: "*Fortasse ad Sophoclis fabulam referenda sunt complura opera Romana quae Hippolytum exhibent litteras Phaedrae*

Hippolytus"[90] – the role in which Byblis implicitly, and perhaps naïvely, cast him.

Perhaps the element most evocative of Phaedra in Byblis' tale is the antithesis between *pudor* (modesty) and *amor* (desire). This dilemma drives not only the narrative but also its forms of discourse, the monologues and the letter, in which Byblis engages. Her entire second speech is a rhetorical exercise in casting off the modesty that ought to curtail further communication with her brother and yielding entirely to desire. Her first speech, however, shows *pudor* and *amor* in true conflict, with either one holding sway at any given moment. In the end, Byblis tries to have it both ways:

> "ipsa petam. poterisne loqui? poterisne fateri?
> coget amor, potero! vel, si pudor ora tenebit,
> littera celatos arcana fatebitur ignes."

> "I will seek him out myself. Will I be able to speak? Will I be able to confess my desire? Love will compel me. I will be able! Or, if modesty curbs my tongue, a secret letter will reveal my inner flames." (*Met.* 9.514–16)

Hers is a partial surrender: if declaring her desire in person is too brazen, writing it down has at least a semblance of modesty: *hanc tibi mittit amans; pudet … edere nomen* (531). Likewise, Ovid's Phaedra rationalizes her own epistle as obedience to both forces:

> qua licet et sequitur, pudor est miscendus amori;
> dicere quae puduit, scribere iussit amor.
> (*Her.* 4.9–10)

We first encountered these verses in Chapter 1, where we observed that Phaedra has rewritten the famous Euripidean double *aidos* (*HS* 383–7) as *pudor* versus *amor*.[91] Byblis deploys the terms as a two-tier allusion,[92] ultimately invoking the extant *Hippolytus* by way of *Her.* 4. More than this, she invokes *pudor–amor* as a dilemma encoded in tragedy.

The Byblis narrative is therefore "contaminated," per tragic practice, with elements of the Phaedra–Hippolytus myth,[93] a sign that Ovid means

a Nutrice allatas proicientem." Leo (ed.) 1878, 178–9, proposed that the Roman representations reflect the method of disclosure in Eur. *HK*; for a contrary view see Halleran 1995, 26.

90 Larmour 1990, 137, following Otis 1970, 220 – though without reference to the visual tradition. Likewise Kenney 2011.

91 Chapter 1, pp. 14–16.

92 E.g., Keith 2002, 265–6, an example of two-tier allusion relevant to Ovid and Roman tragedy.

93 Larmour 1990, a groundbreaking discussion, and the first to apply the term *contaminatio* to the intertextual negotiations of the Byblis narrative (among others). As I discuss in Chapter 6, p. 178, Larmour finds *contaminatio* in the *Metamorphoses* when Ovid seems to gloss over a famous myth (as in the case of Phaedra in book 15) and to transfer its distinctive elements to other stories.

to tell a tragic story. Phaedra's experiences shape those of Byblis. Yet it is equally fair to say that Byblis represents Phaedra in the *Metamorphoses*, whose presence in the epic, unlike in the *Heroides*, is negligible. In book 15 Hippolytus himself, now metamorphosed into Virbius, tells her story in a matter of nine verses (15.497–505), apparently relishing the chance to minimize Phaedra's passion with the sparest of outlines. Byblis' struggles with modesty and desire allow the reader to see Phaedra's own struggles played out in similar circumstances. Yet the Byblis narrative is not the only venue for enacting the dilemma. It recurs in book 10 with Myrrha just before her attempted suicide:

> et modo desperat, modo vult temptare, pudetque
> et cupit, et quid agat non invenit. 372

> She despairs, then wants to try; modesty moves her, then desire, and she has no idea what to do. (*Met.* 10.371–2)

It precedes Byblis with Scylla in book 8, as she deliberates over shearing Nisus' lock:

> "altera iamdudum succensa cupidine tanto
> perdere gauderet quodcumque obstaret amori."

> "Another woman, burning with such desire, would happily have destroyed whatever stood in her love's way." (*Met.* 8.74–5)

And it even extends back to book 7 with Medea, as she wavers between duty to her father and her love for Jason (7.72–3).[94] On its own, each tale can justly be described as "contaminated" with Phaedra's *pudor–amor* dilemma. Collectively, however, these narratives recall less any one incarnation of Phaedra than the genre in which her story flourished. The result is a series of tragic narratives, like a series of plays, in which Ovid explores variations on a theme.

The story of Byblis helps the Ovidian reader transition from the *Heroides* to the *Metamorphoses*, demonstrating the major areas of convergence and divergence in their approaches to the tragic. Most striking are the divergences, for the format of epic differs markedly from that of epistolary elegy. New and seemingly unlimited possibilities for staging attend a genre

[94] So Otis 1970, 172–3: "It is with Medea that the famous duel of *amor* and *pudor* enters the *Metamorphoses* … and points the way for Scylla, Byblis, Myrrha, and Atalanta." Nugent 2008 also clusters the Medea, Scylla, Byblis, and Myrrha narratives, adding Althea (*Met.* 8) and Iphis (9). I will return to Nugent's essay in Chapter 5, pp. 145–7 in my discussion of Medea's struggle with modesty and desire.

narrated in the third person, such that converging displays of pathos and irony can be overshadowed. There is one unequivocal area of convergence, however, in which the *Metamorphoses* continues the Roman tragic program of the *Heroides*: the transformation of tragedy into text. This is not to deny that Ovid's *Medea* existed in textual form; but it was possibly written with performance in mind, if only recitation. Like the works of Catullus and Vergil, the *Heroides* engage the tragic within a new literary form, one not only published as text, but also thematized as text in their epistolarity. Similarly, the *Metamorphoses* unites many tragic stories within a series of books that – as the poet reminds us the end of his work (*ore legar populi*, 15.878) – are texts to be read. Here, too, Byblis provides a transition. Her name was falsely etymologized in antiquity as either βύβλος (*byblos*), the papyrus of which books were made, or βίβλος (*biblos*), the book itself.[95] This bookish heroine, in the course of a spacious narrative, and in the interval between two monologues, finds time to produce a text. However spectacular or rhetorical her tragedy seems, Byblis reminds us that Ovid's audience can only become viewers or listeners through reading.

[95] On the false etymology see Bömer 1977 (after *Met.* 9.449), as well as Raval 2001, 295–6, and Kenney 2011 (after 9.516).

CHAPTER FOUR

Locus exstat et ex re nomen habet

Space, time, and spectacle

The visible world of tragedy is onstage, a world fixed in space and time. The location of a drama typically remains constant, and the time-frame, when the passage of time is marked, is generally narrow. There are notable exceptions, but regardless of the specifics, the reference point for the characters and all onstage action is the here and the now. The boundaries of the here-and-now are permeable to events that either are occurring, have occurred or will occur offstage at other places and times, and these events are brought onstage as necessary. The means of transport are often verbal: messenger-type speeches, prologues or prophecies. The means can be physical as well: stage machinery like the *ekkyklēma* shows the aftermath of deadly events, and characters harmed offstage are conveyed onstage as proof of violence elsewhere.

Sometimes the act of bringing the offstage onstage stretches the fabric of space and time. Consider the preliminaries to Heracles' entrance in the *Women of Trachis*. At verse 632 Lichas departs Trachis for Euboea with a gift for Heracles, the *peplos* charmed by Deianira. Following a brief choral ode (633–62), Deianira confesses her fear that the love-charm might actually be poisonous (663–733). Hyllus enters and confirms the worst: Heracles has been poisoned (734–820). He has been conveyed from Euboea to the mainland by boat and is due to appear, alive or dead, at any moment (καί νιν αὐτίκα | ἢ ζῶντ' ἐσόψεσθ' ἢ τεθνηκότ' ἀρτίως, 805–6). About 100 verses, a matter of moments onstage, separate the exit of Lichas from the return of Hyllus, both of whom must cross the Malian Gulf. It then takes around 150 verses from Deianira's abrupt exit for the afflicted Heracles to be borne onstage from the coast (812–961) – a longer span of lines, but overlapping what should be an inland journey of several miles.

Despite being a showcase for human pathos, the world onstage is not the real world. Oliver Taplin remarks, "Dramatists do not deal in 'clock time' but in 'dramatic time.'"[1] Within the confines of the so-called "tragic day," time may accelerate or decelerate to suit the circumstances. On the one hand, bringing Heracles to Trachis in a dramatically expedient fashion requires that the audience put aside its geographical knowledge and experience. On the other hand, a highly involving speech, such as the Nurse's account of Deianira's suicide (899–946), brings the action to a halt and suspends time. It is the part of a skilled playwright to manipulate the audience's sense of time, even by taking vast liberties. "[T]here is no problem in performance," notes Taplin. "There is no question of days elapsing at some particular point; simply the intervening dramatic time is enough to preserve a semblance of the continuity of action."[2]

The world of epic, which unites many series of actions, is another matter. The genre's access to other places and times minimizes distinctions between "offstage" and "onstage," even in narratives with tragic models. This chapter explores Ovid's manipulations of tragic space and time in the narratives of Hecabe (book 13), Hercules (9), and Medea (7). Sometimes he narrates events no different from those of the source play. At other times he presents directly events originally offstage and out of the audience's view, without need of *ex post facto* reporting. Sometimes a narrative stays within the proximity of the tragic *skēnē*, venturing just behind or beyond it. At other times a narrative ranges well beyond the *skēnē*, as if reveling in the freedom afforded by epic. Unlike the writers of the *Heroides*, whose movements are restricted,[3] the tragic heroes and heroines of the *Metamorphoses* are constantly on the move and transform themselves by crossing key thresholds. Nevertheless, the setting of the source play remains a reference point for their journeys: the original *theatron* has merged with a larger landscape, but there are other viewing places nearby. Before we turn to our case studies, some additional thoughts on theatricality in the *Metamorphoses* are in order, beginning with the notion that a poem of words is also a poem of spectacles.

1 Places in view

Chapter 3 examined theatricality by drawing parallels between the epistolary format of the *Heroides* and the boundaries of the tragic *theatron*. Neither

[1] Taplin 1977, 291. [2] Taplin 1977, 293.

[3] Bolton 2009 observes a correlation between stasis and sexual identity, with virtuous women who remain in place and immoral women who are punished for their transgressions. Kyriakidis 2010 reads the movements of Cydippe's letter in relation to her evolving feelings for Acontius.

genre can rival the spatial and temporal reach of the *Metamorphoses*. The proem boasts a vast chronology, a continuous song from the beginning of the world to the poet's own era (*ab origine mundi | ad mea perpetuum … tempora carmen*, 1.3–4), which in turn portends a global survey of the *mundus*. Such an ambitious project is appropriate for epic – a boundless subject for a boundless genre.

Its format makes the project feasible. Unlike the narrators of tragedy or the *Heroides*, the omniscient narrator of the *Metamorphoses* (Ovid, for purposes of discussion) does not participate in the stories he tells. Although the divide between the teller and his tale is sometimes slender, he stands outside the settings of his myths.[4] Consequently, the narrator can account for long passages of time not only within the poem, but also within a single episode. Likewise, he can accommodate whatever changes in location are necessary – and even ones that can seem unnecessary. The narrator enables the reader to follow the story wherever it leads. Whereas tragedy and epistolary elegy must use indirect means to bring events from other places and times to the attention of the audience, epic can present them to the reader as they occur. The *Metamorphoses* is a potentially limitless sequence of there-and-thens.[5]

A series of epic there-and-thens might appear at odds with the tragic here-and-now, with its unities of time and place. The Ovidian *mundus*, however, provides common ground for many landscapes: mountaintops, promontories, groves, grottoes, springs, and pools – disparate *loci*, all parts of a larger world.[6] Furthermore, a *carmen perpetuum* is inherently concerned with unity and tries to minimize whatever disjunctions arise from presenting myths of different times and places. On the one hand, the poet links episodes wherever possible, exploiting similar themes or situations, or invoking genealogical connections. On the other hand, he duly marks transitions in chronology or locale, especially when they occur within an episode. Ovid's self-conscious manner of introducing new landscapes is particularly well attested, from the opening formula *locus est* and its variants, to reliance on stock scenery such as springs and shade trees.[7] Such

4 On the relationship of narrator to narrative in the *Met.* see Wheeler 1999, especially 34–50.

5 See Clay 2011, a study of Homer's "Trojan theater" – the Trojan landscape and its subdivided spaces in which battles and other events are staged. Purves 2010 surveys the handling of space and time in Greek poetic and prose narratives, emphasizing ancient texts arrayed as landscapes in and of themselves.

6 My list derives from Barchiesi 2005, cv, who offers an even more comprehensive catalogue of Ovidian landscapes and vistas "incluse e forzate tra ostacoli."

7 Hinds 2002 surveys Ovidian landscapes and the ways in which they are introduced. The classic study remains that of Segal 1969. See Curtius 1953, ch. 10, on landscapes in Greco-Roman literature at large.

introductions not only orient the reader, but also serve as preludes to further action. The narrative's pace slows and its focus narrows to accommodate events in the landscape. Through the narrator's verbal stage-dressing the there-and-then of epic can become a dramatic here-and-now.[8]

If the Ovidian landscape often becomes a kind of *theatron*, the reader, in bearing witness, becomes a *theatēs* or spectator.[9] Stephen Hinds's survey of the "aesthetics of place" in the *Metamorphoses* reveals how the poet's scenic descriptions appeal to the visual through analogies with art and architecture. Such analogies place the reader in the position of viewer and create, in the words of Gianpiero Rosati, a poetics of spectacularity ("poetica della spettacolarità").[10] The grove of Diana in book 3, for example, is rich in architectural detail:

> vallis erat piceis et acuta densa cupressu,
> nomine Gargaphie, succinctae sacra Dianae,
> cuius in extremo est antrum nemorale recessu
> arte laboratum nulla; simulaverat artem
> ingenio natura suo, nam pumice vivo
> et levibus tofis nativum duxerat arcum.

> There was a vale thick with pine and barbed cypress, Gargaphie, the sanctum of girded Diana. In its furthest recess is a shady grotto – no work of art, but the work of nature imitating art through ingenuity. For nature had raised an archway of living pumice and pliant tufa. (*Met.* 3.155–60)

Ovid introduces Gargaphie with the formula *vallis erat* (155) and subdivides it with *est antrum* (157), a subtle shift from past to present tense marking a transition from the there-and-then to the here-and-now. This *locus amoenus*, with its pumice-and-tufa arch, is meant to be visualized. But the cost of viewing it is less for the reader than for Actaeon, who will

[8] Barchiesi 2005, cv, calls Ovid's landscapes "teatri di sventura," so named for the protecting and punishing gods overseeing them. The poem's divine hierarchy unites the disparate locales of the *Metamorphoses* as effectively as any of the unifying techniques noted above.

[9] Feldherr 2010, following Konstan 1991, borrows the term *theatēs* from Plato's *Ion* to suggest "the distance required" by the reader "for the thoughtful analysis" of poems like the *Odyssey* – and, by extension, the *Metamorphoses* (22). Feldherr also notes that tragedy and the emotions it conjures can (even in textual form) collapse the distance between observer and observed: Aristotelian "pity depends on some perceived likeness between the character depicted and the audience, while genuine fear comes when we fully accept an identification with such characters to the point of identifying a danger to them as a danger to ourselves" (22–3).

[10] Hinds 2002, especially 136–40, following Rosati 1983, 129–52 (quotation on 152). Linking landscape and spectacularity is now a mainstay of Ovidian criticism: Barchiesi 2005, cli–clvi, and Feldherr 2010, *passim*, especially 168–70. Feldherr explores the tension between visual realism in the *Met.* on the one hand, and its patent fictiveness on the other.

soon face the forbidden sight of the goddess bathing.[11] Note his dramatic entrance: *ecce nepos Cadmi … pervenit in lucum* (3.174–6). Through verbal staging the scenery of Gargaphie becomes a *skēnē*, a backdrop for the punishment of Cadmus' grandson.

Few would deny the theatricality of displays like these. Yet there is something theatrical – or, rather, metatheatrical – about Actaeon himself, whose myth was depicted on the tragic stage. Ancient readers of this episode, or at any rate many of them, would have remembered that Aeschylus and other tragedians had dramatized Actaeon's myth before Ovid.[12] Those for whom the echoes of lost tragedies are too faint may still access the genre through Actaeon's type: the ephebe, a youth whose fatal transgression prevents his crossing over into manhood.[13] Furthermore, a connection between theater and metatheater in the *Metamorphoses* has a precedent in the *Heroides*, where a heroine's prior existence in tragedy is to be juxtaposed with her appearance in elegy. In Actaeon's case, the reader's awareness of him as a tragic character or tragic type (or both) enriches Ovid's already theatrical presentation. Such is the case with Pentheus, another ephebe from the same book:

> monte fere medio est, cingentibus ultima silvis,
> purus ab arboribus spectabilis undique campus.
> hic oculis illum cernentem sacra profanis
> prima videt, prima est insano concita cursu,
> prima suum misso violavit Penthea thyrso
> mater.

> Midway up the mountain was a plain, ringed by forest, vacant of trees, open to view on all sides. Here, as Pentheus was gazing at the rites with uninitiated eyes, his mother was the first to spot him, first to fall upon him in a mad rush, first to hurl the thyrsus and pierce him. (*Met.* 3.708–13)

Verbal scene-setting, with its patent visuality (*hic oculis illum cernentem videt*, 710–11), again joins with metatheater in this adaptation of Euripides' *Bacchae*.[14] Ovid presents the death of Pentheus, which in Euripides takes place offstage, where and when it should occur. The theatrical setting, however, is reminiscent of Pentheus' original genre.

[11] Barchiesi and Rosati 2007 rightly note that Ovid makes his readers complicit in Actaeon's transgressive viewing (*Met.* 3.155–62).
[12] Lost Actaeon plays: *TrGF* I: Phrynichus fr. 1b; Iophon; Cleophon fr. 1. Aesch. *Toxotides TrGF* III.241–6.
[13] On the ephebe in tragedy see Winkler 1990, following Vidal-Naquet 1981.
[14] So Keith 2002, 266.

Theater and metatheater ... and amphitheater? Hinds observes that the setting of Pentheus' demise (*spectabilis undique campus*, 709) suggests "not so much the stage as the arena."[15] This and other instances of so-called amphitheatricality are a natural, and perhaps inevitable, development of Ovid's tragic program. The poet continues the Roman tradition of embellishing tragedy with spectacle, though presumably not the empty variety deplored by Horace (*Epist.* 2.1.188), which seems to have been rampant in Latin tragic productions.[16] Ovid also appeals to his readers' familiarity, if not outright fascination, with the spectacular. Rome in the early principate was a *locus* for every manner of spectacle, from games and athletic contests to political speeches and triumphal processions, to public sacrifices and other religious rituals, and, finally, to the monuments and architecture of the Augustan city – with the emperor himself gazing over all and being gazed at in return.[17] Emblematic of these spectacles is combat in the amphitheater, where audiences witnessed actual bloodshed and sometimes death. The death of Pentheus with its amphitheatrical violence appeals to the Roman experience of watching, appreciating, and even enjoying blood-sport.

The death of Orpheus in book 11 and the death of Actaeon evoke a particular kind of blood-sport: the *venatio*, the staged hunting of wild beasts known from the second century BCE onward. Orpheus is compared to a stag about to fall prey to hounds in the amphitheater: *matutina cervus periturus harena | praeda canum est* (11.26–7). Actaeon, meanwhile, suffers this fate not figuratively but literally, a stag torn apart by his own pack for the amusement of his *comites* (3.242–4).[18] Andrew Feldherr and Philip Hardie have proleptically connected these deaths with an especially dramatic version of the *venatio*, common in the later first century CE, in which beasts executed criminals who were dressed as mythical characters.[19] One such incident in the dedicatory games of the Flavian Amphitheater (80 CE) involved an "Orpheus" torn apart by a bear (a twist on the traditional

[15] Hinds 2002, 139; Barchiesi and Rosati 2007.

[16] Chapter 2, pp. 27, 33–5.

[17] On the Augustan "culture of display" see Zanker 1988; Beacham 1999, ch. 1; and Boyle 2006, 160–76. With reference to Ovid see Hardie 2002, 38–42, and Feldherr 2010, 83–105. Feldherr reminds us that the visuality of Ovid's poetry not only reflects "contemporary taste for spectacle," but also appropriates "problems of seeing" in Augustan Rome, where "who you were was determined by what and how you saw" (162). Of the primary sources perhaps most important are Suet. *Aug.* 43 and the *Res gestae*. On post-Augustan cultures of display see Bartsch 1994. On early republican culture see Boyle 2006, ch. 1.

[18] Orpheus: Hinds 2002, 139–40. Actaeon: Feldherr 1997, 42–4.

[19] Feldherr 1997, 43, with further development in Feldherr 2010, 172–98; Hardie 2002, 40.

band of maenads).[20] Kathleen Coleman has collected this and other reenactments under the rubric "fatal charades," wherein the arena becomes a *locus* for joining myth with violence.[21] Just as the amphitheater would appropriate tragic myth in the decades after Ovid, so tragic myth appropriates amphitheatrical violence in the *Metamorphoses*.[22]

As much as they owe to Ovid's times, the amphitheatrical proportions of his tragic stories are consonant with epic format and epic tradition. Because the genre is a purely verbal form, there are few if any restrictions on what it can display (apart from a poet's own sense of decorum, perhaps). From Homer onward, epic establishes its facility for narrating violence as it occurs. Ovid's visceral descriptions of bloodshed and death uphold the tradition, but in episodes derived from tragedy they are self-consciously recuperative. The narratives of the stage, which developed from epic narrative, are restored to their genre of origin, and with them the presentation of events in sequence.[23] From this standpoint the amphitheater is an apt metaphor for Ovid's reconfiguration of tragedy, like the plain on which Pentheus is murdered: *spectabilis undique campus* (3.709), everything laid open to view on all sides. Ovid, with only words at his disposal, achieves the same conflation as the combination theater/amphitheater of C. Curio five decades earlier.[24] The *Metamorphoses* is a theater of epic with the capacity to display all manner of spectacles, from emotional pathos to violent acts only imagined by tragic audiences, but regularly observed in Rome.

2 Hecabe: off-center stage

The Hecabe narrative of *Met.* 13 is an appropriate first case study of how Ovid transforms the tragic *theatron* for epic. The tale pays homage to Euripides' *Hecabe*, yet seems to glory in displaying what the original play never could or never would, including the murders of Hecabe's children.

[20] *Spect.* 21. Feldherr 1997, 43, supposes that Actaeon-reenactments, although there is no direct evidence that they were staged, are well within the realm of possibility.

[21] Coleman 1990.

[22] Barkan 1986 touches on the amphitheatrical nature of tragic violence by describing the Tereus–Procne–Philomela narrative (*Met.* 6) as a "myth of competitive mutilation" (214, cited in Gildenhard and Zissos 2007, 20). We will see further instances of violent rivalry in Ovid, both in the struggle of one character against another and in Ovid's own struggle to outdo earlier authors.

[23] J. Barrett 2002, xvi–xviii and 1–6, traces the development of tragic messenger speeches from epic narrative.

[24] Chapter 2, pp. 34–5.

The result is an expanded take on tragedy, not so much a revision as an amplification, in which the tragic *skēnē* is self-consciously decentered.

It is impossible to read the Hecabe story without thinking of Euripides. Ovid perpetuates the most distinctive feature of the *Hecabe*, the double deaths of Polydorus and Polyxena, which the Athenian playwright was the first to collate.[25] The epic narrative encompasses other aspects of the Euripidean plot, like the blinding of Polymestor, the *aition* of the Cynossema, and the curious setting of the Thracian Chersonese. Also conspicuous are close renderings of the original text, such as in Polyxena's last act:

> tum quoque cura fuit partes velare tegendas,
> cum caderet, castique decus servare pudoris.

> Even then, as she fell, she took care to cover what should be covered, and to preserve the grace of her unspoiled chastity. (*Met.* 13.479–80)

> ἡ δὲ καὶ θνῄσκουσ᾽ ὅμως
> πολλὴν πρόνοιαν εἶχεν εὐσχήμων πεσεῖν,
> κρύπτουσ᾽ ἃ κρύπτειν ὄμματ᾽ ἀρσένων χρεών.

> Even then, although she was dying, she still had the presence of mind to fall modestly, hiding what should be hidden from the gaze of men. (Eur. *Hec.* 568–70)

The narrative is a kind of translation, not only of Greek into Latin, but also of one genre into another. Translating tragedy into epic involves depicting in proper sequence an event kept offstage and reported after the fact. Although the dying Polyxena was hidden from her original Euripidean spectators, she falls in full view of the Ovidian reader.

We will revisit Polyxena and her noble demise in due course. Perhaps it is better to begin at the beginning, although this is something of a challenge. Ovid's narrative opens not in Euripides' Thrace but in Troy:

> Ilion ardebat, neque adhuc consederat ignis,
> exiguumque senis Priami Iovis ara cruorem
> conbiberat, tractata comis antistita Phoebi
> non profecturas tendebat ad aethera palmas;
> Dardanidas matres patriorum signa deorum,
> dum licet, amplexas succensaque templa tenentes
> invidiosa trahunt victores praemia Grai;
> mittitur Astyanax illis de turribus, unde
> pugnantem pro se proavitaque regna tuentem

[25] Collard 1991, 32–4, and Álvarez Morán and Iglesias Montiel 2006, 40.

saepe videre patrem monstratum a matre solebat.
iamque viam suadet Boreas flatuque secundo
carbasa mota sonant, iubet uti navita ventis;
"Troia, vale! rapimur," clamant, dant oscula terrae
Troades et patriae fumantia tecta relinquunt.

Troy was burning down, and the flames had not yet subsided. The altar of Jupiter had drunk old Priam's meager blood, while the priestess of Phoebus, dragged away by her hair, was stretching her helpless hands to the heavens. The Dardanian matrons, clutching while they can the images of their native gods and thronging their burning temples – these women the Greek conquerors haul away, a spoil worthy of envy. Astyanax is hurled from the turrets where he used to watch his father, singled out by his mother, as he fought for himself and for the safety of his family's realm. And now the North wind ushers them onward, the canvas flaps in the favorable breeze, and the mariner bids them set sail. The Trojan women cry, "Troy, farewell! We are taken captive!" They kiss their home soil and abandon their smoldering houses. (*Met.* 13.408–21)

Ovid converts the destruction of Troy into a prologue. The city's smoldering ruins are hardly a *locus amoenus*, but they are a scene unto themselves, one set for Hecabe, the former Trojan queen:

ultima conscendit classem (miserabile visu)
in mediis Hecabe natorum inventa sepulcris;
prensantem tumulos atque ossibus oscula dantem
Dulichiae traxere manus. tamen unius hausit
inque sinu cineres secum tulit Hectoris haustos.
Hectoris in tumulo canum de vertice crinem,
inferias inopes, crinem lacrimasque reliquit.

The last to embark – a pitiful sight – was Hecabe, who had been discovered among the tombs of her sons. She was embracing their burial mounds and kissing their bones, when the hands of Dulichian Ulysses dragged her away. Nevertheless, she rescued the ashes of one, Hector, and bore them with her in her bosom. On Hector's grave she left a snowy lock, a pauper's offering for the dead, a lock and tears as well. (*Met.* 13.422–8)

Verses 408–21 constitute a catalogue of atrocities – the city burning, the murder of Priam, the rape of Cassandra, the death of Astyanax – all of which might move the reader's pity. But Ovid singles out the former queen as a pitiable spectacle in her own right: *miserabile visu* (422). Revealed in this way she embodies the fall of Troy, the ultimate victim in a line of many. At the same time, our first look at Hecabe affords a glimpse of her future. Neil Hopkinson notes that her behavior borders on the canine: she haunts the graves (*prensantem tumulos*, 424) just as she will haunt the "Bitch's Grave" (Cynos**sema**); she kisses the bones of her sons (*ossibus oscula dantem*, 424) and digs the ground to rescue Hector's remains (*cineres haustos*, 426); even her offering of a *canum crinem* (427) suggests the *canis* she will soon become.[26]

Epic narrative, then, expands the temporal and spatial range of Euripides' *Hecabe* by displaying the destruction of Troy – an event crucial to that drama, but only recalled and lamented, never witnessed. Moreover, Ovid's version is both theatrical and metatheatrical in the reader's awareness of Hecabe as a Euripidean character. In fact, she is Euripidean twice over, the protagonist of not only the *Hecabe* but also the *Trojan Women*. Ovid recalls the latter tragedy in his report of the destruction, particularly the fates of Cassandra and Astyanax, and in the collective and emphatic *Troades* (421), which stamps the preceding narrative with Euripides' title.[27] Tragedy's longstanding reception and transmission as text promote the linking of the plays. Although Euripides' works were produced on separate occasions, Ovid joins them in much the same way that modern editors rearrange Sophocles' "Theban trilogy" in narrative sequence.[28] Hecabe's final act in the *Trojan Women* – her departure from Troy and from the stage – becomes her first act in the *Metamorphoses*. Her exit at 422 is refashioned as an entrance in a spectacular *coup de théâtre*.

With Hecabe aboard ship, the narrative next shifts from Troy to the Chersonese:

> est, ubi Troia fuit, Phrygiae contraria tellus
> Bistoniis habitata viris.
>
> There is a land opposite Phrygia, where Troy was, which the Bistonians inhabit. (*Met.* 13.429–30)

The formulaic *est tellus* (13.429) establishes a landscape new for the poem, but one familiar to audiences of the *Hecabe* (τήνδ' ἀρίστην Χερσονησίαν πλάκα, 8). Euripides' Thracian setting has been puzzled over from time

[26] Hopkinson 2000, duly observing the quantitative difference between *cānus* and *cănis* (*Met.* 13.423–8).

[27] So Hopkinson 2000, who offers additional parallels with Euripides' *Trojan Women*. The collective *Troades* appear three more times during the narrative and always in the service of Hecabe, whether bringing Polyxena's corpse to the queen (481), being asked to bring an urn for water (534), or crying aloud at the discovery of Polydorus' body (538). Ovid's Trojan women are like the choruses in both Euripidean plays, a group of sympathetic women who share Hecabe's confidence.

[28] Compare Álvarez Morán and Iglesias Montiel 2006, who likewise discuss Ovid's linking of the *Troades* and the *Hecabe* into a master Euripidean "script": "[E]l poeta compone sus 'Troyanas' y en especial su 'Hécuba' siguiendo el guión eurípideo" (36).

to time. On the one hand, it facilitates the discovery of Polydorus, who is murdered here. On the other hand, the traditional site of Achilles' tomb, where Polyxena is sacrificed, is the Troad.[29] Given the choice between a Trojan setting, which would have accommodated the death of Polyxena but required a pretext for bringing Polydorus' corpse across the Hellespont, or a Thracian setting, which accommodates the brother's death but requires a pretext for the sister's, Euripides seems to have opted for the latter. The Chersonese also facilitates the appearance of Polymestor, whose palace is apparently near the Greek encampment.[30] Add to all of this the association of Thrace with Dionysus, whose transgressive cult rituals are often reflected in myth as lethal violence against children.[31] Ultimately, the *Hecabe* appears less concerned with geographic plausibility than with geographic identity – or, rather, the loss of it. What happens to a civilized Trojan in a barbarous, Dionysiac land?

Barbarism is a matter of perspective. Throughout the *Metamorphoses*, Ovid presents Thrace as the uncivilized periphery,[32] a perspective that a Roman could easily share with an Athenian, and one that the Hecabe narrative shares with its source play. In adopting Euripides' ideologically motivated but geographically peculiar setting, Ovid shows a Euripidean indifference to geographical reality. We are informed that the Chersonese is the home of the Bistonians (*Bistoniis habitata viris*, 430), a people who actually inhabited the coastal mainland to the west. Rationalizing the discrepancy, commentators have taken *Bistoniis* as a poetic generalization for "Thracian."[33] Nevertheless, Ovid's application of the adjective suggests that space in epic and tragedy can be equally mutable, if not entirely arbitrary.

Hecabe's narrative, although it has left behind the destruction of Troy, has not yet abandoned violence. The newly established scene of the Chersonese becomes the *locus* of Polydorus' murder:

> Polymestoris illic
> regia dives erat, cui te commisit alendum
> clam, Polydore, pater Phrygiisque removit ab armis,
> consilium sapiens, sceleris nisi praemia magnas

[29] Collard 1991, 34.

[30] Polymestor claims to have come to Hecabe by way of central Thrace (ἐν μέσοις Θρῄκης ὅροις, 963), but his status as false friend and deceiver is firmly established by the time of his entrance.

[31] Thus Gildenhard and Zissos 2007, 10, following Schlesier 1988, 124–5. In addition to child murder Gildenhard and Zissos list intra-marital slaughter and cannibalism among acts that surpass "even the rather wide remit of transgressions for which Dionysus is prepared to take responsibility."

[32] See, for example, not only the Hecabe narrative, but also Tereus–Procne–Philomela (book 6) and the death of Orpheus (11).

[33] Bömer 1982; Hopkinson 2000.

adiecisset opes, animi inritamen avari.
ut cecidit fortuna Phrygum, capit impius ensem
rex Thracum iuguloque sui demisit alumni
et, tamquam tolli cum corpore crimina possent,
exanimem scopulo subiectas misit in undas.

In that place was the prosperous house of Polymestor, to whom your father entrusted you, Polydorus, to be brought up in secret, far away from the war at Troy. It was a shrewd plan, except that he had included a mighty treasure, which proved to be an invitation to wrong-doing, a goad for a greedy mind. When the fortune of the Trojans fell, the Thracian king, casting duty aside, seized a sword and drove it into his charge's throat. Then, as if disposing of the corpse could dispose of the crime, he hurled the lifeless boy from a cliff into the waters below. (*Met.* 13.430–8)

The Thracian landscape is the backdrop for a display of bloodshed. Ovid's reader occupies a position of privilege (if that is the right word), witnessing first-hand what the tragic audience learned from the prologue (*Hec.* 1–58).

But there is more at stake than observing tragic events in real time. In the *Hecabe* Polydorus, appearing as a ghost, recalls his own death, an internal narrator speaking in the first person (ἥκω, 1; κεῖμαι, 28). The external narrator of the *Metamorphoses*, however, describes the murder in the third person – even going so far as to address Polydorus directly (*te commisit alendum | clam, Polydore*, 431–2), as if underscoring that the former tragic narrator is now being narrated.[34] Ovid appropriates not only a tragic event, integrating it within the chronology of his epic, but also the narrative instance of the event, as well as its function. The story of Polydorus' death remains a prologue (a second prologue, after the fall of Troy), but the duty of delivering it has shifted. Tragedy has a tradition of presenting ghosts – literally souls, *psychai* – onstage. In addition to Darius in the *Persians* and Clytemnestra in the *Eumenides*, the shade of Achilles delivered the prologue in the lost *Polyxena* of Sophocles (which could have inspired Polydorus' prologue in the *Hecabe*).[35] On the Latin side, the ghost of Deipylus appeared to his mother in the lost *Iliona* of Pacuvius.[36] Yet in

[34] So Álvarez Morán and Iglesias Montiel 2006, 40: "Ovidio … adapta a la *narratio* epica las palabras del prólogo pronunciadas por el espectro de Polidoro y sustituye el parlamento trágico por la interpelacíon directa al joven Priámida." The point with which these authors conclude – "[L]a *narratio* epica permite una mayor plasticidad en la exposición de los sucesos sangrientos, que nunca podrían ser representados en la escena ática" (49) – is more or less the point at which my analysis begins.

[35] Soph. *Polyxena*: *TrGF* IV.522–8 (Achilles' prologue: fr. 523); reconstructions in Calder 1966, Fantham 1982, 57–61, and Mossman 1995, 42–7. Dating the *Polyxena* earlier than the *Hecabe* has been customary since Wilamovitz: Mossman 1995, 45 n. 62.

[36] Chapter 2, pp. 25, 27.

the *Metamorphoses* all that remains is a corpse without a soul, *exanimem* (438). Without an *anima* – that is, a *psyche* – Polydorus can no longer tell his own story. That power now rests with Ovid, whose role as narrator is precisely what grants control over time and space.

The Hecabe narrative has made great strides in crossing from Troy to Thrace, but it does not rest there. Thrace itself offers at least five smaller settings for the action to follow: the house of Polymestor (A), where Polydorus is murdered; the seashore (B), where the boy's body comes to rest; the tomb of Achilles (C), the site of Polyxena's sacrifice; the Greek camp (D), which resembles the original Euripidean *skēnē*, and where Hecabe mourns her daughter; and a remote place (E), the alleged treasure-trove and the site of Hecabe's ultimate transformation. This list is not meant to impart equal weight to all settings. Some are better defined than others, while some contain larger acts, with no correlation between definition and magnitude. The house of Polymestor, although described in concrete terms (*regia dives*, 431), is less important to the narrative than the tomb of Achilles, or even the nondescript scene of Hecuba's lamentations. Although all of these places share a certain proximity, each part of a larger landscape, their number nonetheless shows how much latitude epic has with regard to movement and setting in comparison with tragedy.

The various settings in Ovid's narrative decenter the Euripidean play, which shows only the Greek camp and maintains an almost constant focus on Hecabe. Out of nearly 1,300 verses, there are at most only 160 or so in which she is not onstage: the prologue, the second stasimon (and the very beginning of the third episode, 629–64), the third stasimon (perhaps, 905–52), and the fourth stasimon (1024–43). Though her movements are modest, they are crucial to her emotional arc, each exit and entrance bringing a Hecabe different from before. Her grief over the loss of Polyxena gives way to outrage with the discovery of Polydorus' corpse; her outrage prompts her agreement with Agamemnon and inspires her cunning deception of Polymestor. In the end she stands empowered and terrible, no longer the helpless slave who first took the stage (ἄγετ', ὦ παῖδες, τὴν γραῦν πρὸ δόμων, 59). Ovid's Hecabe takes a parallel path within a shifting landscape. Each movement from setting to setting brings her further from mourning and closer to vengeance. Like her tragic counterpart, she remains mostly in view, and her presence mitigates the decentering effect of Ovid's changing locales.

Mitigates, but does not counteract altogether. There are two settings from which Hecabe is temporarily displaced: the house of Polymestor (A) and the seashore (B). Hecabe is at sea when her son is murdered in

(A), but she eventually comes calling there after plotting her revenge. Polydorus' corpse has already washed ashore at (B), where his unsuspecting mother goes to draw water for Polyxena's funeral. These subtle displacements erode the unifying effect of Hecabe's near-continuous presence. In keeping with a program of tragic amplification, the queen no longer dominates the action as she does in Euripides. There is room for other spectacles and displays. Her marginalization also suits the theme of barbarism. In a tale of violence on the periphery, it is appropriate that Hecabe is sometimes relegated to the periphery of her own narrative.

A third setting from which Hecabe is excluded – completely, this time – is the tomb of Achilles (C), where Polyxena is sacrificed before the Achaean assembly. Hecabe's absence has a Euripidean precedent, since she stays behind while Odysseus leads her daughter offstage (432–7). This is sound dramaturgy, for Hecabe continues to command the attention of the audience, even during Talthybius' report of the sacrifice (484–582). In the *Metamorphoses*, however, the reader witnesses the sacrifice apart from Hecabe. Polyxena is forcibly removed (*rapta sinu matris*, 450) and led off (*ducitur ad tumulum*, 452), with almost no reaction on Hecabe's part. The phrase *rapta sinu matris* suggests resistance, though there is nothing on the order of the play, in which Hecabe rails against the demands of Achilles (154–74), argues with Odysseus (218–333), and bids Polyxena a tearful farewell (402–37). In fact, were it not for *matris*, we might fail to register Hecabe's presence altogether.

The reader follows Polyxena to the tomb of Achilles, which emerges as the most prominent viewing place thus far:

> fortis et infelix et plus quam femina virgo
> ducitur ad tumulum diroque fit hostia busto.
> quae memor ipsa sui, postquam crudelibus aris
> admota est sensitque sibi fera sacra parari,
> utque Neoptolemum stantem ferrumque tenentem
> inque suo vidit figentem lumina vultu,
> "utere iamdudum generoso sanguine," dixit.

> Brave and unfortunate and more than female, the maiden is led to the mound and is made an offering for the dread tomb. She remembered herself after she was brought before the pitiless altar and sensed the savage sacrifice was being readied for her. When she saw Neoptolemus standing there, clutching a sword and piercing her eyes with his, she said, "Take my noble lifeblood at last." (*Met.* 13.451–7)

The space itself, like many in the Hecabe narrative, is nondescript. Although there is little to see here by way of scene-dressing, it is nonetheless a *locus* of heightened visualizing. Whereas the tragic audience hears of the sacrifice along with Hecabe, Ovid allows us to look through Polyxena's eyes as she draws near the altar, where she not only recognizes her fate (*sensit*, 454), but also encounters the forbidding sight of Neoptolemus, whose own eyes reflect the violence to come (*inque suo vidit figentem lumina vultu*, 456).[37]

Beyond sheer visuality, the tomb's unique setting, alien to the Euripidean *skēnē* and sundered from Hecabe herself, renders it a *theatron* in its own right.[38] It is a space reserved for Polyxena, whose moment has come. In the *Hecabe* she shares the stage with her mother, the chorus, and Odysseus (177–437) – a span of over 250 verses, during which she comes to terms with the prospect of dying. What happens offstage, although poignant, is more or less an extension of what has already transpired. Ovid condenses Polyxena's time onstage into a solo vignette, in which she gives her first and final performance before the Greek army. The reader expects a performance from a tragic character, but Polyxena, too, is aware of her role. Upon seeing the altars and the rites in progress she becomes mindful of herself (*memor sui*, 453): self-possessed, remembering her noble station.[39] Yet given the allusive properties of memory in Latin poetry,[40] we can also read *memor sui* as a metatheatrical reference to Polyxena's original genre. She remembers, as if on cue, that she is Polyxena – not merely Trojan nobility, but a Euripidean heroine with a part to play.

Acting the part of a tragic heroine involves displays of bravery:

> "utere iamdudum generoso sanguine," dixit,
> "nulla mora est. at tu iugulo vel pectore telum
> conde meo" – iugulumque simul pectusque retexit.
> "scilicet haud ulli servire Polyxena ferrem."

> She said, "Take at last my noble lifeblood. Do not hesitate. Bury your blade in my throat or in my breast" – and she revealed both her throat and her breast. "I, Polyxena, can bear to be no man's slave." (*Met.* 13.457–60)

[37] See Chapter 6, section 2, a discussion of the scene through the eyes of Iphigenia.

[38] Compare Álvarez Morán and Iglesias Montiel 2006, 44: "El relato de la inmolación de la doncella es otra importante muestra del *modus narrandi* ovidiano, ya que traduce en código épico escenas de tragedia de gran patetismo."

[39] So Bömer 1982 and Hopkinson 2000.

[40] On allusive memory see Hinds 1998, 1–5.

Bold words and bold gestures to suit a theatrical setting, where Polyxena acts and speaks for herself. Upon her exit in Euripides' version, Polyxena can no longer perform. Rather, she is performed by Talthybius, who reports what she did and said at the tomb. Moreover, the herald's performance is fragmented, since he narrates two smaller speeches by Polyxena, which he separates with his own commentary – most notably when he pauses to recall and marvel at the girl's nudity (μαστούς τ' ἔδειξε στέρνα θ' ὡς ἀγάλματος | κάλλιστα, 560–1). Ovid, conversely, yields entirely to Polyxena, interrupting only with a brief and less lascivious aside (*iugulumque simul pectusque retexit*, 459).

Polyxena's speech gives her a measure of control over the narrative:

> "mors tantum vellem matrem mea fallere posset:
> mater obest minuitque necis mihi gaudia, quamvis
> non mea mors illi, verum sua vita gemenda est." 464

> "I only wish that my death could escape my mother's notice: she stands in my way and takes the joy out of being slain – though she should not weep over my death, but her own life." (*Met.* 13.462–4)

Thus far the maiden has echoed many of her Euripidean sentiments on and off the stage. Her rejection of slavery (460), for example, recalls both her words to Odysseus (357–68) and her address to the Achaean assembly (550–2). But nowhere in the *Hecabe* does she utter anything like the passage above, and the patent originality of her statement magnifies her presence. Her wish to die unnoticed further marginalizes her mother, as does her assuming authority over her own body. In the tragedy Hecabe makes the request that Polyxena's corpse remain untouched:

> σὺ δ' ἐλθὲ καὶ σήμηνον Ἀργείοις τάδε,
> μὴ θιγγάνειν μοι μηδέν' ἀλλ' εἴργειν ὄχλον
> τῆς παιδός.

> But you go and tell the Argives this: let no one touch my daughter; keep the crowd away from her. (*Hec.* 604–6)

Her concern for her daughter's purity is justified, given Talthybius' pornographic inclination. The epic Polyxena, however, guards her own virginity:[41]

> "ite procul, si iusta peto, tactuque viriles
> virgineo removete manus." 467

[41] I revisit these lines in Chapter 6, pp. 196–7, where I consider them in light of a request by Polyxena herself at *Hec.* 548–9.

> "Keep back, if there is justice in my request, and take your hands – the hands of men – away from my virgin body." (*Met.* 13.466–7)

In achieving independence from Hecabe, she becomes a protagonist in her own right. In turn, the tragedy of a mother's grief momentarily becomes the spectacle of a daughter's demise.

The reaction of the Achaeans demonstrates that the spectacle, although realized in a theater of epic, has an impact worthy of tragedy:

> dixerat. at populus lacrimas, quas illa tenebat,
> non tenet; ipse etiam flens invitusque sacerdos ...

> She had spoken. But unlike her the throng did not restrain its tears; the officiant himself, also weeping and unwilling ... (*Met.* 13.474–5)

Polyxena moves the pity of her immediate audience, including that of Neoptolemus. Whereas in the tragedy he is divided (ὁ δ᾽ οὐ θέλων τε καὶ θέλων, 566), here he is entirely unwilling to slay the maiden (*flens invitusque*, 475). If the scene reverberates with tragic theatricality, it soon gives way to amphitheatricality:

> ... praebita coniecto rupit praecordia ferro.
> illa super terram defecto poplite labens
> pertulit intrepidos ad fata novissima vultus.

> ... he drove his sword into her breast, just as she had offered. As her knees gave way and she sank to the ground, she kept a brave face until the very end. (*Met.* 13.476–8)

Although he has the option to cut Polyxena's throat, which he does in the play (τέμνει σιδήρῳ πνεύματος διαρροάς, 567), Neoptolemus instead chooses to stab her chest. As Nicole Loraux has shown, the Euripidean Polyxena dies not only as a sacrificial victim, but also as a woman: the neck, especially in tragedy, is where women are most susceptible to violence. Ovid's heroine, however, dies as a man, *plus quam femina virgo* (451), wounded in the chest like a warrior. Loraux is right to suggest that the poet means "to outdo Euripides by giving the fullest meaning to the alternative" between the throat and the chest.[42] That tragic characters can approach the status of gladiators captures the grim spirit of poetic gamesmanship as much as it reflects Ovid's expansion of the *theatron*.

[42] Loraux 1987, 49–61, a discussion of female vulnerability in tragedy with particular emphasis on Polyxena (quotation on 60). Likewise Liveley 2011, 131: "Ovid ... has also transformed the very gender of epic *virtus*."

When at last we reunite with Hecabe, we find her in location (D), the Greek camp, lamenting over her daughter's corpse. In many ways this setting is closest to the tragic *skēnē*, in terms of both where Hecabe is and what she does. Nevertheless, Ovid's portrait of the grieving mother, although inspired by Euripides, has several original touches. In the play, for example, Hecabe mourns Polyxena before her sacrifice, while she is still onstage (415–40); Polyxena then exits, never to return, not even as a corpse. The Euripidean audience witnesses the last living exchange between mother and daughter, but Ovid's reader encounters them together only after Polyxena has died:

> quae corpus complexa animae tam fortis inane,
> quas totiens patriae dederat natisque viroque,
> huic quoque dat lacrimas; lacrimas in vulnera fundit
> osculaque ore tegit consuetaque pectora plangit,
> canitiemque suam concreto in sanguine verrens.

> Hecabe embraced the corpse now devoid of a soul so strong, and the tears, shed so many times for her sons and husband, she now sheds for her daughter. She pours tears into her wound and kisses her lips; she beats her own breast, now used to being beaten, and sweeps her hair over the hardened blood. (*Met.* 13.488–92)

Polyxena is now like Polydorus, a soulless body (*animae inane*, 488). However intently the mother mourns, the daughter cannot reply.

Her urgency surpasses anything on display in the tragedy. The Thracian half of Hecabe's narrative has been a series of set-pieces, with escalating emphasis on characters as performers, and sometimes as violent competitors. In the Polydorus episode, the narrator is in control, and the body is little more than a prop. In the next episode, however, Ovid cedes the stage to Polyxena, who proves so skilled a performer that she rivals her mother for the sympathies of the reader. We are entitled to wonder, given the competitive context of Athenian tragedy, its adversarial structuring of speeches, and its hierarchy of actors, exactly who the protagonist of this narrative is supposed to be. Despite a grand entrance at line 422, Hecabe's presence has thus far been negligible. The histrionics with which she throws herself on the corpse seem to compensate for her absence. Her gestures of lamentation are exaggerated, as if by making a show of mourning she might regain her standing as protagonist. Tears will eventually give way to words as Hecabe delivers her own speech, one of the poem's great monologues.[43]

[43] Chapter 5, which examines tragic rhetoric in the *Metamorphoses*, will consider her oration at length (section 3).

Suffice it for now to say the queen lives up to her reputation, earned from Euripides' plays, of being a dynamic speaker.

Since we are concerned with space and time, let us note how Hecabe's monologue, which brings the narrative to a standstill for nearly forty verses, finally brings renewed momentum:

> "quid moror interea crudelia vulnera lymphis
> abluere et sparsos inmiti sanguine vultus?" 532

> "But why do I delay to wash out her wounds and her face, so crudely spattered with blood?" (*Met.* 13.531–2)

In announcing her intention to gather water, Hecabe annotates her actions as all tragic characters do and paves the way for her exit. Nevertheless, she will remain within the reader's view as the setting changes to match her movements:

> dixit et ad litus passu processit anili
> albentes lacerata comas. 534

> She spoke, and went with an old woman's gait to the shore, tearing at her white hair. (*Met.* 13.533–4)

While the tragic Hecabe sends an old woman to bring water (ἀρχαία λάτρι, 609), her epic counterpart goes for water by herself: she has become the old woman (*passu anili*, 533).[44] Ovid begins to shift the tragic here-and-now, in which things from other places are carried to Hecabe, to a series of epic there-and-thens, the other places to which she carries herself. The first shift brings the discovery of Polydorus' body, which is not borne on, but encountered in a new setting.

In moving from setting (D) to (B), the Thracian shore, Hecabe embarks upon her journey from mourner to avenger. Upon finding her son her every thought is bent on revenge (*ulcisci statuit poenaque in imagine tota est*, 546). The trajectory of Ovid's heroine is similar to that of her Euripidean peer, although it is much more direct – only a few paces separate Hecabe *lugens* from Hecabe *ultrix*. Her movements, becoming more rapid, thematize not only her psychological transformation, but also Ovid's transformation of Euripides' play. No sooner does she arrive at the shore (B), when she visits the house of Polymestor (A) and lures him to the treasure-trove (E) – three changes of setting in nearly twenty lines (533–55). The further

[44] Hopkinson 2000 notes that having the queen "perform even that menial task" illustrates how far she has fallen.

and faster Hecabe ventures from (D), the most Euripidean location, the more her story diverges from its tragic model.

Setting (E), in which Hecabe blinds Polymestor and loses her human form, is the most Ovidian, although not necessarily as we might imagine. Given that the narrative has staged events outside the Euripidean *theatron*, it could conceivably include Hecabe's transformation into a dog, which in the original play is an event fated to happen at sea (1259–65). Ovid obliges, after a fashion:

> at haec missum rauco cum murmure saxum
> morsibus insequitur rictuque in verba parato
> latravit conata loqui. 569

> But with a hoarse growl she chases the stone, and, although her mouth is ready for words, she barks when trying to speak. (*Met.* 13.567–9)

The metamorphosis is sudden and swift, occurring in the midst of a pitched battle between the *Troades* and the Thracians, and occupying less than three verses. It is also somewhat oblique, the only overt signs of the queen's new form being *rauco murmure* (567), *morsibus* (568), and *latravit* (569). We have come a long way from the lucid metamorphosis of Lycaon (*fit lupus*, 1.237).[45]

How surprising is this development? Although Ovid tends to augment tragic stories with spectacles from other times and places, he is also interested, like the tragedians themselves, in emotion and psychology. Here the poet is more concerned with Hecabe's mental transformation than her physical one. Her canine behavior in the Trojan cemetery, for example, has shown that she is well on her way to losing her humanity. In becoming a dog she assumes the form that best clarifies what she has already become. The transformation itself, a modest augmentation of Euripides' play, also clarifies that Ovid shares the playwright's focus on the dehumanizing effect of revenge. Even as she diverges from the Euripidean setting, the epic Hecabe converges with her tragic self.

The poet illustrates Hecabe's bestial tendencies while she still remains human. The last true spectacle in the narrative is not her metamorphosis into a dog, but her blinding of Polymestor scant verses earlier:

[45] Verses 13.404–7, which precede the fall of Troy, have been regularly secluded since the time of Bentley. These lines, which spell out Hecabe's metamorphosis (*perdidit … post omnia formam*, 405; *externasque novo latratu terruit auras*, 406), might be the work of an interpolator looking to make her later metamorphosis more lucid. Then again, Hecabe's transformation has also been foreshadowed as part of Medea's wide-ranging flight to Corinth in book 7 (on which see section 4, below). Pavlock 2009, 56–7, discusses the canine metamorphosis of Maera (7.362) as anticipating the events of book 13.

digitos in perfida lumina condit
expellitque genis oculos (facit ira nocentem)
immergitque manus foedataque sanguine sonti
non lumen (neque enim superest), loca luminis haurit.

She buries her fingers in his treacherous eyes, and gouges them from their sockets (anger led her to this) and submerges her hands; spattered with his guilty blood she tears out not his eyes (for nothing remained of them) but the sockets themselves. (*Met.* 13.561–4)

Repeated references to eyes – *lumina* (561), *oculos* (562), *lumen* and *luminis* (564) – highlight the reader's paradoxical ability to visualize the destruction of Polymestor's sight, which in the tragedy happens within the *skēnē*. Ovid links this latest episode of amphitheatrical carnage to the concept of place:

locus exstat et ex re
nomen habet.

The place still exists and takes its name from what happened there. (*Met.* 13.569–70)

The poet appropriates the original Euripidean etiology (κεκλήσεται … κυνὸς ταλαίνης σῆμα, 1271–3), recasting it as an Alexandrian reference to the Cynossema. Moreover, *locus exstat* (569) echoes the formula *locus est*, whose variant, *est tellus*, had first introduced the violent Thracian landscape. Here, however, *locus exstat* is a formula of exit rather than entry, through which Ovid leaves his seal on the narrative. The brutal display of Polymestor losing his eyes and their sockets, *loca* (564), is visible only in a *locus* of poetic invention.

3 Hercules: tragedy displaced

Close reading of the Hecabe narrative underscores the dynamic of old and new in Ovid's transformations of tragedy. On the one hand, epic streamlines tragic action by reordering it in time and space. On the other hand, the original tragic setting still looms large on the epic horizon, and even new settings operate under the principle of tragic theatricality. The Hercules[46] narrative in book 9, which is as indebted to Sophocles as the Hecabe narrative is to Euripides,[47] ventures even further from its tragic

[46] When comparing Ovid's hero with his Sophoclean counterpart, I take advantage of the difference in spelling of the Latin and Greek names: Hercules versus Heracles, Herculean versus Heraclean.

[47] Bömer 1977 *passim* elucidates many verbal parallels; see also the comparison of the Heraclean and Herculean monologues in Chapter 5, section 4.

model. Ovid treats in sequence events such as Hercules' wrestling match with Acheloüs (1–88) and the death of Nessus (98–133), both of which are only recollected in the *Women of Trachis* (497–530 and 555–81, respectively).[48] Furthermore, Ovid presents the aftermath of Deianira's misguided gambit, the apotheosis of Hercules on Mt. Oeta (159–272). Sophocles concludes with the hero's departure to the mountain, where Hyllus has promised to cremate him (1264). However well known the apotheosis was,[49] the audience's last visible impression is of a fallen and mortal hero. Ovid's reader expects to witness Hercules' deification. What might give pause, particularly given Hecabe's elliptical metamorphosis, is the grand scale on which it takes place. Not only is it well beyond the limits of the original *theatron*, at 114 verses it is also the longest episode in the entire narrative.

Although Oeta is a *locus* worthy of epic, it nonetheless resembles the tragic *skēnē* as a place for displaying heroic pathos. Note, for example, what Heracles says to Hyllus before his house in Trachis:

> καὶ νῦν προσελθὼν στῆθι πλησίον πατρός,
> σκέψαι δ᾽ ὁποίας ταῦτα συμφορᾶς ὕπο
> πέπονθα· δείξω γὰρ τάδ᾽ ἐκ καλυμμάτων.
> ἰδού, θεᾶσθε πάντες ἄθλιον δέμας,
> ὁρᾶτε τὸν δύστηνον, ὡς οἰκτρῶς ἔχω.

> Come close now and stand beside your father; see the sort of misfortunes I suffer. I will show them to you with my coverings removed. Lo and behold, all of you, view my wretched body. See my misery, how pitiful I am. (Soph. *Trach.* 1076–80)

His enjoinders, which emphasize the visibility of his own suffering, highlight the theatricality of this moment. What begins as an address to Heracles' son becomes something more inclusive. The plurals θεᾶσθε (1079) and ὁρᾶτε (1080) reach out to a wider audience: "the world in general as it were," notes Malcolm Davies, though perhaps also Sophocles' spectators.[50] The imperatives, especially θεᾶσθε, implicate the playwright's audience, which has gathered to witness the misfortunes of Heracles in the *theatron*.

[48] On Hercules' bout with Acheloüs, which the river god himself narrates, see Secci 2009. Secci highlights Acheloüs' attempts to elicit pity from his audience by recalling more glorious fights in Homeric, Hellenistic, and Vergilian epic. The river god imbues his account with "tragic overtones" (53) that frame and undermine his ostensibly epic narrative.

[49] On the likelihood that the apotheosis was common knowledge in Sophocles' era see March 1987, 71–2; also Halleran 1997, 157–8.

[50] Davies 1991. Bain 1975, however, denies that Greek tragedy at large makes addresses to the audience.

In much the same way Ovid fashions the mountain into a viewing place, a wider vista on Sophocles. Whereas the tragic audience hears about the effects of Deianira's *peplos* from Hyllus (749–812), and then receives visual confirmation of these effects, Ovid's reader witnesses the hero's destruction as it occurs:

nec mora, letiferam conatur scindere vestem;
qua trahitur, trahit illa cutem, foedumque relatu,
aut haeret membris frustra temptata revelli
aut laceros artus et grandia detegit ossa.
ipse cruor, gelido ceu quondam lammina candens
tincta lacu, stridit coquiturque ardente veneno.
nec modus est, sorbent avidae praecordia flammae
caeruleusque fluit toto de corpore sudor
ambustique sonant nervi.

Without delay he tries to tear away the deadly gown; where it is torn, it tears away the skin as well, and (horrible to tell) it fastens itself to his limbs or exposes his torn muscles and the gigantic bones beneath, though he tried in vain to pull it off. The blood itself sizzles, as when white-hot metal meets cold water, and it boils from the burning venom. Nor is that all: the greedy flames swallow up his midriff, sea-green sweat flows out of his entire body, and his sinews burn and splutter. (*Met.* 9.166–74)

saepe illum gemitus edentem, saepe frementem,
saepe retemptantem totas infringere vestes
sternentemque trabes irascentemque videres
montibus aut patrio tendentem bracchia caelo.

You would have seen him often groaning, often bellowing, often trying and trying to pull the garment to pieces, uprooting trees and raging at the mountains, or stretching out his arms to his father's sky. (*Met.* 9.207–10)

In the first passage the reader is faced once again with violence almost amphitheatrical in its excess (*nec modus est*, 172). The second passage spares more detail, but keeps the hero in focus. The main verb, *videres* (209), insists that Hercules' pain could be visible, while the string of accusative participles (*frementem*, 207; *retemptatem*, 208; *sternentem*, *irascentem*, 209; *tendentem*, 210) makes him the object of the reader's hypothetical gaze.[51]

[51] Compare Gildenhard and Zissos 1999, 165–6, who offer a similar reading of the accusative participles and adjectives in the rape of Philomela (6.555–7; I would add 522–5) and in the murder of Itys (636–41).

It is fitting that Oeta be a space for displaced tragic violence, since Ovid displaces the mountain from its real-world geographical position. The movements of Hercules make this clear. After the siege of Oechalia, the hero is clearly at Cenaeum, the northwestern tip of Euboea:

> victor ab Oechalia Cenaeo sacra parabat
> vota Iovi. 137

> Having sacked Oechalia, he was planning to sacrifice to Jove at Cenaeum. (*Met.* 9.136–7)

In keeping with the plot of the *Women of Trachis* (752–4), Cenaeum is a convenient locale for thanking the gods on Euboea before returning to the mainland. Here, as in Sophocles, Hercules receives the fatal robe:

> capit inscius heros
> induiturque umeris Lernaeae virus echidnae.
> tura dabat primis et verba precantia flammis
> vinaque marmoreas patera fundebat in aras;
> incaluit vis illa mali resolutaque flammis
> Herculeos abiit late dilapsa per artus.

> The unwitting hero accepts the robe, and swathes his shoulders in the poison of the Lernaean hydra. He was offering incense and prayers among the newly lit fires, and pouring wine from the bowl upon the altars. The venom grew warm, activated by the flames, and spread through Hercules' limbs. (*Met.* 9.157–62)

The *aras* (160) on which Hercules pours libations must have been erected as part of his earlier preparations (136–7). If so, the reader next witnesses an instantaneous change of venue, much like a cinematic "jump cut":

> victa malis postquam est patientia, reppulit aras
> implevitque suis nemorosam vocibus Oeten.

> After the pestilence conquered his endurance, he overturned the altars and filled the groves of Oeta with his cries. (*Met.* 9.164–5)

At verse 164 Hercules is wrecking the altars at Cenaeum. By 165 he is ostensibly on the mainland, having bypassed Trachis altogether and shouting atop Mt. Oeta, some thirty miles due west across the Malian Gulf. If we take this discrepancy at face value and assume that Ovid has tacitly relocated Hercules to Oeta, we could read it as a wry commentary on Sophocles' manipulation of space and time in the *Women of Trachis*. Perhaps Ovid has abbreviated a journey already abbreviated by the playwright.

The hero's subsequent movements, however, challenge the limits of plausibility. First, Hercules spies Lichas cowering beneath a rock (*trepidum latitantem rupe*, 211). In Sophocles Hyllus reports that his father killed the herald on Euboea soon after the poison had taken effect (772–82), but in Ovid's version Lichas appears also to be on Oeta, unless Hercules has somehow crossed back over to Euboea unnoticed. Next, Lichas is hurled out into the Euboean Gulf (*mittit in Euboicas tormento fortius undas*, 218) and transformed into a rock, which rises out of the same waters (*nunc quoque in Euboico scopulus brevis eminet alto*, 226). Finally, Hercules gets to work felling trees for his pyre on Oeta (*arboribus caesis, quas ardua gesserat Oete*, 230). The problem, therefore, is that the hero seems to be in two different places at once, both on the island of Euboea and on the mountain near Trachis.[52]

There are essentially four solutions: (1) Hercules, though wracked with pain, manages to wander from Cenaeum to Oeta, then back to Cenaeum to dispatch Lichas, and back to Oeta to build his pyre. (2) Lichas has accompanied Hercules to the mountain, from where he is hurled – *fortius* indeed (218) – across the Malian Gulf and into the waters off Euboea. (3) Ovid has mistakenly placed Oeta on Euboea (or has followed a mistaken tradition). (4) Ovid has intentionally conflated the two locations, prompting his readers to consider the very possibilities we are now considering. The first option, Hercules wandering, is not as bizarre as it might seem. Although it requires the reader to assume not one but three crossings by Hercules, such a journey is possible in light of Medea's flights of fancy in book 7 (220–37 and 350–90, both to be considered in the next section). If the heroine can zoom to and fro over the Aegean, surely the notion of Hercules covering less ground, even under his own diminished power, is within the realm of imagination. Option (2), Lichas catapulted, is nonetheless more probable by comparison. It is easier to imagine the herald having "jumped" to Oeta with his master than Hercules returning to Euboea. Meanwhile, the superheroics required to launch a body on a thirty-mile trajectory are appropriate to the character of Hercules as well as the sheer exuberance of Ovid's poem.

The first two options continue to give Ovid the benefit of the doubt by rationalizing the Lichas episode within the world of the *Metamorphoses*. Option (3), Ovid mistaken, looks outward to the author and finds his

[52] For a summary of the problem see Bömer 1977 (after *Met.* 9.133). Kenney 2011 appreciates the difficulty of imagining an involuntary discrepancy on Ovid's part, although if the poet is alluding to an alternate tradition, there is no trace of it (*Met.* 9.165).

knowledge wanting. Although some might embrace this option, I regard it as the least plausible. Given a poem that scrupulously divides and subdivides the *mundus* into its constituent areas, it seems strange that Ovid neither knew nor remembered to distinguish Oeta from Euboea. What is more, the *Women of Trachis*, with whose text Ovid is as demonstrably familiar as with any of the plays in this chapter, dramatizes the distinction between the two places: Hyllus describes in some detail the voyage back to Trachis (801–6). I cannot theorize the poet's ignorance under these conditions. Which brings us to option (4), Ovid conflating, to my mind the most plausible. The poet knowingly disregards where Mt. Oeta should be, and situates it on Euboea. Ovid creates a self-consciously transgressive landscape emblematic of how epic reconfigures the world vis-à-vis tragedy. This is the Hecabe narrative's *Bistoniis viris* (13.430) writ large. Whereas tragedy offers a fragment of the world, often cut off from the larger whole, epic conceives the world as fragments and strives to piece them together. Sometimes, as with Euboea and Oeta, the seams between them remain visible.

A transgressive landscape is an ideal setting for Hercules' crossing from mortality to immortality, the final leg in his journey from tragic to epic hero.[53] What began as a display of human suffering concludes with divine ascendance, the first of many apotheoses in the poem:

> interea quodcumque fuit populabile flammae
> Mulciber abstulerat, nec cognoscenda remansit
> Herculis effigies, nec quidquam ab imagine ductum
> matris habet, tantumque Iovis vestigia servat.
> utque novus serpens posita cum pelle senecta
> luxuriare solet squamaque nitere recenti,
> sic, ubi mortales Tirynthius exuit artus,
> parte sui meliore viget maiorque videri
> coepit et augusta fieri gravitate verendus.

> Meanwhile, Mulciber stole whatever his flame could plunder, and no likeness of Hercules remained to be recognized. He kept nothing of his mother's image, only traces of Jove. Just as a snake, youthful after sloughing its aged skin, rejoices and shines with fresh scales, in this way when the Tirynthian hero abandoned his mortal limbs, he grew strong in the better part of himself, and he began to seem grander and to become worthy of reverence in his august majesty. (*Met.* 9.262–70)

[53] On Heracles as a liminal and transgressive figure in tragedy see Silk 1985, and Hardie 1997, 320.

Ovid directs the reader's attention to this distinctly un-Sophoclean spectacle not only through simile (266–7), which aids in the visualization, but also through the nouns *effigies* and *imago* (264), which themselves denote visual representations.

Although Sophocles had no place for a deified Heracles in the *Women of Trachis*, the end of his play inspires a sentiment at the end of Ovid's narrative. We learn that Hercules, his mortality burned away, retains vestiges of his father: *tantumque Iovis vestigia servat* (265). Similar is Hyllus' final remark in the *exodos* of the tragedy: κοὐδὲν τούτων ὅ τι μὴ Ζεύς (And there is nothing of these things which is not Zeus, 1278). His meaning is, as Malcolm Davies explains, "Zeus is present in everything that has happened."[54] Yet Ovid seems to read the line more literally and programmatically. Like the narrative and the poem at large, the vestiges of Jupiter now visible in Hercules reify a departure from Sophocles and from tragedy by putting the superhuman on display.

4 Medea: the limits of tragedy

Most events in the Hecabe narrative occur in the vicinity of the tragic *skēnē* – that is, in a Thracian landscape that includes the original Euripidean encampment, but places it off-center. The Hercules narrative, in turn, puts other locations on equal display with Sophocles' Trachis, even to the point of fracturing the poem's continuity. But what are we to make of the Medea narrative in book 7, which not only decenters but also minimizes the setting of Euripides' play, Corinth, to the fullest extent possible? Occupying over 400 verses, the narrative is spacious to the point of sprawling. It is a chronicle of Medea's early, middle, and late exploits, from helping Jason in Colchis (1–158), to arranging the murder of Pelias (297–349), to murdering her own children (391–7). It also sounds the theme of metamorphosis, most notably in the episodes involving the *Spartoi*, the armed men born of serpent's teeth (121–48), and the rejuvenation of Aeson (159–293). Most important of all, however, is the transformation of Medea from helper-maiden to sorceress as she moves from place to place.[55]

[54] Davies 1991.

[55] Newlands 1997 emphasizes the importance of Medea's transformation and finds it (deliberately) disjointed: "The Medea of *Metamorphoses* 7 is not a coherent, rounded character" (178–9). Wise 1982 reads the episode as a showcase for Medea's transformative magic. Buxton 2010 analyzes Medea's movements in Ap. *Ar.* 3 and 4. Instead of a progression such as Ovid offers, Buxton describes a dichotomy between the heroine's "restless movement" and the "controlled stillness" of using magic (29). Nugent 2008 suggests that the reader should "map Medea's moral choices onto geographical coordinates" (159).

Medea covers the most ground of any tragic hero or heroine in the *Metamorphoses*. Looking for a correlation between movement and character development, we might expect to find it in Ovid's account of the Argonautic expedition, an archetypal journey of Greco-Roman myth. But the poet devotes little space to the voyage to or from Colchis. He compresses the outward leg into the book's first six lines, singling out only Phineus and the harpies among the *multa* (5) endured by the Argonauts.[56] The homeward leg with Medea on board is even more compressed:

spolioque superbus
muneris auctorem secum, spolia altera, portans
victor Iolciacos tetigit cum coniuge portus. 158

Glorying in his prize, Jason took with him its provider, another prize, and made a victorious landing with her, now his wife, at the Iolchian harbor. (*Met.* 7.156–8)

Less than three verses for what in Apollonius, say, requires an entire book. So radical a distillation nevertheless has a crucial development for Medea: in Colchis she was a self-described *regia virgo* (21). Taken as Jason's *spolia* (157), she arrives in Iolcus his *coniunx* (158).

Coniugium has profound spatial implications in this narrative, implications familiar from the extant *Medea*. There, for example, Medea's marriage to Jason constitutes a betrayal of her father's house (πατέρα καὶ δόμους προδοῦσ' ἐμούς, 483) in the physical and genealogical senses: to abandon the ancestral dwelling is also to forsake her ancestry. Furthermore, Jason's pursuit of a new marriage necessitates his absence from the house onstage, and therefore his family. In the end he has lost access to both as he stands alone before a locked *skēnē*, his wife and children out of reach (1314–414). In Ovid, *coniugium* brings Medea to Jason's house, where she is obliged to assist in the rejuvenation of his father: *tum sic Aesonides, "o cui debere salutem | confiteor, <u>coniunx</u>"* (164–5). It is ironic that Jason should emphasize both his marriage to Medea and her assistance on the voyage, when in the tragedy he downplays the importance of both.[57]

If undervaluing the ties of marriage fosters separation in the *Medea*, recognizing them at this point in the *Metamorphoses* ought to foster unity and stability. Medea's reciprocation of the term *coniunx* in yielding to Jason's request (172) acknowledges her station, but the task itself requires

[56] Binroth-Bank 1994, 23–5, comments on the compressed voyage with attention to precedents in Vergil and other epic poets.

[57] E.g., his claim that Aphrodite alone was his savior (Κύπριν νομίζω τῆς ἐμῆς ναυκληρίας | σώτειραν εἶναι θεῶν τε κἀνθρώπων μόνην, 527–8)

magic from well beyond the *domus*.[58] Hence Medea again finds herself on the move within thirty verses of becoming Jason's wife:

> egreditur tectis vestes induta recinctas,
> nuda pedem, nudos umeris infusa capillos,
> fertque vagos mediae per muta silentia noctis
> incomitata gradus.
>
> She left the house clad in flowing raiment, her feet bare, her head bare, hair flowing to her shoulders, and wanders alone into the midnight calm. (*Met.* 7.182–5)

She exits the house in ritual garb, which is the opposite of the dress and bearing of a married woman: she goes unshod, uncovered, ungirt, and unaccompanied.[59] Whereas Euripides' Medea, even though separated from Jason, must justify her mere presence out of doors (ἐξῆλθον δόμων, | μή μοί τι μέμφησθ<ε>, 214–15), Ovid's heroine leaves behind the recently adopted role of *coniunx* and starts on the path to becoming the notorious sorceress.

Under an open sky Medea utters a prayer to Night, Hecate, Earth, and other divinities, professing her ability to alter the face of nature:

> "cum volui, ripis mirantibus amnes
> in fontes rediere suos, concussaque sisto,
> stantia concutio cantu freta, nubila pello
> nubilaque induco, ventos abigoque vocoque,
> vipereas rumpo verbis et carmine fauces,
> vivaque saxa sua convulsaque robora terra
> et silvas moveo iubeoque tremescere montes
> et mugire solum manesque exire sepulcris.
> te quoque, Luna, traho, quamvis Temesaea labores
> aera tuos minuant; currus quoque carmine nostro
> pallet avi, pallet nostris Aurora venenis."
>
> "At my will the streams, to the astonishment of their banks, have returned to their sources. With my spell I stir up and lay to rest the seas, I drive the clouds and lead them onward, I dispel the winds and summon them back. I shatter the jaws of serpents with my incantations. The living rocks and

[58] So Masselli 2009 (*Met.* 7.165). The notion of Medea's exploits being too large for the *domus* to contain seems reflected, ironically, in the wall paintings of imperial Roman houses. Carucci 2010 surveys depictions of Medea that expose male viewers' anxieties about women and potential disruptions to the *domus*. Carucci further speculates that the popularity of these and other paintings (attested at *Tr.* 2.521–8) derives from Roman tragedies about Medea, especially Ovid or Seneca.

[59] As Masselli 2009 notes, Medea's dress endows her with "la personalità irregolare" required for a sorceress; also Kenney 2011.

oaks, uprooted from their soil – these and whole forests I move, and I bid the mountains tremble, the earth groan, and spirits rise from their tombs! You also, O Moon, I draw down from the sky, despite Temesaean cymbals to lessen your struggle. The chariot of my grandfather cowers at my song! Aurora fears my poisons!" (*Met.* 7.199–209)

This is a litany of traditional sorcery, as the legions of *comparanda* in ancient literature can attest.[60] For the present, however, we need only observe that Medea's claims of spatial transformation on a global scale are apposite to a character who has already traveled far, and who is about to travel further:

"nec frustra volucrum tractus cervice draconum
currus adest." (aderat demissus ab aethere currus.) 219

"Not in vain is my chariot here, drawn by dragonwing." (The chariot was there, sent from the heavens.) (*Met.* 7.218–19)

The chariot that figures so memorably in the final episode of Euripides' *Medea* (1321–2) makes its first appearance here, but to similar effect.[61] In the play Medea and the chariot are atop the *skēnē*, a place usually reserved for divine characters. Her entrance on high stands in contrast to Jason below: although perhaps not a god in her own right, she has become more than human.[62] Ovid's Medea has not yet ascended her car, but the implications for her humanity, especially in the wake of her earth-shaking prayer, are no less dire.[63]

Whereas the Euripidean audience watches Medea fly away from Corinth, never to return, the Ovidian reader accompanies her from Iolcus on an extensive tour of Thessaly:

sublimis rapitur subiectaque Thessala Tempe
despicit et certis regionibus applicat angues;

[60] For exhaustive lists of parallels see Bömer 1976b and Masselli 2009. Wise 1982, 221, explores a tension between Medea's own self-importance and her appeal to divine aid.

[61] *Pace* Kenney 2011, who sees the chariot cast in "un nuovo ruolo" here. I agree, however, that Medea's subsequent voyages in her car suggest her dominion over both nature and her narrative ("rispecchierà il dominio che Medea ha sia sulla natura sia sulla narrativa").

[62] I single out Rehm 2002 from a long line of critics to recognize the superheroics of Medea's chariot ride: "The play's final image – the chariot of the sun with Medea and her dead children, rising high above the living – suggests a kind of cosmic *erēmia*, in which only Medea can dwell" (266). This line of interpretation has its *locus classicus* in B. M. W. Knox 1977.

[63] Compare Newlands 1997, 189: "The appearance of her chariot ... early in her tale, distances Medea physically and psychologically from the human world with its moral frames of reference." Also Wise 1982: "Since the gods appear to respond to [Medea's] rhetoric and even anticipate her need for the dragon car, the sense of her power is briefly reinforced" (22, brackets mine).

et quas Ossa tulit, quas altum Pelion herbas,
Othrysque Pindusque et Pindo maior Olympus
perspicit et placitas partim radice revellit,
partim succidit curvamine falcis aenae.
multa quoque Apidani placuerunt gramina ripis,
multa quoque Amphrysi, neque eras immunis, Enipeu;
nec non Peneos, nec non Spercheides undae
contribuere aliquid iuncosaque litora Boebes;
carpsit et Euboica vivax Anthedone gramen,
nondum mutato vulgatum corpore Glauci.

She is borne on high, looking down upon the expanse of Thessalian Tempe, and she drove her dragons to regions known to her. The herbs Ossa and lofty Pelion bore, and Othrys and Pindus and Olympus greater than Pindus – all these she surveyed. Of those that caught her fancy, some she plucked at the root and others she sheared with a bronze scythe. Many grasses, too, from Apidanus' bank were pleasing, and those from Amphrysus' also; nor were you exempt, Enipeus. The waters of Peneus and Spercheus yielded something, as did Boebe's marshy banks. And she culled from Euboean Anthedon a revitalizing grass not yet known from Glaucus' metamorphosis. (*Met.* 7.222–33)

What is the point of this? Naturally Medea, requiring herbs for her rejuvenating draught, must gather them where they grow. Yet the herbs are only a fraction of what is required. Other ingredients include such curiosities as oriental stones (*extremo lapides Oriente petitos*, 266), a lycanthrope's entrails (*ambigui prosecta lupi*, 271), and a thousand more (*mille aliis sine nomine rebus*, 275) – all of which Medea either has on hand or has gathered without the reader's awareness. Why, then, does Ovid allow us to witness the gathering of herbs when there are more exotic ingredients to be had? Thessaly, being the quintessential hotbed of magic and sorcery (especially in Roman thinking), is apt territory for Medea to explore. Nor is it wrong to suspect that Ovid is advertising his credentials as a learned poet – credentials subject to doubt in book 9 – by displaying geographical mastery. It is a particularly erudite and clever display, with Medea traveling clockwise among the mountains that ring the plain of Thessaly, and then among the various bodies of water within them.[64] The only exception is her visit to Anthedon (232–3), which faces Euboea well south of Thessaly on the Boeotian coast – the sole detour in an otherwise tidy itinerary.

[64] So Masselli 2009, after Maggiulli 2007, 90. The catalogue has two halves, one devoted to naming mountains (*l'orografica*); the other, to naming the waters (*l'idrografica*).

Alexandrian erudition, however, goes only so far. The point of Medea's long journey (*nona dies … nonaque nox*, 234–5) seems to be its transformative effect on Medea herself. Borne aloft by her dragons (*sublimis*, 222), she uses Thessaly as a proving ground in which she tests her magic. She returns in the role of a full-fledged sorceress, a role now antithetical to her role as *coniunx*:

> constitit adveniens citra limenque foresque
> et tantum caelo tegitur refugitque viriles
> contactus statuitque aras e caespite binas,
> dexteriore Hecates, at laeva parte Iuventae.

> Returning, she stopped just short of the threshold and its doors. Only the sky covered her, and she avoided her husband's touch. She built two altars out of turf, one to Hecate at right, and one to Youth at left. (*Met.* 7.238–41)

Medea's abandonment of *coniugium*, which began at 182 with her departure from the house, has taken hold. She stays on the outer side of the threshold (*citra limen*, 238), which delineates her magical self from her conjugal self, and avoids physical contact with Jason (*refugitque viriles | contactus*, 239–40). Although she does this to keep herself pure for the ritual to follow,[65] the separation becomes permanent. In subsequent episodes Medea will remain outside Jason's house, beyond his grasp, as she remains at the end of Euripides' play.

The outdoors, in turn, become a *theatron* for the rejuvenating rite. The double altars (240–1) suggest an otherworldly version of the *paraskēnium*, with its set of doors on either side, each leading into a *domus*. However, Medea's stage, the setting in which she will continue to contravene the laws of nature, is anything but domestic. There is no room for anyone from the household except herself: her servants and even Jason himself are turned away:[66]

> hinc procul Aesoniden, procul hinc iubet ire ministros
> et monet arcanis oculos removere profanos.
> diffugiunt iussi, passis Medea capillis
> bacchantum ritu flagrantes circuit aras.

> She ordered Jason away, her attendants, too, and warned them not to profane her sacred rites with their eyes. They left as bidden. Medea, her hair flowing, circled the flaming altars like a bacchant. (*Met.* 7.255–8)

[65] Kenney 2011.

[66] Aeson is present as well, but he is little more than a corpse (*exanimi similem*, 254) – another ingredient in the ritual.

This is a stage for a solo performance, through which Medea assumes her most extreme incarnation thus far, disavowing all human contact, loosening her hair once more (*passis capillis*, 257), and circling the altars like a maenad (*bacchantum ritu*, 258). In particular, Medea resembles the Ariadne of Catullus 64.63–5, whose maenadic acts of unbinding precede her Medea-like monologue. At the end of the rite we learn that Dionysus himself has been in the audience, watching from on high and planning to turn Medea's rite to his own advantage (294–6). If Ovid's brand of tragic theatricality assimilates the violence of the amphitheater, here it seems to reach in a new direction as both tragic and ritual performance merge in Medea's sorcerous bacchanal.

Medea's long, strange journey is not yet complete, for Ovid has not explored fully the implications of sorcery. Magic has proven a boon for Jason and his father; it will soon prove a bane for Pelias and his daughters:

> neve doli cessent, odium cum coniuge falsum
> Phasias adsimulat Peliaeque ad limina supplex
> confugit; atque illam, quoniam gravis ipse senecta est,
> excipiunt natae.

> Lest treachery be lacking, the Phasian incurred her husband's hatred – that was the pretense – and fled as a suppliant to Pelias' house. His daughters, since he himself was weighed down by old age, took her in. (*Met.* 7.297–300)

The heroine effortlessly crosses the line from beneficent to maleficent magic, as if deceit were motivation enough: *neve doli cessent* (297). Barbara Pavlock observes that *dolus* is the Latin equivalent of the Greek μῆδος (pl. μήδεα, *mēdea*).[67] By embarking on a career in deception, Medea begins to realize her quintessential self. This self publicly rejects the bonds of *coniugium* through a feigned quarrel with Jason: *odium cum coniuge falsum* (297). Marital strife, even simulated, takes Medea further from Jason's threshold. It also brings her closer to Corinth, where martial strife will become genuine. Moreover, in this episode she acquires a new label: *venefica*, poisoner (316), which both reflects Roman attitudes toward magic and suggests Medea's duplicitous methods in Euripides (τοιοῖσδε χρίσω φαρμάκοις δωρήματα, 789).[68]

[67] Pavlock 2009, 49.

[68] So Newlands 1997, 189, also citing Hypsipyle's use of the term when condemning Medea at *Her.* 6.19. It is worth noting that both Sophocles and Euripides wrote tragedies concerning Medea and the Peliads: Soph. *Rhizotomoi*: *TrGF* IV.534–6; Eur. *Peliades*: *TrGF* V.601–16. Hence Medea's nascent transformation into her quintessential tragic self might already be predicated on affiliations with tragic models.

After murdering Pelias (339–49, a gruesome, amphitheatrical spectacle that rivals Hecabe's vengeance against Polymestor), Medea soars to safety:

> quod nisi pennatis serpentibus isset in auras
> non exempta foret poenae.

> Had she not flown into the air with her winged serpents, she would not have evaded punishment. (*Met.* 7.350–1)

The magical chariot, which made a surprising appearance before, now arrives in almost laconic fashion, without fanfare or anticipation: by what other means does a sorcerous *venefica* travel? If the chariot is expected, so is Medea's destination. In Euripides' prologue, the Nurse declares that, following the death of Pelias, Medea exiled herself in Corinth with Jason and their sons (ξὺν ἀνδρὶ καὶ τέκνοισιν, 11). Ovid's Medea ought now to proceed to the site of her most (in)famous deeds, to which the narrative has ostensibly been leading up.

Although she ultimately reaches Corinth, she takes a most circuitous route, which for our purposes is worth examining in full, or nearly so:

> fugit alta superque
> Pelion umbrosum, Philyreia tecta, superque
> Othryn et eventu veteris loca nota Cerambi;
> hic ope nympharum sublatus in aera pennis,
> cum gravis infuso tellus foret obruta ponto,
> Deucalioneas effugit inobrutus undas.
> Aeoliam Pitanen a laeva parte relinquit
> factaque de saxo longi simulacra draconis
> Idaeumque nemus, quo nati furta iuvencum
> occuluit Liber falsi sub imagine cervi,
> quaque pater Corythi parva tumulatus harena est,
> et quos Maera novo latratu terruit agros,
> Eurypylique urbem, qua Coae cornua matres
> gesserunt tum cum discederet Herculis agmen,
> Phoebeamque Rhodon et Ialysios Telchinas,
> quorum oculos ipso vitiantes omnia visu
> Iuppiter exosus fraternis subdidit undis.
> transit et antiquae Cartheia moenia Ceae,
> qua pater Alcidamas placidam de corpore natae
> miraturus erat nasci potuisse columbam.
> inde lacus Hyries videt et Cycneia Tempe,
> quae subitus celebravit olor … 372
> adiacet his Pleuron, in qua trepidantibus alis 382
> Ophias effugit natorum vulnera Combe.
> inde Calaureae Letoidos aspicit arva

in volucrem versi cum coniuge conscia regis.
dextera Cyllene est, in qua cum matre Menephron
concubiturus erat saevarum more ferarum.
Cephison procul hinc deflentem fata nepotis
respicit in tumidam phocen ab Apolline versi
Eumelique domum lugentis in aere natum.

She flees on high over shady Pelion, the home of Philyra, and over Othrys and the places famed for the fortune of old Cerambus: he with the nymphs' aid was borne aloft on wings, when the earth was sunken deep beneath the sea, and so he avoided drowning in Deucalion's flood. On her left she passes Aeolian Pitane, and the stone statue of the dragon. She passes the grove of Ida, where Bacchus hid the bull stolen by his son under the guise of a stag, and where Corythus' father is interred beneath a small dune of sand, and the fields where Maera once wrought terror with her strange barking. She passed Eurypylus' city, where the matrons of Cos grew horns as Hercules' band departed. She passed Rhodes, Phoebus' island, and the Telchines of Ialysos, whose all-devastating gaze Jupiter hated and buried beneath his brother's waves. She crosses over the walls of Carthaea on ancient Cea, where Alcidamas would marvel that a gentle dove could be born from his daughter's body. Next she sees the lake of Hyrie and Cycnus' vale, famed for the sudden appearance of the swan … Nearby lies Pleuron, where Combe, Ophius' daughter, avoided injury on her sons' fluttering wings. Next she sees the lands of Calaurea, Leto's island, which knows all about the pair, the king and his wife, changed into birds. On the right is Cyllene, where Menephron would mount his mother, as wild animals do. Far from Cyllene she looks upon Cephisus as he laments the fate of his grandson, whom Apollo turned into a swollen seal, and upon the house of Eumelus, who mourns his airborne son. (*Met.* 7.351–72, 382–90)

Unlike her prior flight, in which Medea circled mainly over Thessaly, this voyage covers much of Greece and Asia Minor – almost a one-woman Argonautica in its scope. Rather than flying directly to Corinth from Iolcus, a southern course over eastern Aetolia and the Corinthian Gulf, she heads east across the Aegean, along the Asian coast, and back over to the mainland, where she zigs and zags over the northern Peloponnese.

As Medea has no herbs to gather this time, readers have to work all the harder to make her meanderings relevant. One approach is to connect the heroine with the legends of the various sites. For instance, it is appropriate that she fly over Ialysus, the home of the Telchines, whose dark magic is comparable to her own (365); or that she see the stone dragon of Pitane from her dragon-chariot (*simulacra draconis*, 358); or that most legends involve avian transformations, which is the more typical way for Ovidian characters to take flight; or that many involve the loss of children, as

Medea's own myth will.[69] Despite these connections, it is most tempting to construe the heroine's voyage as another scholarly exercise, whereby Ovid catalogues abstruse transformations that might otherwise remain untold. Her journey is delineated less by geography than by mythography.[70]

Nevertheless, we can read Medea's flight in terms of tragic movement and the continuing metamorphosis of her character. At some point she must again be Jason's *coniunx* in order for her narrative to achieve a tragic denouement.[71] But not quite yet: her tour of the Aegean in Ovid is really a detour, in which she, along with the reader, hesitates over her place within her own legend. The sense of delaying the inevitable heightens, particularly in the latter legs of the voyage. After her second crossing of the sea and her sighting of Carthaea, Medea passes over the vicinity of Corinth no fewer than four times (if we assume a relatively straight trajectory): first on the way from Carthaea to Hyrie, then from Pleuron to Calaurea, next from Calaurea to Mt. Cyllene, and finally from Cyllene to the Cephisus.

As the inevitable is postponed, Medea's journey transcends her own narrative and adds a metapoetic dimension to her character. Pavlock has described the catalogue of sites as "an image of the second half of the *Metamorphoses*," a preview of themes and even individual stories in books 8 and beyond.[72] Pavlock rightly stresses the connections between "Ovid's problematic heroine [and] Ovid's own production of clever plots that subvert traditional mores."[73] Yet the connections arrive by way of an underappreciated transformation in Medea herself. As often in the *Metamorphoses*, the external narrator adopts the personae of his characters, who in turn become internal narrators. Here Medea's perspective shifts outwards and assimilates to that of the external narrator. The voyage empowers her to look beyond the limits of her own story and to see, with Ovidian eyes, into the stories of others. In the epilogue of the extant tragedy, Medea attains prophetic vision and forecasts Jason's inglorious end from her

[69] On these and other connections between Medea and the sites over which she passes see Binroth-Bank 1994, 140, and Pavlock 2009, 50–9.

[70] Binroth-Bank 1994, 139: "Ihre Reiseroute wird demnach nicht von der Geographie, sondern von der Mythographie bestimmt." Compare Anderson 1972 (after *Met.* 7.349): "In this section, we are not interested in Medea as a dramatic character at all. She merely serves as a vehicle for the amusing display of Ovid's erudition." Likewise Newlands 1997, 190, and Kenney 2011. Tarrant 2005 notes Ovid's "dazzling display of arcane learning," but finds in Medea's itinerary a deliberate marginalization of the heroine, "who is now less interesting than the places over which she passes in her flight" (71).

[71] Kenney 2011 notes the conspicuous absence of Jason from the narrative at this point, with no mention of how he must arrive in Corinth before Medea.

[72] Pavlock 2009, 41, with further analysis on 49–60.

[73] Pavlock 2009, 60 (brackets mine).

chariot (1386–8). She sees beyond the tragic here-and-now into the there-and-then, momentarily crossing the boundaries of her own story. From this perspective the airborne heroine of the *Metamorphoses*, whose metapoetic sight has made her most Ovidian, is also most Euripidean.

Medea's arrival in Corinth makes for an elegant segue:

> tandem vipereis Ephyren Pirenida pennis
> contigit; hic aevo veteres mortalia primo
> corpora vulgarunt pluvialibus edita fungis. 393

> At last by dragonwing she reached Pirenian Ephyre: here the old tales say that in the beginning the bodies of mortal men arose from mushrooms in the rain. (*Met.* 7.391–3)

Those who have wondered when the heroine's chariot would come to rest find validation in *tandem* (391): at last, it seems, the long-expected moment when Medea reaches Corinth and commits her most infamous deeds. At the same time, Ovid's introduction of the city, with its myth of mushrooms-turned-men, is obscure. The poet nowhere mentions Corinth by name, neither here nor in what follows. Instead he uses the archaic and much less common Ephyre (391), modified by an adjectival form of the spring, Pirene, which might (or might not) clarify the city in question. Corinth appears, when it does appear, as one more point on the heroine's itinerary of metamorphic places. *tandem* aside, Ovid depends on the erudition of his readers to know that Medea's narrative arc is winding down.

Even after a cryptic prelude, some might anticipate a full account of Jason's infidelity and Medea's revenge on Glauce, as well as insight into the murder of her sons. Yet Medea flees after only four verses, making Corinth less a destination than a way-station:[74]

> sed postquam Colchis arsit nova nupta venenis
> flagrantemque domum regis mare vidit utrumque, 395
> sanguine natorum perfunditur impius ensis,
> ultaque se male mater Iasonis effugit arma.
> (*Met.* 7.394–7)

The salient points of the Euripidean play are here, as well as an Ovidian detail, the burning of the palace (*flagrantemque domum regis*, 395), which might derive from the poet's lost *Medea*.[75] Certainly there is nothing on the order of the preceding episodes, with their psychological and supernatural

[74] So Binroth-Bank 1994, 143.

[75] Chapter 2, p. 43, where these lines are translated in full.

embellishment.[76] Rather, Ovid offers a synopsis grossly out of proportion with the reader's expectations, a deliberate anticlimax. No narrative about Medea would be complete without the events at Corinth, and yet Ovid's perversely abbreviated account seems to ask how necessary these events actually are. What can they add to a narrative that has already displayed Medea as maiden, wife, sorceress, poisoner, and narrator? Perhaps only that the heroine is also a mother, *mater* (397), the only instance in which the word is applied to her.

After the heroine's departure from Corinth there would seem little left to tell. Yet one episode remains. Accordingly, the heroine flies – directly, this time – from Corinth to Athens, a fulfillment of the famous oath scene in Euripides, in which Aegeus promises Medea asylum (663–758). Along the way she takes notice of two other avian transformations, those of Periphas and Phene (399–400) and of Alcyone (400–1, not the heroine of book 11). Medea's metanarrative powers are still intact, and prompt us to ask how much further she can go. At first glance, it seems that her arrival in Athens is a step backward. She revisits two of her earlier roles, guest and wife, courtesy of Aegeus, who receives her as the Peliads did (*excipiunt natae*, 300; *excipit hanc*, 402) and marries her as Jason did (*thalami quoque foedere iungit*, 403). Lest her story repeat itself, Medea tries to poison Theseus with aconite, but Aegeus intervenes without harm to himself or his son (404–24). Thus ends Medea's brief career as a *noverca*, a label Ovid does not grant, but which readily comes to mind from his account of the Iron Age and its atrocities: *lurida terribiles miscent aconita novercae* (1.147). With this latest role Medea pushes the time-frame of the Euripidean tragedy to its limit, embodying a future only suggested in the play.

The (amphi)theatrical spectacles of the *Metamorphoses* depend upon the reader, who brings to bear metatheatrical knowledge of the original stories and their genre. We are more alive to tensions and synergies between epic and tragedy because we remember, or because we are made to remember, the dramas that Ovid retells. Our mindfulness extends to the travels of individual characters through the poem's landscapes, as we track their proximity to or the distance from the settings of their model plays. Although the original *skēnē* is now one *locus* among many, it nonetheless exerts a certain pull within the narrative. Ovid's Hecabe remains within the orbit of the Euripidean *skēnē*, the Achaean camp. Hercules does

[76] Tarrant 2005 calls the passage an "implicit comment on the development (or more precisely the degradation) of Medea's character over the course of the first half of [b]ook 7" (71).

manage to avoid Sophocles' Trachis on his way to achieving godhood, but his overall trajectory – even if it follows a dotted line from Euboea to Mt. Oeta – had already been mapped out on the tragic stage.

Not even Medea, Ovid's signature heroine, can escape the pull of Corinth. But once in Athens, she travels even further than Hercules, who though a god remains within the sphere of the poem (*sensit Atlas pondus*, 9.273). After the botched attempt to poison Theseus, the narrator shifts his focus away from Medea to Athens and its legends, where it will remain until book 9. Medea escapes under her own power – without her chariot – vanishing in a conjured puff of smoke: *effugit illa necem nebulis per carmina motis* (7.424). This is her most impressive metamorphosis yet. Throughout the narrative Medea has used song to change the world around her, and on her journey from Iolcus to Athens she has partaken in the narrator's song. Now she musters *carmina* through which she eludes even the poet and takes leave of his *mundus* for good.

CHAPTER FIVE

Tollens ad sidera palmas exclamat
Staging rhetoric

The *Metamorphoses* contains places that function as stages, and these stages offer displays of many kinds. In addition to visual displays of the violent and the supernatural, the Ovidian *locus* also permits the display of words: prayers, songs, conversations, debates, stories, and especially monologues. This chapter examines Ovid's monologues in relation to the rhetoric of tragedy, a genre grounded in the physical realities of the *theatron* yet dependent on words to accomplish its business. If the *Metamorphoses* is a further milestone in Ovid's career as a Roman tragedian, the solo speeches of his heroes and heroines ought to be legible in these terms.[1] The poet's affinity for spectacle, we have seen, correlates with Roman tastes, which tragedians and tragic productions had a hand in shaping. His affinity for rhetoric, however, evokes Roman tragic theatricality more than any other aspect of his poetry and preserves the Latin tragedians' most distinctive contribution to the genre. My discussion will focus on the monologues of Medea (*Met.* 7), Hecabe (13), and Hercules (9), three of the epic's longest solo speeches. Each follows conventions of tragic rhetoric, which Ovid manipulates to create original dramatic vignettes. Not only are these pieces emblematic of his tragic program in the *Metamorphoses* (and, by extension, in the *Heroides*), they also hint at the rhetorical masterpiece we have lost in his *Medea*.

As a preface, let us consider the short speech of Philomela (*Met.* 6), who matches the violence done to her by Tereus with a violent rebuke:

> mox ubi mens rediit, passos laniata capillos,
> lugenti similis, caesis plangore lacertis,[2]
> intendens palmas, "o diris barbare factis,

[1] The topic of Ovid and rhetoric is immense. Let me here recommend Auhagen 1999 as a comprehensive introduction, appropriately focused on monologues throughout the Ovidian corpus. See especially 22–6 on monologues in drama; 45–53, the *Heroides*; 123–30, the *Metamorphoses*. Further thoughts and reflections, much more general, in Auhagen 2007.

[2] I follow the text of Rosati 2009, which retains lines 532 and 537–8.

o crudelis," ait, "nec te mandata parentis
cum lacrimis movere piis nec cura sororis
nec mea virginitas nec coniugialia iura?
omnia turbasti; paelex ego facta sororis,
tu geminus coniunx, hostis mihi debita Procne.[3]
quin animam hanc, ne quod facinus tibi, perfide, restet,
eripis? atque utinam fecisses ante nefandos
concubitus; vacuas habuissem criminis umbras.
si tamen haec superi cernunt, si numina divum
sunt aliquid, si non perierunt omnia mecum,
quandocumque mihi poenas dabis. ipsa pudore
proiecto tua facta loquar. si copia detur,
in populos veniam! si silvis clausa tenebor,
implebo silvas et conscia saxa movebo!
audiet haec aether, et si deus ullus in illo est!"

When her faculties returned, she tore her tangled hair, and slashing her arms and beating her breast like a mourner she put forth her hands and said to Tereus, "What you have done is an abomination, you barbarian! You have no pity! My father's wishes, his tears, they meant nothing to you! What of my sister's love, my virginity, your marriage? Everything is out of place because of you. You have shamed my sister by making me your whore. You have become a husband twice over. Procne has to be my rival. Liar! Why not kill me? You've done everything else. I wish you had before you raped me, so I would have died pure, an innocent ghost. If the gods above witness these things, if they have any power at all, if it hasn't all been lost with me, then someday you will pay the price. I myself – modesty be damned – will tell what you have done. If I have the chance, I will proclaim it in public! If held captive I will fill the forest with my voice and call the stones to witness! The very heavens will hear of these things, and whatever god there is as well!" (*Met.* 6.531–48)

Although not a true solo *rhesis* (speech, pl. *rheseis*), Philomela's rebuke can inform our appreciation of Ovid's monologues. First and foremost, this is a display of strong emotion, a mixture of sorrow, despair, and anger. Time and again in the *Metamorphoses* a character reaches a high emotional pitch, often after a period of protracted inner turmoil. At this point the narrator seems to step aside and let the hero or heroine speak for himself or herself. The narrator is still in control and is simply speaking in character. Yet he need not do so, since he is able to explicate his characters' inner thoughts, desires, and fears in his own persona as easily as he might describe a landscape or a work of art. Ovidian characters speak because

[3] *Procne*: Withof's emendation of *poena*; see the apparatus of Tarrant 2004.

the poet has decided that their emotions are best conveyed in their own words.

Second, Philomela's speech is inextricable from its *locus*. She harangues Tereus inside stables, *stabula* (521), which have already served as the setting of the rape.[4] The stables are described in modest terms (we learn they are *alta* and *silvis obscura*, also 521), but they are substantial enough to house a brutal spectacle of sexual violation. Ovid has turned the *skēnē* of the tragic stage inside out and allowed the reader to venture within. This small demonstration of how epic transcends barriers to storytelling is enough to demarcate the rape spatially – to create an uncomfortably intimate *theatron*. And just as there is something to "see" (however much one might not wish to), there is also something to "hear": the stables now become a listening place, wherein Philomela gives voice to her plight. She thematizes her own audibility, highlighting her potential to convert any setting, however nondescript, into an auditorium – even the trees, the rocks, and the air above (547–8). Philomela substantiates the rather tenuous here-and-now of the *stabula* through rhetoric and creates a genuine sense of place.

Finally, this forceful rebuke exemplifies how Ovid uses rhetoric to create original and distinctive drama, particularly when a narrative has had a prior existence on the tragic stage. We know of no fewer than three plays entitled *Tereus* by Sophocles, Livius Andronicus, and Accius, respectively – all of which are now lost, and at least one of which (Sophocles') featured Philomela.[5] In uttering her speech Philomela evokes the rhetoric of her former genre without necessarily repeating her tragic counterparts verbatim. Her speech cannot have echoed Sophocles' heroine in any case, since Sophocles most likely presented Philomela as a mute, taking the stage after Tereus had cut out her tongue. The *rhesis* of Ovid's Philomela is nothing less than extraordinary, for it enables her to be heard as a tragic heroine, perhaps for the first (and last) time in her literary history.[6]

1 Talking to oneself

The *Metamorphoses* boasts thirteen extended monologues of fifteen lines or more: Narcissus (3.442–73), Boreas (6.687–701), Medea (7.11–71), Scylla

[4] *OLD s.v. stabulum* 1.

[5] On the fragments of Tereus plays see Chapter 3, n. 33. Philomela is attested in Soph. *Tereus*, *TrGF* IV.581.5–10, 589.1–2, and 595. On the relationship of Ovid's Tereus narrative to the Sophoclean fragments see Fitzpatrick 2001, Curley 2003, and March 2003.

[6] See further Curley 2003, 190–3.

(8.44–80 and 108–42), Althaea (8.481–511), Hercules (9.176–204), Byblis (9.474–516 and 585–629), Iphis (9.726–63), Myrrha (10.320–55), Hecabe (13.494–532), and the other Iphis (14.718–32).[7] This list reveals an essential characteristic of Ovidian monologues, of which Philomela's *rhesis* is also exemplary: women are the great orators of the poem, delivering nine of the thirteen soliloquies, or 363 of 454 total verses.[8] The dominance of female oratory continues the enterprise begun with the *Heroides*, which are rhetorical in the extreme.[9]

The ostensible purpose of an Ovidian monologue is the same as that of tragic *rheseis* in general: to articulate thoughts, laments, questions, plans, and rationales that might otherwise go unexpressed or that are best expressed in the first person.[10] In particular, Ovid's speakers attempt (in Georgia Nugent's useful formulation) "to regain agency through the power of redescription": that is, to redefine and even transform the self by interrogating social conventions and their vocabulary.[11] Often the act of articulation becomes an end in itself, a validation of rhetorical form. The monologue does not necessarily result from desire or despair. Rather, these emotions might occur in order to be expressed out loud, artificially and self-consciously so. In this regard, Ovidian soliloquies again recall the single letters of the *Heroides*. Without hope of a reply, the introspective form of the letter sends its own message and helps to shape the content. Literary self-reflection might well be uniquely Roman,[12] but there is no denying that talking to oneself at length is unrealistic.[13] Ironically, the artificial

[7] Monologues excluded under this criterion are those of Pyramus (4.108–15, 118), Thisbe (4.148–61), Procne (6.631–5), Deianira (9.143–51), Apollo (10.196–208), and Ajax (13.387–90). Fifteen verses is an admittedly arbitrary length, but shorter monologues afford little room to explore emotion and have lesser dramatic impact. I also exclude the song of Polyphemus (13.789–869), which is more monody and panegyric than monologue, and the didactic *rhesis* of Pythagoras (15.75–478), which is addressed to an audience that ostensibly includes Numa.

[8] Thus Solodow 1988: "[E]xamples abound of dramatic monologues, especially those of women in distress" (19); and Auhagen 1999, 12. Female rhetorical dominance is still true under a more inclusive count of monologues in the poem. For example, if the six speeches catalogued in the previous note were considered along with the thirteen extended monologues, women would still account for twelve out of the eighteen, or 391 out of 511 verses.

[9] Chapter 3, pp. 60–1.

[10] Compare the thematic groups of monologues in the *Met.* proposed by R. Heinze 1919, 110–11 (and cited in Auhagen 1999, 124): (1) indignation/threats, (2) last words, (3) laments for the dead, and (4) inner conflicts between two opposing forces. Medea's monologue belongs to Heinze's fourth category; Hecabe's, to the third; Hercules', the first and second.

[11] Nugent 2008, 171. Compare Bate 1993: "The character's 'self' is both created and transformed by the very process of verbal articulation; her or his 'being' is invented rhetorically" (5).

[12] So Auhagen 1999, 30–1, with examples from Cicero, the younger Seneca, and others.

[13] Auhagen 1999, 16–18, takes stock of scholarly reactions to the artificiality of Ovid's monologues, particularly how the form cultivates "pathos at any price" (17, the formulation applied by Sabot

convention of the dramatic monologue is used, as Jonathan Bate puts it, to "create the illusion that a fictional character has an interior life."[14]

I use the term "artificial," but only to highlight the strangeness of monologues outside the contexts of epic and dramatic poetry. They have always made sense within those genres, beginning with Homer, whose characters routinely talk to themselves πρὸς θυμόν. These interior moments, like other techniques of epic narrative, found their way to the tragic stage, whose great *rheseis* thrust their speakers into the proverbial spotlight, holding the attention of the audience and prolonging dramatic time. Although later poets of epic reincorporated tragic rhetoric back into its genre of origin, the speeches themselves preserved the rhetorical traditions of the stage in all their sophistication. The Medea of the *Argonautica*, for example, delivers monologues that anticipate her expressive "future" in Euripides. Ariadne in Catullus 64 and Dido in the *Aeneid* likewise narrate their own suffering. Their soliloquies respond to Medea in Apollonius and Euripides, and to as many other tragic heroines and heroes as readers are prepared to seek out. That said, all three epic poets mobilize tragic monologues as code, that is, as a system of discourse that flourished in tragedy. For Vergil in particular, these rhetorical displays provide direct access to the tragic, a point of entry into an eminent Greek genre, which in Rome had traveled from the stage to recital halls and to the page on the strength of rhetoric.[15] The result, by Ovid's day, was that any monologue by itself could evoke the tragic. As Georges Lafaye noted long ago, "[I]l est impossible de séparer la rhétorique de la tragédie."[16]

One point about setting, also obvious upon reflection. The promulgation of tragedy in textual form makes possible what is relatively rare on the stage: true monologues, or speeches delivered by characters who are utterly alone. In classical Greek tragedy the almost constant presence of the chorus leaves little room for solitude.[17] Even Medea's great monologue

1976 to the *Heroides*, but an apt descriptor of speeches in the *Met.*). Auhagen, 25, also cites Pfister 1988, who goes so far as to equate self-conversation in reality with pathological deviance (131–3).

[14] Bate 1993, 5.

[15] Chapter 2, pp. 26–7 and 36–7.

[16] Lafaye 1904, 153, whose study of rhetoric in the *Met.* was incorporated into his discussion of tragedy. Similar verdicts in R. Heinze 1919, 124; Binroth-Bank 1994, 33–5; and Auhagen 1999, 127–8. Jouteur (ed.) 2009, 7, correlates the textualization of tragedy with the migration of rhetoric from the legal and political spheres.

[17] A point central to Leo 1908: "Es kann nach allem wohl mit Sicherheit behauptet werden, daß die Tragiker und besonders Euripides dem Monolog deshalb eine so geringe Ausbildung gegeben haben, weil die Existenz des Chors sie daran verhinderte, nicht weil sie den Monolog aus künstlerischen Erwägungen verwarfen" (35).

(Eur. *Med.* 1021–80) is not really a monologue in the strict sense, since it occurs in front of the Corinthian women as well as the children themselves. For true solo speeches in extant tragedy, we must look to plays in which the chorus leaves the stage after the *parodos*, or in which characters are alone before the *parodos*.[18] Of the five plays in the first category, three contain solo *rheseis*: *Alcestis*, in which Heracles resolves to go down to Hades (837–60); *Helen*, in which Menelaus laments his misfortunes after Troy (386–434); and *Ajax*, in which the titular hero makes preparations for his suicide (815–65).[19] Although plays in the second category are too many to list individually,[20] their sheer number is not significant in itself: prologues, which contextualize a drama, rarely bear the emotional burden of an Ovidian soliloquy.[21] Perhaps we should look also to instances of monody or solo song. In the *Trojan Women* Hecabe, alone onstage after the departure of Athena and Poseidon, sings a lament for the fall of Troy (98–152).[22] This and other examples of monody in Greek tragedy, which typically operate at high emotional registers, are the forerunners of *cantica* in Roman tragedy. Ovid's monologues probably incorporate the traditions

[18] I pass over so-called "entrance monologues," speeches delivered by entering characters who believe they are alone, without realizing others are already present onstage (e.g., Theseus entering at Eur. *Supp.* 87, and noticing Aethra at 92; Athena entering at *Eum.* 397, and noticing Orestes and the Furies at 406). Most of these monologues are brief, and therefore contain limited emotional interest, with one notable exception: Pentheus at *Bacch.* 215–47, in which he reveals his deep distrust of Dionysus and his rituals before noticing Cadmus and Teiresias. On entrance monologues see Bain 1977, 61–6 (re. Euripides) and 67–70 (re. Aeschylus), who notes the suspension of dramatic time in such *rheseis*: "[T]here is … a kind of freezing of the action, with all attention concentrated on one actor to the exclusion of the others" (70). See also Tarrant 1978, 231–41, who, following Leo 1908, traces the development of entrance monologues from Athenian tragedy to New Comedy.

[19] There is an additional monologue at *Alc.* 747–72, delivered by a servant who expresses misgivings about Heracles' merry-making; at *Hel.* 483–514, moreover, Menelaus has a second monologue after his encounter with the porter. The two other classical instances of the chorus exiting after the *parodos*, *Eum.* 232–43 and *Rhes.* 565–673, do not yield extended monologues. In the former play, Orestes utters a brief prayer to Athena before the Furies re-enter, while the latter contains dialogue between Athena, Odysseus, and Diomedes, and later between Athena and Aeneas.

[20] It is easier, in fact, to note extant plays that open with two or more characters onstage than to note those opening with only one: Aesch. *Pers.*, *PV* (but note Prometheus' monologue, discussed below), *Sept.*, and *Supp.*; Eur. *Heracl.* (though the children with Iolaus do not speak), *HF*, *IA*, and *Rhes.*; Soph., all but one (*Trach.*).

[21] Closest, perhaps, are the prologues of *Trach.*, in which an anxious Deianira speculates about her husband's fate; *Andr.*, in which Andromache recounts her new life of servitude; and *PV*, in which Prometheus agonizes over being fettered to the rock (88–113, following the departure of Might, Violence, and Hephaestus).

[22] Other monodies in Athenian tragedy before the *parodos* include those by the eponymous characters at *Hec.* 59–97, *Andr.* 103–16, *Hel.* 164–78, *Ion* 82–183, Soph. *El.* 86–120, *PV* 114–27 (which Taplin 1977, 247, describes as a "gesture in the direction of monody"). Standard discussions of monody include Barner 1971 and the introduction of Barlow 1986 (with emphasis on Euripides).

of solo song as much as solo speech, particularly when his characters are under extreme duress.[23]

Although opportunities for true monologues or monodies were relatively rare on the Greek stage, they seem to have been more frequent on the Roman stage, which apparently was more spacious. Over time tragic choruses became detached from their dramas. The process was already under way in the late fifth century: Aristotle reports that Agathon composed choral odes on stock themes (ἐμβόλιμα, *Poet.* 18.1456a), which replaced odes composed for specific plays. This practice likely continued with tragedy of the Roman republic and beyond. Further detachment occurred through the practice of restricting the chorus from the stage altogether, except for the performance of odes. Richard Tarrant argues plausibly that the frequent absence of the chorus from the episodes of Senecan tragedies is conventional from Agathon onward.[24] A stage less populated by choruses might have yielded more instances of pure monologue. One such instance, already discussed in Chapter 2, seems preserved in a fragment of Pacuvius' *Periboea* (*SRF* 1.284–6), in which Diomedes speaks directly to his *animus* and *mens*.[25] Certainly, a detached chorus helps to explain the frequency of *cantica* in Roman tragedy, to judge from their considerable representation in the fragments. Just as Ovidian monologues perpetuate the rhetorical traditions of Roman tragedy at large, so the absolute isolation in which his characters perform might reflect conventions of tragic staging closer to his own era.

Of course, the solitude of speakers has been a trope of epic from the very beginning: Hector, in a celebrated example, debates with himself outside the walls of Troy (*Il.* 22.98–130). It is easy for epic narrators, with their all-encompassing perspectives, to isolate their characters and afford them privacy. Yet while Ovid often revels in the mutability of epic time and space, the private settings of his monologues nevertheless evoke individual performances on the tragic stage, even those which occur in the presence of other characters. On the one hand, Ovid exploits the theatrical potential of the *locus* by supplying it with sounds as well as sights. As Philomela reminds us, any viewing place easily becomes a listening place. When

[23] It is worth remembering that fr. 2 of Ovid's *Medea* is from a *canticum* in which the heroine wrestles with a dilemma, and which recalls her great monologue in Euripides. See Chapter 2, p. 42.

[24] Tarrant 1978, 221–8: "Seneca … thought, at least in some scenes, of a chorus which took the stage only to perform its lyric pieces and which retired from sight during the episodes; this is just the sort of chorus one would expect to find in Greek tragedy after Agathon" (225). Leo 1908 charts the rise of pure comic monologue in the absence of the chorus in New Comedy (35–46).

[25] Pacuv. *Periboea*: see Chapter 2, pp. 26–7.

speaking with themselves, Ovid's heroes and heroines are truly center stage, the solitude of each creating a vacuum to be filled with rhetoric. On the other hand, the great *rheseis* of tragedy are expressions of the self – of an "I."[26] This singular perspective, when combined with a speaker's emotional or psychological detachment, adds a distancing effect[27] and creates a semblance of solitude. Hence Medea's great monologue in Euripides, regardless of who else is onstage, is a moment of profound isolation and loneliness. Ovid's solitary *loci* map out in physical terms the inner desolation that tragic speakers must put into words.

2 Medea: a heroine's debut

The monologue of Medea (*Met.* 7.11–71) will bear out many of these principles, even as it points us in new directions. W. S. Anderson claims that Medea offers the "first dramatic soliloquy in the *Metamorphoses*."[28] That honor actually belongs to Narcissus, whose extended monologue in book 3 is perhaps a further "echo of Oedipus."[29] Nor is Medea the first woman to speak in solitude: Thisbe utters a brief solo *rhesis* before committing suicide (4.148–61, mourning over Pyramus' corpse). Nevertheless, the speech of Medea is the poem's first *fully* dramatic monologue, and at just over sixty verses, it is the longest in the poem by man or woman. Programmatically speaking, Medea becomes a prototype for other Ovidian heroines, even as she responds to incarnations of herself in other texts and authors. Her speech, in which she "creates, rather than describes, a relationship with Jason,"[30] offers hesitant and formative versions of tragic rhetorical commonplaces and heralds flights of imagination still to come. This is the portrait of a heroine gradually coming into her own.

[26] So Auhagen 1999: "[E]in ‚Individuum' — ein ‚Ich' — in ‚Einsamkeit' sich äußert (laut redend, schriftlieb oder gedanklich), wobei es keine Rolle spielt, ob dieses Individuum (physisch) wirklich allein ist" (22). Auhagen, 22–5, draws upon the work of Leo 1908 and Schadewaldt 1926, who expanded Leo's criterion of physical isolation to include inner or psychological isolation.

[27] Distancing effect: Auhagen 1999 *passim* offers "distanzierte Perspektive" as a structural criterion for evaluating monologues in Ovid and elsewhere.

[28] Anderson 1972 (before *Met.* 7.1).

[29] I allude to the subtitle of Gildenhard and Zissos 2000, "echoes of Oedipus." Upon recognizing his reflection in the pool, Narcissus utters a series of rhetorical questions – *quid faciam? roger anne rogem? quid deinde rogabo?* (3.465) – a prelude to a desperation speech (on which *topos* see pp. 147–50, below).

[30] Wise 1982, 18. Wise focuses on the transformative power of language in the Medea narrative, especially in magical incantations. Compare Pavlock 2009, 41–9, who describes how the structure of Medea's speech "lends a concreteness to her expectations" (41).

As suggested earlier, it is to Euripides first and foremost that we owe our association of Medea with powerful speeches. But her reputation as a rhetorician is also much indebted to book 3 of Apollonius' *Argonautica*, and the love-struck heroine made famous there. In comparison with her Ovidian counterpart, the Apollonian Medea speaks volumes, including dialogues with Chalciope (674–738) and Jason (975–1145), as well as three monologues (464–70, 636–44, and 771–801).[31] Apollonius, in giving his young Medea so many different opportunities to speak, tried to match the grand rhetoric of Euripides' play and even (within the chronology of the myth) to anticipate it. Medea's speech in *Met.* 7, however, is less a matter of output than of emphasis. Her *rhesis*, for all intents and purposes, is her great monologue in the poem, whereby Ovid recuperates her rhetorical facility in Apollonius back to Euripides.[32]

Ovid establishes his rhetorical focus on Medea not only by consolidating many speeches into one, but also by presenting the one as soon as possible. In Euripides Medea delivers her monologue toward the end of both her tragedy and her mythological career. In Apollonius her first monologue comes early in her career, but late in the book: about 220 verses separate it from the heroine's first appearance. In Ovid Medea delivers her monologue at the earliest possible moment in her narrative and in her career. The outward voyage of the *Argo*, occupies only six verses (1–6),[33] and once it is moored on the Phasis (6), Jason fades into the background while Medea comes to the forefront:

> dumque adeunt regem Phrixeaque vellera poscunt
> lexque datur Minyis magnorum horrenda laborum,
> concipit interea validos Aeëtias ignes
> et luctata diu, postquam ratione furorem
> vincere non poterat, "frustra, Medea, repugnas:
> nescioquis deus obstat," ait.

While the Minyans approach the king and demand the fleece of Phrixus, and while a terrifying mandate for mighty deeds is given, the daughter of Aeëtes is seized with a powerful passion and, though she struggled against it for a long time, after she was unable to beat back her madness with rea-

[31] Binroth-Bank 1994, 31, also comments on the trio of monologues in Apollonius.

[32] Compare Wise 1982, who finds in Medea's "romantic musings" an "Alexandrian context for her infatuation" (16). The only other speech of Medea in *Met.* 7 with the scale of her initial monologue is her prayer to Night, Hecate, and Earth (192–219). This is technically a solo *rhesis*, but it operates on a global instead of a personal scale, with Medea exploring not her emotions but her ability to alter the face of nature: see Chapter 4, pp. 123–4.

[33] Chapter 4, p. 122.

> son, she says, "Resistance is useless, Medea: some or other god stands in your way." (*Met.* 7.7–12)

The *locus* of her speech is unknown, but it is substantiated by Medea's very presence as subject of the main verbs *concipit* (9) and *ait* (12). The latter provides her initial *raison d'être* in the poem. Though she ostensibly experiences a long struggle (*luctata diu*, 10) beforehand, the narrator introduces Medea, and therefore her speech, as soon as possible. What follows is not only her great monologue, but also her rhetorical debut, in which she speaks with "a self-consciousness that suggests [her] awareness of her own literary past."[34]

The impetus of Medea's *rhesis* is her desire for Jason, first glimpsed in the *validos ignes* of verse 9. This is a tidy summary, but Medea's own rhetoric is anything but tidy, at least at first. She initially struggles to define her terms:

> "frustra, Medea, repugnas:
> nescioquis deus obstat," ait, "mirumque nisi hoc est,
> aut aliquid certe simile huic, quod amare vocatur." 13
>
> She says, "Resistance is useless, Medea: some god or other stands in your way. I wonder whether this is not that thing called 'love,' or something very close to it." (*Met.* 7.11–13)

The heroine who in other texts will outwit her enemies time and again and demonstrate mastery of the spoken and the written word, can scarcely describe *amor*, let alone recognize it: *mirumque nisi hoc est ... quod amare vocatur* (12–13) is patent circumlocution.[35] So awkward an attempt to verbalize her emotions calls attention to the monologue itself, a mode of discourse disposed toward verbalizing emotion.

Opposing Medea's desire, however tentatively described, is not indifference on Jason's part, but her own anxiety over betraying Aeëtes:

> "nam cur iussa patris nimium mihi dura videntur?
> sunt quoque dura nimis!" 15
>
> "For why else do my father's commands seem too harsh? Surely they are!" (*Met.* 7.14–15)

Her father's precepts (*iussa patris*, 14) represent the rational and the familiar. In articulating them, Medea at last defines their opposite, *cupido* or desire:

[34] Pavlock 2009, 40 (brackets mine).

[35] Kenney 2011 regards Medea's "pseudo-innocenza" more skeptically. See further on 7.19–20: "[L]o sa o no che sta nominando proprio quel *nescioquis deus* che sospetta?"

> "sed trahit invitam nova vis, aliudque cupido,
> mens aliud suadet; video meliora proboque,
> deteriora sequor. quid in hospite regia virgo
> ureris et thalamos alieni concipis orbis?"

> "But a strange power attracts me against my will – desire urges one thing, reason another. I see the better way, and I approve of it, but I follow the worse way. Why do you, a maiden of royal blood, burn for a stranger and dwell on marriage in a foreign land?" (*Met.* 7.19–22)

Much neater than her awkward periphrasis, *cupido* (19) finds its antithesis in the equally efficient *mens* (20), her capacity for reason.[36] In fact, her antithetical formulation is proof of this capacity, as is Medea's next statement, her first rhetorical triumph: *video meliora proboque, | deteriora sequor* (20–1), a stylish chiasmus marking the heroine's increasing oratorical competence.[37]

Medea's fateful declaration creates another kind of chiasmus, one founded on allusion. Here are the penultimate words of Medea's great *rhesis* in Euripides:

> καὶ μανθάνω μὲν οἷα τολμήσω[38] κακά,
> θυμὸς δὲ κρείσσων τῶν ἐμῶν βουλευμάτων.

> And I understand the misdeeds I will dare, but my anger is stronger than my resolve. (Eur. *Med.* 1078–9)

Ovid links the Medea of epic, naïve and untested, to her more experienced tragic counterpart. The allusion, less a matter of wording than sentiment, spans the gulf of time and experience: Medea's choice to pursue the worse course of action in Corinth, despite understanding the better one, originates in Colchis.[39] Nugent finds in the statements of both heroines a rhetorical commonplace or *topos*. Specifically, the *topos* reflects the Aristotelian state of *akrasia* (ἀκρασία), which Nugent defines as a "paralysis of the will, in which a moral agent correctly perceives the 'better' course but fails to act on it."[40] The *topos* is rhetorical not only for being featured in rhetoric – another tragic example is Phaedra in the *Hippolytus*

[36] Thus Auhagen 2007, 419.

[37] So Bömer 1976b: "Der Chiasmus hebt in rhetorisch wirksamer Weise den Gegensatz hervor." Likewise Auhagen 1999, 143: "Genauso eindrücklich sind Antithesen."

[38] I read τολμήσω for δρᾶν μέλλω: see Page 1938.

[39] Compare Anderson 1972: "When Euripides had her say something similar in his tragedy *Medea* … the statement then epitomized her barbaric irrationality."

[40] Nugent 2008, 155–9 (quotation on 155), following Arist. *Eth. Nic.* 7.1–10.

(τὰ χρήστ᾽ ἐπιστάμεσθα καὶ γιγνώσκομεν, | οὐκ ἐκπονοῦμεν δ<έ>, *HS* 380–1)[41] – but also for using rhetoric to formulate it and to negotiate its implications.[42] The state of *akrasia*, Ovid suggests, is what makes Medea Medea, especially in providing opportunities to speak at length.[43]

The *akrasia-topos* also shows the difficulty in imagining a Medea who, regardless of where she is in her career, is not caught up in a tragic dilemma.[44] For Ovid's Medea *cupido* or desire for Jason conflicts with her *mens* or rational capacity. As noted, this is a tidy antithesis, though *mens* does not represent a state of being as much as the intellectual faculty to formulate opposing pairs. Hence Medea continues to define the terms of her dilemma, even at the end of her monologue:

> "coniugiumne putas speciosaque nomina culpae
> imponis, Medea, tuae? quin aspice quantum
> adgrediare nefas, et, dum licet, effuge crimen!"

> "Do you call it marriage, Medea, and do you apply seemly names to what deserves blame? Observe what a great wrong you approach, and avoid the crime while you may!" (*Met.* 7.69–71)

Words such as *culpa* (69), *nefas*, and *crimen* (both 71) are clearer moral antitheses to *cupido*. To reject Jason is to avoid wrongdoing in the eyes of her family, her society, and perhaps even the gods.[45] Yet it is the narrator who has the final say:

> dixit et ante oculos rectum pietasque pudorque
> constiterant et victa dabat iam terga cupido.[46] 73

> She finished speaking, and before her eyes stood propriety, reverence, and modesty, while desire began to turn tail. (*Met.* 7.72–3)

The terms *rectum*, *pietas*, and *pudor* (72) all belong to the same semantic matrix of forthright behavior – *rectum* designates moral correctness; *pietas*, dutiful conduct toward family and the gods; yet *pudor*, the last word

[41] "We understand and recognize what is right, but we do not do it." On the mores of Phaedra's statement see W. S. Barrett 1964. Bömer 1976b and Kenney 2011 both note the allusion at *Met.* 7.20–1, whose syntax is closer to this passage than to *Med.* 1078–9.

[42] Nugent 2008 finds a dramatic context for *akrasia* in Arist. *Eth. Nic.* 7.3.8: "Aristotle draws the analogy that under those circumstances [i.e., passion negating knowledge of what is right] a person apparently speaking the language of knowledge is simply mouthing the words, like an actor speaking a part" (157, brackets mine).

[43] Compare Nugent 2008, 157: "The poster child for akratic conflict clearly is Medea." Nugent shows *akrasia* at work in six narratives in the *Met.*: Medea, Scylla, Althea, Byblis, Iphis, and Myrrha.

[44] Thus Binroth-Bank 1994, 39–40.

[45] *OLD s.v. culpa* 3c–d, 4a; *nefas* 1–2; *crimen* 2.

[46] I follow Anderson 1972 in decapitalizing *rectum*, *pietas*, *pudor*, and *cupido*.

in the sequence, denotes self-conscious modesty and best contrasts with *cupido* (73), which is confirmed as the other force in the dilemma Medea has struggled to articulate.[47]

Thus another tragic *topos*, modesty versus desire, drives the *akrasia-topos* of Medea's rhetoric. Our exploration of modesty–desire thus far has led us from the extant *Hippolytus*, in which Phaedra comments on the helpful/harmful *aidos* or modesty (*HS* 385–6), to Ovid's own *Heroides* 4, where Phaedra reinscribes the double *aidos* as *pudor* versus *amor* (9–10).[48] Between the *HS* and *Her.* 4 there is room for other intertexts. For example, the Medea of Apollonius seems to have been the first to encounter the double *aidos* as two separate forces:

> ἤτοι ὅτ᾽ ἰθύσειεν, ἔρυκέ μιν ἔνδοθεν αἰδώς·
> αἰδοῖ δ᾽ ἐργομένην θρασὺς ἵμερος ὀτρύνεσκεν. 654

> Whenever she resolved to set out, modesty kept her within; yet desire spurred her on, though she was barred by modesty. (Ap. *Ar.* 3.653–4 Hunter)

And Dido encounters the Latin version of these forces, *pudor* and *amor*, well before Ovid's Phaedra does:

> his dictis impenso animum flammavit amore,
> spemque dedit dubiae menti, solvitque pudorem.

> These words[49] kindled Dido's heart with costly desire, gave hope to her troubled mind, and overcame her modesty. (Verg. *Aen.* 4.54–5 Mynors)

The Medea of *Met.* 7, therefore, is the latest in a line of heroines to experience the modesty–desire *topos*, which encodes the stories in which it appears as tragedies. Furthermore, Ovid's Medea is the first in a line of tragic heroines within her own poem who struggle with modesty and desire: as noted in Chapter 3, they include Scylla (book 8), Byblis (9), and Myrrha (10).[50] Although we previously considered these characters in relation to Phaedra, we can also read them as increasingly incestuous departures from the paradigm of Medea, with *pudor–amor* presenting itself in degrees of difference. Just as a lifetime of experience divides Medea in Colchis from Medea in Corinth, so the transgressions of Myrrha against culture and kin clearly separate her from Medea. These variations suggest

[47] *OLD rectus* 10; *pietas* 2–3; *pudor* 2a–b.

[48] Chapter 1, pp. 14–16.

[49] The *dicta* of verse 54 are those of Anna, Dido's sister, the actual subject of all three verbs in this quotation.

[50] Chapter 3, pp. 92–3.

the transformative effects of modesty and desire – its capacity to manifest in almost endless permutations.[51] On all accounts, whether it appears inside or outside the *Metamorphoses*, the *topos* engenders rhetoric worthy of the tragic stage as heroines endeavor to talk themselves into and out of love.

A third *topos* of tragic rhetoric appears near the middle of Medea's speech in the form of several rhetorical questions:

> "prodamne ego regna parentis
> atque ope nescioquis servabitur advena nostra
> ut per me sospes sine me det lintea ventis
> virque sit alterius, poenae Medea relinquar?"

> "Am I to betray my father's kingdom, and will my aid save some stranger, so that, once safe and sound because of me, he might sail away without me and become the husband of another, while I, Medea, am left behind to pay the price?" (*Met.* 7.38–41)

This kind of self-interrogation has a precedent in Euripides' *Medea* – not her great monologue, but an earlier dialogue with Jason:

> νῦν ποῖ τράπωμαι; πότερα πρὸς πατρὸς δόμους;
> οὓς σοὶ προδοῦσα καὶ πάτραν ἀφικόμην;
> ἢ πρὸς ταλαίνας Πελιάδας; καλῶς γ' ἂν οὖν
> δέξαιντό μ' οἴκοις ὧν πατέρα κατέκτανον.

> Where am I to go now? To my father's house and my fatherland, betraying which I went with you? To the daughters of Pelias? A fine welcome they would give me for murdering their father! (Eur. *Med.* 502–5)

This passage is the *locus classicus* of what Robert L. Fowler has called "the rhetoric of desperation." The hallmark of the *topos* is a series of questions, raised in a state of utter helplessness or *aporia* (ἀπορία), which enumerate the speaker's alternatives. In most instances, none but suicide are viable.[52]

Although the rhetoric of desperation appears in many genres, poetry and prose, like the monologue itself it becomes inseparable from tragedy. Catullus and Vergil, for example, have Ariadne and Dido employ the *topos* in their tragic monologues.[53] Furthermore, the device is a mainstay of

[51] I thank Reader "A" for encouraging this line of thought.

[52] R. L. Fowler 1987, a groundbreaking study. For a taxonomical classification of questions in tragic rhetoric, see Mastronarde 1979.

[53] Catullus 64.177–85; Vergil, *Aen.* 4.534–47.

Medea's rhetoric. In addition to the Ovidian and Euripidean passages, it appears in a fragment of Ennius' *Medea exul*:[54]

> quo nunc me vortam? quod iter incipiam ingredi?
> domum paternamne? anne ad Peliae filias? 218

> Where am I to turn? Upon what path am I to embark? To my father's house? Or to the daughters of Pelias? (Enn. *M. exul* fr. 104.217–18 Jocelyn)

Consider also this excerpt from the *Argonautica*:

> ἑζομένη δἤπειτα δοάσσατο, φώνησέν τε·
> "δειλὴ ἐγώ, νῦν ἔνθα κακῶν ἢ ἔνθα γένωμαι;
> πάντῃ μοι φρένες εἰσὶν ἀμήχανοι ...
> "φθίσθω ἀεθλεύων, εἴ οἱ κατὰ νειὸν ὀλέσθαι
> μοῖρα πέλει. πῶς γάρ κεν ἐμοὺς λελάθοιμι τοκῆας
> φάρμακα μησαμένη; ποῖον δ' ἐπὶ μῦθον ἐνίψω;
> τίς δὲ δόλος, τίς μῆτις ἐπίκλοπος ἔσσετ' ἀρωγῆς;
> ἦ μιν ἄνευθ' ἑτάρων προσπτύξομαι οἶον ἰδοῦσα;"

> Being of two minds, [Medea] sat down and said, "Wretched me, now in what place of misery am I to be, here or there? My mind is entirely at a loss ... Let him perish in his trial, if his fate is to die among the furrows. For how could my parents not notice the drugs as my contrivance? What story could I tell them? What trick, what cunning skill will be of help? Or shall I greet him when I see he is alone and without his companions?" (Ap. *Ar.* 3.770–2, 778–82 Hunter)

Once again Apollonius makes his Medea a precursor to her tragic self not merely through rhetoric, but through the most Medeaesque of all rhetoric.

Ovid likewise incorporates the *topos* into Medea's speech, opening up an allusive dialogue between the Colchian maiden and her Corinthian counterpart: *prodamne ego regna parentis* (38) is an inverted echo of πότερα πρὸς πατρὸς δόμους, | οὓς σοὶ προδοῦσα (502–3). In Ovid's epic the young Medea can scarcely summon the courage to betray her father and leave Colchis for Jason's sake. In the tragedy, however, the older and more experienced Medea, who has long ago betrayed her father, reminds Jason that she has no hope of returning. As with *akrasia*, Ovid recalls the Euripidean passage as a *topos*, but within the chronology of the myth reconfigures it as his own *locus classicus*, to which the tragic Medea now

[54] Vahlen 1928 suspected that Cicero (who cites these verses at *De or.* 3.217) truncated Medea's speech. See R. L. Fowler 1987, 5–6, who reports Vahlen's remarks verbatim, including the old notion that the Ennian fragment is a translation of Euripides. For fuller discussion of the fragment itself see Jocelyn 1967.

seems to respond. Other heroines in the *Metamorphoses* will respond to the *exemplum* of Medea. Two in particular, Althaea (book 8) and Deianira (9), are also heroines from tragedy, and to hear them employ desperation rhetoric is to recognize a *topos* of their former genre.[55] But when Scylla, who has no prior tragic history, verbalizes the *topos*, she becomes a tragic heroine.[56]

Up until now we have seen in Medea's debut *topoi* mobilized to prototypical effect, becoming first instances of devices found either in her "later" Euripidean rhetoric, or in the stories of heroines elsewhere in the *Metamorphoses*. Now I want to expand the notion of the prototype to the *Heroides* and to show how Medea's monologue can anticipate Ovid's epistles. One possible tack is to highlight the inexperience of Medea in matters of love versus the broader experience of Ovidian correspondents, which results in a prospective stance from the former and retrospection from the latter. Another is to contrast the spoken discourse of Medea with the literacy of the epistolary mode, the letters offering more calculated reflections on love versus Medea's sometimes faltering efforts. Such an approach might apply to instances of desperation rhetoric in the epistles of Ariadne and Hypermestra:

> quid faciam? quo sola ferar? vacat insula cultu.
>   non hominum video, non ego facta boum.
> omne latus terrae cingit mare; navita nusquam,
>   nulla per ambiguas puppis itura vias.
> finge dari comitesque mihi ventosque ratemque –
>   quid sequar? accessus terra paterna negat.

> What am I to do? Where am I to go on my own? The island is barren. I see no sign of people, no sign of cattle. The sea hems in every shore; nowhere is there a sailor, or a ship to venture out on the uncertain waves. Suppose I mustered a crew and winds and a ship – what path am I to follow? My homeland forbids my approach. (*Her*. 10.59–64)

> "finge viros meruisse mori – quid fecimus ipsae?
>   quo mihi commisso non licet esse piae?
> quid mihi cum ferro? quo bellica tela puellae?
>   aptior est digitis lana colusque meis."

[55] Althaea: *Met*. 8.486–97; Deianira, 9.147–8 (on which see Chapter 6, pp. 204–5).

[56] *Met*. 8.113–17. We possess some tantalizing evidence that the story of Scylla was staged in antiquity, though probably not as a tragedy. Ovid himself stipulates that the heroine was a tragic character (*impia nec tragicos tetigisset Scylla cothurnos*, *Tr*. 2.393), but his word is about all the evidence we have. *TGF*^{2}, *adesp*. 9, and *TrGF* II.8m refer Ovid's comments to the lost *Scylla* of the dithyrambist Timotheus. See also Lyne 1978, 6–7, and the preface of Bömer 1977 to Ovid's Scylla narrative.

> "Suppose our husbands deserved death – what did we wives do? What crime have I committed that I am not allowed to be virtuous? What has a sword to do with me? What are the weapons of war to girl? Wool and the distaff suit my hands better." (*Her.* 14.63–6)

Given the long history of reading the letters rhetorically, it is surprising not to encounter the *topos* more often: of all twenty-one epistles, these are the only two instances.[57] Their inscription into an epistolary text colors them as sequels to Medea's questions in *Met.* 7. In *Her.* 14, Hypermestra is quoting a monologue she claims to have uttered with the blade at Lynceus' throat (*dixi talia verba*, 52). She not only invokes the tragic *topos*, but also highlights its conventionally spoken delivery. Ariadne's questions in *Her.* 10, however, are written as they arise – a fact we might have missed the first time around, since they also recall the heroine's spoken questions in Catullus 64.

Medea's anticipation of the *Heroides* becomes specific with regard to poem 12, written by Medea during the dissolution of her marriage. When read as a "prequel"[58] to her future epistolary tirade, the younger heroine's monologue seems hopelessly optimistic:[59]

> "si facere hoc aliamve potest praeponere nobis,
> occidat ingratus! sed non is vultus in illo,
> non ea nobilitas animo est, ea gratia formae,
> ut timeam fraudem meritique oblivia nostri."

> "If he can do this, if he can prefer another woman to me, let that ingrate go to hell! But his bearing, his nobility of mind, the charm of his beauty are not the sort to make me afraid that he will deceive me or forget my service." (*Met.* 7.42–5)

These verses demonstrate how Ovidian monologues, like his letters, can foster dramatic irony when a speaker contravenes the knowledge of the reader. Medea's first impression of Jason will become a point of self-reproach in *Her.* 12:

[57] On several occasions Ovid's correspondents ask isolated deliberative questions, e.g., *quid precor infelix?* (2.103); *quid mihi cum Lesbo?* (15.52); *an sequar … laudataque Pergama visam?* (17.205). Paris flirts with the *topos* briefly: *quid faciam, dubito* (16.235). Perhaps the closest thing to extended self-interrogation outside *Her.* 10 and 14 is in the letter of Hypsipyle (6.75–8), as she considers whether to keep her vows for Jason's safety – though her deliberations leave no room for the refutations characteristic of desperation speeches.

[58] On this terminology see Hinds 1993, 40, with reference to *Her.* 12 as a prequel to Eur. *Med.* (and to Ovid's own play).

[59] Wise 1982 likewise explores Medea's visions of her future, even where they are "mutually exclusive" (17).

et formosus eras, et me mea fata trahebant;
  abstulerant oculi lumina nostra tui.

You were handsome, too, and my destiny began to drag me under; your eyes stole away my own capacity to see. (*Her.* 12.35–6)

Here Medea chides herself for not seeing her husband as he was: his beauty (*formosus*, 35; cf. *gratia formae, Met.* 7.44) blinded her to consequences now obvious in hindsight. These consequences are the very ones the Colchian Medea dismisses as unworthy of anxiety: that Jason would deceive her (*fraudem, Met.* 7.45; cf. *sua pars et fraudis in illis, Her.* 12.91), forget the services she rendered (*meritique oblivia*, 45; *inmemor Aesonides, Her.* 12.16), and prefer another woman to her (*aliamve potest praeponere nobis*, 42; *paelex amplectitur artus, Her.* 12.173). Perhaps the greatest irony of Medea's conjectures in the epic is that, should she pay them heed, she would avoid becoming the prototype of her elegiac and tragic selves.

Let me conclude with a fourth and final *topos* of Medea's monologue, which is prototypical for other heroines within and without the *Metamorphoses*. A permutation appears in Catullus 64, in Ariadne's harangue of Theseus:

"quaenam te genuit sola sub rupe leaena,
quod mare conceptum spumantibus exspuit undis,
quae Syrtis, quae Scylla rapax, quae vasta Charybdis."

"For she who birthed you was a lioness beneath a lonely crag; or the sea, which conceived and vomited you forth in its foaming waves, or the Syrtis, or greedy Scylla, or immense Charybdis." (Cat. 64.154–6 Thomson)

The basic parameters are clear: a friend or lover, who has proven faithless, is characterized as an inhuman prodigy, whether a freak of nature or the offspring of a monster. The figure is a timeless one, with origins in Patroclus' harangue of Achilles at *Il.* 16.33–5.[60] Especially relevant is a version by Euripides' Medea following the murder of the children:

πρὸς ταῦτα καὶ λέαιναν, εἰ βούλῃ, κάλει
καὶ Σκύλλαν ἣ Τυρσηνὸν ᾤκησεν πέτραν:[61]
τῆς σῆς γὰρ ὡς χρὴ καρδίας ἀνθηψάμην.

In return for this call me a lioness, if you wish, and Scylla, who inhabits a crag in the Tyrrhenian sea: for I have touched your heart as I should. (Eur. *Med.* 1358–60)

[60] So Quinn 1973 on Cat. 60. Kenney 2011 (*Met.* 7.32–3) lists many pre-Ovidian examples.
[61] I accept Elmsley's πέτραν for obelized πέδον of Page 1938.

Here Medea assumes ownership of her Otherness, daring Jason to use the *topos* so that she can gauge the depths of his misery.[62]

Ovid's heroines, no strangers to the pathos of love, avail themselves of this *topos* just as they do others from tragedy. Most often it serves as a bitter reproach: thus Dido chastises Aeneas (*Her.* 7.37–8); Ariadne, Theseus (*Her.* 10.131–2); and Scylla, Minos (*Met.* 8.120–5).[63] The figure appears in *Met.* 7, but as a formative version in two parts, the speculations of a Medea whose marriage to Jason lies ahead of her:

> "hoc ego si patiar, tum me de tigride natam,
> tum ferrum et scopulos gestare in corde fatebor." 33

> "If I allow [Jason to perish], then I shall declare myself born of a tigress, and bearing iron and stone in my heart!" (*Met.* 7.32–3)

Like her Euripidean counterpart, Medea turns the *topos* against herself. Yet her inhumanity is predicated not on the dire things she has done, but on the things she might leave undone. Other Ovidian heroines will have no qualms about turning the figure against their former lovers and their misdeeds.

The second part finds Medea marveling at the wonders of the world:

> "quid quod nescioqui mediis concurrere in undis
> dicuntur montes ratibusque inimica Charybdis
> nunc sorbere fretum, nunc reddere cinctaque saevis
> Scylla rapax canibus Siculo latrare profundo?" 65

> "What about the strange mountains that are said to clash together among the waves, and Charybdis, the bane of ships, who swallows the sea in, then spews it back out, and voracious Scylla surrounded by fierce dogs, who bays on the Sicilian deep?" (*Met.* 7.62–5)

Once again, the *topos* reflects her vast inexperience, for Charybdis, the Symplegades, and Scylla are real dangers to be marveled at and braved first-hand.[64] They will remain real, at least real enough for Medea to recall them in *Her.* 12 as challenges she faced with Jason (121–6). But for wiser heroines, including Euripides' own, monsters like these are mere figures

[62] Pavlock 2009, 43–5, discusses this and other examples of the *topos* in the *Medea* to support the thesis that Ovid's heroine "employs poetic figures that recall her unspeakable act of infanticide … in Euripides' play" (43).

[63] A counter-example: Byblis uses the *topos* to convince herself that Caunus is *not* inhuman (9.613–5).

[64] Real dangers, though conceived "with a specificity that suggests the mental pleasure one takes in imagining things that do not exist or that do not pose an immediate threat to one's existence": Wise 1982, 17.

of speech, which exist in rhetoric for the purpose of denouncing faithless men.

3 Hecabe: a mother's lament

Turning to the speech of Hecabe (13.494–532), we transition from the poem's first full monologue to its last, also delivered by a woman. Hecabe's monologue therefore enables us to assess the development of female oratory in the *Metamorphoses*. Where Medea's speech was appropriately tentative and incipient, Hecabe's is refined and polished. We also mark a subtle yet significant transition in purpose. Hecabe, like Medea, appropriates the conventions of tragic *rheseis* in her soliloquy. Nevertheless, the speech of the Colchian maiden was an expression of erotic pathos and so overlapped with erotic elegy. The speech of the Trojan queen, which she delivers over the corpse of her slain daughter, also has an elegiac quality, except that it falls squarely within the tradition of funerary elegy.[65] Between them Medea and Hecabe unite under the discourse of the monologue both major strains of elegy, the medium of love as well as lament.

The occasion of Hecabe's speech resembles that of Medea's speech in many respects, some of which are fit to list now, and some of which will become clear as the discussion unfolds. For each heroine the monologue serves as an introductory showcase, a vignette (albeit each with a rather nondescript setting) that reveals the woman's inner mind and establishes her definitively as the protagonist. Medea's showcase comes early in her narrative; Hecabe's comes later, but at a crucial juncture. In the previous chapter we noted the challenges to spatial readings of the Hecabe narrative. For example, her story begins with her dramatic entrance after the fall of Troy (13.422). But this entrance is also an exit, for the queen takes leave of Troy as well as her own narrative for over fifty verses. In her absence the spectacle of Polyxena's death occupies center stage, including a stirring oration before the Achaean assembly. When the mother re-enters her narrative, she must direct the sympathy of the reader back toward herself.[66] Hecabe rises to the occasion, asserting control over her narrative with a speech whose rhetorical competence surpasses even that of Polyxena.

Another similarity between the speeches of Medea and Hecabe is the aptness of the speakers themselves. Just as Medea enters the *Metamorphoses*

[65] In this sense, her monologue is like that of Thisbe, the poem's first female solo speaker, who laments over the body of Pyramus in book 4.

[66] Chapter 4, pp. 112–13.

bearing strong associations with rhetoric and inaugurates the conventions of solo *rheseis* within the poem, so Hecabe is a fitting last speaker, for in Euripides she participates in three separate debates with men, her command of rhetoric growing with each contest or *agon*. Her first is with Odysseus, whom she fails to dissuade from leading Polyxena to sacrifice (*Hec.* 218–401); the second is with Agamemnon, whom she persuades to support her revenge against Polymestor (726–904); the third is with Polymestor himself, whose claim that Polydorus' murder was a service to the Greeks she systematically demolishes (1109–251). Ann Michelini has noted the importance of rhetoric to interpretations of the *Hecabe*, both as a dominant part of the onstage action and as a motif in and of itself. Michelini reads Hecabe's increasing oratorical skill as a sinking moral barometer, which measures the queen's descent into a "world of change and degeneration." In learning how to argue, in adopting the same sort of demagoguery that sanctioned Polyxena's death, she compromises the nobility her daughter takes to the grave.[67] Judith Mossman, in turn, attempts to divorce rhetoric from characterization by demonstrating that Hecabe is more or less constant in character, but her rhetorical techniques vary depending on her relationship with her interlocutor.[68] Whatever we are to make of Hecabe's speeches in the tragedy, her Euripidean prowess as an orator carries over into *Met.* 13, where her monologue validates rhetoric as a critical facet of Hecabe's identity.

Although Hecabe is an apposite last speaker, we must not expect her speech in the *Metamorphoses* to do the exactly same work as in the play. In fact, like Medea, Hecabe speaks on a different occasion from her tragic counterpart. Whereas in Ovid the queen laments over the body of Polyxena, in Euripides she refrains from doing so, partly because the discovery of Polydorus' body leads to a new course of action, and partly because (as she herself says) Polyxena's noble death has lessened her grief:

> καὶ νῦν τὸ μὲν σὸν ὥστε μὴ στένειν πάθος
> οὐκ ἂν δυναίμην ἐξαλείψασθαι φρενός·
> τὸ δ᾽ αὖ λίαν παρεῖλες ἀγγελθεῖσά μοι
> γενναῖος.

> And now I could not forget your suffering so as not to mourn it. But because I have heard you were noble, you have alleviated the need for excess grief. (Eur. *Hec.* 589–92)

[67] Michelini 1987, 142–57 (quotation on 142).

[68] Mossman 1995, ch. 4, 94–141, with additional bibliography on rhetorical analyses of the *Hecabe*.

Ovid's heroine, who (per Polyxena's wish at 13.462) has no one to report her daughter's death, is unrestrained:

> quae corpus complexa animae tam fortis inane,
> quas totiens patriae dederat natisque viroque,
> huic quoque dat lacrimas; lacrimas in vulnera fundit
> osculaque ore tegit consuetaque pectora plangit,
> canitiemque suam concreto in sanguine verrens.
> (*Met.* 13.488–92)

In this passage, discussed in Chapter 4,[69] Hecabe's torrent of grief is little different from her behavior in the Trojan cemetery, the site of her introduction. Although the Euripidean heroine is liberated from displaying excessive mourning (τὸ λίαν, 591), Ovid's heroine has only excess to give. Indeed, the narrator suggests that the reported monologue is only an excerpt:

> plura quidem, sed et haec laniato pectore dixit.
>
> She spoke rather many words, but especially these after gashing her bosom. (*Met.* 13.493)

Those who find the queen's speech long should bear in mind that it might have run longer, if not for the poet's judicious editing.[70]

Even though Hecabe delivers only one *rhesis* instead of many, and even though the occasion is unique, she still bears some resemblance to Euripides' heroine. Paolo Venini catalogues several parallels between her Ovidian speech and her reaction in the *Hecabe* upon hearing of Polyxena's death.[71] Of particular note are the initial apostrophes to Polyxena (ὦ θύγατερ, *Hec.* 585; *nata*, 13.494 and 495) as well as references to Priam:

> ὦ πλεῖστ' ἔχων μάλιστά τ' εὐτεκνώτατε
> Πρίαμε, γεραιά θ' ἥδ' ἐγὼ μήτηρ τέκνων,
> ὡς ἐς τὸ μηδὲν ἥκομεν!
>
> O Priam, most wealthy and most fortunate in your children, and I, too, their aged mother, how we have come to nothing! (Eur. *Hec.* 620–2)

> "quis posse putaret
> felicem Priamum post diruta Pergama dici?
> felix morte sua est."

[69] Chapter 4, p. 112.
[70] So Hopkinson 2000.
[71] Venini 1952, 370 ("Qualche particolare ricorda tuttavia Euripide," with examples) and nn. 4–7.

> "Who would think Priam can be called fortunate after the destruction of Troy? He is only fortunate in death." (*Met.* 13.519–21)

There is, however, as much difference here as similarity. Although both passages lament the misfortunes of Priam, Ovid adds the unexpected sentiment that the king is fortunate to have died, since he has escaped the sight of his fallen daughter (*nec te, mea nata, peremptam | aspicit*, 521–2). On the whole, the resemblance between these and other lines is a passing one.[72]

Hecabe's Ovidian soliloquy, however much it resonates with her speeches in the tragedy, stands with Medea's soliloquy in *Met.* 7 as an original tragic *rhesis*. Apart from the new occasion of its delivery and the addition of novel sentiments, Hecabe's monologue manipulates the very conventions of tragic monologues, such as the rhetoric of desperation *topos*:

> "quo ferrea resto?
> quidve moror? quo me servas, annosa senectus?
> quo, di crudeles, nisi uti nova funera cernam,
> vivacem differtis anum? quis posse putaret
> felicem Priamum post diruta Pergama dici?"

> "For what purpose do I, a woman made of iron, remain? Why do I linger on? Why do you preserve me, chronic old age? For what purpose do you, pitiless gods, extend an old crone's life, except to witness funeral after funeral? Who would think Priam can be called fortunate after the destruction of Troy?" (*Met.* 13.516–20)

This is a sophisticated take on the *topos*. Quite often the rhetorical questions are practical in nature, employing interrogatives like who, where, or what (e.g., *What shall I do? Where shall I go?*), or framing statements as questions (e.g., *Shall I go to X?* from *I shall go to X.*). Hecabe's questions, however, mainly ask *Why?*, a query of a different order. Her inquiries are not so much options as acknowledgments of the futility of action. *For what purpose do I continue to live?*, she asks: *quo* (516) … *quid* (517) … *quo* (517) … *quo* (518). The ostensible answer to all of these is that there is no purpose, no other option besides death, which is a happy one for Priam and presumably herself.

Equally sophisticated is how Hecabe's *topos* proceeds from, instead of culminating in, a death-wish. Consider this excerpt from the queen's

[72] So Hopkinson 2000 (*Met.* 13.494): "[T]he Euripidean Hecuba … begins a long speech with the words 'O daughter' (494), though this speech of the Ovidian Hecuba bears little resemblance to it."

introductory monody in Euripides, which she sings in response to news of Polyxena's impending sacrifice.

> τίς ἀμύνει μοι; ποία γενεά,
> ποία δὲ πόλις; φροῦδος πρέσβυς,
> φροῦδοι παῖδες.
> ποίαν ἢ ταύταν ἢ κείναν
> στείχω; ποῖ δὴ σωθῶ; ποῦ τις
> θεῶν ἢ δαίμων ἐπαρωγός;
> ... οὐκέτι μοι βίος
> ἀγαστὸς ἐν φάει.

> Who protects me? What is my family? My city? Gone is my husband; gone, my children. What road am I to take, either nearby or far off? Where am I to find safety? Where is some guardian god or spirit? ... There is no longer life for me to enjoy in the light of day. (Eur. *Hec.* 159–64; 167–8)

Even as it exemplifies the *topos* at work in lyric – Hecabe enumerates and dispenses with her options for protecting herself and her daughter – the passage demonstrates how naturally death-wishes follow from this type of discourse. Her declaration that life is no longer worth living (οὐκέτι μοι βίος | ἀγαστὸς ἐν φάει, 167–8) is the only logical conclusion.

Hecabe's death-wish in the *Metamorphoses*, in contrast, initiates her rhetoric: a question like *quid moror?* (517) ought to be one of the last a speaker would ask, and should require no refutation. Yet the queen supplies one in the *uti*-clause that explains why the gods have extended her life: in order to witness the funeral of child after child (*uti nova funera cernam*, 518). Such a purpose seems hardly preferable to dying. Yet it becomes so for Hecabe, who soon thereafter announces her intention to bury Polyxena, albeit in modest fashion:

> "at, puto, funeribus dotabere regia virgo,
> condeturque tuum monumentis corpus avitis.
> non haec est fortuna domus; tibi munera matris
> contingent fletus peregrinaeque haustus harenae."

> "But, I imagine, as a regal maiden you will receive funeral rites, and the monuments of your forefathers will cover your body. This is not our house's lot; your mother's tears will be your offerings, and the handfuls of dust will consist of foreign sand." (*Met.* 13.523–6)

Her initial *at* plus *puto* (523), the former a stronger adversative than *sed*, the latter a rhetorically self-conscious aside, signals a clear break from the *topos*: here is a new phase of the monologue, in which Hecabe will come to terms with her remaining work. Emblematic of this phase is her ultimate question, *quid moror?* (531), which repeats the one she had asked only moments ago. Then the question was one of *aporia*: *Why do I linger on in life?* Now, however, it is deliberative, combining with the infinitive *abluere* (532) and calling attention to the duty at hand: *Why do I delay to wash my daughter's wounds?*

This inquiry also interrogates the very conventions of the Ovidian monologue. The notion of delaying draws attention to how Hecabe's speech substantiates her setting and suspends narrative time: *Why do I linger here over tragic discourse?* Indeed, the queen has lingered for fifteen verses past her initial *quid moror?* at 517, which should have marked the end of her rhetoric. In her zeal to answer her own question Hecabe prolongs both her soliloquy and her life. Instead of talking herself into death, she talks herself out of it, citing the *funera* of Polyxena as a reason to persevere. However, the rites for her daughter, although an immediate concern, are but one reason:

> "omnia perdidimus; superest, cur vivere tempus
> in breve sustineam, proles gratissima matri,
> nunc solus, quondam minimus de stirpe virili,
> has datus Ismario regi Polydorus in oras."

> "All is lost. Still, there remains one reason why I should tolerate living a little longer: Polydorus, his mother's favorite, now her one and only, the youngest son, given up to the Ismarian king on these shores." (*Met.* 13.527–30)

The reader, who has already witnessed the murder of Polydorus at 429–38, finds irony in Hecabe's resolve: she might as well have decided to die, because she in fact has nothing left to live for. In choosing death she would have concluded her monologue, rendering her second instance of *quid moror?* unnecessary. As it stands, her final question becomes a formula of closure, a transition from rhetoric back to narrative, which is approaching its end sooner than Hecabe can foresee.

Before taking leave of Hecabe I want to highlight another *topos* within her soliloquy, which confirms the queen as the last great speaker of the *Metamorphoses*. We have observed that her speech is both excessive in its display of lamentation, and innovative in its approach to tragic convention. These qualities are well suited to the poem's ultimate *rhesis* as it concludes the enterprise of the tragic monologue. They are also appropriate qualities for the character of Hecabe herself, who has lost everything and whose losses were dramatized so memorably on the Euripidean stage in both the *Hecabe* and the *Trojan Women*. In Chapter 4, when considering the speech of Polyxena, we raised the possibility that the girl is performing herself: the phrase *memor sui* (453), in conjunction with the depiction of the tomb as a viewing place, suggests that Polyxena remembers her tragic history and plays her part accordingly.[73] Similarly, Medea's negotiation of *pudor* and *amor*, complete with its own passage of desperation rhetoric, reveals her as the tragic heroine she is destined to be. Hecabe's monologue in book 13, therefore, is an opportunity for her to be seen and heard as Hecabe – to embody the paradigm of the grieving mother from not one but two Euripidean plays.

Just before her spate of rhetorical questions, Hecabe imagines a life of servitude in Ithaca:

> "nunc trahor exul, inops, tumulis avulsa meorum,
> Penelopes munus, quae me data pensa trahentem
> matribus ostendens Ithacis 'haec Hectoris illa est
> clara parens, haec est' dicet 'Priameia coniunx!'"

> "Now I am dragged off into exile, into poverty, torn from my sons' tombs, a gift for Penelope, who will point me out to the matrons of Ithaca as I spin out my allotment of wool: 'This is the famous mother of Hector,' she will say, 'this is Priam's wife!'" (*Met.* 13.510–13)

These lines recall Hector's words to Andromache in *Iliad* 6:

> "καί κεν ἐν Ἄργει ἐοῦσα πρὸς ἄλλης ἱστὸν ὑφαίνοις,
> καί κεν ὕδωρ φορέοις Μεσσηΐδος ἢ Ὑπερείης
> πόλλ' ἀεκαζομένη, κρατερὴ δ' ἐπικείσετ' ἀνάγκη.
> καί ποτέ τις εἴπῃσιν ἰδὼν κατὰ δάκρυ χέουσαν·
> "Ἕκτορος ἥδε γυνή, ὃς ἀριστεύεσκε μάχεσθαι
> Τρώων ἱπποδάμων.'"

> "And when you are in Argos you might ply the loom of another woman, and you might carry water from the Messeis or Hypereia against your will, but a powerful necessity will burden you. And sometime someone who sees you weeping will say, 'This is the wife of Hector, the mightiest warrior of the Trojans, breakers of horses.'" (Homer *Il.* 6.456–61 Monro and Allen)

Few would disagree with Neil Hopkinson's assessment of the relationship between these two passages: "Ovid has transferred to [Hecabe] a vision of the future given by Homer to her son Hector."[74]

Although Ovid places *Iliad* 6 in view, there is room for several Euripidean variations on the Homeric passage. Here, for example, is an excerpt from one of Polyxena's speeches in the *Hecabe*:

[73] Chapter 4, pp. 109–10. [74] Hopkinson 2000.

νῦν δ᾽ εἰμὶ δούλη. πρῶτα μέν με τοὔνομα
θανεῖν ἐρᾶν τίθησιν οὐκ εἰωθὸς ὄν·
ἔπειτ᾽ ἴσως ἂν δεσποτῶν ὠμῶν φρένας
τύχοιμ᾽ ἄν, ὅστις ἀργύρου μ᾽ ὠνήσεται,
τὴν Ἕκτορός τε χἀτέρων πολλῶν κάσιν,
προσθεὶς δ᾽ ἀνάγκην σιτοποιὸν ἐν δόμοις,
σαίρειν τε δῶμα κερκίσιν τ᾽ ἐφεστάναι
λυπρὰν ἄγουσαν ἡμέραν μ᾽ ἀναγκάσει.

Now I am a slave. In the first place, the name makes me want to die because it is not customary. In the second place, I might find cruel-minded masters, one of whom will buy me with silver – me, the sister of Hector and many others – and, assigning me to make bread in his house, he will force me to spend a grievous day sweeping and tending the loom. (Eur. *Hec.* 357–64)

We recognize in Polyxena's words many of the same motifs: a prospective view of servile life in a foreign land, which stands in sharp contrast to the woman's noble station, and which includes the performance of menial tasks, such as sweeping and baking bread, in addition to spinning, weaving, and fetching water. Also included is an identification of the enslaved woman in relation to a famous Trojan man: whereas Andromache is the wife of Hector (Ἕκτορος γυνή, *Il.* 6.460) and Hecabe is his mother (*Hectoris parens*, 13.512–13) as well as the wife of Priam (*Priameia coniunx*, 513), Polyxena is the sister of Hector and others (τὴν Ἕκτορός τε χἀτέρων πολλῶν κάσιν, *Hec.* 361). The only substantial difference is that the identification comes from Polyxena herself, rather than from an imagined third party.[75]

Two additional passages, both from Euripides' *Trojan Women*. The first comes from a *rhesis* by none other than Hecabe:

δούλη γυνὴ γραῦς Ἑλλάδ᾽ εἰσαφίξομαι.
ἃ δ᾽ ἐστὶ γήρᾳ τῷδ᾽ ἀσυμφορώτατα,
τούτοις με προσθήσουσιν, ἢ θυρῶν λάτριν
κλῇδας φυλάσσειν, τὴν τεκοῦσαν Ἕκτορα,
ἢ σιτοποιεῖν.

As a poor old serving woman I will reach Greece. They will assign me things most inconvenient to my old age, such as guarding the door bolts or making bread – me, the mother of Hector. (Eur. *Tro.* 490–4 Murray)

The second is part of Andromache's invocation to the deceased Hector:

[75] Collard 1991 places quotation marks around his translation of *Hec.* 361 – "the sister of Hector and many others" – almost as if this clause were the thoughts of a prospective buyer, and thus an implicit third-party identification of the enslaved.

καὶ νῦν ὄλωλας μὲν σύ, ναυσθλοῦμαι δ' ἐγὼ
πρὸς Ἑλλάδ' αἰχμάλωτος ἐς δοῦλον ζυγόν. 678

And now you, Hector, have perished, and I will sail to Greece, bound to a slave's yoke. (Eur. *Tro.* 677–8 Murray)

Hecabe's passage is clearly cut from the same cloth as the others we have seen, touching upon the motifs of slavery versus nobility, a foreign land, menial labor (with door-keeping now added to the list of drudgeries), and the identification of blood kinship (the mother of Hector, τὴν τεκοῦσαν Ἕκτορα, 493, as in Ovid). Andromache's passage, meanwhile, is less specific, omitting one of the familiar parameters (no explicit mention of herself as Hector's wife[76]) and generalizing another (Andromache is bound to the yoke of slavery – δοῦλον ζυγόν, 678 – but does not imagine what tasks await her). Nevertheless, her speech does convey the sentiments of a Trojan noblewoman bound for servitude in Greece. Even this context is enough to cast her words as a response to Hector in *Iliad* 6, a fulfillment of her husband's sorrowful vision.[77]

These examples from Euripides demonstrate how the Homeric concept of a Trojan woman's future as a Greek slave, and the ways of articulating this concept, had become a *topos* with currency in tragedy. Ovid memorializes its tragic associations by situating it in the ultimate tragic *rhesis* of his poem, which is uttered by the foremost of his *Troades*. The *topos* not only enumerates the woes of Trojan women, but also – as in the tragic versions – allows the Trojan women to do the enumerating and to display themselves as objects of pity. This is a defining moment of Hecabe's speech, which bears the rhetorical burden of all her speeches in Euripides, and which aspires to be the "mother" of all laments in the *Metamorphoses*.

4 Hercules: a heroic body of work

Finally, the monologue of Hercules (9.176–204), which the hero delivers atop Mt. Oeta after donning the poisoned robe. His speech presents several points of contrast with the speeches of Medea and Hecabe. First, as one of the poem's extended monologues delivered by men, it presents an occasion to evaluate a masculine *rhesis* – especially from the mouth

[76] At least Andromache does not mention being Hector's wife in this excerpt; two lines earlier, however, she nostalgically recalls her marriage (675–6).

[77] A response more easily heard in concert with other allusions to *Il.* 6 in her speech: see Lee 1976 and Barlow 1986.

of Hercules, who is a pillar of masculinity in the epic. Second, the hero's speech is a display of not only male rhetoric, but also male pathos, which in this case is entirely physical. Third, Hercules' soliloquy is more intertextually involved with a tragic model. Medea and Hecabe, we have noted, speak more or less independently of their Euripidean plays. Hercules, however, when describing the effects of the hydra's poison, recalls a similar speech by Heracles in the *Women of Trachis* (1046–111). We should consider how this speech, a kind of script for Ovid's hero, furnishes ways of proclaiming misery in a most tragic fashion.[78]

An overview of both speeches. The Sophoclean speech, which spans sixty-six verses, has five main sections: (1) an introduction, in which Heracles describes his pain – both its effects and its unprecedented nature (1046–61); (2) blame for Deianira, the author of his illness (1062–75); (3) an invitation to view his suffering, which also includes prayers to Zeus and Hades (1076–89); (4) a catalogue of his labors (1089–102); and (5) a brief restatement of his condition (1103–11). The Ovidian speech, in turn, lasts about twenty-eight verses, and falls into three sections: (1) an address to Juno, whom Hercules blames for his downfall (176–81); (2) a catalogue of labors (182–98); and (3) outrage over the unfairness of his affliction (198–204). One of the most striking differences from these summaries, apart from the disparity in the speeches' lengths, is that Hercules says nothing whatsoever about Deianira. He holds Juno accountable instead (*cladibus, Saturnia, pascere nostris*, 176). In the tragedy, however, Heracles condemns his wife while making only passing mention of Hera, and even then as causing him nothing so evil as his current plight (τοιῦτον οὔτ' ἄκοιτις ἡ Διὸς | προὔθηκεν, 1048–9). In fact, Ovid's speech is an indictment of divine justice from start to finish. His conclusion, in which he questions the practice of believing in gods at all (*et sunt, qui credere possint* | *esse deos?* 203–4), is a far cry from the appeals of Heracles, which divulge his belief in the divine order (ὦναξ Ἀΐδη, δέξαι μ', | ὦ Διὸς ἀκτίς, παῖσον, 1085–6).

Despite these overall differences, both Heracles and Hercules glorify their pasts in light of their present miseries. The centerpiece of each speech is a catalogue of labors, which conjures images of him as victor rather than victim:

[78] Kenney 2011 finds Ovid maximizing the rhetorical potential of Hercules' situation with no interest in verisimilitude (*Met.* 9.176). Silk 1985 asserts that in tragedy it is virtually impossible to portray Heracles outside of disastrous circumstances (the *Alcestis* notwithstanding). Ovid's hero, by virtue of his anguish alone, ought to recall his tragic incarnations.

ὦ χέρες χέρες,
ὦ νῶτα καὶ στέρν', ὦ φίλοι βραχίονες,
ὑμεῖς ἐκεῖνοι δὴ καθέσταθ', οἵ ποτε
Νεμέας ἔνοικον, βουκόλων ἀλάστορα,
λέοντ', ἄπλατον θρέμμα κἀπροσήγορον,
βίᾳ κατειργάσασθε, Λερναίαν θ' ὕδραν,
διφυᾶ τ' ἄμεικτον ἱπποβάμονα στρατὸν
θηρῶν, ὑβριστήν, ἄνομον, ὑπέροχον βίαν,
Ἐρυμάνθιόν τε θῆρα, τόν θ' ὑπὸ χθονὸς
Ἅιδου τρίκρανον σκύλακ', ἀπρόσμαχον τέρας,
δεινῆς Ἐχίδνης θρέμμα, τόν τε χρυσέων
δράκοντα μήλων φύλακ' ἐπ' ἐσχάτοις τόποις.

O hands, hands! O back and chest! O arms, my allies! You have come to this, you who once overcame with force that plague of herdsmen, the lion of Nemea, a terrible and savage creature; and the Lernaean hydra; and the biform, galloping, bellicose army of beasts, an outrageous, lawless, overbearing force; and the Erymanthian boar; and Hades' three-headed hound under the earth, an unassailable monster, the whelp of dread Echidna; and the dragon, guardian of the golden apples far, far away. (Soph. *Trach.* 1089–100)

"ergo ego foedantem peregrino templa cruore
Busirin domui saevoque alimenta parentis
Antaeo eripui nec me pastoris Hiberi
forma triplex, nec forma triplex tua, Cerbere, movit?
vosne, manus, validi pressistis cornua tauri?
vestrum opus Elis habet, vestrum Stymphalides undae
Partheniumque nemus, vestra virtute relatus
Thermodontiaco caelatus balteus auro
pomaque ab insomni concustodita dracone.
nec mihi centauri potuere resistere nec mi
Arcadiae vastator aper, nec profuit hydrae
crescere per damnum geminasque resumere vires.
quid, cum Thracis equos humano sanguine pingues
plenaque corporibus laceris praesepia vidi
visaque deieci dominumque ipsosque peremi?
his elisa iacet moles Nemeaea lacertis,
hac caelum cervice tuli."

"For this I conquered Busiris, who defiled temples with the blood of strangers? For this I deprived savage Antaeus of his mother's aid? For this the triple body of the Spanish herdsman held no fear, nor your triple form, Cerberus? You, O hands, did you check the horns of the powerful bull? Elis has known your work, as do the Stymphalian waves and the Parthenian grove. The belt embossed in Thermodontian gold I brought back through

> your strength, and the apples guarded by the unsleeping dragon. Neither were the centaurs able to stand against me, nor the boar who ravaged Arcadia, nor did the hydra gain anything by growing after losing a head and regaining twice its strength. What, when I saw the Thracian's horses, fattened on human blood, and the mangers stuffed with body parts, and I cast them down and killed both master and the steeds themselves? Crushed by these arms, the Nemean monster lies low; on this neck I bore the heavens." (*Met.* 9.182–98)

The catalogues share six exploits, five of the canonical twelve labors[79] and one *parergon* or side-labor: the Nemean lion (*Trach.* 1092–4; *Met.* 9.197), the Lernaean hydra (1094; 192–3), the centaurs (1095–6; 191), the Erymanthian boar (1097; 191–2), Cerberus (1097–9; 185), and the apples of the Hesperides (1099–100; 190). The Ovidian hero clusters the tragic labors toward the end of his catalogue (the one exception is Cerberus, whom he mentions earlier) and preserves, with the centaurs and then the boar, some of the tragic sequence.

Although there is much common ground between the catalogues, there is also considerable difference in content and structure. To begin with, Ovid's catalogue is more comprehensive. Hercules not only lists the same exploits as Heracles, but also includes an additional seven labors to make the canonical twelve: the cattle of Geryon (184–5), the Cretan bull (186), the Augean stables (*opus Elis habet*, 187), the Stymphalian birds (187), the Ceryneian hind (*Parthenium nemus*, 188), the girdle of Hippolyte (188–9), and the mares of Diomedes (194–6). To these he adds three other *parerga*: Busiris (182–3), Antaeus (183–4), and the vault of the heavens (198). It is tempting to read Ovid's expanded catalogue as an indicator of the expansiveness of epic in general. In the previous chapter we observed that Oeta, the setting for this monologue, takes a wider view of the Sophoclean stage.[80] The smaller catalogue in the *Women of Trachis* accords with the play's conception of Heracles as more vulnerable and more mortal. The tragic *theatron*, having little room for a superhuman hero, confines his labors to six: enough to highlight his former glory, but not too many to undercut his current plight.[81] Ovid's theater of epic, however, leaves space

79 Canonical twelve labors: canonical, at least, in Ovid's time. The canon of labors in Sophocles' time, although approaching formation (the best example being the metopes of the temple of Zeus at Olympia, *c.* 470–456 BCE), was not yet set: see Bond 1981, who discusses the canon with the first stasimon of Eur. *HF* (348–450).

80 Chapter 4, pp. 117–20.

81 So Silk 1985, describing the problems of putting Heracles on the tragic stage: "His presence dislocates the overall structure. On the level of character, it produces a huge imbalance of sympathy in [the] *Trachiniae*" (19, brackets mine).

for the Sophoclean catalogue and more – almost to the point of minimizing the *nova pestis* (200) of the robe.

The Ovidian catalogue is also more varied in its presentation, not only in comparison to Sophocles but also within itself. Heracles' list is roughly chronological, opening with the Nemean lion and the hydra (1092–5), the hero's earliest labors (they are, in fact, the canonical first and second),[82] and concluding with two of his latest labors, Cerberus and the apples, with which the hero tested the boundaries of mortality itself (1097–100). Hercules' list, however, is decidedly unchronological, seeming to delight in the juxtaposition of early and late labors, as happens with the lion and the heavens in the final two verses. The Sophoclean catalogue, in addition, is paratactic: the entire list stems from the relative pronoun οἵ (1091) which agrees with βραχίονες a line earlier, but which includes all the named parts of his body, and is the subject of κατειργάσασθε (1094). Virtually everything else is either the direct object of this verb or an object complement (adjective or appositive); the coordinating enclitic τε connects the objects themselves. In Ovid's catalogue, by contrast, the only unifying factor appears to be *variatio*, for Hercules utters not a parallel list, but a series of elegant yet asymmetrical constructions, each different from the ones before it. Such mannered variation, in turn, pushes the limits of clarity, because which labor comes next or even how it is identified can be unpredictable. Perhaps the most obscure section of the Ovidian catalogue comes after the hero names three places as the beneficiaries of his hands' work: *vestrum opus Elis habet, vestrum Stymphalides undae | Partheniumque nemus* (187–8). The *locus* designates the labor, since there is nothing else to identify the stables, birds, and the hind, respectively – no reference to the nature of the various *opera*, and certainly no mention of *stabula*, *aves* or a *cerva*.[83]

This analysis reveals the Ovidian catalogue, and by extension the surrounding monologue, as a more self-consciously rhetorical enterprise than its Sophoclean predecessor, despite being briefer overall. This is not to say that the Heraclean speech lacks rhetorical skill or polish: Malcolm Davies does a thorough job of highlighting both qualities.[84] But the Herculean speech is more rhetorical by turns. In the example cited above, the hero's use of places to indicate labors borders on the obscure, and yet displays

[82] See Davies 1991.

[83] On these places and their associated labors see Anderson 1972 and Bömer 1977.

[84] An exemplary comment: "Here begins his great speech's third and final priamel ..., leading to the climactic restatement of [Heracles'] suffering at 1103ff.": Davies 1991 (*Trach.* 1089 and following, brackets mine).

artful expression. The places themselves become the subjects of *habet* through personification; *vestrum* is repeated through anaphora in the first two clauses, while *opus* and *habet* are suppressed through brachylogy in the last two.

A higher order of rhetoric appears in other parts of the monologue. Hercules' closing question, for instance, *et sunt, qui credere possint | esse deos?* (203–4), which we noted for its skepticism regarding the divine, is also an excellent specimen of irony, since the hero is on the verge of becoming a god himself.[85] Equally noteworthy is the artifice of verses such as *defessa iubendo est | saeva Iovis coniunx; ego sum indefessus agendo* (198–9). Of these lines Anderson writes, "To round off the list of his exploits Hercules contrives a rhetorical antithesis, with a rhyme arrangement of gerunds, positive and negative forms of *defessus*, and the chiastic placing of subjects."[86] Anderson's choice of verbs, "contrives," implies a disconnect between Hercules' rhetorical *ingenium* and his pathetic circumstances, which might render a lesser hero inarticulate. Brooks Otis makes the disconnect explicit, calling the hero's monologue "altogether too rhetorical for its agonized setting."[87] Yet realism is perhaps the last thing we should expect in the rhetoric of grandiose genres like epic and tragedy, especially Roman tragedy in textual form.

Before we write off Hercules' speech as artifice for its own sake, we should consider its overall effect. The astute construction of the hero's *rhesis* reflects an idealized construction of his past self, which is couched in corporeal terms – the self as a body strong, whole, and well ordered. Both epic and tragedy harbor considerable interest in the human form, the *soma* or *corpus*, and in ways to display it. We think immediately of epic battle scenes, which yield high body counts when not describing individual wounds, abrasions, and other injuries of warfare; or of tragic messenger speeches, which often relate bodily suffering in great detail. Both genres traditionally fashion the body as a *locus* for violence, such that corporeal pathos becomes one of their defining motifs. This motif, in turn, assures the genres' places in (to quote Charles Segal) "the grander reaches of the poetic tradition."[88]

[85] See Galinsky 1972 for a negative evaluation of these verses: "The sentiment can be traced back to the *Heracles* of Euripides (1340–6), where it admirably fits into the context of the play, but here it merely serves to undercut Hercules' deification … Ovid's rhetorical question, put in the hero's own mouth, warns us not to take Hercules' apotheosis seriously" (101).

[86] Anderson 1972. [87] Otis 1970, 200, also cited by Galinsky 1972.

[88] Segal 1998, 13. Segal retroactively accords Ovid's poem a prominent status in theoretical discussions of the body in literature: "It is peculiar that the *Metamorphoses*, … whose main subject, in one sense, is the body, has not played as significant a role in this discussion as it should" (9); see also

The skillful composition of both heroes' *rheseis*, then, is inversely proportionate to the pitiful decomposition of their bodies. In the *Women of Trachis*, even before Heracles' entrance, Hyllus offers a grisly first-hand account of the robe and its maleficent work (749–812). It begins with his father's skin (χρωτί, 767) and sides (πλευραῖσιν, 768), and finds its way into his joints (ἅπαν κατ' ἄρθρον, 769) and his bones (ὀστέων, 769). Soon thereafter this account receives visual confirmation in the unusual manner by which Heracles takes the stage. Rather than walking under his own power, his body upright, he is borne horizontally on a litter (964). Awakened, the hero augments this image of infirmity with agonized cries, brief anapestic and lyric outbursts whose urgency and emotion convey the enormity of his torment. So great is his pain that he calls for his own decapitation (οὐδ' ἀπαράξαι <μου> κρᾶτα βίου θέλει, 1015), a wish that, if fulfilled, would leave him disembodied, and paradoxically unable to narrate his affliction further.

All of this is a preface to the *rhesis* proper, in which Heracles elevates the play's already heightened somatic interest by offering an *epideixis* (exhibition) of himself.[89] He begins with a reminder of his body's glorious exploits:

> ὦ πολλὰ δὴ καὶ θερμά, καὶ λόγῳ κακά,
> καὶ χερσὶ καὶ νώτοισι μοχθήσας ἐγώ! 1047
>
> O the many labors, blazing hot, evil to speak of, that I performed with my hands and my back! (Soph. *Trach*. 1046–7).

This is, however, not the moment to rehearse the past – at least not yet. Rather, the hero launches out on a graphic description of his present suffering:

> καθῆψεν ὤμοις τοῖς ἐμοῖς Ἐρινύων
> ὑφαντὸν ἀμφίβληστρον, ᾧ διόλλυμαι.
> πλευραῖσι γὰρ προσμαχθὲν ἐκ μὲν ἐσχάτας
> βέβρωκε σάρκας, πλεύμονός τ' ἀρτηρίας

Segal 2005. Compare Gildenhard and Zissos 1999, 162 n. 2: "If a concern with (disfigured) corporeality nowadays helps to bestow canonical status upon a text … the *Metamorphoses* must surely count as a postmodern classic." Enterline 2000, chs. 1 and 2, draws "close connections between language, sexuality, and violence" in her corporal study of the *Met.* (quotation, 6).

[89] This paragraph and the two following are indebted to Rehm 2002, 169–75, from a chapter entitled "Space and the Body." Rehm provides a theoretical overview of how characters in tragedy evoke, respond to, and perform the body, from addressing one another synecdochically as κάρα (head) and ὄμμα (eye) to displaying their own actions as movements of the body: "How a character treats his or her body helps create that character's reality, establishing a dramatic context and 'fleshing it out'" (169).

ῥοφεῖ ξυνοικοῦν· ἐκ δὲ χλωρὸν αἷμά μου
πέπωκεν ἤδη, καὶ διέφθαρμαι δέμας
τὸ πᾶν, ἀφράστῳ τῇδε χειρωθεὶς πέδῃ

She cast a woven net of the Furies, by which I am destroyed, upon my shoulders and ensnared them. For plastered to my sides it has devoured my innermost flesh, and taking up residence in my lungs it empties the air-passages. It has already drained my living blood to the dregs, and I am ruined, my entire body ruined, remanded to these ineffable shackles. (Soph. *Trach.* 1051–7)

Just as Hyllus' messenger speech brought the offstage events at Cenaeum onstage, so Heracles exposes parts of his body normally hidden from view. He begins with his shoulders (ὤμοις, 1051) and sides (πλευραῖσι, 1053), both of which are visible to Hyllus and his attendants, as well as to the Sophoclean audience. Thereafter his focus is beneath the skin, on his lungs (πλεύμονος, 1054), his blood (αἷμα, 1055), and his innermost flesh (ἐσχάτας σάρκας, 1053–4). He in effect picks up where his son left off, following the inward trajectory of the poison and turning his body inside out.

Heracles' description of the actual robe shares this somatic interest. As a covering for the human body, the *peplos* is already anthropomorphic; in the hero's account it becomes personified and embodied. In the excerpt above, the robe has taken up residence in his body (ξυνοικοῦν, 1055), devoured him (ἐκβέβρωκε, 1053–4; ῥοφεῖ, 1055), drained him dry (ἐκπέπωκεν, 1055–6), and, most remarkably, taken him in hand (χειρωθείς, 1057). The personification of the *peplos* also entails the depersonalization of Heracles: the body, which should ideally be the subject of all action, has been reduced to an object, a place in which to dwell, mere fodder. This reversal serves the purpose of the *rhesis*, which is to reveal the hero at the height of his pathos. In describing his body as the object of the robe's pernicious actions, Heracles simultaneously fashions his body into the object of the audience's gaze. At line 1057 the hero calls the shackles (πέδῃ, literally a binding for the foot) into which he has been remanded ἀφράστῳ, unspeakable. This characterization is false: Heracles has already said much about the *peplos* and its poison. True, however, is that without the body as a template for his speech – providing both labels for pinpointing where it suffers and metaphors for describing how – his pain would be far less vivid in the imagination and less conducive to sympathy.

Soon after his account of the hydra's poison Heracles offers a second cluster of somatic references that frames his catalogue of labors:

ὦ χέρες χέρες,
ὦ νῶτα καὶ στέρν', ὦ φίλοι βραχίονες,
ὑμεῖς ἐκεῖνοι δὴ καθέσταθ', οἵ ποτε ...
ἄλλων τε μόχθων μυρίων ἐγευσάμην,
κοὐδεὶς τροπαῖ' ἔστησε τῶν ἐμῶν χερῶν.

O hands, hands! O back and chest! O arms, my allies! You have come to this, you who once ... And I have tasted myriad other labors, yet no one has ever won trophies from my hands. (Soph. *Trach.* 1089–91; 1101–2)

The apostrophe at 1089–91 finds the hero once again directing his attention, and therefore the audience's attention, to his body. If his earlier bodily inventory defined his condition in the here-and-now, the direct invocation of his hands, back, chest, and arms defines Heracles as he was in various there-and-thens (οἵ ποτε, 1091), when he had a body capable of performing countless exploits – and not simply performing, but tasting (ἐγευσάμην, 1101). This is not an original metaphor,[90] but is it an embodied one, resonating with the eating and drinking metaphors applied earlier to the *peplos*: whereas Heracles was once the consumer, he is now the consumed.

The hero, therefore, contrasts not only the glorious past with the inglorious present, but also his former body with his current one. His current body, however, dominates the *theatron*. The former is not available for viewing *per se*, but it almost becomes so through the catalogue of labors, which is an offshoot of the initial apostrophe. The hero's address to his own body provides a physical context for the labors that follow, rendering them more real than they might otherwise be, similar to how the earlier somatic references substantiate the deadly effects of the robe. The labors, in turn, afford the healthy but absent body a certain presence by enabling the audience to visualize the hero in action. We are reminded again of how messenger speeches permit access to the offstage world. Heracles' rhetoric transforms his body into a conduit to other places and times by presenting the labors as lived experiences – or, more precisely, by presenting the hero in the act of reliving his experiences. As is also true of messenger speeches, the conduit between the past and the present is only temporary. In the case of Heracles, the former body and its former glory, although within the bounds of recollection, are beyond recovery. What remains – νῦν δ' ὧδ' ἄναρθρος καὶ κατερρακωμένος (1103) – is a body all

[90] Kamerbeek 1959 lists prior instances, beginning with *Il.* 21.60–1.

but dismembered, its fragments representing a body of work fragmented over distance and time.

The monologue of Hercules in *Met.* 9, when read in light of the Sophoclean *rhesis*, shows similar concerns about the hero's body as it was and as it is. As in the tragedy, the epic speech begins after an account of the *vestis* at work on Hercules' anatomy (166–74, cited in Chapter 4 as exemplifying a visual display of agony).[91] However, unlike the Sophoclean account, a messenger speech delivered by Hyllus, the Ovidian description is part of the external narrative. As such it documents the hero's suffering while it occurs, not after the fact. Furthermore, Ovid's version immediately precedes Hercules' monologue, forming a preface of extensive somatic references that the hero himself need not reinforce – at least not at the beginning of his speech. Rather, he reserves a description of bodily pathos for the end:

> "pulmonibus errat
> ignis edax imis perque omnes pascitur artus."
>
> "A ravenous flame wanders within my lungs and grazes on all my limbs." (*Met.* 9.201–2)

These lines are a compendium of Heracles' report at *Women of Trachis* 1049–57, with *pulmonibus* (201) corresponding roughly to πλεύμονος ἀρτηρίας (1054), *edax imis* (202) to ἐσχάτας βέβρωκε (1053–4), and *omnes artus* (202) to δέμας τὸ πᾶν (1056–7).[92] Because the omniscience of the external narrator blurs the boundaries between offstage and onstage, statements like the one above are somewhat superfluous: Hercules says little about himself that the poet did not already say. Nevertheless, that Ovid sees fit to allow the hero to describe his body highlights the importance of these later somatic references, theatrical displays of the self in torment.

Hercules likewise follows his Sophoclean counterpart in associating his body with his many labors. Heracles, as noted earlier, apostrophizes his hands, back, chest, and arms (ὦ χέρες χέρες, | ὦ νῶτα καὶ στέρν', ὦ φίλοι βραχίονες, 1089–90). Hercules, in turn, apostrophizes his hands (*vosne, manus*, 186), and later mentions his arms (*his lacertis*, 197), and neck as well (*hac cervice*, 198), which, to judge from its work of supporting the sky, approximates the Sophoclean νῶτα. The Ovidian references also share the demonstrative focus of the tragedy. The apostrophizing force of *vosne, manus* (186), which suggests that Hercules is holding his hands

[91] Chapter 4, p. 117. [92] On the parallels see Bömer 1977.

before him, carries over into the next two verses with the second-person possessives of *vestrum opus* (187) and *vestra virtute* (188). Note, too, the demonstratives in the phrase *his lacertis* (197) and *hac cervice* (198), which imply that Hercules is gesturing to these parts of his anatomy while he speaks. Like the tragic hero, the epic hero provides in his monologue a simultaneous *epideixis* of both his body and his body of work.

At the same time, Hercules' association of *corpus* with *opus* is more deliberate. His somatic references, which appear within his catalogue, are more fully "incorporated" than those of Heracles, who addresses his body first, his labors second. Each body part in the Ovidian catalogue, moreover, is explicitly linked to one or more exploits. Although the Sophoclean hero locates his deeds within a relative clause, which clearly presents them as accomplishments of his body, he leaves unspecified which parts accomplished which deeds. Hercules, however, frequently gives credit where it is due. His hands are responsible for subduing the Cretan bull (186), cleansing the Augean stables and expelling the Stymphalian birds (both 187), capturing the Ceryneian hind (188), retrieving the girdle of Hippolyte (188–9), and securing the apples of the Hesperides (190) – although this last feat requires the assistance of Atlas, who can pick the apples by hand. Hercules' arms, in turn, receive credit for crushing the Nemean lion (197); his back, for supporting the heavens (198). Eight out of sixteen total deeds, seven canonical labors and one *parergon*, are attributed to a specific part of the hero's anatomy. The result is a clearer sense, already clear in Sophocles, of the labors as lived experiences, and of the body as a sum of its accomplishments.

The Ovidian catalogue is also interested in other bodies, not only those of Hercules' opponents, but also those of their victims. For example, the hero describes his encounters with Busiris and Antaeus in somatic terms:

> "ergo ego foedantem peregrino templa cruore
> Busirin domui saevoque alimenta parentis
> Antaeo eripui?" 184
>
> (*Met.* 9.182–4)

He brought down Busiris for spilling the blood of strangers (*peregrino cruore*, 182), while he defeated Antaeus by depriving him of the earth-mother's restorative touch (*alimenta parentis*, 183). The same notion of corporeal regeneration informs the description of the hydra:

> "nec profuit hydrae
> crescere per damnum geminasque resumere vires." 193
>
> (*Met.* 9.192–3)

Its abilities to grow after an injury (*crescere per damnum*, 193) and regain its physical strength twice over (*geminas resumere vires*, 193) were of no help to the monster. Geryon and Cerberus, in turn, have very unusual bodies:

> "nec me pastoris Hiberi
> forma triplex, nec forma triplex tua, Cerbere, movit?"
> (*Met.* 9.184–5)

Though twice outnumbered three bodies to one (*forma triplex ... forma triplex*, 185), the hero prevailed on both occasions. The mares of Diomedes, finally, revisit the corporeal horrors of Busiris:

> "quid, cum Thracis equos humano sanguine pingues
> plenaque corporibus laceris praesepia vidi
> visaque deieci dominumque ipsosque peremi?"
> (*Met.* 9.194–6)

Once again the hero decries the inappropriate shedding of human blood, this time as fodder for the horses (*equos humano sanguine pingues*, 194). To this incongruous image he adds another, a macabre glimpse into the feeding troughs filled with *corporibus laceris* (195). By depicting his labors as encounters with dangerous bodies, or as involving dangers to the body (not necessarily his own), Hercules depicts himself as the embodiment of heroism.[93]

Ingo Gildenhard and Andrew Zissos, describing the transformation of tragic violence in the Theban narratives of *Met.* 3, observe that Ovid "reproduces vital aspects of tragedy's theatrical dimension by 'staging' the events with the limited formal resources available to him in epic."[94] I agree in general, taking issue only with the word "limited," for which I would substitute "unlimited." What the poet has done with the Sophoclean *rhesis* as a whole – both its substance and its staging – is to free it from the limitations of the tragic *theatron*. Hercules' monologue, although briefer than that of Heracles, nevertheless achieves a grandeur exceeding the tragedy by being uttered atop a mountain, and more importantly by depicting

[93] Other labors in the Herculean catalogue display somatic interest, although in more nuanced ways. In describing his encounter with the Amazons, the hero evokes the girded body of Hippolyte by way of her *balteus* (189). Hercules also claims that neither the centaurs nor the Erymanthian boar were able to stand against him: *nec potuere resistere* (191), a phrase whose embodied metaphor is easily overlooked. Finally, we have previously noted the personification of Elis, Stymphalus, and Pathenium at 187–8; although these examples are less striking than, say, the personification of the robe at *Trach.* 1053–7, they nevertheless contribute to Hercules' overall vision of an embodied past in which he tested the limits of his own body.

[94] Gildenhard and Zissos 1999, 172.

the hero as larger than life. Hercules' greatness depends upon his body, not only in how large it bulks within the monologue, but also from its position as he speaks. The *Women of Trachis* presents a hero formerly larger than life, but now reduced to being borne onstage and off by others. The *Metamorphoses*, however, presents a hero still able to move himself, who just before speaking strikes the same oratorical pose (*tollens ad sidera palmas*, 175) as Aeneas when making his first *rhesis* (*tendens ad sidera palmas*, *Aen.* 1.93 Mynors).[95] Regardless of whether his speech measures up to that of Vergil's hero, the position of Hercules' body is a gesture toward the grandest reaches of the poetic tradition.

One point more, which returns to the issues of male rhetoric and male pathos raised at the beginning of this section. In our discussion of Polyxena's sacrifice in the previous chapter, we noted how Ovid's depiction of the sword plunging into her chest contravenes the norms of feminine death in tragedy, which tends to portray the neck as a woman's "weak point."[96] The notion that the tragic body is gendered accords with Greco-Roman conceptions of the body at large, according to which bodily actions may be classified as either male or female – the most female of which is the act of being penetrated (although, as Polyxena demonstrates, some forms of penetration are less female than others).[97] In the *Women of Trachis* the internal pathway of the robe's poison, reaching all the way into Heracles' ἐσχάτας σάρκας (his innermost flesh, 1053–4), is the pharmaceutical equivalent of penetration. This interpretation finds support from the hero himself, who laments his condition as a transgression against his gender:

> οἴκτιρόν τέ με
> πολλοῖσιν οἰκτρόν, ὅστις ὥστε παρθένος
> βέβρυχα κλαίων, καὶ τόδ' οὐδ' ἂν εἷς ποτε
> τόνδ' ἄνδρα φαίη πρόσθ' ἰδεῖν δεδρακότα,
> ἀλλ' ἀστένακτος αἰὲν εἰχόμην κακοῖς.
> νῦν δ' ἐκ τοιούτου θῆλυς ηὕρημαι τάλας.

Pity me, who am pitiful to many, who have wailed aloud, crying like a maiden. And no one could ever claim to have seen this man here act in this way. Rather, even among troubles, I used to carry myself without so much

[95] Compare Galinsky 1972: "Ovid cannot resist the temptation to let Hercules play Aeneas even now" (100). On the hero's gesture as angry and defiant see O'Bryhim 1992. Compare Philomela's gesture, *intendens palmas* at *Met.* 6.533.

[96] Chapter 4, p. 111. Weak point: Loraux 1987, 50.

[97] See Sharrock 2002, 95–9 (with bibliography), on penetration in Greco-Roman culture, with particular emphasis on Latin poetry.

as a groan. But now, after this misfortune, I am revealed a woman. (Soph. *Trach.* 1070–5)

I am revealed a woman (θῆλυς ηὕρημαι, 1075): the *peplos* has both penetrated him and left him exposed to further penetration by the audience's gaze.[98]

Although such a correlation between penetration and femininity is absent from Ovid's account, it is present elsewhere. As Segal observes, the *Metamorphoses* tends "to pay rather more attention to the male body when it is dealing with ... anxiety about maintaining the integrity of the body, keeping its surface areas intact, and protecting its cavities from painful penetration."[99] Nor does Ovid neglect the invasive effects of the poison. Hercules declares that a flame is wandering deep within in his lungs (*pulmonibus errat | ignis edax imis*, 201–2); and the string of accusative participles modifying the hero at 207–10, cited in Chapter 4,[100] renders him vulnerable to the gaze of others. Although the potential for emasculating Hercules exists, Ovid does not follow Sophocles' lead. Instead he presents a hero who, despite being penetrated, retains vestiges of masculinity. His monologue is a declaration of manhood, in which he stands upright and shouts down the *pestis* that would turn him into a woman.[101]

In the hero's self-glorification there is another instance of tragedy and epic made amphitheatrical. His *incipit* is particularly reminiscent of the masochistic relationship between gladiators and their spectators:

tollens ad sidera palmas
"cladibus," exclamat "Saturnia, pascere nostris,
pascere et hanc pestem specta, crudelis, ab alto
corque ferum satia!"

[98] Rehm 2002 contrasts the feminine pathos of Heracles, who laments being killed by a woman (*Trach.* 1062–3), with the masculine death of Deianira, who commits suicide by means of the sword (ἀμφιπλῆγι φασγάνῳ, 930). Rehm also demonstrates how role-doubling (the same actor would have played both Heracles and Deianira) portrays both casualties as transgressions against gender: "By means of role-doubling, Sophocles blurs the spatial separation and social difference between men and women" (174).

[99] Segal 1998, 26, a summation of a larger discussion of impenetrable men in the *Metamorphoses*: Cycnus and Caeneus (both book 12).

[100] Chapter 4, p. 117.

[101] The next chapter will revisit the masculine qualities of Hercules' monologue in a discussion of *Her.* 9, in which Deianira reviews her husband's deeds from a decidedly feminine and erotic point of view; see pp. 213–15.

> Raising his hands to the heavens, he shouts, "Glut yourself, daughter of Saturn, on my disasters! Glut yourself and gaze upon this plague from on high, cruel goddess, and satiate your savage heart!" (*Met.* 9.175–8)

This is rhetoric not of desperation, but of resignation and defiance – resignation in that Hercules has accepted this latest disaster, defiance in that he dictates the terms under which his pathos is to be observed. He invites Juno, and through her the reader, not only to witness his downfall (*hanc pestem specta*, 177), but also to take pleasure in it (*cladibus pascere*, 176; *cor ferum satia*, 178).[102] To be a gladiator was to embody a contradiction: to endure the debasement of one's body in the sight of others and yet to find empowerment in that debasement. Of this paradox Carlin Barton writes,

> The gladiator's existence offered a form of simplified, purified soldiering, a means of gaining honor within a dishonorable situation and a way of transforming one's humiliation into a pattern of self-sacrifice, even while it was clear to the gladiator and to the would-be gladiator [i.e., the spectator] that those who would give him honor and glory were the very ones who despised him and who would take positive pleasure in his pain and death as well as in his vindication.[103]

Hercules' opening verses, like the speech that follows, capture this very sense of submission and exaltation, to the ostensible delight of his audience.

This survey of tragic monologues in the *Metamorphoses* has illustrated how epic poetry can be configured as a *theatron* for not only spectacles but also speeches. The stories of Medea, Hecabe, and Hercules are alive to the spatial extremes of epic, regardless of the degree to which those spaces resemble the original tragic *skēnai*. With regard to rhetoric, however, the stories streamline and compress instances of speech from their model plays into single, sustained monologues, which are intertextually engaged both with their models and with other tragic texts. Such engagements, in turn, focus the reader's attention on the constructedness of Ovidian speeches, as do frequent rhetorical *topoi*, many of which were current in tragedy. In tracing a program of rejuvenating Roman tragedy across Ovid's career, we must expect that he would have aimed for the rhetorical heights of the Roman stage with novel speeches suited to traditional tragic characters. Medea, Hecabe, and Hercules are protagonists both familiar from tragedy and renowned for delivering powerful speeches. Yet Ovid's program is no less apparent in episodes without tragic models, whose characters engage

[102] For hedonistic connotations of these verbs see *OLD s.v. pasco* 5a, *s.v. satio* 3.

[103] Barton 1992, 35 (brackets mine).

in original monologues, and so become tragic protagonists in a theater of epic.

Also evident from our survey is the potential of Ovidian speakers not only to perform rhetoric, but also to perform themselves. Self-performance goes beyond adopting a general type, though typology is important: Medea takes the stance of helper-maiden; Hecabe, a grieving widow and mother; Hercules, a gladiator about to die. Each hero or heroine also performs a dramatic version of himself or herself. Hecabe becomes the downtrodden queen of Euripidean tragedy. Hercules offers a speech of Herculean proportions. Medea begins to settle into her role as Medea.[104] The notion of mythological characters performing themselves is arresting, but consonant with the metatheatrics of Ovid's tragic program.

No less arresting is the notion of mythological characters performing other characters. Each monologue, to some degree, presents its speakers with an opportunity of this sort. Hercules, at the outset of his speech, poses as Aeneas. Hecabe's use of the Trojan-woman-as-slave *topos* suggests a certain interchangeability of experience among herself, Polyxena, and Andromache, as if to imagine the plight of one Trojan woman is to imagine the plight of them all. Medea's ambivalent struggle with modesty and desire implicates her in a network of heroines, some Ovidian, some not, each of whom faces the same struggle and becomes in her turn a paradigm for the rest. Hence Medea plays the part of Phaedra or Dido or Byblis; or Byblis plays Scylla, Myrrha, or Medea. As we will see in the next chapter, Ovid's paradigmatic deployment of characters is systemic in both the *Metamorphoses* and the *Heroides*. For now, let us observe how Ovidian monologues, as platforms for negotiating identity, suggest the metamorphic power of words themselves.[105]

[104] Compare Nugent 2008, 157: "Ovid's akratic heroines ... in several instances clearly recall dramatic heroines and at other times seem to conceive themselves almost as actors in a play."

[105] Nugent 2008, 171, remarks that the rhetoric of Medea, Scylla, Althea, Byblis, Iphis, and Myrrha rarely have the desired transformative effect, namely "freeing [them] from the perceived constraints of [their] circumstances" (brackets mine). Apart from Medea's incantations or Iphis' prayer, the "exercise of language in a transformative effort" by most heroines "results in the unmaking both of themselves and of the family."

CHAPTER SIX

Medeae Medea forem

Tragic intratextuality

Thus far reading the tragic in Ovid has involved looking outward and backward, following the referential pathways typical of an intertextual approach. This chapter presents another strategy of reading, one that involves looking inward and exploring how Ovid's poetry cultivates the tragic from within, whether from narrative to narrative or letter to letter.

Such a strategy is best described as **intra**textual. Although intratextuality might seem little more than a theoretical conceit, its principles are beneficial, if not essential, to the study and interpretation of Greco-Roman literature. Alison Sharrock, in her introduction to the first major volume on the topic, characterizes intratextual reading as "looking at the text from different directions ... chopping it up in various ways, building it up again, contracting and expanding its boundaries both within the *opus* and outside it." Moreover, "the hypothesis of intratextuality [is] that a text's meaning grows not only out of the reading of its parts and its whole, but also out of readings of the relationships between the parts, and the reading of those parts as parts, and parts as relationship."[1]

Under this hypothesis it is possible to recoup readings from other chapters as already being intratextual. In Chapter 4, for example, it was clear that Polyxena's sacrifice occupies a place of privilege within the Hecabe narrative (book 13): the daughter temporarily relegates the mother to the margins of her own story.[2] An intratextual reading might clarify that the mother–daughter relationship is temporarily inverted. In making a spectacle of her own demise, Polyxena assumes the autonomy and authority of her mother in the original tragedy. This reversal of roles extends to the hierarchy of the episodes themselves, as the daughter-episode comes into its own and upstages the glory of the mother-episode. Furthermore, in Chapter 5, the antithesis between modesty and desire in Medea's rhetoric opened up dialogues with other Ovidian heroines and their responses to

[1] Sharrock 2000, 5 and 6–7. [2] Chapter 4, pp. 108–13.

the same dilemma.[3] Intratextually speaking, these heroines are implicated in a kind of matrix in which modesty and desire manifest themselves in distinctive and defining ways.

The close relationship among tragic narratives in the *Metamorphoses* has received due attention. David Larmour published a comprehensive study of "tragic *contaminatio*" in the poem, demonstrating that elements of the Medea legend are played out in the Procne narrative (book 6); likewise elements of the Phaedra myth in the narratives of Scylla (8), Byblis (9), and Myrrha (10). His usage of the term *contaminatio* is a compelling shorthand for the Ovidian practice. Larmour suggests that Ovid's primary motivation is narrative variety: "Ovid chooses not to retell a very familiar tale in its full form – either because it was hackneyed or because it could not be given a metamorphosis."[4] Yet *contaminatio* also situates Ovid among the Roman dramatists, who when reworking Greek plays "contaminated" the plot of one play with another, a practice allegedly begun by Naevius.[5] Following Larmour are Carole Newlands, who discovers Medea in the narratives of Orithyia (book 6), Procris (7), and Scylla, and Ingo Gildenhard and Andrew Zissos, who amplify Narcissus' "echoes of Oedipus" (3).[6]

I acknowledge a debt to these studies, but I want to take a somewhat larger view of the intratextual network of the *Metamorphoses*, which implicates Ovid's tragic stories and their characters. Accordingly, I will draw parallels between Iphigenia (12) and Polyxena (13), and between Medea (7) and Deianira (9), in an effort to extrapolate principles that govern the poem in general. At the same time, I will also consider the *Heroides* and their connections not only among the women of the collection, but also between the collection and the *Metamorphoses*. My discussion is based on a mode of reference I call the *intratextual footnote*, a signal that activates and mobilizes Ovid's tragic network. Like other referential pathways in the poet's repertoire, the intratextual footnote is emblematic of the often "peculiar logic of Ovidian poetics."[7]

[3] Chapter 5, pp. 145–7.

[4] Larmour 1990, who also includes parallels between Polyxena and Iphigenia (on whom see below, section 2).

[5] On Naevius and *contaminatio* see Chapter 2, p. 24.

[6] Newlands 1997; Gildenhard and Zissos 2000. Binroth-Bank 1994, 20, also discusses the appearances of other Medeas prior to *Met.* 7.

[7] Gildenhard and Zissos 2000, 130.

1 Intratextual footnotes

Intratextuality encourages close readings of the relationships between Ovid's tragic stories. Another enabling concept, not exclusive to intratextual negotiations, but helpful for interrogating them, is synchrony. Synchrony is the antithesis of diachrony, which involves the sequential arrangement of events from earliest to latest. A diachronic approach to narrative (or an episode thereof) tends to follow the plot, beginning at the beginning and ending at the end. Chapter 4, for example, offered a diachronic approach to the narratives of Hecabe, Hercules, and Medea in tracking the movements of these characters from their origins to their final destinations. A synchronic approach to narrative, however, is concerned not with following the order of events, but with compiling and comparing them regardless of when they occur. Events are treated as though occurring simultaneously, the better to compare them side-by-side. Structuralist analyses, which arrange recurrent motifs by category, are perhaps the best known examples of synchrony in close readings of classical texts and myths.

Just as diachrony can be deployed in studies of individual heroes or heroines – the Ovidian character arcs of Hecabe and the rest are eminently diachronic – such studies can avail themselves of synchrony as well. The result is less a character's progression from one state to another than a collation of a character's most significant actions or roles. The synchronies inherent in mythical characterization were recognized in antiquity. A fragment of Antiphanes' comedy, *Poiesis*, describes the synchronic possibilities of a character's very name:

ὥσθ᾽ ὑπομνῆσαι μόνον
δεῖ τὸν ποιητήν· Οἰδίπουν γὰρ ἂν μόνον
φῶ, τἆλλα πάντ᾽ ἴσασιν· ὁ πατὴρ Λάιος,
μήτηρ ᾽Ιοκάστη, θυγατέρες, παῖδες τίνες,
τί πείσεθ᾽ οὗτος, τί πεποίηκεν.

> A poet need only remind. I have just to say, "Oedipus," and they know all the rest: father, Laius; mother, Jocasta; their sons and daughters; what he will suffer; what he has done. (Antiphanes, *CAF* II.191.4–8, tr. Burian 1997)

The speaker exaggerates, but only a little. The mention of Oedipus' name triggers a synchronic recollection of his myth, in which details can be arranged without regard for linear plotting. Much the same can be said of (say) Medea, who is synonymous with, in no particular order, child-killer, helper-maiden, sorceress, and more.[8] From this perspective mythical characters are synchronic incarnations or embodiments of their stories.

As embodiments, characters become codes in their own right. In the previous chapter the *topoi* of *akrasia*, modesty/desire, and desperation speech were key parameters of a distinct, Medeaesque strain of tragic rhetoric.[9] To these add now the various identities the heroine assumes over the course of her career. The sum of these parameters is a master Medea code, a synchronic compilation of actions, roles, intentions, speeches, and anything else that makes a Medea. By privileging certain parameters within a character's code, authors and readers privilege characters as exemplars or paradigms: Medea, therefore, may be considered a paradigm of infanticide, as well as of sorcery, maidenly assistance, vengeance, cleverness, and rhetoric, perhaps individually, perhaps all at the same time.

A character's paradigmatic status enables another kind of synchrony, a kind that collates actions or motifs not within a single myth but between different myths, and hence between different characters. One character can become a paradigm for another, and vice versa. Tragedy is particularly well known for mobilizing paradigms, and the dire outcomes associated with the genre are often the result of one character consciously or unconsciously conforming to the destructive type of another. Charles Segal demonstrates this process with the *Women of Trachis*, which is "suspended between two simultaneous and opposing paradigms, the myth of the *Odyssey* and the myth of the *Oresteia*." In Segal's schema, Deianira attempts to play the part of Penelope, waiting for Heracles to return, but unwittingly becomes Clytemnestra in destroying her husband. Heracles, in turn, becomes not Odysseus but Agamemnon; and Hyllus, Orestes rather than Telemachus.[10] A fundamental dynamic of the *Women of Trachis*, and of tragedy at large, is the shifting of characters between paradigms.

The *Heroides* are alive to the possibilities of synchrony. To begin with, the rather rigid constraints of the epistolary here-and-now encourage the reader to bring a heroine's past and future into dialogue with her present. Although from a diachronic perspective a heroine's career has yet to achieve fullness – Medea (*Her.* 12), for instance, has already been the

[8] In the introduction to their volume on Medea (1), Bartel and Simon 2010 offer an extensive list of her identities, "echoes from antiquity that reverberate into the present day." I paraphrase: vengeful wife, wicked witch, multiple murderer, scorned and mistreated wife, marginalized Other, psychologically frail heroine, exotic princess, beautiful and smitten maiden, semi-divine woman, strong-yet-abused victim.

[9] Chapter 5, pp. 144–50.

[10] Segal 1983, 179–80 (quotation on 180).

helper-maiden and the sorceress, but has not yet become the infanticide – a synchronic perspective allows access to her full career. Her identity cannot easily be separated from her exploits, even those belonging to the future. Within the framework of any given letter synchrony allows ample opportunity for tragic irony, as we have repeatedly seen at the end of Medea's epistle: *nescio quid certe mens mea maius agit* (212). Across letters, however, synchrony allows the heroines to serve as mutually deconstructing paradigms for one another, especially since all find themselves in the position of somehow being abandoned by their lovers. As in tragedy, the failure of a heroine to conform to the paradigm of another is just as important, if not more so, than actually conforming. Laodamia (*Her.* 13) will never be a Penelope (1), try as she might. Where Phaedra (4) has failed to combine familial and sexual relations, Canace (11) has succeeded. Briseis (3) longs to return to Achilles, while Hermione (8) despairs of ever escaping his son, Pyrrhus. Both Oenone (5) and Helen (17) write to Paris, each aware of the other's claim.

Out of the many pleasures of reading the *Heroides*, perhaps the most underappreciated is the drawing of such imperfect parallels, despite encouragement from the heroines themselves. The letter of Hypsipyle issues a most provocative invitation:

> paelicis ipsa meos implessem sanguine vultus,
> quosque veneficiis abstulit illa suis!
> Medeae Medea forem!
>
> I would have spattered my own face with the blood of my rival, and your face, too – the face she poisoned and took from me. I would have become Medea to Medea! (*Her.* 6.149–51)

After working hard to differentiate herself from Medea, Hypsipyle now imagines herself playing the part of that heroine. The irony is that, diachronically speaking, the paradigm would extend only as far as betraying her father and killing her brother. The reader, who holds the synchronic view, knows Hypsipyle must go even further to become a true Medea – further than even Medea can imagine in her own letter.[11]

Ovid's letters share the synchronic capacity of tragedy, but with one key difference. Whereas tragic synchrony is generally intertextual – the *Women of Trachis*, for example, deploys paradigms familiar from Homer and Aeschylus – in the *Heroides* it is intratextual, involving epistles within the

[11] Fulkerson 2005 reads the *Heroides* as a self-consciously intratextual enterprise: Ovid's heroines are a community of authors cognizant of – and responding to – each other's letters. On Medea's ignorance of her tragic future see Chapter 3, p. 82.

same collection. Synchrony opens a new window on reading the *Heroides* as a tragic enterprise. Even as an individual letter, or all of them, adopts tragic subject matter and devices or recalls tragic modes of performance, the collection as a whole constitutes a paradigmatic network, fully responsive unto itself, that approximates the network established by Greek and Roman tragedians over many generations. The *Heroides* come equipped with a built-in literary tradition, to which the synchronies of intratextual reading provide access.

The *Metamorphoses* likewise fashions its own tragic network, a fine example being the connections between Hecabe and Procne.[12] The Trojan queen, effusive in grieving over the corpse of Polyxena, greets the body of Polydorus with stunned silence:

> obmutuit illa dolore,
> et pariter vocem lacrimasque introrsus obortas
> devorat ipse dolor …
> ulcisci statuit poenaeque in imagine tota est. 546

> She is stricken dumb with grief, grief itself consumes both her voice and her tears welling up from inside … She decided to seek vindication, utterly absorbed by the thought of revenge. (*Met.* 13.538–40, 546)

This is a transformative moment, when Hecabe first abandons rhetoric for vengeance. It is also a moment familiar to readers of Procne, who undergoes virtually the same metamorphosis after learning that Tereus has raped and mutilated Philomela:[13]

> dolor ora repressit,
> verbaque quaerenti satis indignantia linguae
> defuerunt, nec flere vacat, sed fasque nefasque
> confusura ruit poenaeque in imagine tota est.

> Grief weighed down her lips, and sufficiently indignant words failed her tongue, try as it might to find them. Nor is there time to weep, but she quickly confuses right and wrong, utterly absorbed by the thought of revenge. (*Met.* 6.583–6)

The passages are reciprocally allusive, activating paradigmatic links between the two women. Both Hecabe and Procne are displaced from their homelands and have loved ones who fall prey to Thracian

[12] The following discussion of Hecabe and Procne, as well as of Pentheus and Medea, revisits Curley 2003, 185–8.

[13] On the correspondences see Rosati 2009 (*Met.* 6.583 and 586).

brutality.[14] They respond in animalistic fashion. Hecabe pursues Polymestor like a lioness:

> utque furit catulo lactente orbata leaena
> signaque nacta pedum sequitur, quem non videt, hostem ... 548

> Just as a lioness, bereft of her suckling cub, falls into a frenzy, finds the tracks of her unseen foe, and follows them ... (*Met.* 13.547–8)

Procne, in turn, is compared to a tigress:

> nec mora, traxit Ityn, veluti Gangetica cervae
> lactantem fetum per silvas tigris opacas. 637

> Without delay she drags Itys off, like a Ganges tigress drags a deer's suckling fawn through the shadowy forest. (*Met.* 6.636–7)

Here, however, the paradigms diverge. Although both women direct their rage toward the authors of the crimes, Procne's vengeance involves killing her own son – a step too far for a Hecabe. Hecabe and Procne are mutually deconstructing figures, each one providing points of comparison and contrast for the other. And all of this within the confines of a single poem.

The intratextuality of the Hecabe and the Procne narratives is somewhat atypical of the *Metamorphoses*. Although each story enhances the reading of the other, each is nonetheless independent and may stand on its own. More typical is the interdependence of tragic narratives, whereby Ovid underplays certain elements in one story and expands upon them in another; this is a tenet of Larmour, Newlands, and Gildenhard and Zissos. We already have a sense of this tendency in characters like Scylla, Byblis, and Myrrha, all doubles for Phaedra, whose story (in Ovid's epic, at least) is reduced to the bare essentials.[15] Another example from the *Metamorphoses* comes late in the Medea narrative, a passage first discussed in Chapter 2 and again in Chapter 4:[16]

> tandem vipereis Ephyren Pirenida pennis
> contigit; hic aevo veteres mortalia primo
> corpora vulgarunt pluvialibus edita fungis.
> sed postquam Colchis arsit nova nupta venenis

[14] Gildenhard and Zissos 2007, 10 n. 34, point out that Ovid links the authors of the Thracian brutality, Polymestor and Tereus, with the epithet *Odrysius* (13.554 and 6.490), "the only two occurrences in the poem."

[15] Chapter 3, pp. 90–3. As noted in that discussion, *Her.* 4 gives Phaedra a platform for expressing her desire in the fullest possible terms.

[16] Chapter 2, p. 43; Chapter 4, pp. 131–2.

flagrantemque domum regis mare vidit utrumque,
sanguine natorum perfunditur impius ensis,
ultaque se male mater Iasonis effugit arma.
(*Met.* 7.391–7)

As mentioned earlier, both Larmour and Newlands demonstrate that the events abbreviated in this tragic narrative are more fully explored through the events of other narratives. Most notable is the murder of the children, which finds a more comprehensive analogue in the narrative of Procne, who is a paradigm for Medea as well as Hecabe.

The passage above is of particular interest because of its bold abridgement, which becomes a kind of footnote, a signpost pointing to more expansive tragic stories elsewhere in the *Metamorphoses*. The concept of footnoting in Latin poetry achieved currency with David Ross's *Alexandrian footnote*, a general statement that points to an established tradition.[17] There is an Alexandrian footnote in the second and third lines of the passage: *hic aevo veteres mortalia primo* | *corpora vulgarunt pluvialibus edita fungis* (392–3). With *veteres vulgarunt* Ovid styles himself a researcher of abstruse lore, now lost to us, on old Corinth. Whereas the Alexandrian footnote uses precise markers like *vulgarunt* or *ferunt* or *fama est*, the marker of the footnote I am describing – an intratextual footnote – is more ambiguous. In this case the cursory nature of Medea's Corinthian episode, which has what Gildenhard and Zissos might call an "absent presence"[18] in the narrative, serves as the actual footnote. The less the poet narrates, the clearer the reference, and the more the reader is encouraged to seek out analogies elsewhere in the poem.[19]

Sometimes the marker of an intratextual footnote involves not how little is said, but what escapes mention altogether. An excerpt from the Pentheus narrative of book 3:

perstat Echionides nec iam iubet ire, sed ipse
vadit, ubi electus facienda ad sacra Cithaeron
cantibus et clara bacchantum voce sonabat.

[17] Ross 1975, 78. For the impact of Ross's formulation in the scholarship see Hinds 1998, 1–3.

[18] Gildenhard and Zissos 2000, 143, discussing the "presence" of Narcissus versus the glaring "absence" of Oedipus.

[19] Tarrant 2005, 69, likens the abridgement of Medea's Colchis episode and other notoriously abridged passages to the "fast forward" mode of a videorecording. Tarrant focuses on the **inter**textuality of these passages, whether a "gesture of deference toward a canonical predecessor" or a "rejection of the same" (70–1). Tarrant's "fast forward" passages exemplify "untold stories" in the *Metamorphoses*, through which Ovid's narrative choices "create an added dimension of metamorphosis at the textual level" (87).

> But the son of Echion persists, no longer ordering others to go forth, but goes forth himself, where Cithaeron, chosen for performing the sacred rites, was resounding with the songs and loud cries of the bacchants. (*Met.* 3.701–3)

Pentheus' journey to Cithaeron seems to happen without his dressing as a maenad, which is perhaps the most distinctive parameter of the Pentheus code established in Euripides' *Bacchae*. The intratextual footnote, therefore, consists in the blatant absence of this detail, which prompts the reader to look for counterfeit maenads in another story. The story in question is, once again, the Procne narrative:

> nocte sua est egressa domo regina deique
> ritibus instruitur furialiaque accipit arma:
> vite caput tegitur, lateri cervina sinistro
> vellera dependent, umero levis incubat hasta.

> By night the queen leaves her house and adorns herself for the rites of the god, putting on the panoply of fury: ivy wreathes her head, the fawnskin hangs from her left side, a light spear upon her shoulder. (*Met.* 6.590–3)

Why Ovid's Pentheus avoids playing the bacchant is really the subject of another discussion.[20] For the present we need only observe that the footnote in book 3 invokes Procne and her story as a central node in Ovid's intratextual network, making her a paradigm for no fewer than three tragic figures in the *Metamorphoses*.

2 Iphigenia and Polyxena: (re)playing the victim

With the concept of the intratextual footnote established, let us put it to work in a synchronic reading of the sacrifices of Iphigenia and Polyxena in *Met.* 12 and 13, respectively. Polyxena's demise, particularly her initial experience at the tomb of Achilles, helps augment the succinctly narrated experience of Iphigenia at Aulis. Although the following discussion might seem tendentious in the parallels it draws, tragic intratextuality in the *Metamorphoses* is generally no less tendentious than tragic intertextuality, which requires that some allusive pathways be intentionally taken over others. Ovid challenges the reader to make sense of tragic narratives that are lacunary or otherwise problematic. To accept this challenge requires

[20] Briefly: the absence of Bacchic dress might be apposite to a Latin narrative, one based not the *Bacchae*, but on the lost *Pentheus* of Pacuvius, which to judge from its Servian summary omitted the maenadic disguise. So Keith 2002, 265–6, after D'Anna 1959 and Currie 1981, 2716–18. See also Barchiesi and Rosati 2007 (*Met.* 3.701–33). Pacuv. *Pentheus*: *SRF* I.

the radical redrawing of the boundaries between narratives, leaving open to negotiation where one ends and another begins.

Book 12 begins with Helen, who abandons Sparta for Troy (4–6). There follows a rather perfunctory account of the Greek fleet's confinement at Aulis, which culminates in the sacrifice of Iphigenia:

> postquam pietatem publica causa
> rexque patrem vicit castumque datura cruorem
> flentibus ante aram stetit Iphigenia ministris,
> victa dea est nubemque oculis obiecit et inter
> officium turbamque sacri vocesque precantum
> supposita fertur mutasse Mycenida cerva.

> After what the people wanted defeated what is right, and Agamemnon the king defeated Agamemnon the father, and Iphigenia, about to spill her virgin blood, stood before the altar while the attendants were weeping, the goddess was overcome and threw a cloud over their eyes, and amid the business and hubbub of the rite and the chants of the worshippers she is said to have transformed the Mycenaean girl by substituting a hind. (*Met.* 12.29–34)

Here we have a summary – much of it within subordinate clauses, no less – where we might otherwise expect a full-fledged narrative, especially since Iphigenia's situation is ripe with that Ovidian mainstay, pathos.[21] Moreover, it is a summary of a story depicted on the Greek and Roman stage, most notably in the extant *Agamemnon* and *Iphigenia at Aulis* (*IA*).[22] A patent abbreviation of a tragedy should by now strike us for what it is: an intratextual footnote, a reference to the trauma of a maiden elsewhere in the poem, whose ordeal can supplement that of the maiden at hand.

Which maiden? There is good reason to take Philomela and the atrocities inflicted upon her as the referent of the footnote. As Larmour observes, the experiences of Iphigenia and Philomela both involve "brutal male violence, coupled with deceit, and defenseless female innocence."[23] Nevertheless, since the inherent ambiguity of intratextual footnotes allows for multiple referents, *Met.* 12.29–34 also points to the Polyxena episode of book 13. Indeed, Iphigenia and Polyxena are so similar that they are almost

[21] Although Ulysses later fills in some of the background in his *agon* with Ajax, describing how he convinced Agamemnon to think of the public welfare (*ingenium ad publica commoda verti*, 13.188) and deceived Clytemnestra (*quae astu decipienda fuit*, 193–4), he says nothing about the ritual itself.

[22] Lost tragedies about Iphigenia: Aesch., *TrGF* III.94; Naev., *SRF* I.18; Enn., *SRF* I.177–203. On both Latin plays see Jocelyn 1967.

[23] Larmour 1990, 136, one of many observations on how the *Metamorphoses* links the Tereus–Procne–Philomela legend with the house of Atreus.

mirror images: regal virgins, sacrificed for the greater good of the Greek war effort, which is deferred due to unfavorable winds.[24] One difference of note, apart from one heroine being Greek and the other Trojan, or the position of their sacrifices within the chronology of the Trojan War, is the fact that Iphigenia survives. We learn from 12.32–4 that Diana intervened at the last moment, substituting a hind for the girl. Even here, however, there is ambiguity: the goddess' intervention is couched as an Alexandrian footnote (*supposita fertur mutasse Mycenida cerva*, 34). It is the reader's part to decide whether or not Iphigenia lives on, and consequently how far her parallel with Polyxena extends.

In conflating these two tragic heroines Ovid not only replicates in a general sense the synchrony of tragedy, but also continues the synchronic work of the tragic poets themselves. It is one thing to note how Ovidian characters like Medea and Procne correspond within the framework of the *Metamorphoses*. But we can go further and trace their correspondence back to the original plays, one of which might have served as the inspiration for the other. Jennifer March, for example, has argued that Euripides' tragedy motivated Sophocles to place the Athenian Procne in circumstances similar to those of Medea at Corinth.[25] Similarly, the conflation of Polyxena and Iphigenia is not Ovid's innovation, but a practice with demonstrable origins in Athenian tragedy. The *Agamemnon*, the *Hecabe*, and the *IA* together establish a network in which the maidens serve as each other's paradigm.[26] This network is worth exploring in some detail, for it will clarify the relationship between Polyxena and Iphigenia in the *Metamorphoses*.

The earliest extant presentation of Iphigenia's sacrifice in tragedy is in the *parodos* of Aeschylus' *Agamemnon*, which portrays Iphigenia as a victim of circumstances outside her control. For example, the chorus describes the dilemma of Agamemnon, torn between the welfare of the expedition and the welfare of his family:

> "βαρεῖα μὲν κὴρ τὸ μὴ πιθέσθαι,
> βαρεῖα δ', εἰ
> τέκνον δαΐξω, δόμων ἄγαλμα,
> μιαίνων παρθενοσφάγοισιν

[24] Both are also potential brides of Achilles: see pp. 189–90, below.

[25] March 2003, 151.

[26] In addition to Eur. *Hec.*, lost tragedies about or featuring Polyxena include Soph., *TrGF* IV.522–8; Eur. II, *TrGF* I.17; Nic. Alex., *TrGF* I.127.9; Enn. *Hec. SRF* I.162–76; Acc. *Hec. SRF* I.481. My discussion of the dialogue between Iphigenia and Polyxena in extant Greek plays is largely a matter of circumstance. Who knows what these other poets might have contributed to the discussion?

ῥείθροις πατρῴους χέρας πέλας βω-
μοῦ· τί τῶνδ' ἄνευ κακῶν;"

"It is a dire fate not to heed, and a dire fate to sacrifice my child, the glory of my house, polluting my fatherly hands with streams of maiden-slaughter at the altar. Which of these choices is without evil?" (Aesch. *Ag*. 206–11)

He eventually decides in favor of the fleet, donning the notorious ἀνάγκας λέπαδνον (necessity's yoke, 218), against which there is no recourse:

λιτὰς δὲ καὶ κληδόνας πατρῴους
παρ' οὐδὲν αἰῶνα παρθένειόν <τ'>
ἔθεντο φιλόμαχοι βραβῆς.
φράσεν δ' ἀόζοις πατὴρ μετ' εὐχὰν
δίκαν χιμαίρας ὕπερθε βωμοῦ
πέπλοισι περιπετῆ παντὶ θυμῷ
προνωπῆ λαβεῖν ἀέρ-
δην, στόματός τε καλλιπρῴ-
ρου φυλακᾷ κατασχεῖν
φθόγγον ἀραῖον οἴκοις,

βίᾳ χαλινῶν τ' ἀναύδῳ μένει.
κρόκου βαφὰς δ' ἐς πέδον χέουσα
ἔβαλλ' ἕκαστον θυτή-
ρων ἀπ' ὄμματος βέλει φιλοίκτῳ,
πρέπουσά θ' ὡς ἐν γραφαῖς, προσεννέπειν
θέλουσ', ἐπεὶ πολλάκις
πατρὸς κατ' ἀνδρῶνας εὐτραπέζους
ἔμελψεν, ἁγνᾷ δ' ἀταύρωτος αὐδᾷ πατρὸς
φίλου τριτόσπονδον εὔποτμον παι-
ῶνα φίλως ἐτίμα.

The chieftains, eager for battle, valued as nothing her pleading and cries of "Father!" and her virginal youth. After prayers, her father ordered the attendants to lift her up above the altar like a she-goat, as she fell forward about his robes, pleading with all her heart, and he ordered them to suppress with a restraint on her beautiful mouth any curse upon the house, with violence and the ineffable strength of the bit. Pouring saffron garments toward the ground, her eyes darted pitiably, striking each of the celebrants. She stood out as if in a painting, wishing she could address them, since she often sang in her father's hospitable banquet halls, and, not yet married, did justice to the joyous paean at the third libation with her pure voice. (Aesch. *Ag*. 228–46)

Iphigenia supplicates the Achaean leaders and her father (λιτὰς δὲ καὶ κληδόνας πατρῴους, 228), moving pity with her eyes when she cannot use words (ἀπ' ὄμματος βέλει φιλοίκτῳ, 240), held over the altar like a goat (δίκαν χιμαίρας, 232) with a bit in her mouth (βίᾳ χαλινῶν, 238). Here Iphigenia is submissive and dehumanized, her body and voice controlled by others, a paradigm of maidenly victimization.

Polyxena's death in the *Hecabe* provides a stark contrast (Talthybius reporting):

> ἡ δ', ὡς ἐφράσθη, τόνδ' ἐσήμηνεν λόγον:
> "ὦ τὴν ἐμὴν πέρσαντες Ἀργεῖοι πόλιν,
> ἑκοῦσα θνῄσκω· μή τις ἅψηται χροὸς
> τοὐμοῦ· παρέξω γὰρ δέρην εὐκαρδίως.
> ἐλευθέραν δέ μ', ὡς ἐλευθέρα θάνω,
> πρὸς θεῶν, μεθέντες κτείνατ'· ἐν νεκροῖσι γὰρ
> δούλη κεκλῆσθαι βασιλὶς οὖσ' αἰσχύνομαι."
> λαοὶ δ' ἐπερρόθησαν, Ἀγαμέμνων τ' ἄναξ
> εἶπεν μεθεῖναι παρθένον νεανίαις ...
> λαβοῦσα πέπλους ἐξ ἄκρας ἐπωμίδος
> ἔρρηξε λαγόνας ἐς μέσας παρ' ὀμφαλόν,
> μαστούς τ' ἔδειξε στέρνα θ' ὡς ἀγάλματος
> κάλλιστα, καὶ καθεῖσα πρὸς γαῖαν γόνυ
> ἔλεξε πάντων τλημονέστατον λόγον:
> "ἰδού, τόδ', εἰ μὲν στέρνον, ὦ νεανία,
> παίειν προθυμῇ, παῖσον, εἰ δ' ὑπ' αὐχένα
> χρῄζεις, πάρεστι λαιμὸς εὐτρεπὴς ὅδε."
>
> When she saw [the preparations], she delivered this speech: "Argives, destroyers of my city, I go to death willingly. Let no one touch my body, for I shall offer my neck wholeheartedly. Allow me to be free when you kill me, by the gods, so that I may die free. Since I come from a royal line, being called a slave among the dead shames me." The host shouted in agreement, and lord Agamemnon told the youths to release the maiden ... She grasped her gown and tore it open from the tips of her shoulders to her sides near the navel, revealing her breasts – most beautiful, like a statue. Kneeling upon the earth she spoke her saddest word of all: "Look, young man, if you want to strike my chest, strike here. Or, if you want to strike below my throat, this neck of mine is ready." (Eur. *Hec.* 546–54, 558–65)

Unlike Iphigenia, Polyxena goes willingly and enthusiastically to her death (ἑκοῦσα, 547; εὐκαρδίως, 549). Although initially restrained, she is released (554). Nowhere on her body are there fetters, not least on her mouth. Whereas Iphigenia can only wish to speak, Polyxena speaks openly. Hers is a self-sacrifice, a showcase for her bravery and humanity, a paradigm of virginal nobility.

William Thalmann successfully argues that Euripides, in establishing Polyxena as the paradigmatic antithesis of Iphigenia, offers a calculated response to Aeschylus. In particular, Thalmann sees in Polyxena's act of disrobing (558–61) an amplification of a puzzling Aeschylean line, κρόκου βαφὰς δ' ἐς πέδον χέουσα (*Ag.* 239), for which there are several interpretations. Perhaps Iphigenia's robe is touching the earth as she is lifted up; perhaps she has removed a veil from her head and placed it on the ground; or perhaps she has in fact disrobed completely. Common to all of these readings is a sexual display, either incidental, deliberate, or prescribed by ritual. The veil in particular carries associations with marriage, regardless of whether Iphigenia is in Aeschylus' version betrothed to Achilles or more generally the "bride of death," and its removal signifies the maiden's displaced sexual maturation. In any event, Thalmann rightly stresses that Iphigenia's sexuality is implicit, while that of Polyxena is explicit. She does not simply remove her *peplos*, she tears it open down the front (ἔρρηξε, 559); Talthybius, in turn, commenting on the beauty of her breasts (μαστούς τ' ἔδειξε στέρνα <τε> κάλλιστα, 560–1), renders the heroine the object of the male gaze.[27] To Thalmann's insights I might add that the *Hecabe* expands upon a reference to the visual arts in the *Agamemnon*. The chorus likens the sight of Iphigenia at the altar to a painting (πρέπουσα ὡς ἐν γραφαῖς, 241), while Talthybius compares the nude Polyxena to a statue (ὡς ἀγάλματος, 560). Here again is a sense of amplification, with Euripides adding a third dimension to his victim.

The *Hecabe* places Polyxena in opposition to the Iphigenia of the *Agamemnon*. In his posthumous *IA*, however, Euripides closes the gap by aligning Iphigenia with his own Polyxena. At first the maiden appears very much like the Aeschylean heroine.[28] A naïf who knows little of the world (ποῦ τοὺς Φρύγας λέγουσιν ᾠκίσθαι, πάτερ; 662), she pleads with Agamemnon for her life after learning of the impending sacrifice:

> ἱκετηρίαν δὲ γόνασιν ἐξάπτω σέθεν
> τὸ σῶμα τοὐμόν, ὅπερ ἔτικτεν ἥδε σοι,
> μή μ' ἀπολέσῃς ἄωρον· ἡδὺ γὰρ τὸ φῶς
> βλέπειν· τὰ δ' ὑπὸ γῆς μή μ' ἰδεῖν ἀναγκάσῃς.
> πρώτη σ' ἐκάλεσα πατέρα καὶ σὺ παῖδ' ἐμέ·
> πρώτη δὲ γόνασι σοῖσι σῶμα δοῦσ' ἐμὸν
> φίλας χάριτας ἔδωκα κἀντεδεξάμην.

> I bind my body, which my mother here bore for you, to your knees in supplication. Do not obliterate my life. How sweet to live, to see the light! Do

[27] Thalmann 1993, 136–48, a thoughtful and nuanced discussion, one of many highlighting Euripides' responses to Aeschylus in the *Hecabe*.

[28] The more general discussion of Luschnig 1988, 3–5, has guided my observations here.

not make me see the Underworld. I was the first to call you father, and you the first to call me your child. I was the first to kiss you as I sat upon your knee, and we would greet each other. (Eur. *IA* 1216–22)

Her words, particularly her reminder that she was Agamemnon's first child, the first to call him father (πρώτη σ' ἐκάλεσα πατέρα, 1220), evoke the cries of "Father!" reported in the *Agamemnon* (κληδόνας πατρῴους, 228). Moreover, her remembrance of their mutual affection (1221–2) recalls the girl who once sang at his libations (*Ag.* 243–6). She concludes by endorsing life, no matter how miserable:

τὸ φῶς τόδ' ἀνθρώποισιν ἥδιστον βλέπειν,
τὰ νέρθε δ' οὐδέν· μαίνεται δ' ὃς εὔχεται
θανεῖν. κακῶς ζῆν κρεῖσσον ἢ καλῶς θανεῖν.

It is sweetest for mankind to see the light, and what lies below is nothing. Whoever prays for death is mad. Better to live wretchedly than to die nobly. (Eur. *IA* 1250–2)

Her sentiments are the reverse of Polyxena's, who claims that living dishonorably is worse than dying (*Hec.* 375–8, especially τὸ γὰρ ζῆν μὴ καλῶς μέγας πόνος, 378). Agamemnon, too, echoes his Aeschylean precursor:

δεινῶς δ' ἔχει μοι ταῦτα τολμῆσαι, γύναι,
δεινῶς δὲ καὶ μή· τοῦτο γὰρ πρᾶξαί με δεῖ.

To dare this deed, wife, is horrible, and it is horrible not to dare. For it is necessary that I do it. (Eur. *IA* 1257–8)

This aphorism recalls the sense and syntax of the dilemma articulated in the *Agamemnon* (βαρεῖα μέν … βαρεῖα δ<έ>, 206–7), while his appeal to the needful (τοῦτο γὰρ πρᾶξαί με δεῖ, 1258) is a more prosaic version of Aeschylus' yoke of necessity (ἀνάγκας λέπαδνον, 218).

At this point in the *IA* it would seem that Iphigenia will be sacrificed unwillingly and forcefully, as she was in the *Agamemnon*. Before she can be led away, Achilles enters, vowing to defend Iphigenia and his honor at the cost of his own life (1345–68). Instead of a battle, however, an unexpected shift in the Aeschylean paradigm occurs. Iphigenia offers herself to the sword:

κατθανεῖν μέν μοι δέδοκται· τοῦτο δ' αὐτὸ βούλομαι
εὐκλεῶς πρᾶξαι, παρεῖσά γ' ἐκποδὼν τὸ δυσγενές.
δεῦρο δὴ σκέψαι μεθ' ἡμῶν, μῆτερ, ὡς καλῶς λέγω·
εἰς ἔμ' Ἑλλὰς ἡ μεγίστη πᾶσα νῦν ἀποβλέπει,
κἀν ἐμοὶ πορθμός τε ναῶν καὶ Φρυγῶν κατασκαφαί.

I am determined to die. I wish to do this very thing nobly, casting aside the unseemly. Mother, come and see how well I speak. Hellas in all its might looks to me, and to me falls the passage of ships and the destruction of Trojans. (Eur. *IA* 1375–9)

Her new-found self-possession and worldliness constitute not only a complete reversal of her character, but also a shift toward the paradigm of Polyxena.[29]

The conflation of the two maidens carries over into the play's posthumous epilogue and the messenger's account of the sacrifice. After walking freely into the grove of Artemis, Iphigenia addresses Agamemnon with unfettered mouth:

"ὦ πάτερ, πάρειμί σοι·
τοὐμὸν δὲ σῶμα τῆς ἐμῆς ὑπὲρ πάτρας
καὶ τῆς ἁπάσης Ἑλλάδος γαίας ὕπερ
θῦσαι δίδωμ' ἑκοῦσα πρὸς βωμὸν θεᾶς."

"Father, I am here. My body I commit willingly to sacrifice on the goddess' altar for the sake of my homeland and all of Hellas." (Eur. *IA* 1552–5)

These are not words of resistance, but of acquiescence, the sort of thing a Polyxena might say. In fact, Iphigenia repeats almost verbatim two of Polyxena's lines in the *Hecabe*:

"πρὸς ταῦτα μὴ ψαύσῃ τις Ἀργείων ἐμοῦ·
σιγῇ παρέξω γὰρ δέρην εὐκαρδίως."

"Therefore let none of the Argives touch me, for I shall offer my neck wholeheartedly, without a word." (Eur. *IA* 1559–60)

"μή τις ἅψηται χροὸς
τοὐμοῦ· παρέξω γὰρ δέρην εὐκαρδίως." 549

"Let no one touch my body, for I shall offer my neck wholeheartedly." (Eur. *Hec.* 548–9)

Not only does Iphigenia quote Polyxena, she quotes her at her most Polyxenaesque, standing before the assembly and declaring her willingness to die. The play seems to engage in the *contaminatio* favored by Roman playwrights.

[29] Whether Ennius associated his Iphigenia with Polyxena is unknown, but *SRF* 1.202, in which Iphigenia declares her resolution to die (*Acherontem obibo, ubi Mortis thesauri obiacent*), is suggestive.

These conflations are not Euripidean in the strict sense, since the entire epilogue of the *IA* has long been marked as interpolated. D. L. Page, for instance, proposed that a fourth-century poet composed all of the messenger speech (with the exception of 1554, an even later insertion).[30] Nevertheless, such textual difficulties, although relevant to an appreciation of Euripides' play in itself, should not hamper our discussion of Ovid. On the one hand, we are privileging the conflation of Iphigenia and Polyxena as a tradition established by tragic poets. The interpolator, although not Euripides, participates in this tradition, and Iphigenia's speech before the altar responds to and continues the paradigmatic shift already under way in the original Euripidean text.[31] On the other hand, if the maiden's speech is a fourth-century addition, it must have survived into Ovid's own era, by which time it had become the tradition.

To return to Ovid, his dialogue between the paradigms of Iphigenia and Polyxena resumes a dialogue begun by tragedians over four centuries earlier. That said, we also expect Ovid to contribute something new to the discussion, which he does by way of the intratextual footnote in book 12. Although the *IA* had assimilated the two maidens of the *Agamemnon* and the *Hecabe*, the plays were, and remain, autonomous texts. However interconnected they seem, they can stand alone – much like Ovid's own Hecabe and Procne narratives, which are mutually allusive but distinct. His Iphigenia and Polyxena episodes, however, are structured such that drawing parallels is almost compulsory. Ovidian narrative indulges in vivid presentations of characters in turmoil, and on this score the experience of Iphigenia in the *Metamorphoses* is underwhelming. Condensed into six verses, it requires the pathos of another heroine to attain a tragic register.

The Polyxena episode recovers what is absent from the Iphigenia episode. In fact, several elements of Polyxena's sacrifice make better sense when read with Iphigenia in mind. Consider how the heroine is taken to Achilles' tomb:

> rapta sinu matris, quam iam prope sola fovebat ...
>
> Stolen from her mother's embrace, now her only solace ... (*Met.* 13.450)

[30] Page 1934, 196.

[31] Our excerpts from the *IA* before the epilogue (1216–22, 1250–2, 1257–8, and 1375–9) might well be genuine, and therefore part of the interpolator's text: see Page 1934, as well as his general observations following verses 1270 and 1391. Even if these passages are spurious, however, they were still probably part of the play as Ovid knew it.

In Chapter 4 *rapta sinu matris* was interpreted as denoting resistance on Hecabe's part, as if she were unwilling to release her daughter.[32] Now, perhaps, it signifies the daughter's unwillingness to release her mother. If so, this reading seems out of place in an episode based on Euripides, where Polyxena assures Odysseus that she will neither supplicate nor resist him (*Hec.* 342–50) and asks Hecabe not to stand in her way (372–4). Yet from Iphigenia's point of view, resistance of some sort is to be expected. This is true whether we are thinking of the *Agamemnon* or the *IA*, for both plays feature maidens who are (at first) unwilling to die.

Polyxena's approach to the tomb can also be seen through Iphigenia's eyes:

> quae memor ipsa sui postquam crudelibus aris
> admota est sensitque sibi fera sacra parari. 454

> She remembered herself after she was brought before the pitiless altar and sensed the savage sacrifice was being readied for her. (*Met.* 13.453–4)

Let us treat these three clauses not in order of appearance, but in order of action. First, Polyxena is conveyed to the altar (*aris* | *admota est*, 453–4). The presence of an altar at a sacrifice, even at what is essentially a libation, is not in itself problematic. Euripides, however, portrays Polyxena's death as a libation to the dead, a *choē*, in two stages: Neoptolemus empties a golden cup over his father's tomb (δέξαι χοάς μοι τάσδε, *Hec.* 535), and then sheds the maiden's blood, which he has invited the shade to drink (ἐλθὲ δ', ὡς πίῃς, 536).[33] Whereas liquid might be poured onto an altar in other kinds of libation (as Hercules demonstrates: *vinaque marmoreas patera fundebat in aras*, 9.160), in *choai* the usual practice was to pour directly onto the earth, over the mound of the deceased.[34] Accordingly, there is no mention of an altar in the *Hecabe*, while in the *Metamorphoses*, the *arae* seem little more than scene-dressing.[35] Yet an altar is a prominent fixture in literary treatments of Iphigenia's sacrifice. One is reported in the *Agamemnon* (ὕπερθε βωμοῦ, 232) and the *IA* (πρὸς βωμὸν θεᾶς, 1555; 1589); another appears in Ovid's account in *Met.* 12 (*ante aram stetit*

[32] Chapter 4, p. 108.

[33] I thank Leslie Mechem for this suggestion. Collard 1991 also endorses Polyxena's death as a libation.

[34] See Zaidman and Pantel 1992, 39–41, on libations in Greek religion, including *choai*.

[35] Compare the famous Tyrrhenian amphora by the Timiades painter (British Museum 1897.7–27.2), which depicts Neoptolemus cutting the throat of Polyxena who is held aloft over the tomb of Achilles, on top of which rests a flaming altar. Since Polyxena's blood is clearly flowing onto the mound, the altar appears ornamental, perhaps included only to emphasize the sacrificial context of the girl's death.

Iphigenia, 31), one of few concrete details. The altar is an essential apparatus for a virgin who is meant to replace a sacrificial animal (and vice versa, through the intervention of Diana).

Next, Polyxena observes the ritual preparations (*sensitque sibi fera sacra parari*, 454). The verb *sentire* can denote both visual and mental perception.[36] Given the psychological tendencies of Ovidian narrative, as well as the use of the more common verb for seeing two verses later (*vidit*, 456), the latter sense seems preferable with *sibi*: Polyxena realizes the rites are for her.[37] This is another problematic reading, since realization implies ignorance or surprise, and neither is a state of mind one might attribute to Polyxena – at least, not to Euripides' heroine, who exits knowing exactly what is in store (*Hec.* 435–7). At least one commentator has suggested that such matters are of no concern to Ovid, the implication being that readers ought not be concerned with them, either.[38] An intratextual reading of this line both acknowledges and embraces the problem, for surprise is representative of Iphigenia's mental state, especially of a girl lured to an altar under false pretenses.

Arriving at the tomb, and realizing she is the victim, Polyxena becomes mindful of herself (*memor* [*erat*] *ipsa sui*, 453). In Chapter 4 this expression, in line with the intertextual properties of memory in Latin poetry, signified Polyxena's recognition of herself as Polyxena – a tragic character who must deliver a tragic performance.[39] An intratextual reading builds upon this interpretation: perhaps Polyxena remembers not only that she is Polyxena, but also that she is *not* Iphigenia, despite appearances to the contrary. Or, perhaps she remembers that for intratextual intents and purposes she *is* Iphigenia, or as close to an Iphigenia as readers of the *Metamorphoses* are going to find.

An intratextual memory encourages us to seek out other traces of Iphigenia's experience, even after what seems for Polyxena a definitive moment of self-realization:

> utque Neoptolemum stantem ferrumque tenentem
> inque suo vidit figentem lumina vultu …

> And when she saw Neoptolemus standing there, holding his sword, and fixing his eyes upon hers … (*Met.* 13.455–6)

[36] *OLD s.v. sentio* 1 versus 2b. [37] So Hopkinson 2000.

[38] Bömer 1982: "Ovid schaltet mit dem für ihn nicht wichtigen Detail nach Belieben."

[39] Chapter 4, p. 109.

We have been looking through Polyxena's eyes, and we continue to do so through the vivid sequence of accusative present participles describing Neoptolemus. At the same time, Neoptolemus reciprocates the gaze, his eyes locked upon hers: *in figentem lumina vultu*, 456. *figere* has palpable connotations of piercing and wounding,[40] appropriately so for a sacrificial ritual, and doubly so for a son of Achilles, who looks darkly at Hector during their fateful duel in the *Iliad* (ὑπόδρα ἰδών, *Il.* 22.344 Monro and Allen). Perhaps the father's hostility transfers to Hector's sister. Or perhaps Neoptolemus is looking for signs of Iphigenia, who in the *Agamemnon* is gagged and can only launch piteous missiles with her eyes (ἀπ’ ὄμματος βέλει φιλοίκτῳ, 240). With his own eyes, therefore, he makes a preemptive strike against a visual assault from his victim. Furthermore, *figere* has strong erotic overtones in line with other Latin sexual metaphors, such as striking, cutting, wounding, and even killing.[41] An erotic, penetrating gaze upon Polyxena seems fitting, given Talthybius' objectification of her in the *Hecabe* (560–1), and given that the gaze comes from Neoptolemus, a stand-in for his father, to whom Polyxena will be married in death. Yet it would apply equally to Iphigenia, who was lured to Aulis under the pretext of marrying Achilles (*IA* 128–32) and also sexualized in death (*Ag.* 239).

In the speech that follows, Polyxena makes it clear that she is Polyxena (*Polyxena ferrem*, 460; *Priami … filia regis*, 470). Despite these self-identifications, she sometimes sounds like an Iphigenia, as in her wish to die untouched:

> "ite procul, si iusta peto, tactuque viriles
> virgineo removete manus." 467
> (*Met.* 13.466–7)

These lines appropriate Hecabe's command to Talthybius that none of the Achaeans touch her fallen daughter (*Hec.* 604–8).[42] In the present discussion they also imitate *Hec.* 548–9, where Polyxena beseeches the Achaeans not to touch her (μή τις ἅψηται χροός, 548). Moreover, Ovid's Polyxena alludes to the *IA* and Iphigenia's request to remain untouched (μὴ ψαύσῃ τις Ἀργείων ἐμοῦ, 1559). Although this verse is modeled after the *Hecabe*,

[40] *OLD s.v. figo* 1b.

[41] On violent sexual metaphors in Latin see Adams 1982, ch. 4, especially 145–59. The fact that Adams does not include *figere* does not hinder a sexual reading of the verb at *Met.* 13.456. My thanks to Reader "A" for suggesting this line of inquiry.

[42] Chapter 4, pp. 110–11.

it recommends itself for epitomizing the very conflation Ovid seeks to exploit. His Polyxena imitates Iphigenia in the act of imitating Polyxena.

As already noted, the request of Ovid's Polyxena is bound up with general concerns for her virginity. More specifically, she is concerned with pleasing Achilles:

> acceptior illi,
> quisquis is est, quem caede mea placare paratis,
> liber erit sanguis. 469

> Blood that is free will be more acceptable to him, whoever he is, whom you placate with my sacrifice. (*Met.* 13.467–9)

The parenthesis *quisquis is est* (468) has engendered some debate. Franz Bömer and others take it as a contemptuous dismissal of Achilles, on the grounds that Polyxena, like her Euripidean precursor, should know to whom she is being sacrificed.[43] Indeed, her knowing pun two words earlier, ***acceptior illi*** (467), betrays her knowledge and her contempt.[44] Elsewhere in Ovid, however, *quisquis is est* and its variants express genuine ignorance: recall Laodamia, who advises Protesilaus to beware Hector (*Hectora, quisquis is est, si sum tibi cura, caveto*, *Her.* 13.65).[45] If, as with *sensit* (454), it is too much to believe that Polyxena has no prior knowledge of either the ritual or Achilles, *quisquis is est* becomes another evocation of Iphigenia's experience, not only her general ignorance of her impending demise, but also a specific instance in which Achilles' identity is in question. At *IA* 1338 she sees a throng of approaching men, among them Achilles, come to defend his bride from the Achaean mob. Yet the task of identifying him falls to Clytemnestra, for Iphigenia has never met the hero in person. Rather, her first impulse is to defer their meeting by running away in shame (Ἀχιλλέα τόνδ᾽ ἰδεῖν αἰσχύνομαι, 1341). Thus *quisquis is est* recalls Iphigenia's inability to recognize Achilles, while signifying Polyxena's refusal to do the same.

In the remainder of her performance Polyxena says and does more or less what we would expect of a Polyxena, such as falling modestly onto Achilles' tomb (479–80), which is a virtual translation of *Hec.* 568–70.[46] The reaction of the Achaeans to her speech, however, seems out of character:

[43] Bömer 1982, following Shackleton Bailey: "Stolz einer *virgo regia*." Compare Hopkinson 2000, who nevertheless allows for the possibility that Polyxena might not know Achilles.

[44] I thank Reader "A" for calling the pun to my attention.

[45] Chapter 3, p. 83.

[46] Observed in Chapter 4, p. 202.

dixerat. at populus lacrimas, quas illa tenebat,
non tenet; ipse etiam flens invitusque sacerdos …
(*Met.* 13.474–5)

In Chapter 4 this outpouring of grief was a measure of Polyxena's oratorical competence, an appropriate response to a tragic spectacle.[47] Yet this is an altogether different reaction to what is reported in the *Hecabe*. Although Talthybius admits to weeping during the sacrifice (518–20), tears are noticeably absent from his account. Instead Hecabe hears that the Achaeans shouted their approval of Polyxena's words (λαοὶ δ' ἐπερρόθησαν, 553), while Neoptolemus was divided in purpose (ὁ δ' οὐ θέλων τε καὶ θέλων, 566); and that the soldiers threw leaves upon the corpse and gathered logs for a pyre, while reproaching any and all stragglers (571–80). But there is nothing like the grieving from Ovid's *populus* and *sacerdos*, who unlike his tragic counterpart is weeping and wholly unwilling to slay Polyxena (*flens invitusque*, 475).

In accounts of Iphigenia's sacrifice, however, tears are a common reaction to her situation. In the *IA*, for example, Agamemnon weeps openly at his daughter's approach:

ἀνεστέναξε, κἄμπαλιν στρέψας κάρα
δάκρυε, πρόσθεν ὀμμάτων πέπλον προθείς.

He groaned and turned his head, weeping and covering his eyes with his robe. (Eur. *IA* 1549–50)

Likewise the officiants in Ovid's version:

flentibus ante aram stetit Iphigenia ministris.
(*Met.* 12.31)

The *Agamemnon* offers the most dispassionate account, with Iphigenia's pleas falling on deaf ears (παρ' οὐδὲν ἔθεντο, 229–30). Yet there are tears in this play: the chorus notes that the Atreidae wept upon hearing Artemis' demands:

χθόνα βά-
κτροις ἐπικρούσαντας Ἀτρεί-
δας δάκρυ μὴ κατασχεῖν.

Striking the earth with their staves, the sons of Atreus could not curb their tears. (Aesch. *Ag.* 202–4)

[47] Chapter 4, p. 111.

None of this is to say that Polyxena's death is unworthy of the grief it inspires. Rather, the tears of Ovid's Achaeans complete the experience of Iphigenia even as they acknowledge the tragic heroism of Polyxena; they cry not for one maiden or the other, but for both. So doing, they activate a final link in the intratextual network of the *Metamorphoses*, which like tragedy avails itself of codes under which the sacrificial victim may be played and replayed.

As an epilogue, let us briefly consider one last account of Iphigenia's sacrifice, perhaps the closest Latin antecedent to Ovid's version in book 12:

> cui simul infula virgineos circumdata comptus
> ex utraque pari malarum parte profusast,
> et maestum simul ante aras adstare parentem
> sensit et hunc propter ferrum celare ministros
> aspectuque suo lacrimas effundere civis,
> muta metu terram genibus summissa petebat.

> As soon as the sacrificial fillets wreathed her virginal locks and flowed down either side in equal lengths, and she realized that her father was mourning as he stood by the altars and that beside him the officiants were concealing a sword, and that the host was weeping at the very sight of her, her knees gave way and she sank to the ground in silent terror. (Lucr. *DRN* 1.87–92 Martin)

This is an excerpt from book 1 of the *De rerum natura*, in which Lucretius offers Iphigenia (here called Iphianassa[48]) as proof of the atrocities committed in the name of religion. The passage recreates Iphigenia's experience in terms familiar from Ovid – the altar (*aras*, 89), the girl's growing awareness (*sensit*, 90), the grief of her father (*maestum parentem*, 89) and of the assembly (*lacrimas effundere civis*, 91) – so familiar that we cannot doubt it influenced Ovid in depicting both maidens' ordeals.[49] I draw attention to Lucretius not to complicate the dialogue between Ovid and the tragedians (there is plenty of room for another Latin poet), but to make a final point. Although the intratextual footnote in the Iphigenia episode prompts us to seek her paradigm in the Polyxena episode, the shifting of the paradigms in Athenian tragedy enhances our search, if not guides it:

[48] The *Cypria*, *EGF* fr. 17, appears to have distinguished Iphigenia from Iphianassa, who is also one of the daughters (with Chrysothemis and Laodice) Agamemnon pledges to Achilles (*Il.* 9.144–7). Lucretius, however, seems to have conflated the two: see M. P. Brown 1984 (*DRN* 1.85).

[49] For a general discussion of Lucretian echoes in Ovid's Polyxena sacrifice see Venini 1952, 369; also Keith 2000, 122–3. On Lucretius' debt to Roman tragedy in his account of Iphigenia see Goldberg 2005, 133–4.

we are more receptive to the footnote in light of the exchange between Euripides and Aeschylus. What is more, the sacrifice of Polyxena in the *Metamorphoses* takes stock of these earlier treatments. Nor, as our parting glance at Lucretius has shown, does it confine itself to tragic poetry. The corollary, then, is that intertextuality and intratextuality are hardly mutually exclusive: in Ovid's poetic *mundus* reading inward benefits from reading outward, and vice versa.

3 Medea and Deianira: pernicious text(ile)s

This principle is worth bearing in mind as we explore another intratextual link between two tragic narratives, Medea (book 7) and Deianira (9). As was the case with Polyxena, Deianira's story contains a puzzling detail that defies literal explanation but admits an intratextual one. As was also the case, tragic intertextuality will be crucial in making intratextual connections within the *Metamorphoses.*

We plunge *in medias res* and into the difficulty in Deianira's narrative. Having heard a rumor about Hercules and Iole, she decides on a course of action:

> in cursus animus varios abit; omnibus illis
> praetulit imbutam Nesseo sanguine vestem
> mittere, quae vires defecto reddat amori. 154

> Although her mind wanders various paths, to all others she prefers to send the garment steeped in the blood of Nessus, and so to restore the vigor of lost love. (*Met.* 9.152–4)

These lines seem consonant with the plot of the *Women of Trachis.* The problem, however, begins to take shape in light of the encounter between Nessus and Deianira in the tragedy, which (as the heroine recounts it) occurred just after Heracles struck the centaur with a poisoned arrow:

> "ἐὰν γὰρ ἀμφίθρεπτον αἷμα τῶν ἐμῶν
> σφαγῶν ἐνέγκῃ χερσίν, ᾗ μελάγχολος
> ἔβαψεν ἰὸς θρέμμα Λερναίας ὕδρας,
> ἔσται φρενός σοι τοῦτο κηλητήριον
> τῆς Ἡρακλείας, ὥστε μήτιν' εἰσιδὼν
> στέρξει γυναῖκα κεῖνος ἀντὶ σοῦ πλέον."

> "For if you carry in your hands the clotted blood of my wound, where the black bile of the Lernaean hydra has tainted it, you will have a charm to control the passion of Heracles, such that if he looks at another woman, he will not love her more than you." (Soph. *Trach.* 572–7)

Deianira says that she has kept the blood hidden in a copper cauldron (λέβητι χαλκέῳ κεκρυμμένον, 556). It has been in the house, well sealed (δόμοις γὰρ ἦν … ἐγκεκλῃμένον καλῶς, 578–9), untouched by light and heat (ἄπυρον ἀκτῖνός τ᾽ ἀεὶ | θερμῆς ἄθικτον, 685–6). But when did the cauldron come into play? Did Deianira happen to be carrying it as Nessus was dying, or did she transfer the blood into one later on? If so, how did she collect the blood in the first place? By removing the arrow from the wound and securing it on her person?[50] (It does not help that the passage quoted above is a "notorious crux."[51]) Whatever the case, Sophocles seems to have been less concerned with how Deianira took the blood than with how she preserved it in liquid form to dye Heracles' robe (χιτῶνα τόνδ᾽ ἔβαψα, 580).

The means of collection appears to have caused Ovid some concern, since his version of the exchange is rather different:

> quod simul evulsum est, sanguis per utrumque foramen
> emicuit, mixtus Lernaei tabe veneni.
> excipit hunc Nessus, "neque enim moriemur inulti,"
> secum ait et calido velamina tincta cruore
> dat munus raptae velut inritamen amoris.

> When Nessus tore out the shaft, blood and gore of the hydra's poison gushed forth from both ends of the wound. This he gathered, saying to himself, "May I not die unavenged." He gave his bloody garment to the woman he had stolen, a gift to stimulate passion. (*Met.* 9.129–33)

The *velamina* of Nessus (132) seem to be an attempt at greater plausibility. We need not suppose that Deianira took the arrow or had a *lebes* on hand, if the centaur gives her a blood-stained garment. Nevertheless, in providing this solution, Ovid creates a problem for his own text. In the *Women of Trachis* Deianira smears the blood on a *peplos* she herself has woven (δώρημ᾽ ἐκείνῳ τἀνδρὶ τῆς ἐμῆς χερός, 603). But in the *Metamorphoses* the *vestis* sent to Hercules for his victory sacrifice (*imbutam Nesseo sanguine vestem*, 153) appears to be the same gory *velamina* she received from Nessus – a situation far more paradoxical than anything in Sophocles. Perhaps Deianira has sent the centaur's *vestis* to remind Hercules of his past victories: as Nessus fell, so Oechalia has fallen; if so, the hero does not

[50] So Kamerbeek 1959: "[Deianira] had to take the [admixture of blood and venom] from the arrow, when removed from the wound" (brackets mine). The arrow is a plausible solution, especially since the noun ἰός can mean either "venom" (*LSJ* s.v. ἰός B) or "arrow" (*LSJ* A, and the meaning at *Trach.* 567). If Sophocles had intended to have Nessus instruct Deianira to remove the arrow, this would render Ovid's version of events (see below) even stranger.

[51] So Davies 1991, with a useful summary of the interpretive problems.

recognize it (*capit inscius heros*, 157). Or perhaps Deianira has managed to extract the venom from the centaur's *velamina* and has applied it to an altogether different garment.[52] Who knows? No simple explanation comes of reading literally.

Reading intratextually, however, affords an opportunity to resolve the paradox. Ovid emphasizes the twice-given garment – Nessus gives it to Deianira, and she in turn gives it to Hercules – at the expense of narrative plausibility. Prompted in this way to consider poisoned robes in a mythical and tragic context, we are reminded of Medea, who in Euripides' play sends her rival an enchanted gown (and a diadem). Our association of the Deianira and Medea paradigms is intertextual, but the footnoting at work in the perfunctory Corinthian episode of *Met.* 7.391–7 activates a simultaneous intratextual association. The severely abbreviated demise of Jason's new bride (*Colchis arsit nova nupta venenis*, 394) finds a more expansive analogue in the motives and methods on display in book 9. For example, although Nessus presents his *velamina* as a boon (*munus*, 133), his stage-whisper tells otherwise: *"neque enim moriemur inulti," | secum ait* (131–2). Ovid, unlike Sophocles, highlights the centaur's dissimulation at the moment of his death. Such irony is on par with Euripides' *Medea*, where the gown and diadem, which the audience already knows to be deadly (774–97), are offered as benevolent wedding gifts (φερνάς, 956). In using a garment to avenge himself on a rival, Nessus follows the Medea code adumbrated in book 7.

The analogy between the offerings of Medea and Nessus plays out in Hercules' gruesome pathos, previously observed in Chapter 4:[53]

> nec mora, letiferam conatur scindere vestem;
> qua trahitur, trahit illa cutem, foedumque relatu,
> aut haeret membris frustra temptata revelli
> aut laceros artus et grandia detegit ossa. 169
> (*Met.* 9.166–9)

Although the *Women of Trachis*, through a messenger speech by Hyllus, depicts the workings of the *peplos* in great detail, including how it clings to Heracles' sides (προσπτύσσεται | πλευραῖσιν ἀρτίκολλος, 767–8), nowhere is there anything as graphically *foedum relatu* (167) as in Ovid's account. The image of the hero tearing away his own flesh is not

[52] Anderson 1972 (*Met.* 9.152–3) notes that in Apollod. *Bibl.* 2.7.7 Heracles sends Lichas to Trachis to fetch clothing worthy of the sacrifice to Zeus at Cenaeum. Even if this scenario was what Ovid had in mind, the terseness of his account is still problematic.

[53] Chapter 4, p. 117.

Sophoclean, but it is not wholly Ovidian, either. As W. S. Anderson has noted, it has much in common with the messenger speech in Euripides' *Medea*, in which Creon tries to extricate himself from his daughter's fatal embrace:[54]

> χρῄζων γεραιὸν ἐξαναστῆσαι δέμας
> προσείχεθ' ὥστε κισσὸς ἔρνεσιν δάφνης
> λεπτοῖσι πέπλοις, δεινὰ δ' ἦν παλαίσματα·
> ὃ μὲν γὰρ ἤθελ' ἐξαναστῆσαι γόνυ,
> ἣ δ' ἀντελάζυτ'· εἰ δὲ πρὸς βίαν ἄγοι,
> σάρκας γεραιὰς ἐσπάρασσ' ἀπ' ὀστέων.

> Although he longed to lift his aged frame, he was held fast to the delicate gown like ivy to branches of laurel, and there was a dire grappling. For whenever he would raise his knee to stand up, she would pull him back down. And if he struggled hard he tore the flesh from his limbs. (Eur. *Med.* 1212–7)

Nessus enacts the same sort of venomous revenge as Medea. Even as we read Hercules' demise in *Met.* 9 as an expansion of *Met.* 7.394, we must acknowledge how large the intertext of Euripides' play looms on the intratextual horizon.

Although the centaur's machinations transform the story of Deianira into one of Medeaesque proportions, we remain cognizant of the fine line separating one heroine's paradigm from the other's. Whereas Medea means to destroy Creon and his daughter, Deianira has only the best of intentions for her husband and for herself (*nescia*, 155). Nevertheless, the threshold between good intentions and bad is sometimes immaterial. This is a truth not only explicit in the treachery of Nessus, which is disguised as benevolence, but also implicit in the brief monologue of Deianira prior to sending the robe:

> mox deinde "quid autem
> flemus?" ait "paelex lacrimis laetabitur istis.
> quae quoniam adveniet, properandum aliquidque novandum est,
> dum licet et nondum thalamos tenet altera nostros." 146

> Soon she says, "But why do I weep? My rival will be glad of such tears. Since she will soon be here, I must plan something, and quickly, while I can, before the other woman takes control of my bed." (*Met.* 9.143–6)

Ovid's heroine takes a more adversarial view of Iole than Sophocles' heroine. In the *Women of Trachis* Deianira refers to the girl as "offensive

[54] Anderson 1972.

merchandise" (λωβητὸν ἐμπόλημα, 538), and hopes that the love potion will defeat her (φίλτροις δ' ἐάν πως τήνδ' ὑπερβαλώμεθα, 584). But such statements are balanced by her acceptance of Heracles' passions (445–6, 459–62), her refusal to blame Iole (447–8, 462–3), her sympathy for the girl's misfortunes (463–6), and her will to remain sensible and to avoid anger (552–3, 582–3). In the *Metamorphoses*, however, she shows no ambivalence: Iole is a rival (*paelex*, 144), and a haughty one at that, for whom Deianira's tears would be a source of amusement (*lacrimis laetabitur*, 144). The girl's arrival is tantamount to an invasion, a struggle for control of the marriage bed (*nondum thalamos tenet*, 146). Such a threat must be neutralized quickly and decisively (*properandum ... novandum est*, 145). At this point the reader is justified in wondering exactly what the intentions of Deianira are.

Ovid's narrative finds Deianira at a crux, one without precedent in the *Women of Trachis*, where the heroine meets Iole before hearing of Heracles' infidelity and adopts the stratagem of the robe without any kind of self-debate, at least none depicted onstage.[55] Although we are outside the Sophoclean *theatron*, we are nevertheless within the bounds of tragedy, as Deianira's next lines demonstrate:[56]

> "conquerar an sileam? repetam Calydona morerne?
> excedam tectis an, si nihil amplius, obstem?" 148

> Shall I complain or be silent? Shall I go back to Calydon or linger here? Shall I leave this house or, if there is nothing more I can do, stand my ground?" (*Met.* 9.147–8)

This is, as observed in Chapter 5, the rhetoric of desperation, which Ovid employs to evoke the *aporia* of tragic monologues. From an intertextual perspective, Deianira's rhetorical questions appropriate the tragic *topos*, an appropriation independent of Sophocles, whose heroine remains more or less sure of herself. However, intertextual perspectives can inform intratextual ones, and the passage above resonates with the *locus classicus* of desperation speeches: *Med.* 502–5, in which the heroine weighs her options

[55] The Sophoclean Deianira asks the chorus whether using the love charm is rash (εἴ τι μὴ δοκῶ | πράσσειν μάταιον, 586–7). But she does so only after deciding on the *peplos* and dipping it in the blood. Unlike Ovid, Sophocles devotes no time to the decision itself.

[56] Tarrant 2004 contravenes editorial practice, including Kenney 2011, by bracketing these lines. I believe them to be genuine on the grounds that they constitute yet another instance of desperation rhetoric, and support the connection between Deianira and Medea (on both grounds see below). If interpolated, however, they nonetheless demonstrate a subsequent poet's recognition of Deianira as a tragic heroine, whose words are suited to her deeds.

following Creon's decree of exile.[57] In particular, Medea's initial questions about whether to return to her native Colchis (502–3), find an echo in Deianira's *repetam Calydona?* (147). More generally, Medea's speech is a code model for Deianira, who asks not only similar questions, but also questions of a similar type. In the wake of her misgivings about Iole, Deianira's rhetoric places the paradigm of the Corinthian Medea, conspicuously minimized in book 7, in view.

This alignment with Medea raises the question of whether Deianira can be reconciled with her Sophoclean paradigm. It is, moreover, a question Deianira herself raises:

> "quid si me, Meleagre, tuam memor esse sororem
> forte paro facinus, quantumque iniuria possit
> femineusque dolor, iugulata paelice testor?"

> "What if, Meleager, I remember I am your sister and plan a wicked deed, proving how far an injured and anguished woman can go by cutting my rival's throat?" (*Met.* 9.149–51)

An inquiry worthy of Medea, whose preliminary deliberations in Euripides' play include entering the palace and slaying Jason's bride with the sword (ἢ θηκτὸν ὤσω φάσγανον δι᾽ ἥπατος, 379). To witness Deianira considering the part of Medea is arresting, and provides yet another intratextual link between these women in the *Metamorphoses*. True, Deianira ultimately takes the Sophoclean course, eschewing violence in favor of what she believes is a more productive option (*vestem mittere*, 153–4). Yet what matters is less the outcome of the deliberation than the deliberation itself, a moment in which she contemplates the kind of gladiatorial carnage on display in the poem's other tragic stories – whose ranks will soon include her own story. After this Medeaesque interlude comes the grisly spectacle of the *vestis*, through which Deianira's story finally becomes a revenge tragedy. It is the revenge of Nessus, but it was very nearly her own.

Conjuring Medea, Deianira not only suggests an alternative code for handling her situation, but also comments on her own literary history. Just as Polyxena's death in book 13 takes its bearings from how tragedy aligns and realigns the figures of Iphigenia and Polyxena, so Deianira's monologue evokes a fundamental realignment of her character in the *Women of Trachis*. Jennifer March has proposed that Sophocles transformed the heroine from an angry and vindictive wife in an earlier version

[57] Chapter 5, pp. 147–9.

of the myth to an anxious and fearful one. Furthermore, she advertises her own paradigmatic shift: her hatred of daring women (τάς τε τολμώσας στυγῶ, 583), though seemingly an allusion to other vindictive wives like Clytemnestra and Medea, also invokes the old Deianira, who deliberately punished Heracles for his infidelity.[58] In the *Metamorphoses* her threat to remember that she is Meleager's sister (*quid si me, Meleagre, tuam memor esse sororem*, 149) – that is, courageous and proud as well as quick to anger, as Ovid depicts him in book 8 – functions in much the same way, an allusion to her pre-Sophoclean incarnations.[59] At the same time, her conditional memory activates the possibility of reincorporating those paradigms, whereas she all but rejects them in the *Women of Trachis*. Ovid's heroine threatens to do for her Sophoclean precursor what that heroine failed to do for her own precursors: to become Deianira to Deianira.

4 Deianira(s) and Hercules: expanding the intratext

In this chapter I have treated the *Heroides* and the *Metamorphoses* in isolation, with instances of tragic intratextuality observed between epistle and epistle or between book and book. In what remains I want to expand the concept to include connections between epistle and book, and vice versa. Although a relationship between two different works might at first seem intertextual, it is more properly intratextual. First, both works are by the same poet, a poet renowned for using his poetry to define and redefine his corpus. As Alessandro Barchiesi and Philip Hardie have put it, Ovid's texts "talk to each other."[60] Second, and more important, Ovid links the *Heroides* to the *Metamorphoses* with the intratextual footnote, whose markers are identical to the footnotes already observed. Both works are therefore implicated in a single super-text, an alliance between epic and elegy held together by the tragic.

Some examples. In *Met.* 8 Ovid describes what happens to Ariadne after helping Theseus to slay the Minotaur:

> protinus Aegides rapta Minoide Dian
> vela dedit comitemque suam crudelis in illo

[58] March 1987, 66–71.

[59] In Bacchyl. 5, which dates to 476 BCE, Heracles asks the shade of Meleager whether he has any sisters like himself (σοὶ φυὰν ἀλιγκία, 168 Campbell); Meleager singles out Deianira. The inference is that she is bold and bellicose like her brother (μενεπτολέμου, 170), and thus a good match for Heracles. See March 1987, 52.

[60] Barchiesi and Hardie 2010, 59. In the introduction to that essay's volume, Hardie and Moore (2010, 1) affirm the "intratextual relationships" of an author's oeuvre as a focal point of career criticism.

litore destituit. desertae et multa querenti
amplexus et opem Liber tulit.

Straightaway the son of Aegeus took the daughter of Minos and set sail for Dia, and then cruelly abandoned his companion on that shore. To her, deserted and lamenting much, Bacchus brought affection and help. (*Met.* 8.174–7)

Ariadne has a reputation, richly deserved from Catullus 64, as Theseus' harshest critic, and Ovid's reader has every right to expect her to denounce him now. Instead the poet reduces her speech to a mere two words, *multa querenti* (176), the briefest possible representation of a long complaint (her monologue in poem 64 lasts seventy verses). It would be rash to deny that Ovid is concerned with repeating Catullus. Nevertheless, even though *multa querenti* should be read intertextually as an allusion to her famous soliloquy, the phrase also functions as an intratextual footnote to poem 10 of Ovid's own *Heroides*, which has no qualms whatsoever about recalling Catullus.[61] Moreover, *querenti*, as a signifier of lamentation, is perhaps more suggestive of elegy than epic.[62] A. S. Hollis' terse comment on verse 176, "Cf. *Heroides* 10," invites one to consider the Ovidian epistle as an elaboration of Ariadne's abridged pathos; but Hollis might as well be paraphrasing Ovid's unwritten instructions to his own reader.[63]

Intratextual footnoting of the *Heroides* also occurs in book 14, where Ovid narrates Aeneas' landing at Carthage and Dido's suicide in a matter of seven lines:

hunc ubi Troianae remis avidamque Charybdin
evicere rates, cum iam prope litus adessent
Ausonium, Libycas vento referuntur ad oras.
excipit Aenean illic animoque domoque
non bene discidium Phrygii latura mariti
Sidonis, inque pyra sacri sub imagine facta
incubuit ferro deceptaque decipit omnes.

After the Trojan fleet evaded Scylla and gluttonous Charybdis, and although they had nearly reached the Ausonian coast, the winds bore them backward to the shores of Libya. There the Sidonian allowed Aeneas into her heart and house, although she would not bear his departure well – her Phrygian husband. On a pyre assembled under the pretext of a sacrifice,

[61] So Newlands 1997, 198, with additional parallels (n. 34) between Ariadne in *Met.* 8 and *Her.* 10.

[62] Note, however, that Ariadne's speech in poem 64 receives the label *querellis* (130), perhaps appropriate for Catullus' brand of epic.

[63] Hollis 1983.

she threw herself upon the sword, deceiving everyone after being deceived herself. (*Met.* 14.75–81)

Once again, we marvel at the poet's audacity in abbreviating the misery of a famous heroine, perhaps the most famous in all of Latin poetry. The assertion that Dido would not bear Aeneas' departure well, *non bene discidium latura* (79), is, to say the very least, an understatement. Such a maneuver is typical of Ovid with regard to the *Aeneid*, with whose main character and storylines he seems unwilling to engage on their own terms, relegating them to the background while placing Vergilian transformation stories in the foreground.[64] Thus *non bene discidium latura* is an intertextual footnote to *Aen.* 4, the premier treatment of Dido's jealousy, anger, and suicide, as if Ovid were conceding this particular episode to Vergil. Yet Ovid's own *Her.* 7 offers further proof that canonicity, especially of the most Augustan epic, cannot deter the poet's *ingenium*. We have, then, an intratextual footnote to Dido's letter, a footnote that reveals a poet concerned less with repeating Vergil than with repeating himself.

Returning to *Met.* 7, and the summary of Medea's deeds at Corinth (391–7), we find Ovid's concerns about self-repetition doubled. Throughout the chapter, this passage has already served as both an intertextual and an intratextual footnote. As the former it abridges the tragedy by Euripides, Ennius, and others in a deliberate anticlimax. As the latter it directs the reader to at least two other narratives, those of Procne and Deianira, in which the respective "Medeaness" of infanticide or poison is explored at length. Now the passage acquires not one but two more intratextual referents beyond the *Metamorphoses*: not only *Her.* 12, but also Ovid's lost *Medea*. On the one hand, readers who want a fuller treatment of Medea's anguish before making the fateful choice to murder her children, Creon, and his daughter will find ample disclosure in her epistle. On the other hand, those who want to see her choices played out (used to) have Ovid's own tragedy at their disposal. In either case, there is little need to pull a different author from the shelf. Moreover, the *flagrantem domum* of 7.395 is out of place in a summary of the Greek play, in which Medea only contemplates arson (*Med.* 378). If the burning house is a recapitulation of Ovid's *Medea*,[65] then the Corinthian episode of *Met.* 7

[64] Hinds 1998, 104–22, offers a wide-ranging analysis of the intertextual dynamics in the Ovidian "Little *Aeneid*"; on the notions of backgrounding and foregrounding see especially 104–6. On Ovid's reception of the *Aeneid* vis-à-vis tragedy, see Chapter 7, pp. 222–3.

[65] Chapter 2, p. 43.

is not casually intratextual, but inherently and deliberately so, and other tragedies become the odd texts out.

Although these expanded uses of the intratextual footnote are couched in familiar terms – conspicuous abridgement or understatements – they point to a different sort of intratext, which not only lies outside the boundaries of the *Metamorphoses*, but also constitutes a full version of the same myth. *Met.* 7.391–7 exemplify the difference. In footnoting Procne and Deianira the passage recommends narratives that follow paradigms similar to Medea's. The narratives represent, but cannot fully present, the heroine's experiences in Corinth. In footnoting *Her.* 12 and the lost tragedy, however, the passage refers to texts featuring Medea herself. Likewise the footnotes in *Met.* 8 and 14, which point to poems about none other than Ariadne and Dido.[66] The result is both an expanded view of the *Metamorphoses*, which annexes other Ovidian treatments of these heroines, as well as a more narrow view of the *Heroides*, whose framework now derives solely from Ovid. In Chapter 3 the intertextual dynamic of the collection was one of borrowing. Ovid temporarily appropriates his heroines from other authors and myths, only to have them be re-appropriated at the end: a Penelope on loan from the *Odyssey*, no matter how Ovidian she becomes in the course of writing, must ultimately return to the *Odyssey*. Under an intratextual dynamic the women of *Her.* 7, 10, and 12 are now on loan from the *Metamorphoses*. They need not become Ovidian because, it seems, they already are. In the case of *Her.* 12, it could be that Medea was always Ovid's to begin with, if we consider the poet's own tragedy the framework for her letter. If so, the *Metamorphoses*, in laying claim to Medea's epistle, actually continues the intratextual negotiations begun there.

The annexation of the *Heroides*, although it provides a point from which certain heroines may depart and to which they may return, does not necessarily render the act of writing a letter any more plausible. For example, Duncan Kennedy's comment about the implausibility of Ariadne's situation in poem 10 – "[I]t is by no means unreasonable to wonder how [she] is going to have her letter delivered, and even where she has managed to find writing materials"[67] – applies regardless of whether she is the heroine of Catullus 64 or of *Met.* 8. Whether an epistle is framed by the

[66] Hollis 1983 rightly notes that Ariadne's *multa querenti* are of appropriate length after Scylla's vituperative complaints to the departing Minos (8.108–42). That is, the phrase is an intratextual footnote not only to *Her.* 11, but also to Scylla's lament in the same book.

[67] Kennedy 1984, 416 (brackets mine).

Metamorphoses or by the text of another author, the problems that attend placing the epistle within that framework remain. Furthermore, new problems arise in the transition from spoken to written discourse and vice versa. Markers like *multa querenti* and *non bene discidium latura* not only invoke *Her.* 10 and 7, respectively, but also invoke them as substitutes for tragic monologues. Just as the *Metamorphoses* elides listening with reading in the direct speech of its characters, so the intratextual footnote, when applied to the *Heroides*, elides speaking with writing.

Nowhere are these problems more pronounced than in *Her.* 9, which like poems 7, 10, and 12, can be read as an offshoot of Ovid's epic. Here is Deianira's initial response after hearing about Hercules and Iole in book 9:

> credit amans Venerisque novae perterrita fama
> indulsit primo lacrimis flendoque dolorem
> diffudit miseranda suum. 143
>
> The lover believes, and terrified at the prospect of a new love gave way to tears, and, poor woman, poured out her grief in weeping. (*Met.* 9.141–3)

This passage is clearly an intratextual footnote to *Her.* 9, in which Deianira offers full disclosure of her grief: her copious weeping has a patent elegiac resonance (the last word of Deianira's first epistolary couplet is in fact *queror*). The transition to the heroine's epistle, however, is far from seamless. Her lamentation in *Met.* 9 comes before the arrival of Iole in Trachis, as her subsequent monologue makes clear: *quae quoniam adveniet* (145); *nondum thalamos tenet altera nostros* (146). *Her.* 9, if we read it as being composed in a single sitting, belongs to a time in which Iole has already arrived: *ante meos oculos adducitur advena paelex* (121). The narrative seems to place two discursive acts from the same heroine side-by-side: the footnoted letter, which she writes "offstage," and the monologue she delivers soon thereafter.

Such difficulties should not deter us from reading the *Metamorphoses* as a framework for the *Heroides*, any more than they should deter us from reading the letters in light of other authors. In fact, these problems are to be expected from reading intratextually, especially where tragic texts are concerned. We have seen that making connections between the tragic heroines of the *Metamorphoses* is a self-consciously transgressive enterprise. To draw parallels between Iphigenia and Polyxena or between Medea and Deianira is in its fullest sense to transcend the boundaries between one narrative and another – to let them permeate into one another in various, if sometimes incongruous, ways. To draw parallels between the heroines in the *Metamorphoses* and the *Heroides* requires the same sort of tendentious adventurousness on the reader's part.

Not to reconcile the Deianira of *Her.* 9 with the Deianira of *Met.* 9 is to shirk an opportunity to take stock of how Ovid reconfigures the same tragedy for elegy and epic. Both heroines, for example, learn of Iole from *fama* or rumor:[68]

> Gratulor Oechaliam titulis accedere nostris;
> victorem victae succubuisse queror.
> fama Pelasgiadas subito pervenit in urbes
> decolor et factis infitianda tuis,
> quem numquam Iuno seriesque inmensa laborum
> fregerit, huic Iolen inposuisse iugum.
>
> I am thankful that Oechalia is added to our honorific titles, I lament that the victor has fallen beneath his victim. A rumor has suddenly pervaded the Pelasgian cities, an indecorous rumor, fit for your deeds to disavow: upon that man, whom Juno and an endless series of labors never broke, Iole has imposed her yoke. (*Her.* 9.1–6)

> victor ab Oechalia Cenaeo sacra parabat
> vota Iovi, cum Fama loquax praecessit ad aures,
> Deianira, tuas, quae veris addere falsa
> gaudet et e minimo sua per mendacia crescit,
> Amphitryoniaden Ioles ardore teneri.
>
> The conqueror of Oechalia was preparing to fulfill his sacred vows to Jupiter at Cenaeum, when garrulous Rumor reached your ears, Deianira, Rumor who rejoices in adding falsehoods to the truth, and who grows through her lies out of something very small: The son of Amphitryon (she said) was held fast by a burning desire for Iole. (*Met.* 9.136–40)

In both passages Ovid has severely abridged the mystery and intrigue of the initial episodes of the *Women of Trachis*, in which Deianira hears of her husband's passion through a combination of messenger reports and direct inquiry. The presence of *fama* in both texts provides a link through

[68] In *Met.* 9 it is conventional to print *fama* with a capital F – that is to personify rumor as a goddess. This convention accords *Fama* a status in keeping with epic practice, beginning with Homer and Hesiod and continuing on through Vergil, who describes Rumor's lineage and workings at *Aen.* 4.173–97. Ovid himself offers four set-pieces in the *Metamorphoses* that feature deified abstractions, one of which is the house of *Fama*, with its infinite apertures and resounding murmurs (12.39–63). The *Fama* of book 9 offers a glimpse of the goddess revealed later in the poem. On the four set pieces, and their place in the epic tradition, see Feeney 1991, 241–9. Feeney demonstrates that the house and the function of *Fama* have ramifications for Ovid's own poetic authority, particularly at the very end of the *Met.* (*per omnia saecula fama*, 15.878: see 247–9).

which *Her.* 9 and *Met.* 9 may be read as mutually reinforcing takes on Deianira's ordeal, rather than as one absorbing the other. In the earlier discussion of *Her.* 7, 10, and 12, and how these texts are footnoted in the *Metamorphoses*, the epic frames the individual elegies, drawing them into its totalizing orbit. Such appears to be the case with Deianira. Her querulous reaction in book 9 (141–3) encapsulates the complaints and lamentations of her epistle, which constitutes one possible response to *fama*. It is, moreover, an elegiac response, but as Chapter 3 has shown, the heroine's display of pathos is not alien to the tragic stage. Yet the epic Deianira has a second response: we have already seen how she puts aside her grief and begins to weigh her options – a discourse motivated less by *dolor* than by *ira* (143–51). Her self-inquiry is worthy of Ovid's epic, in which the terrible consequences of female subjectivity are depicted again and again; nevertheless, this discourse is also a staple of tragedy. Together *Her.* 9 and *Met.* 9 offer two distinctive portraits of a tragic heroine in turmoil, each attuned to the genre in which she appears, but neither far removed from the genre in which she originated.

The portraits are mutually dependent and must be intentionally juxtaposed in order to see the whole picture. Although it is tempting to think of the epic Deianira as active, and the elegiac Deianira as merely reactive, we should remember that in *Her.* 9 she has already decided to send her husband the tunic:

> sed quid ego haec refero? scribenti nuntia venit
> fama, virum tunicae tabe perire meae. 144

> But why rehash the past like this? While I write word has come that my husband is dying from the poison I placed on the cloak. (*Her.* 9.143–4)

This new *fama* (144) confirms that the heroine is capable of decisive action, although the decisions themselves are conspicuously absent from the text of her letter. Indeed, upon hearing the news, she responds not with an aporetic *quid faciam?* (What shall I do?) but with *quid feci?* (145, What have I done?). Just as *Met.* 9 footnotes *Her.* 9 as a more comprehensive display of erotic pathos, so poem 9 footnotes the deliberations in which Deianira elects to send Hercules the charmed robe in book 9. Under this reading *Her.* 9 provides a framework for *Met.* 9, a point from which the heroine departs to conduct her self-interrogation in the epic, and to which she returns to lament the disastrous result. And not only to lament, but also to die (*inpia quid dubitas, Deianira, mori?* 146, 152, 158, 164), for the epic loses all track of the heroine once the robe leaves her hands. Deianira's epistle takes precedence over the epic, not in terms of publication (although it was published first), but in terms of establishing an authoritative "voice" for the heroine, to which the monologue of book 9 responds.

The notion of *Met.* 9 responding to *Her.* 9 is also helpful later in the narrative, when Hercules delivers his great monologue atop Mt. Oeta (176–204). As discussed in Chapter 5, the hero catalogues both his labors and the *corpus* with which he accomplished them – a display at once biographical and anatomical.[69] Although we noted that his speech is indebted to the *Women of Trachis*, in which Heracles offers a catalogue of his body and its victims (1089–100), albeit a less inclusive one, we are now in a position to appreciate the influence of *Her.* 9 as well. Deianira, too, has taken a page from Sophocles in associating her husband's labors with his body. The context of her catalogue, however, is not the hero's mortal agony, but his enslavement to Omphale:

> Maeandros, terris totiens errator in isdem,
> qui lassas in se saepe retorquet aquas,
> vidit in Herculeo suspensa monilia collo
> illo, cui caelum sarcina parva fuit.
> non puduit fortis auro cohibere lacertos,
> et solidis gemmas opposuisse toris?
> nempe sub his animam pestis Nemeaea lacertis
> edidit, unde umerus tegmina laevus habet?
> ausus es hirsutos mitra redimire capillos!
> aptior Herculeae populus alba comae.
> nec te Maeonia lascivae more puellae
> incingi zona dedecuisse putas?
> non tibi succurrit crudi Diomedis imago,
> efferus humana qui dape pavit equas?
> si te vidisset cultu Busiris in isto,
> huic victor victo nempe pudendus eras!
> detrahat Antaeus duro redimicula collo,
> ne pigeat molli succubuisse viro!

The Meandrus, a frequent wanderer in these same lands, who often turns his tired streams back upon themselves, has seen necklaces hung from Hercules' neck, upon which the heavens were mere baggage. Was there no shame in binding your strong arms with gold and in bejeweling your firm muscles? Can it be that the plague of Nemea gave up the ghost under these very arms, the plague from which your left side has a covering? You dared to crown your thick locks with a mitra! The white poplar was better suited to the hair of Hercules. And did you not find it unseemly to wear

[69] Chapter 5, pp. 170–1.

> the Maeonian girdle like a lusty girl? Did the image of cruel Diomedes not occur to you, that savage who pastured his mares on a human feast? Had Busiris seen you in that outfit, surely you, the victor, would have shamed your victim! Antaeus would tear from your hardy neck these bands, lest he be mortified at falling to a delicate man! (*Her.* 9.55–72)

As in the catalogues of Heracles/Hercules, the hero's inglorious present contrasts with his glorious past. Nevertheless, given his role as a love-slave, a *servus amoris* whose feminine finery is ill suited to his masculinity, his present circumstances contain more bathos than pathos – although for Deianira they are no less offensive.

Her. 9 sets a standard for *Met.* 9 in the sheer comprehensiveness of Deianira's catalogue, which all told occupies forty-six verses (55–100), incorporating all of the labors in the Sophoclean catalogue (the apples of the Hesperides, *Trach.* 1099–100, are represented by *caelum … fuit*, 58) and surpassing it by six: two of the canonical twelve (mares of Diomedes, 67–8 and 89–90; Geryon, 91–2), three *parerga* (Busiris, 69–70; Antaeus, 71–2 and 97–8; centaurs, 99–100), and the serpents sent by Hera (85–6). In the *Metamorphoses*, therefore, Hercules continues the comprehensive trend begun by Deianira, incorporating all of the labors and *parerga* mentioned in her epistle and adding the Cretan bull (186), the Augean stables (187), the hind of Artemis (188), the Amazons (188–9), and an explicit reference to the Hesperides (190). The hero's catalogue not only rivals his wife's in expansiveness, but in two instances appears to follow her arrangement of the labors. Hercules leads off with Busiris and Antaeus (182–4), listing these two *parerga* in the same order in which Deianira lists them (69–72), and continues with Geryon and Cerberus (184–5), which likewise appear in that sequence in the heroine's epistle (91–4, although they do not immediately follow Busiris and Antaeus). Furthermore, Hercules even borrows the wording of Deianira's catalogue when describing two of his labors: Geryon (*pastoris Hiberi* | *forma triplex*, *Met.* 9.184–5; *prodigiumque triplex, armenti dives Hiberi*, *Her.* 9.91) and the Nemean lion (*his … iacet moles Nemeaea lacertis*, *Met.* 9.197; *sub his animam pestis Nemeaea lacertis* | *edidit*, *Her.* 9.61–2). In these three respects – comprehensiveness, patterning, and phrasing – the hero acknowledges that his wife has already reviewed his body of work.

More than an acknowledgement, however, Hercules' catalogue is an appropriation of Deianira's – an attempt to summarize his career in an epic context, and hence to recuperate the poignancy of the catalogue in the *Women of Trachis*. His inclusion of four additional (and canonical) labors is one measure of this effort; the circumstances in which he delivers his catalogue are another. Deianira's synopsis of her husband's heroic exploits has two main parts: 55–72, quoted above, which she herself offers, and 81–100, which she imagines Hercules offering as he sits at Omphale's feet (*ante pedes dominae*, 81). The latter catalogue, she insists, is inappropriate for a *servus amoris*:

> haec tu Sidonio potes insignitus amictu
> dicere? non cultu lingua retenta silet? 102

> You can tell of these things while decked out in your Sidonian gown? Does your tongue, restrained by your dress, not fail you? (*Her.* 9.101–2)

In *Met.* 9 Hercules clarifies that his present travails are an appropriate time to utter the sort of catalogue Deianira ascribes to him – a time of mortal peril, in which he stands beneath the gaze of Juno (*Saturnia*, 176; *hanc pestem specta*, 177) instead of sitting at the feet of his lover. Mortal peril, moreover, is an inappropriate time for invoking erotic exploits: although Hercules lists the girdle of Hippolyte (189), who in at least one version of the story promised it freely,[70] the adjective *Thermodontiaco* is as close as the hero comes to mentioning Hippolyte by name. Nor does he mention any of his lovers – neither Megara nor Omphale nor Iole nor even Deianira herself. His situation likewise calls for a more streamlined approach to his body. Hands (186), arms (197), and neck (198) all receive their due as instruments of masculine labor, while in his wife's epistle these and other parts, including his hair (63–4), his fingers (79), and even his thumb (77), are occupied with the dress and work of women. An intratextual reading of *Met.* 9 and *Her.* 9 shows Hercules, made effeminate in Deianira's letter, remaking himself as an epic hero with a *gravitas* both imitating and exceeding the Sophoclean stage. Perhaps most important of all, tragic intratextuality makes possible for one of the single *Heroides* that which is normally thought to be impossible: the lover's reply.

Our survey of tragedy in Ovid has taken us from the poet's lost *Medea*, to displays of pathos and irony in the theatrical epistles of the *Heroides*, to the spectacles and rhetoric of the *Metamorphoses*, and finally to the intratextual network of heroes and heroines connecting all of these works. Along the way we have taken stock of Ovid's career, his relationship to the Greek stage, his handling of myth, and his flair for theatricality – all concerns of the Roman playwrights who preceded him. Moreover, these concerns found their fullest expression in the medium of the book more so than

[70] Apollod. *Bibl.* 2.5.9.

on the living stage, and the efforts of Catullus and Vergil, who had transformed and revitalized tragedy in textual form, must have been instructive models. If we are to appreciate fully Ovid's tragic program, we must examine the socio-political implications of his works, as we would for any Roman tragedian. Just as Chapter 2 attempted to situate the *Medea* in the context of the early principate, my last chapter will consider the *Heroides* and the *Metamorphoses* in a similar light. What can a myriad network of tragic characters say about the age of Augustus?

CHAPTER SEVEN

Carmen et error

Tragedy's end

This book is about building bridges. It began with the notion of Ovid as a bridge between the Athenian tragedians and Seneca, but other bridges have presented themselves along the way. The early Roman tragedians, for example, link the Attic playwrights to Vergil, while Vergil is Ovid's most important link to the Roman tragedians. To extend the metaphor, this book has attempted to bridge certain milestones in the Ovidian *cursus litterarum* – to link the *Medea*, the *Heroides*, and the *Metamorphoses* as tragic texts. Close readings have identified a tragic project spanning Ovid's career, a project described in literary terms by decoding the material and the modalities of tragedy. Yet tragedy was always a socio-political enterprise: this is true regardless of whether we mean the works of the Greek dramatists, their Latin successors, Seneca, or even Vergil.

It must also be true of Ovid's tragic texts. In Chapter 2 we considered his *Medea* within the context of its times, as a work with *gravitas* to suit the burgeoning principate. The *Heroides* and the *Metamorphoses* deserve similar consideration, although for a long time it seemed as though there was little, if anything, to consider. Ovid's reputation for self-conscious ingenuity, which the poet himself had a hand in cultivating, suggested a tragic program frivolous, fragmented, and detached from contemporary events. His position between Vergil and Seneca, the former complicit in the formation of Augustan ideology, the latter a victim of Neronian excess, also contributed to this aura of detachment. Nevertheless, critics of recent decades, bolstered by the effort to recall Ovid from the alleged desert of Silver Latin, have found in his tragic texts a program serious, sustained, and attuned to the Augustan age.

Accordingly, my final chapter considers the implications of reading tragically in a world prescribed by *imperium Romanum*. Tragic readings of the *Heroides* and the *Metamorphoses*, I maintain, benefit rather than suffer from reading Ovid as a bridge between Vergil and Seneca. Ovid constructs

Vergil as a precursor to his own career as a tragedian. Meanwhile, Seneca's *Medea* and *Thyestes*, composed in an era of imperial abuses, seem to follow the trajectory of Ovidian tragedy. I will conclude with some thoughts on the tragedy of Ovid's exile, brought on by transgressions against the *imperium* reflected in his prior tragic texts. Because these issues are predicated on earlier chapters, a brief retrospective will be useful.

1 Ovid as a tragic poet

First, the question of genres, and the connections between epic and tragedy. What the Aeschylean banquet of Homer (Ath. 8.347e) offered tragedians like Aeschylus, Sophocles, Euripides, Ennius and others, apart from characters and stories, are thematic and narrative devices. The former include motifs such as divine will, justice, the destiny of mortals, honor, revenge, and friendship. The latter include Aristotelian devices, such as reversals and recognitions, the storytelling principles at work in messenger speeches and other accounts of past events, and first-person *rheseis*. Homer originated many of these motifs and devices, but it is equally true to say that tragedy appropriated them and others as the genre progressed, with Roman tragedy emphasizing rhetoric and spectacle to even greater degrees. Following Apollonius, Catullus, and Vergil, Ovid's achievement in the *Metamorphoses* was to re-appropriate the stories, themes, and techniques of tragedy back into epic. Only these elements are not quietly assimilated into the poet's text. Rather, they are appropriated with a full measure of metatheatricality, retaining their associations with tragedy and fulfilling the totalizing ambitions of the *Metamorphoses*. As Alison Keith writes, "Th[e] process of generic exploration culminates in [Ovid's] comprehensive summation of *epos* with the return of all literary streams to their generic origin."[1]

Tragic appropriation opens both a play of tensions and a play of synergy between the genres. Tensions obtain when Ovid expands the spatial and temporal boundaries of the *theatron* for his tragic stories and facilitates the presentation of offstage events, often visceral and supernatural. The poem's visual appeal, even as it takes advantage of epic's boundless medium, is also an appeal to Roman experience. Although the predilection of Roman tragedy for spectacle was part of this experience, Rome

[1] Keith 2002, 269 (brackets mine). For an equally helpful formulation see Scodel 2005, 195: "Epic, having created tragedy, recreated itself on the model of its creation."

was the ultimate venue for spectacle, including displays of blood-sport in the amphitheater. Ovid's penchant for presenting offstage violence often merges with amphitheatrical carnage, most notably in the death of Polyxena (book 13), whom Neoptolemus puts to the sword. All in all the *Metamorphoses* seems to revel in its own spectacularity, that is, its capacity to stage events that tragedy either could not or, as seems more likely, would not stage in the open.

The lack of distinction between offstage and onstage in Ovid's theater of epic ensures that his protagonists are almost constantly in view. Whereas tragic characters enter into and exit from the here-and-now of the spectators' vision, the Ovidian reader is usually able to track the movements of characters from one there-and-then to the next. These movements can be of relatively short distance or they can be global in proportion, such as Medea's fantastic chariot voyage over Greece, the Aegean, Asia Minor, and back again, in what should otherwise have been a relatively direct flight from Iolcus to Corinth (book 7). As Ovid's tragic characters pass from one location to another and from one physical or emotional state to another, the sense of place within a given narrative, often introduced by the formula *locus est* and its variants, becomes magnified. Mt. Oeta (book 9) demonstrates to an incongruous extreme the mutability of space in epic, the genre in which Hercules' passage from mortal to immortal is afforded room to play out.

Still, for all its expansiveness and directness, the *Metamorphoses* synergistically adopts the conventions of the stage. The prominent position of Hercules on Oeta at the apex of his suffering captures the essence of visual theatricality. Likewise the sacrifice of Polyxena at Achilles' tomb, kept offstage in the *Hecabe* but occurring in full view of the reader. The vivid settings in which to view Polyxena, Hercules, and others are also places in which to hear them, their speeches remaining essential to the theatrical experience of an epic text. No less significant are the soliloquies of Medea and Hecabe, whose speeches are performed in nondescript settings, but create a static here-and-now in the suspension of narrative time. Furthermore, the many soliloquies of the *Metamorphoses* remain the poem's closest link with tragedy, despite the fact that relatively few opportunities exist in extant plays for characters to be alone onstage and to engage in bouts of self-psychologizing and self-moralizing. In this respect Ovid has taken a page from postclassical tragedians, whose diminished use of the chorus ostensibly allowed more occasions for solo *rheseis*, and from Roman tragedians in particular, whose predilection for rhetoric is well attested. Moreover, his speakers' solitude, easily arranged in epic poetry, reflects the emotional and psychological desolation of the tragic stage.

Treating Ovidian monologues as performances, particularly when these performances feature so-called desperation rhetoric or aporetic dilemmas (the dilemma between *pudor and amor* being one example), means hearing the speakers themselves as tragic characters. As tragic characters, they represent mutually deconstructing paradigms or embodiments of tragic code. Appropriately for a poem about sudden transformations, characters are made to stand in for another, a phenomenon recalling Roman tragic *contaminatio* and signaled by the intratextual footnote. As a transgressive strategy of composition, intratextuality thematizes at the level of narrative the transgressive acts of the tragic stage, removing barriers between one narrative and another. The reader becomes the ultimate transgressor, crossing thresholds between stories, characters, and even genres in the service of connecting Ovid's tragic texts.

As a strategy of reading, intratextuality not only reveals the *Metamorphoses* as a boundless poem unto itself, but also expands the poem's boundaries by annexing Ovid's earlier *Heroides*. Here again the intratextual footnote is put to use, referencing letters by heroines who appear in the epic narratives, but whose amatory pathos seems better remembered in an epistolary context. The footnote, moreover, reminds us that the *Heroides* are a highly responsive intratextual network all their own. Penelope (*Her.* 1), Laodamia (13), and Hero (19) are all paradigms of a lover expecting a *nostos*; Hypsipyle (6), whom Jason abandoned first, threatens to turn Medea's own methods against her; Oenone (5) lays claim to Paris, while Helen rebukes him (17). In these and other examples the *Heroides* anticipate the meticulous intraconnectivity of the *Metamorphoses*.

The *Heroides* equal, and perhaps exceed, the *Metamorphoses* in propagating tragic modalities, especially in exploiting myth to create irony and to convey the magnitude of erotic pathos. The epic is especially indebted to the elegies in its monologues, whose conceit that articulating pathos is a feminine act originates in the collection's rhetorical and univocal epistles. This is not to say that the *Heroides* are merely tragic soliloquies in epistolary form; they are clearly much more than that. However, the intratextual footnotes of the *Metamorphoses* often refer to the letters not as written texts, but as substitutes for the spoken monologues that would have been delivered. Ovid's epistles offer a close approximation of what a heroine would have said, had she been given the opportunity to speak in the epic.

The epistolary mode and its intrinsic univocality replicate the narrative viewpoint of tragedy, in which characters provide context for their letters by describing the present, narrating the past, and noting entrances, exits, or any other changes (as Deianira does in *Her.* 9). Furthermore, Ovid's epistolographers operate, like the characters in a *theatron*, in a highly boundaried here-and-now, which makes them the focus of the reader's attention. This dynamic changes radically in the *Metamorphoses*, whose external narrator has access to the there-and-thens surrounding the here-and-now. When seen from the perspective of the earlier collection, as the Byblis narrative allows (*Met.* 9), the sheer exuberance with which the epic grants access to other times and places seems a determined effort to break free of the spatial and temporal constraints of the *Heroides* – to move beyond the epistles by thematizing movement in the tragic narratives of the epic. Whereas the *Metamorphoses* offers an expansive view of tragic storytelling, typically presented from the outside and working inward, the *Heroides* offer a minimalist view from the inside out.

Ovid's lost *Medea*, his one and only attempt to engage tragedy on its own terms, encouraged his pursuit of tragedy in other genres. Why the poet wrote no more plays than this – especially given its reputed success, its probable composition during a boom in Roman theater construction, and its apparent launching of a new phase in his career – remains a mystery. But earlier poets, chief among them Vergil, had succeeded in transforming tragedy into texts, opting for the play of genres rather than actual plays. Inspired by the fusion of tragedy and epic in the *Aeneid*, Ovid followed suit with the *Heroides* and the *Metamorphoses*, continuing the genre he had abandoned. Abandoned, but not forgotten, because the *Medea* is also bound up in the intratextuality of the epic and the epistles. Between the three works Ovid cultivated a robust network of tragic heroines and heroes, who collectively embody the dramaturgical career that would otherwise never have materialized.

2 Staging *imperium*: Vergil, Ovid, and Seneca

Vergilium vidi tantum (*Tr.* 4.10.51). This understated remark from Ovid's autobiography in exile is, as Richard Tarrant describes, a "terse disclaimer of personal acquaintance" with Vergil's poetry, his place in Roman literary history, and his career.[2] No other poet had as much influence on Ovid as Vergil, and the sheer amount of industry Ovid devotes to the

[2] Tarrant 2002, 23; I have added Vergil's career to the list of Ovid's acquaintances.

reception of his predecessor is astonishing. Equally striking is the industry critics have devoted to affirming Vergil's originality at the expense of his successor. Such parochialism is apparent even in the "sympathetic and engaged criticism"[3] that has given the Ovidian renascence its impetus. For example, Brooks Otis' *Ovid as an Epic Poet*, for all its insights into the *Metamorphoses* and its negotiation of genre (including tragedy), nevertheless privileges Vergilian seriousness at the expense of Ovidian cleverness.[4] Sara H. Lindheim has aptly summarized this critical era: "Ovid is not Vergil, and for a long time this was considered a liability ... Ovidian scholarship constructed a poet congenitally prone to trivialization, and then responded to its own creation by trivializing his work."[5]

Critics have since progressed from Ovid's reception of Vergilian poetry to his reception of Vergil himself. Careerist readings by Joseph Farrell and others, in which Ovid places his own spin on the Vergilian *rota*, are one such mode of criticism.[6] Stephen Hinds has taken a slightly different tack in his analysis of metamorphic tales in the *Aeneid*, which Ovid avoids retelling not to fashion himself as a post-Vergilian epicist, but rather to fashion Vergil as pre-Ovidian:

> Ovid is engaged in a tendentious poetic appropriation of his predecessor – a kind of bid for teleological control. Rather than construct himself as an epigonal reader of the *Aeneid*, Ovid is constructing Vergil as a hesitant precursor of the *Metamorphoses*. There is a *Metamorphoses* latent in the *Aeneid*, Ovid's treatment tells us: in Circe and in the biform Scylla, as also in the transformation of Aeneas' ships into nymphs and in the transformation of Diomedes' companions into birds. But in Vergil these myths are fragmented, scattered, unresolved: not until Ovid's own poem are they gathered into perfection and system.[7]

[3] Sympathetic and engaged criticism: so Hardie in Hardie, Barchiesi, and Hinds 1999, 1, in reference to Fränkel 1945, Wilkinson 1955, Otis 1970, and Due 1974. Of these Due probably best lives up to Hardie's billing.

[4] Otis 1970. Some representative remarks: "An intense and serious poet like Vergil could greatly heighten the *ethos* of his epic: a less serious poet like Ovid could considerably relax the tension" (73); "Ovid could conceivably have written his *continuous poem* so that it would, quite naturally, have terminated in epic battles, philosophic soliloquies, and apotheoses. But he certainly did no such thing. His humor and pathos proved fatal to his heroics. The latter, at best, was clever imitation; at worst dreadful exercise in the incongruous and the grotesque" (281, author's emphasis, with reference to the "dignity and solemnity" of Vergil's conclusion to the *Aeneid*). Compare Kennedy 2002, 219, assessing Jacobson 1974, in its time a sympathetic treatment of Ovid's epistles: "Much though Jacobson wants to like and admire the *Heroides*, his book is pervaded by a profound sense of disappointment."

[5] Lindheim 2003, 135.

[6] Farrell 2004; Barchiesi and Hardie 2010; Kilgour 2010, from whose title the phrase "spin on the Vergilian *rota*" derives.

[7] Hinds 1998, 106, one of the central points in a discussion of "Ovid's *Aeneid*" in *Met.* 13–14.

Hind's description of Vergil as a "hesitant precursor" to Ovid offers perspectives from which to view the *Metamorphoses* and the *Heroides* as tragic enterprises in a post-Vergilian era. For instance, the widespread and sustained application of tragic coding throughout Ovid's oeuvre is by itself enough to trope Vergil as an incipient tragedian, and Ovid himself as an accomplished and consummate one.

Nevertheless, Tarrant wonders whether "by defining himself in opposition to Vergil in matters relating to Augustus Ovid did not help create the image of Vergil the pure 'Augustan' that much recent criticism has been at pains to complicate."[8] Indeed, Vergil's restrained and classicizing take on tragedy seems even more so – almost "hyper-classicizing" – in light of Ovid's exuberant and totalizing approach to the genre. All the same, Philip Hardie has shown through a nuanced reading of Ovid's "Theban History" in *Met.* 3–4 that Vergilian tragedy can be both classicizing and complicated at the same time. Ovid, Hardie argues, structures his ktistic narrative of Cadmus' efforts to found Thebes with reference to the *Aeneid* as the foundational epic of Rome. In effect, Ovid creates an "anti-*Aeneid*," with his problematic use of Thebes parallel to how classical tragedians constructed that city-state as a kind of "anti-Athens," in which political matters could be explored and dramatized.[9]

The *Metamorphoses*, then, presents an *Aeneid* with ideological concerns similar to those of classical Athenian tragedy, which reflects the tempests of its own era. The fundamental richness of drama in the fifth century derives from the political and social upheaval in those years. Even if the subject matter of tragedy was by and large mythical, the plays themselves, framed within the civic contexts of the Dionysia and the Lenaea, remained tied to the world outside. Furthermore, the diffusion of tragedy is bound up in the decline of its *polis*: as the imperial hegemony of Athens waned, so did her hegemony within the genre, which gave over to internationalization and the cultivation of repertoire.[10] The socio-political background to the *Aeneid* is likewise cognizant of factionalism and civil war, and the still-valid question of understanding both *imperium* and the *imperator* wielding it. Lily Panoussi writes,

> [A]t the time Vergil was composing his poem, Rome too was undergoing momentous changes in its social and political structure. The *Aeneid* was

[8] Tarrant 2002, 25.

[9] Hardie 1990, especially 227–30. Reception and refinement of Hardie's reading in Gildenhard and Zissos 2000 and Janan 2009.

[10] Chapter 2, p. 22 and pp. 50–1.

> written at a time when the triumph of Augustan order with its promise of peace and stability for the Roman state was still being measured against the fresh memories of the civil struggle which preceded it and which had depleted the country's resources and decimated its manpower.[11]

These conditions, which resemble those under which Athenian drama reached its zenith, made tragedy a necessary component in Vergil's attempt to write a new Augustan classic, a document of that era's social and political conflict.[12]

The conflict of Ovid's era is less pronounced, but no less valid. Whereas Vergil witnessed first-hand the civil strife leading to empire, Ovid flourished at a time when the principate had already taken hold. Even his earliest poetry, the *Amores*, is suffused with the imagery and the language of conquest and imperialism.[13] This is not to say that Ovid's view of *imperium* is static or inert. Indeed, the Lycaon story of *Met.* 1 is a political allegory that exposes the tension – a true tension – between the will of the *imperator* and his subjects.[14] Such pressures, already present in the poem's inaugural metamorphosis, carry over to the poem's end. In the closing verses of his epic Ovid raises a panegyric for the emperor, at face value an endorsement of the *pax Augusta*:

> Iuppiter arces
> temperat aetherias et mundi regna triformis,
> terra sub Augusto est; pater est et rector uterque …
> tarda sit illa dies et nostro serior aevo,
> qua caput Augustum, quem temperat, orbe relicto
> accedat caelo faveatque precantibus absens.

> Jupiter rules the citadels of heaven and the kingdoms of the triform universe, while the earth is under Augustus' power. Each is the father and the director … Let it come late, past my own era, that day when Augustus leaves behind the world he rules, enters the heavens, and looks with favor on our prayers from afar. (*Met.* 15.858–60, 868–70)

Whether we read it as genuinely laudatory or as disingenuous,[15] this imperialist passage displays true anxiety, not necessarily about the nature

[11] Panoussi 2002, 97. [12] Thus Hardie 1997, 316–19 and 322.

[13] Habinek 2002 traces the "political commitments of Ovid's poetry" (46). On the *Amores* see 47–50, where "images of war and conquest, slavery and imperialism, clemency and triumph" (48) find their way into supposedly tender elegies.

[14] The Lycaon story, narrated by Jupiter to his fellow gods, is a quintessentially Augustan display of authority, disagreement with which is dangerous as it is inevitable: see Feldherr 2002, 169–72.

[15] For a pessimistic reading of this passage see Barchiesi 1997, 195–6; Salzman 1998, meanwhile, offers a generally favorable interpretation of apotheosis in Ovid.

or origins of *imperium*, but about its perpetuation after Augustus. The prospect of the current emperor reigning *in absentia* from the heavens (*faveat absens*, 870) is comforting more in the abstract, and offers no lasting solution to the question of succession – both who would govern in Augustus' wake, and how he would do so.[16]

To judge from imperial history, such questions were well founded. The tragedies of the younger Seneca are not only rife with their own anxieties about *imperium*, but they also expose similar anxieties in the tragic program of Ovid. Just as the tragedy in the *Aeneid*, especially when viewed from the perspective of the *Metamorphoses*, holds up a mirror to its own complicated times, so the *Metamorphoses* and the *Heroides* find a greater poignancy when viewed from the later tragic stage. Senecan tragedy borrows constantly from Horace, Vergil, and Ovid. And for a long time the overall effect of these borrowings on Seneca's reputation has been detrimental, much like the impact of Ovid's Vergilian borrowings on his own reputation.[17] To consider how Senecan tragedy constructs Ovid as a poet, therefore, is a more productive approach both to Ovidian tragedy and to Seneca himself. What emerges is a dynamic similar to that between Vergil and Ovid: Seneca is not so much a post-Ovidian tragedian as Ovid is a pre-Senecan one.[18]

The extent of Seneca's debt to Ovid is well known, at least at the level of word and idea. In his edition of the *Thyestes*, for example, Tarrant catalogues over thirty instances of Ovidian echoes and imitations throughout the play, most of which derive from the *Metamorphoses*, and of these a good percentage from the tragic narratives of that poem.[19] Two of Tarrant's items are especially instructive for our purposes. In this excerpt from the messenger scene (623–788), the chorus hears about the murder of Thyestes' sons at Atreus' hand:

[16] So Liveley 2011, 6: "[T]he unbroken continuity of [the] *pax* would and could not have been taken for granted ... The threat that chaos might return to devastate the order of the Augustan cosmos remained" (brackets mine).

[17] Modern readers of Seneca are more encouraging, e.g., Trinacty 2007: "Intertextuality allows for the incorporation of diverse voices into Seneca's tragedies, and when he incorporates elegy and epic, the reader must decide how the genre of the source material alters the meaning of the line in its new tragic context" (64). On the so-called Latin Silver Age see Boyle 1997, 20, and Hinds 1998, 83–4, both with bibliography.

[18] Hinds 2011 surveys "impressions of the dramatic, rhetorical and conceptual space which Ovid and his poetry occupy in Seneca's tragic imagination." Although Hinds's survey is more comprehensive than mine, and our *exempla* overlap in a few instances, our conclusions were conceived independently of one another.

[19] Tarrant 1985, Index II s.v. "Ovid," under the heading "echoed or imitated by S[eneca]."

ac pueri statim
pectore receptus ensis e tergo exstitit.
cadit ille et aras sanguine extinguens suo
per utrumque vulnus moritur.

At once the sword, inserted into the boy's chest, protruded from his back. He went down and, tainting the altars with his own blood, dies from his wounds on either side. (Sen. *Thy.* 740–3)

There are clear parallels between this passage and the death of Nessus in *Met.* 9:

missa fugientia terga sagitta
traicit; exstabat ferrum de pectore aduncum.
quod simul evulsum est, sanguis per utrumque foramen
emicuit.

[Hercules] let fly an arrow and struck [Nessus] in the back as he fled; the barbed iron tip protruded from his chest. As soon as it was removed, blood spurted from the wound on either side. (*Met.* 9.127–30)

Of interest are not only the verbal similarities, which show Seneca an attentive reader of Ovid, but also the systemic parallels enabling the similarities in the first place. As Tarrant notes, a "fascination with bizarre forms of physical violence and mutilation is part of the *Metamorphoses*' legacy to later poets."[20] And not just to later poets, one could add, but to Seneca in particular, whose affinity for both violent images and violent deeds in his plays seems in retrospect most Ovidian. Furthermore, the reminiscences of *Met.* 9 call attention to the fluidity between epic and tragic narrative. We have observed that messenger speeches and other reflective *rheseis* in tragedy, such as Deianira's account of Nessus' demise in the *Women of Trachis* (555–81), are heavily indebted to epic narrative technique. In *Met.* 9 Ovid re-appropriates the heroine's tragic narrative as epic, while Seneca's messenger reclaims Ovidian narrative for tragedy.

A second instance of Ovidian imitation in the *Thyestes* lets us reflect on both the *Metamorphoses* and the *Heroides*. Here is Atreus, attempting to define the limits of vengeance:

nescioquid animus maius et solito amplius
supraque fines moris humani tumet
instatque pigris manibus; haud quid sit scio,
sed grande quiddam est.

[20] Tarrant 1985 (*Thy.* 741).

My mind swells with something larger and more powerful than what is customary, something beyond the limits of human habits, and it urges my idle hands to act. I hardly know what it is, but it is something great. (Sen. *Thy.* 267–70)

His certainty that his revenge will have some magnitude (*grande quiddam*, 270), coupled with his uncertainty about the specifics (*haud quid sit scio*, 269), recalls Procne as she prepares to retaliate against Tereus in *Met.* 6:

"magnum quodcumque paravi;
quid sit, adhuc dubito." 619

"I have prepared something great; what it is I do not know." (*Met.* 6.618–19)

In addition, the inchoate plans of Atreus' mind (*nescioquid animus maius … tumet*, 267–8) resemble the ones coming to Medea's mind at the end of *Her.* 12:

nescio quid certe mens mea maius agit. (*Her.* 12.212)

Tarrant follows an allusive chain from Seneca to Ovid to Ovid: Atreus invokes Medea in *Her.* 12, whose *nescio quid maius* invokes the "revenge-plot" of the lost *Medea*, the same kind of plot that drives the Thyestes.[21]

Although such inferences are plausible, Medea's *nescio quid maius* can be the words of a tragic heroine independent of Ovid's lost play. Seneca's allusion to *Her.* 12 already recalls Medea at her most self-consciously tragic – the moment when she takes her leave of elegy and returns, through her ironic contemplation of revenge, to the Euripidean, Ennian, and Ovidian stages from which she was appropriated.[22] The allusion to Procne in *Met.* 6, a heroine renowned from the Sophoclean and Accian stages (and an intratextual Medea herself), likewise recalls her at a moment representative of tragedy. Although her participation in the deliberative conventions of the tragic monologue is brief – the great revenge monologue of the *Metamorphoses* belongs to Althaea in book 8 – the conventions are evident enough for Seneca to recall them as such.

A further resonance with Ovid, apparent not only in *Thyestes* but also throughout the Senecan corpus, consists in the paradigmatic value

[21] Tarrant 1985 (*Thy.* 269–70).

[22] Trinacty 2007, 67, notes that Seneca's Medea, who feels a heavier pain (*gravior dolor*, 49) and favors greater misdeeds (*maiora scelera*, 50), "appears to be taking up where Ovid's Medea left off in the *Heroides*." In turn, "Seneca is bringing forth a plot 'greater' … than the 'light' … deeds of elegy."

of names. Atreus, for example, begins his deliberations with a startling self-awareness:

> post tot scelera, post fratris dolos
> fasque omne ruptum questibus vanis agis
> iratus Atreus?
>
> After so many wrongs, after your brother's deception and the destruction of all that is right, are you, if you are Atreus moved by anger, acting with empty laments? (Sen. *Thy.* 178–80)

Much like Polyxena in *Met.* 13, whose remembrance of herself at the tomb of Achilles engenders a performance worthy of the stage, Atreus realizes that his being Atreus, and an *iratus* Atreus at that (180), requires a more drastic response to his brother's affronts than lamentation (*questibus vanis*, 179).[23]

Such self-dramatization is most fully developed in the *Medea*, the play with which this book began. Moments before she murders her sons, the heroine meditates on the reciprocal relationship between her identity and her exploits:

> prolusit dolor
> per ista noster: quid manus poterant rudes
> audere magnum, quid puellaris furor?
> Medea nunc sum; crevit ingenium malis …
> quaere materiam, dolor:
> ad omne facinus non rudem dextram afferes.
>
> My anguish has practiced on those other crimes: what great deed were inexperienced hands and girlish rage able to dare? Now I am Medea; my genius has grown with my evil … Seek, my anguish, a new subject: you will turn a skilled hand toward every misdeed. (Sen. *Med.* 907–10, 914–15)

Here Medea fulfills her vow at the play's beginning to become Medea (*Medea – fiam*, 171), with full awareness of what the role entails. Hypsipyle, let us recall, demonstrates similar awareness in *Her.* 6 when contemplating how she would confront her rival: *Medeae Medea forem* (151).[24] Seneca, however, transfers the moment of becoming Medea from Ovid's conditional future to the actual present: *Medea nunc sum* (910).[25] His heroine, by slaying both sons in view of the audience, and especially one in front of Jason (1019), dramatizes her own Medeaness. She asks her husband

[23] Tarrant 1985. [24] Tarrant 1985 notes the parallel.
[25] So Trinacty 2007, 72, noting Medea's use of *fiam* at 171.

whether he now recognizes his wife (*coniugem agnoscis tuam?* 1021). The maiden he married is perhaps unrecognizable, but Medea herself is unmistakable in both word and deed.[26]

As Ovid refashions Vergil, so Seneca refashions Ovid as his own hesitant precursor. The latter's tendencies toward tragic paradigms and violent spectacle are clearly intended not only to recall but also to perfect these tendencies in the former. Although Ovid's characters display awareness of their literary histories, especially where their histories involve tragedy, and take on the paradigmatic function of tragic characters, Seneca's characters return tragic paradigms to the stage, where they constantly guide their performances. Medea becomes her own self-authorizing model.[27] Atreus is equally aware of himself as a paradigm, but his evocation of Procne's words at *Thy.* 269–70 also reveals his familiarity with that heroine's legend as a kind of blueprint for his actions. As Alessandro Schiesaro observes, "Atreus has read his Ovid, and displays through a number of revealing allusions a detailed knowledge of Tereus' story, and in particular of Procne's avenging plans."[28] With regard to violence, we have seen that the distinction between "offstage" and "onstage" in Ovid is often negligible. Nevertheless, these labels are figurative ones, applicable only insofar as we regard the *Metamorphoses* as a theater of epic. In Seneca, whose plays observe conventions of the stage regardless of whether or not they were actually written for the theaters, the labels become literal, and the blurring of offstage and onstage action all the more pronounced. Thyestes, for instance, is revealed in the act of feasting on his children, while Medea kills her sons outside and on top of the *skēnē*. It is one thing to view such acts in Ovid from the perspective of tragic epic, but quite another to visualize them on an actual tragic stage.

Beyond paradigms and spectacles we can point to other features of Ovidian tragedy that seem to have influenced Seneca – or features of Senecan tragedy that Ovid seems to have anticipated. Tarrant highlights many aspects of Senecan dramaturgy, among them the confinement of the chorus to odes, the resulting isolation of the characters, and the overall "dissolution of the dramatic structure." Of the latter aspect he writes,

[26] Boyle 1997, 131–3, discusses self-dramatization and metatheatricality in the final act of the *Medea*.

[27] Trinacty 2007, 75, discusses Medea's use of *materiam* as the object of her *dolor* (914). Seneca's self-conscious heroine, in constructing her own plot, "points both to the means of revenge and the way this telling of the Medea story will be rendered." *OLD* s.v. *materia* 6, 7.

[28] Schiesaro 2003, 77, noting also Thyestes' failure to remember the plight of Tereus. Boyle 1997, 133, notes Jason's failure to understand Medea's and his own literary history.

"[L]ater scenes contradict earlier ones, scenes are juxtaposed without any connecting material, and even within a scene transitions may be sudden and unresolved."[29] Following Leo, Tarrant attributes these and other aspects to postclassical drama.[30] Yet they also seem, in the context of a discussion of Seneca and Ovid, to be a fundamental part of the Ovidian tragic program, as if the *Metamorphoses* and the *Heroides* were Seneca's closest dramaturgical antecedents, quite apart from the putative influence of Ovid's *Medea*.[31] Schiesaro, in turn, believes that the playwright's epicized brand of tragedy lends itself to the exaggerated conception of vengeance in the *Thyestes*: "[E]pic appears from the very beginning of the *Thyestes* as the voice of destruction and violence, of endless horrors and cruel, often excessive revenges"; such a reading applies to Seneca's *Medea* as well.[32] The epic elements within Senecan tragedy call attention to "the constructedness of the tragic experience and [encourage the audience's] speculation on the specific literary features of the tragedy."[33] Much like Tarrant's postclassical and essentializing take on Seneca, Schiesaro's take on the poet's own literary reflexivity could pass for an analysis of Ovid's engagements with tragedy in the *Metamorphoses* and the *Heroides*.

Socio-political readings of Senecan Ovid could take various avenues. We might, as we have begun to do with issues of stage violence, seek to elucidate Roman customs and mores. Or we might try to uncover political allegory in dramas about power abused, a project that brings both Ovid and Seneca in line with Accius, whose stage tyrants (one of whom was Atreus) were clearly a caution against the tumult of the dying republic.[34] But let us instead take a cue from Schiesaro's reading of epic atrocities in the *Thyestes* and see how Senecan tragedy reflects upon *imperium* in Ovidian terms. In the second choral ode of the *Medea*, the Corinthian

[29] Tarrant 1978, both quotations on 228. Schiesaro 2003 explicitly links Ovidian and Senecan disconnectedness: "[B]oth authors have been censured for what critics have seen as their inability to create a coherent continuum between scenes" (250).

[30] Chapter 5, pp. 138–40.

[31] Thus Schiesaro 2003, 84: "Seneca imitates Ovid not only in the subject matter and expressive opinions of his work, but also in his intricate intertextual protocols." Such protocols for Schiesaro are grounded in Ovid's allusions to tragic and epic texts, but I would also include among them the poet's emulation of tragedy itself. Tarrant 1978 is doubtless right in presuming that Seneca's *Medea* was indebted to Ovid's: "His *Medea* and *Thyestes* (which are among his most effective productions) ... were undoubtedly shaped by the corresponding plays by Ovid and Varius" (261).

[32] Schiesaro 2003, 85.

[33] Schiesaro 2003, 251 (brackets mine).

[34] Panoussi 2005 reads the Tereus narrative of book 6 in general social and political terms. On Accian stage tyrants see Chapter 2, pp. 28–9.

men bemoan the transgressive voyage of the *Argo*, which has made the world smaller:

> terminus omnis motus et urbes
> muros terra posuere nova;
> nil qua fuerat sede reliquit
> pervius orbis: Indus gelidum
> potat Araxen, Albin Persae
> Rhenumque bibunt – venient annis
> saecula seris, quibus Oceanus
> vincula rerum laxet et ingens
> pateat tellus Tethysque novos
> detegat orbes nec sit terris
> ultima Thule.

> Every boundary line has shifted and cities place their walls over new territory; the world, now accessible, has left nothing in its original place: the Indian drinks from the chilly Araxes; the Persians, from the Elbe and the Rhine – the age will dawn in later years when Ocean will relax the bonds holding the world together, the broad earth will lie open, Tethys will uncover new worlds, and Thule will not be the furthest of lands. (Sen. *Med.* 369–79)

In Cindy Benton's view, these verses illustrate the dire consequences of Vergil's *imperium sine fine* (*Aen.* 1.279) as boundaries between countries and cultures become permeable. Within the milieu of Seneca's play, such permeability allows the Other, represented by Medea, to journey from the periphery to the center with murderous results. In the milieu of imperial Rome, the dissolution of borders erodes core Roman values such as *frugalitas* and *simplicitas* through the importation and display of foreign goods and treasures, which stimulate unwholesome appetites. Perhaps gravest of all is the loss of Roman national identity, as Rome herself becomes the Other heretofore kept at arm's length.[35]

These concerns are embodied in the very character of Seneca's heroine, reified in the gradual alignment of her identity with the Medea famous from Euripides, Ennius, Ovid, and who knows how many other plays: *Medea nunc sum* (910), the ultimate outsider. As we noted above, her identity is linked to her actions, which depict spatially and visually the process of becoming Medea. Whereas in Euripides' play Medea's sudden appearance atop the *skēnē* signifies a transformation that has already occurred,

[35] Benton 2003, 282–3, citing examples of Senecan disdain for excess from his treatises. Benton follows Boyle 1997, 128, in connecting the second ode of the *Medea* with Vergilian *imperium sine fine.*

in Seneca the heroine climbs to the top of her house, enacting her transformation through vertical movement. Likewise her killing of the children onstage, as opposed to behind the *skēnē*, which violates the Horatian *dictum* that violent deeds are best kept offstage and out of view (*AP* 179–88). In particular she contravenes Horace's precept that a Medea should not murder her children in front of the audience (*ne pueros coram populo Medea trucidet*, 185 Rudd).[36] Such transgressive acts reflect the transgressions of *imperium* at the level of the person and illustrate the dangers of individual excess to the whole. Seneca's configuration of theatrical space brings Ovid's theater of epic center stage, on the one hand feeding the Roman appetite for spectacle, and on the other hand calling that appetite into question by leaving little to the imagination. The poet himself fosters a sense of decadence and decline, presenting his audiences with a certain inevitability:[37] barbarous acts must occur, and they must occur in plain sight. What alternatives does empire offer?

When viewed in a Senecan light, Ovid's enlarged and expanded tragedies reveal nascent anxieties about *imperium* and its ends. For example, Medea's extended tour of the Aegean in *Met.* 7 is at once a display of erudition on the part of the poet, a demonstration of spatial mutability in epic, and a journey with transformative consequences for Medea herself. The last quality is particularly apposite to the vertical movement of Seneca's heroine, which, as in Ovid, is part and parcel of the drama. Yet the scope and speed of Medea's travels are virtually unthinkable outside an imperial context. Just as the voyage of the *Argo* coincides with the ever-expanding boundaries of the empire, so the heroine's one-woman Argonautica, which is itself an expansion of her earlier tour of Thessaly, regards geography in the abstract. The world becomes a collocation of seemingly random points, unified only by the whims of Ovid and Medea, whose every move tests the limits of how much further she can go. Also present is a nascent Senecan inevitability: try as she might, Medea must eventually reach Corinth and take part in the horrors for which she is renowned. This same sense of inevitability also pervades *Her.* 12, whose lovelorn heroine is ultimately obliged to move on to something greater than an amatory epistle.

Ovid's theaters of epic and elegy begin the imperialistic transgressions fully played out in Seneca's tragic theater. As incipient gestures, Ovid's

[36] Note also the Horatian *dictum*, violated in the *Thyestes*, that Atreus' banquet should be kept behind the *skēnē* (*aut [ne] humana palam coquat exta nefarius Atreus*, *AP* 186 Rudd).

[37] On the self-imposed sense of decline among so-called Silver Latin poets see Hinds 1998, 83–91, following G. W. Williams 1978.

negotiations of tragedy have a certain experimental flair, almost a playfulness that contrasts with Senecan *gravitas*. Perhaps this sense owes something to the reign of Augustus, which although hardly a golden age must have seemed so from Seneca's point of view, which was consumed with the political theatrics of Nero. As Ingo Gildenhard and Andrew Zissos suggest, Ovid's strategy in transforming tragedy was to "[deconstruct] centers of Greek civilization en route to Roman ascendancy."[38] Ovid knew not only the dangers of imperialism, but also its possibilities, which when filtered through the poet's characteristic *ingenium* manifest themselves in the almost infinite series of tragic heroes and heroines. The intratextual tragic network of the *Metamorphoses* is suited to epic in its sheer complexity. Yet the network of the *Heroides* is likewise full and intricate, which qualities make it a project suited to the grandeur of the Augustan age. The connections between letters – such as the ones Hypsipyle makes with Medea in poem 6 – enable the heroines to transcend the restrictive boundaries of their letters. Likewise the annexation of the collection within Ovid's epic, an ambitious and sometimes spectacularly problematic appropriation of elegy that encourages the epistles to be read as tragic poems, even speeches. In breaking down boundaries between characters, myths, texts, and genres, Ovid enacts a tragic program that, more than any one play ever could, does what *imperium* does. His transgressive poetry fashions itself after the very spirit of empire, under which the *Heroides* and the *Metamorphoses* become *carmina sine fine*.

3 Exodos

Ovid's literary transgressions, although facilitated by the relatively stable *pax Augusta*, eventually caught up with him. Relegated to Tomis in 8 CE,[39] he cites the causes in *Tr.* 2, his epistle to Augustus:

> perdiderint cum me duo crimina, carmen et error.
>
> Two offenses ruined me, a poem and a mistake. (*Tr.* 2.207)

The *carmen* was the *Ars amatoria*, whose infractions against Augustan mores are alluded to early in the letter (7–9). Bound up with the content of the *Ars* is its format, which is transgressive in its own right: an elegiac experiment in which the code of elegy adulterates the code of didactic, all

[38] Gildenhard and Zissos 2007, 23 (brackets mine).
[39] Syme 1978, ch. 12, remains a useful study of Ovid's relegation.

in the service of defining the rules of adultery in Augustan Rome. The *Ars* in effect shows what the *Metamorphoses* and the *Heroides*, with their abundant displays of obsessive *eros*, might have looked like in a contemporary rather than mythical context.

Along with the transgressive *carmen* went some kind of transgressive act – *error* – which implies that Ovid somehow found himself in the wrong place at the wrong time. The poet's recollection of the incident in *Tr.* 2 supports this implication:

> cur aliquid vidi? cur noxia lumina feci?
> cur imprudenti cognita culpa mihi? 104

> Why did I see something at all? Why did I make my vision culpable? Why was I so imprudent as to have knowledge of a fault? (*Tr.* 2.103–4)

Whatever Ovid saw was better left unseen.[40] His misfortune in viewing the unviewable prompts a mythical comparison:

> inscius Actaeon vidit sine veste Dianam: 105
> praeda fuit canibus non minus ille suis.

> Actaeon, although it was not his intent, saw Diana undressed: nevertheless he fell prey to his own pack. (*Tr.* 2.105–6)

The mention of Actaeon associates the poet's own *error* with tragedy. In particular, it recalls *Met.* 3, where Actaeon's story is recounted in full as tragic epic. Here, however the prior treatment is invoked less as epic than as tragedy. Jennifer Ingleheart writes, "Ovid elevates the disaster of his exile to the same level as the [pathos] found in tragedy, evoking for his own fate the pity and terror usually felt by the audiences of … tragedy."[41] Not only does Ovid highlight generic synergy in the *Metamorphoses*, validating readings that privilege the tragic, he retroactively encodes one of his tragic narratives with political awareness born of personal and bitter experience.[42] His prior work becomes an intratext for his "after-career,"[43] a backdrop against which his current sorrows are displayed. The poet presents in his transgressions and complaints the tragic types familiar from

[40] On the consequences of forbidden sight in the exile poetry see Ingleheart 2006, who correlates the many ironies among Ovid's accidental viewing, the publication of the *Ars*, Augustus' viewing of the poem, and his sanctioning corrupt spectacles in Rome.

[41] Ingleheart 2006, 74–5. See also Liveley 2011, 4–5: "Ovid regarded his punishment as akin to the tragic transformations described in his own *Metamorphoses*."

[42] On the rewriting of the *Metamorphoses* in Ovid's exile poetry see Hinds 1985 and 1999.

[43] After-career: Hardie and Moore 2010, 6.

his oeuvre: the ephebe who traverses the wrong threshold, and the heroine whose letter has no hope of a reply.[44] The difference is that both roles are played by Ovid himself, an erstwhile tragic poet but now the protagonist in a tragedy he cannot – for once – transform.

[44] Rosenmeyer 1997 compares the *Heroides* and the *Tristia* in epistolary terms. Compare Barsby 1978, 44: "[T]he laments of heroines separated from their lovers have become the laments of the poet separated from his fatherland and friends."

Bibliography

Abbreviations of journal titles follow the conventions of *L'Année Philologique* (Paris 1924–). Other abbreviations follow the *Oxford Classical Dictionary* (4th edn., 2012).

Adams, J. N. (1982) *The Latin Sexual Vocabulary*. Baltimore, Md.

Álvarez Morán, M. C. and R. M. Iglesias Montiel (2006) "Hécuba, «mater orba» (Ov. *Met.* XIII 399–575)," in *«Koinòs lógos»: homenaje al profesor José García López*, ed. E. Calderón Dorda, A. Morales Ortiz, and M. Valverde Sánchez. Murcia: 35–50.

Anderson, W. S. (ed.) (1972) *Ovid's Metamorphoses: Books 6–10*. Norman, Okla.

(1973) "The *Heroides*," in *Ovid*, ed. J. Binns. Boston: 49–83.

(1989) "Lycaon: Ovid's deceptive paradigm in *Metamorphoses* 1," *ICS* 14: 91–101.

(ed.) (1997) *Ovid's Metamorphoses: Books 1–5*. Norman, Okla.

Arcellaschi, A. (1990) *Médée dans le théâtre latin d'Ennius à Sénèque*. Rome.

Armstrong, R. (2006) *Cretan Women: Pasiphae, Ariadne, and Phaedra in Latin Poetry*. Oxford.

Auhagen, U. (1999) *Der Monolog bei Ovid*. Tübingen.

(2007) "Rhetoric in Ovid," in *A Companion to Roman Rhetoric*, ed. W. J. Dominik and J. Hall. Malden, Mass.: 413–24.

Austin, R. G. (ed.) (1955) *P. Vergili Maronis Aeneidos Liber Quartus*. Oxford.

Bain, D. (1975) "Audience address in Greek tragedy," *CQ* 25: 13–25.

(1977) *Actors and Audience: A Study of Asides and Related Conventions in Greek Drama*. Oxford.

Barchiesi, A. (1993) "Future reflexive: two modes of allusion and Ovid's *Heroides*," *HSPh* 95: 334–65.

(1996) Review of Heinze 1903/1993. *JRS* 86: 229–31.

(1997) "Endgames. Ovid's *Metamorphoses* 15 and *Fasti* 6," in *Classical Closure: Reading the End in Greek and Latin Literature*, ed. D. H. Roberts, F. M. Dunn, and D. Fowler. Princeton: 181–208.

(ed.) (2005): See *Ovidio, Metamorfosi*, vol. I.

Barchiesi, A. and P. Hardie (2010) "The Ovidian career model: Ovid, Gallus, Apuleius, Boccaccio," in Hardie and Moore (eds.), 59–88.

Barchiesi, A. and G. Rosati (eds.) (2007): See *Ovidio, Metamorfosi*, vol. II.

Barkan, L. (1986) *The Gods Made Flesh: Metamorphosis and the Pursuit of Paganism*. New Haven, Conn.
Barlow, S. A. (ed.) (1986) *Euripides: Trojan Women*. Warminster.
Barner, W. (1971) "Die Monodie," in *Die Bauformen der griechischen Tragödie*, ed. W. Jens. Munich: 277–320.
Barrett, J. (2002) *Staged Narrative: Poetics and the Messenger in Greek Tragedy*. Berkeley, Calif.
Barrett, W. S. (ed.) (1964) *Euripides: Hippolytus*. Oxford.
Barsby, J. A. (ed.) (1973) *Ovid's Amores: Book I*. Oxford.
(1978) *Ovid*. Greece & Rome New Surveys in the Classics 12. Oxford.
(1996) "Ovid's *Amores* and Roman comedy," *PLLS* 9: 135–57.
Bartel, H. and A. Simon (eds.) (2010) *Unbinding Medea: Interdisciplinary Approaches to a Classical Myth from Antiquity to the 21st Century*. London.
Barton, C. (1992) *The Sorrows of the Ancient Romans*. Princeton.
Bartsch, S. (1994) *Actors in the Audience: Theatricality and Doublespeak from Nero to Hadrian*. Cambridge, Mass.
Bate, J. (1993) *Shakespeare and Ovid*. Oxford.
Beacham, R. C. (1992) *The Roman Theatre and Its Audience*. Cambridge, Mass.
(1999) *Spectacle Entertainments of Early Imperial Rome*. New Haven, Conn.
Beare, W. (1965) *The Roman Stage: A Short History of Latin Drama in the Time of the Republic*. 3rd edn. London.
Benton, C. (2003) "Bringing the other to center stage: Seneca's *Medea* and the anxieties of imperialism," *Arethusa* 36: 271–84.
Bessone, F. (ed.) (1997) *P. Ovidii Nasonis Heroidum Epistula XII: Medea Iasoni*. Florence.
Bilinski, B. (1957) *Accio ed i Gracchi: Contributo alla storia della plebe e della tragedia romana*. Rome.
Binroth-Bank, C. (1994) *Medea in den Metamorphosen Ovids: Untersuchungen zur ovidischen Erzähl- und Darstellungsweise*. Frankfurt am Main.
Bloch, D. J. (2000) "Ovid's *Heroides* 6: preliminary scenes from the life of an intertextual heroine," *CQ* 50: 197–209.
Boedeker, D. (1997) "Becoming Medea: assimilation in Euripides," in Clauss and Johnston (eds.), 127–48.
Bolton, M. C. (2009) "Gendered Spaces in Ovid's *Heroides*," *CW* 102: 273–90.
Bömer, F. (ed.) (1969–86) *P. Ovidius Naso: Metamorphosen*. 8 vols. Heidelberg.
(1969) Vol. I. *Buch I–III*.
(1976a) Vol. II. *Buch IV–V*.
(1976b) Vol. III. *Buch VI–VII*.
(1977) Vol. IV. *Buch VIII–IX*.
(1980) Vol. V. *Buch X–XI*.
(1982) Vol. VI. *Buch XII–XIII*.
(1986) Vol. VII. *Buch XIV–XV*.
Bond, G. W. (ed.) (1981) *Euripides: Heracles*. Oxford.
Bonner, S. F. (1949) *Roman Declamation in the Late Republic and Early Empire*. Berkeley, Calif.

Booth, J. (ed.) (1991) *Ovid: Amores II*. Warminster.

Boyd, B. W. (ed.) (2002) *Brill's Companion to Ovid*. Leiden.

Boyle, A. J. (1997) *Tragic Seneca: An Essay in the Theatrical Tradition*. London and New York.

(2006) *An Introduction to Roman Tragedy*. London and New York.

Braund, D. (1993) "Dionysiac tragedy in Plutarch, *Crassus*," *CQ* 43: 468–74.

Brown, M. P. (ed.) (1984) *Lucretius: De Rerum Natura I*. Bristol.

Brown, S. A. (1999) *The Metamorphosis of Ovid: From Chaucer to Ted Hughes*. New York.

Burian, P. (1997) "Myth into *muthos*: the shaping of tragic plot," in Easterling (ed.), 178–208.

Bushnell, R. W. (ed.) (2005) *A Companion to Tragedy*. Malden, Mass.

Buxton, R. (2010) "How Medea moves: versions of a myth in Apollonius and elsewhere," in Bartel and Simon (eds.), 25–38.

Cahoon, L. (1998) "Myrrha's tears: Roman epic in performance," American Philological Association. 130th Annual Meeting. Washington, D.C.

Calder, W. M. (1966) "A reconstruction of Sophocles' *Polyxena*," *GRBS* 7: 31–56.

(1974) "Sophocles' *Tereus*: a Thracian tragedy," *Thracia* II: 87–91.

Cameron, A. (1968) "The second edition of Ovid's *Amores*," *CQ* 18: 320–33.

Campbell, D. A. (ed.) (1982). *Greek Lyric Poetry*. 2nd edn. Bristol.

Camps, W. A. (ed.) (1961–7) *Propertius: Elegies*. 4 vols. Cambridge.

(1961) Vol. I. *Book I*.

(1965) Vol. IV. *Book IV*.

(1966) Vol. III. *Book III*.

(1967) Vol. II. *Book II*.

Carucci, M. (2010) "The representation of Medea in the Roman house," in Bartel and Simon (eds.), 53–65.

Casali, S. (1995a) "Strategies of tension (Ovid, *Heroides* 4)," *PCPhS* 41: 1–15.

(1995b) "Tragic irony in Ovid, *Heroides* 9 and 11," *CQ* 45: 505–11.

Casanova-Robin, H. (2009) "Canacé, une héroïne tragique? (Ovide, *Hér*. XI)," in Jouteur (ed.), 53–66.

Cheney, P. (1997) *Marlowe's Counterfeit Profession: Ovid, Spenser, Counter-nationhood*. Toronto.

(2002) "'Jog on, jog on': European career paths," in Cheney and de Armas (eds.), 3–23.

(2004) *Shakespeare, National Poet-Playwright*. Cambridge.

(2010) "Did Shakespeare have a literary career?" in Hardie and Moore (eds.), 160–78.

Cheney, P. and F. A. de Armas (eds.) (2002) *European Literary Careers: The Author from Antiquity to the Renaissance*. Toronto.

Clauss, J. J. (1993) *The Best of the Argonauts: The Redefinition of the Epic Hero in Book 1 of Apollonius' Argonautica*. Berkeley, Calif.

Clauss, J. J. and S. I. Johnston (eds.) (1997) *Medea: Essays on Medea in Myth, Literature, Philosophy, and Art*. Princeton.

Clay, J. S. (2011) *Homer's Trojan Theater: Space, Vision, and Memory in the Iliad*. Cambridge.

Coleman, K. M. (1990) "Fatal charades: Roman executions staged as mythological enactments," *JRS* 80: 44–73.
Collard, C. (1975) "Medea and Dido," *Prometheus* 1: 131–51.
(1981) *Euripides*. Greece & Rome New Surveys in the Classics 14. Oxford.
(ed.) (1991) *Euripides: Hecuba*. Warminster.
Conte, G. B. (1985) *Memoria dei poeti e sistema letterario: Catullo, Virgilio, Ovidio, Lucano*. Turin.
(1986) *The Rhetoric of Imitation: Genre and Poetic Memory in Virgil and Other Latin Poets*. Ithaca, NY.
(1994a) *Genres and Readers: Lucretius, Love Elegy, Pliny's Encyclopedia*. Baltimore, Md.
(1994b) *Latin Literature: A History*. Baltimore, Md., and London.
Costa, C. D. N. (ed.) (1973) *Seneca: Medea*. Oxford.
Courtney, E. (ed.) (1993) *The Fragmentary Latin Poets*. Oxford.
Cowan, R. (2010) "A stranger in a strange land: Medea in Roman republican tragedy," in Bartel and Simon (eds.), 39–52.
Csapo, E. and W. J. Slater (eds.) (1995) *The Context of Ancient Drama*. Ann Arbor, Mich.
Cunningham, M. P. (1949) "The novelty of Ovid's *Heroides*," *CP* 44: 100–6.
Curley, D. (1999) "Metatheater: Heroines and Ephebes in Ovid's *Metamorphoses*." PhD diss. University of Washington, Seattle.
(2003) "Ovid's *Tereus*: theater and metatheater," in Sommerstein (ed.), 163–97.
Currie, H. MacL. (1981) "Ovid and the Roman stage," *ANRW* 2.31.4: 2701–42.
Curtius, E. R. (1953) *European Literature and the Latin Middle Ages*. New York.
Dangel, J. (2009) "Tragédie et élégie en interface dans l'oeuvre ovidienne: essai sur les frontières génériques," in Jouteur (ed.), 21–39.
D'Anna, G. (1959) "La tragedia latina arcaica nelle *Metamorfosi*," in *Atti del convegno internazionale Ovidiano*, vol. II, 217–34. Rome.
(ed.) (1967) *M. Pacuvii Fragmenta*. Rome.
Davies, M. (ed.) (1988) *Epicorum Graecorum Fragmenta*. Göttingen.
(ed.) (1991) *Sophocles: Trachiniae*. Oxford.
Davis, P. J. (1995) "Rewriting Euripides: Ovid, *Heroides* 4," *Scholia* n.s. 4: 41–55.
Denniston, J. D. and D. L. Page (eds.) (1957) *Aeschylus: Agamemnon*. Oxford.
Depew, M. and D. Obbink (eds.) (2000) *Matrices of Genre: Authors, Canons, and Society*. Cambridge, Mass., and London.
Diggle, J. (ed.) (1981–94) *Euripidis Fabulae*. 3 vols. Oxford.
Dodds, E. R. (ed.) (1960) *Euripides: Bacchae*. 2nd edn. Oxford.
Dué, C. (2006) *The Captive Woman's Lament in Greek Tragedy*. Austin, Tex.
Due, O. S. (1974) *Changing Forms: Studies in the Metamorphoses of Ovid*. Copenhagen.
Easterling, P. E. (1997) "From repertoire to canon," in Easterling (ed.), 211–27.
(ed.) (1997) *The Cambridge Companion to Greek Tragedy*. Cambridge.
Enterline, L. (2000) *The Rhetoric of the Body from Ovid to Shakespeare*. Cambridge.
Erasmo, M. (2004) *Roman Tragedy: Theatre to Theatricality*. Austin, Tex.
Ernout, A., A. Meillet, and J. André (eds.) (2001) *Dictionnaire étymologique de la langue latine: histoire des mots*. 4th edn., revised. Paris.

Faider, P. (1922) "Sénèque *De ira* 1.1.4 et la *Médée* d'Ovide," *Musée Belge* 27: 131–3.
Fantham, E. (ed.) (1982) *Seneca's Troades*. Princeton.
(2004) *The Roman World of Cicero's De Oratore*. Oxford.
Farrell, J. (1998) "Reading and writing the *Heroides*," *HSPh* 98: 307–38.
(2002) "Greek lives and Roman careers in the classical *Vita* tradition," in Cheney and de Armas (eds.), 24–46.
(2004) "Ovid's Virgilian career," *MD* 52: 41–55.
Feeney, D. C. (1987) "Following after Hercules, in Virgil and Apollonius," *PVS* 18: 47–85.
(1991) *The Gods in Epic: Poets and Critics of the Classical Tradition*. Oxford.
Feldherr, A. (1997) "Metamorphosis and sacrifice in Ovid's Theban narrative," *MD* 38: 25–55.
(2002) "Metamorphosis in the *Metamorphoses*," in Hardie (ed.), 163–79.
(2010) *Playing Gods: Ovid's Metamorphoses and the Politics of Fiction*. Princeton.
Fitzpatrick, D. (2001) "Sophocles' *Tereus*," *CQ* 51: 90–101.
Fordyce, C. J. (ed.) (1961) *Catullus: A Commentary*. Oxford.
Fowler, D. (2000) "The didactic plot," in Depew and Obbink (eds.), 205–19.
Fowler, R. L. (1987) "The rhetoric of desperation," *HSPh* 91: 5–38.
Fränkel, H. F. (1945) *Ovid, a Poet between Two Worlds*. Berkeley, Calif., and Los Angeles.
Fulkerson, L. (2002) "(Un)Sympathetic magic: a study of *Heroides* 13," *AJPh* 123: 61–87.
(2005) *The Ovidian Heroine as Author: Reading, Writing, and Community in the Heroides*. Cambridge.
Furneaux, H. (ed.) (1939) *Opera Minora*. Oxford.
Galinsky, G. K. (1972) "Hercules Ovidianus (*Metamorphoses* 9, 1–272)," *WS* n.s. 6: 93–116.
(2003) "Greek and Roman Drama and the *Aeneid*," in *Myth, History, and Culture in Republican Rome: Studies in Honour of T. P. Wiseman*, ed. D. Braund and C. Gill. Exeter: 275–94.
Gentili, B. (1979) *Theatrical Performances in the Ancient World: Hellenistic and Early Roman Theater*. Amsterdam.
Gibert, J. C. (1997) "Euripides' *Hippolytus* plays: which came first?" *CQ* 47: 85–97.
Gildenhard, I. and A. Zissos. (1999) "'Somatic economies.' Tragic bodies and poetic design in Ovid's *Metamorphoses*," in Hardie, Barchiesi, and Hinds (eds.), 162–81.
(2000) "Ovid's Narcissus (*Met.* 3.339–510): echoes of Oedipus," *AJPh* 121: 129–47.
(2007) "Barbarian variations: Tereus, Procne and Philomela in Ovid (*Met.* 6.412–674) and beyond," *Dictynna* 4: 1–25.
Glare, P. G. W. (ed.) (1982) *Oxford Latin Dictionary*. Oxford.
Goldberg, S. M. (1996) "The fall and rise of Roman tragedy," *TAPhA* 126: 265–86.
(2005) *Constructing Literature in the Roman Republic: Poetry and Its Reception*. Cambridge.
Graf, F. (2002) "Myth in Ovid," in Hardie (ed.), 108–21.

Gratwick, A. S. (1982) "Drama," in *The Cambridge History of Classical Literature II: Latin Literature*, ed. E. J. Kenney and W. V. Clausen. Cambridge: 77–137.
Gregory, J. (ed.) (2005) *A Companion to Greek Tragedy*. Malden, Mass.
Gruen, E. (1996) *Studies in Greek Culture and Roman Policy*. Berkeley, Calif.
Habinek, T. (2002) "Ovid and empire," in Hardie (ed.), 46–61.
Hall, F. W. and W. Geldart (eds.) (1906) *Aristophanis Comoediae*. 2 vols. Oxford.
Halleran, M. R. (ed.) (1995) *Euripides: Hippolytus*. Warminster.
(1997) "It's not what you say: unspoken allusions in Greek tragedy?" *MD* 39: 151–63.
Halliwell, S. (ed.) (1995) *Aristotle: Poetics*. Cambridge, Mass., and London.
Hammond, N. G. L. and H. H. Scullard (eds.) (1970) *The Oxford Classical Dictionary*. 2nd edn. Oxford.
Hardie, P. (1990) "Ovid's Theban history: the first 'anti-*Aeneid*'?" *CQ* 40: 224–35.
(1995) "Virgil's epic techniques: Heinze ninety years on," *CP* 90: 267–76.
(1997) "Virgil and tragedy," in Martindale (ed.), 312–26.
(2002) "Ovid and early imperial literature," in Hardie (ed.), 34–45.
(ed.) (2002) *The Cambridge Companion to Ovid*. Cambridge.
(2004) "Ovidian middles," in Kyriakidis and De Martino (eds.), 151–82.
Hardie, P. and H. Moore (eds.) (2010) *Classical Literary Careers and Their Reception*. Cambridge.
Hardie, P., A. Barchiesi, and S. Hinds (eds.) (1999) *Ovidian Transformations: Essays on Ovid's Metamorphoses and Its Reception*. Cambridge.
Harrison, E. L. (1972–3) "Why did Venus wear boots? Some reflections on *Aeneid* 1, 314f." *PVS* 12: 10–25.
Harrison, S. J. (2002) "Ovid and genre: evolutions of an elegist," in Hardie (ed.), 79–94.
Haupt, M. and K. Ehwald (eds.) (1916) *Die Metamorphosen des P. Ovidius Naso*. 2 vols. Berlin.
Heinze, R. (1903/1993) *Virgil's Epic Technique*, tr. H. Harvey, D. Harvey, and F. Robertson. Berkeley, Calif.
(1919) *Ovids elegische Erzählung*. Leipzig.
Heinze, T. (ed.) (1997) *Der XII. Heroidenbrief: Medea an Jason; mit einer Beilage: Die Fragmente der Tragödie "Medea."* Mnemosyne Supplementum 170. Leiden and New York.
Helgerson, R. (1983) *Self-Crowned Laureates: Spenser, Jonson, Milton, and the Literary System*. Berkeley, Calif., and Los Angeles.
Henkel, M. D. (1929) *Illustrierte Ausgaben von Ovids Metamorphosen im XV., XVI., und XVII. Jahrhundert*. Vorträge der Bibliothek Warburg 6. Leipzig.
Hinds, S. (1985) "Booking the return trip. Ovid and *Tristia* 1," *PCPhS* 31: 13–32.
(1987a) "Generalising about Ovid," *Ramus* 16: 4–31.
(1987b) *The Metamorphosis of Persephone: Ovid and the Self-conscious Muse*. Cambridge.
(1993) "Medea in Ovid: scenes from the life of an intertextual heroine," *MD* 30: 9–47.
(1998) *Allusion and Intertext: Dynamics of Appropriation in Latin Poetry*. Cambridge.

(1999) "After exile: time and teleology from *Metamorphoses* to *Ibis*," in Hardie, Barchiesi, and Hinds (eds.), 48–67.

(2000) "Essential epic: genre and gender from Macer to Statius," in Depew and Obbink (eds.), 221–44.

(2002) "Landscape with figures: aesthetics of place in the *Metamorphoses* and its tradition," in Hardie (ed.), 122–49.

(2011) "Seneca's Ovidian *loci*," *SIFC* 9: 5–63.

Hine, H. M. (ed.) (2000) *Seneca: Medea*. Warminster.

Hollis, A. S. (ed.) (1977) *Ovid: Ars Amatoria Book I*. Oxford.

(ed.) (1983) *Ovid: Metamorphoses Book VIII*. 2nd edn. Oxford.

Hopkinson, N. (ed.) (2000) *Ovid: Metamorphoses Book XIII*. Cambridge.

Hornblower, S. and A. Spawforth (eds.) (2003) *The Oxford Classical Dictionary*. 3rd edn., revised. Oxford.

Horsfall, N. (1976) "The *Collegium Poetarum*." *BICS* 23: 79–95.

(ed.) (2000) *Virgil, Aeneid 7: A Commentary*. Leiden and Boston, Mass.

Hunter, R. L. (ed.) (1989) *Argonautica Book III*. Cambridge.

(1993) *The Argonautica of Apollonius: Literary Studies*. Cambridge.

Ihm, M. (ed.) (1978) *C. Suetoni Tranquilli Opera*. Vol. I. *De Vita Caesarum Libri VIII*. Stuttgart.

Ingleheart, J. (2006) "What the poet saw: Ovid, the error and the theme of sight in *Tristia* 2," *MD* 56: 63–86.

Jacobson, H. (1974) *Ovid's Heroides*. Princeton.

Jäkel, S. (1979) "The *Aiolos* of Euripides," *GB* 8: 101–18.

Janan, M. (2009) *Reflections in a Serpent's Eye: Thebes in Ovid's Metamorphoses*. Oxford.

Jocelyn, H. D. (ed.) (1967) *The Tragedies of Ennius: The Fragments*. Cambridge.

(1969) "The poet Cn. Naevius, P. Cornelius Scipio and Q. Caecilius Metellus," *Antichthon* 3: 32–47.

(1980) "The fate of Varius' *Thyestes*," *CQ* 30: 387–400.

Jolivet, J.-C. (2009) " Quelques remarques sur la péripétie et la reconnaissance dans l'oeuvre ovidienne," in Jouteur (ed.), 41–52.

Jouteur, I. (2009) "Une lettre dans les coulisses de la tragédie (*Hér.* XII)," in Jouteur (ed.), 67–88.

(ed.) (2009) *La théâtralité de l'oeuvre ovidienne*. Paris.

Kamerbeek, J. C. (ed.) (1959) *The Plays of Sophocles: Commentaries: Part 2, The Trachiniae*. Leiden.

Kannicht, R. (ed.) (2004): See *Tragicorum Graecorum Fragmenta*, vol. V.

Kannicht, R. and B. Snell (eds.) (1981): See *Tragicorum Graecorum Fragmenta*, vol. II.

Karakasis, E. (2010) "Generic consciousness and diction in Ovid: a reading of *Amores* 3, 1," *RFIC* 138: 128–42.

Kauer, R., Lindsay, W. M., and O. Skutsch (eds.) (1958) *P. Terenti Afri Comoediae*. Oxford.

Keith, A. M. (1992) *The Play of Fictions: Studies in Ovid's Metamorphoses Book 2*. Ann Arbor, Mich.

(2000) *Engendering Rome*. Cambridge.

(2002) "Sources and genres in Ovid's *Metamorphoses* 1–5," in Boyd (ed.), 235–69.
Kempf, K. F. B. (ed.) (1888) *Valerii Maximi Factorum et Dictorum Memorabilium Libri Novem*. Leipzig.
Kennedy, D. (1984) "The epistolary mode and the first of Ovid's *Heroides*," *CQ* 34: 413–22.
(2002) "Epistolarity: the *Heroides*," in Hardie (ed.), 217–32.
Kenney, E. J. (ed.) (1961) *P. Ovidi Nasonis Amores, Medicamina Faciei Femineae, Ars Amatoria, Remedia Amoris*. Oxford.
(1976) "Ovidius Prooemians," *PCPhS* n.s. 22: 46–53.
(1979) "Two disputed passages in the *Heroides*." *CQ* 29: 394–431.
(1996) *Ovid: Heroides XVI–XXI*. Cambridge.
(2011): See *Ovidio, Metamorfosi*, vol. IV.
Kilgour, M. (2010) "New spins on old rotas: Virgil, Ovid, Milton," in Hardie and Moore (eds.), 179–96.
Kirby, J. T. (1989) "Humor and the unity of Ovid's *Metamorphoses*," in *Studies in Latin Literature and Roman History* 5, ed. C. Deroux. Brussels: 233–51.
Kiso, A. (1984) *The Lost Sophocles*. New York.
Klingner, F. (ed.) (1959) *Q. Horati Flacci Opera*. Leipzig.
Klotz, A. (ed.) (1953) *Scaenicorum Romanorum Fragmenta*. 2 vols. Vol I. *Tragicorum Fragmenta*. Munich.
Knox, B. M. W. (1977) "The *Medea* of Euripides," *YClS* 25: 193–225.
Knox, P. E. (1986a) "Ovid's *Medea* and the authenticity of *Heroides* 12," *HSPh* 90: 207–23.
(1986b) *Ovid's Metamorphoses and the Traditions of Augustan Poetry*. Cambridge.
(ed.) (1995) *Ovid: Heroides: Select Epistles*. Cambridge.
(2002) "*Heroides*: elegiac voices," in Boyd (ed.), 117–39.
(ed.) (2009) *A Companion to Ovid*. Malden, Mass.
Kock, T. (ed.) (1880–8) *Comicorum Atticorum Fragmenta*. 3 vols. Leipzig.
Konstan, D. (1991) "The death of Argus, or what stories do: audience response in ancient fiction and theory," *Helios* 18: 15–30.
Kovacs, D. (1986) "On Medea's great monologue (E. *Med*. 1021–80)," *CQ* 36: 343–52.
(2005) "Text and transmission," in Gregory (ed.), 379–93.
Kroll, W. (1924) *Studien zum Verständnis der römischen Literatur*. Stuttgart.
Kyriakidis, S. (2010) "*Heroides* 20 and 21: motion and emotions," *LICS* 9: 13 pp.
Kyriakidis, S. and F. De Martino (eds.) (2004). *Middles in Latin Poetry*. Bari.
La Penna, A. (1979) *Fra teatro, poesia e politica romana*. Turin.
(1980) "Mezenzio. Una tragedia della tirannia e del titanismo antico." *Maia* 32: 3–30.
Lafaye, G. (1904) *Les Métamorphoses d'Ovide et leurs modèles grecs*. Paris. Reprinted 1971. Hildesheim.
Laird, A. (2003) "Roman epic theatre? Reception, performance, and the poet in Virgil's *Aeneid*," *PCPhS* 49: 19–39.

Larmour, D. H. J. (1990) "Tragic *contaminatio* in Ovid's *Metamorphoses*: Procne and Medea; Philomela and Iphigeneia (6.424–674); Scylla and Phaedra (8. 19–151)," *ICS* 15: 131–41.

Lee, K. H. (ed.) (1976) *Euripides: Troades*. Basingstoke.

Lefkowitz, M. (1973) "Critical stereotypes and the poetry of Sappho," *GRBS* 14: 113–23.

Leo, F. (1878) *De Senecae Tragoediis Observationes Criticae*. Berlin.

(ed.) (1878–9) *L. Annaei Senecae Tragoediae*. 2 vols. Berlin.

(1908) *Der Monolog im Drama: Ein Beitrag zur griechisch-römischen Poetik*. Berlin.

(1913) *Geschichte der römischen Literatur*. Berlin.

Lexicon Iconographicum Mythologiae Classicae. (1981–) Zurich.

Liddell, H. G., R. Scott, H. S. Jones, and R. McKenzie (eds.) (1996) *A Greek–English Lexicon*. Oxford.

Lindheim, S. H. (2003) "To be or not to be a 'new formalist': Ovidian studies in 2003," *Vergilius* 49: 135–51.

Lipking, L. I. (1981) *The Life of the Poet: Beginning and Ending Poetic Careers*. Chicago.

(2010) "Inventing a life – a personal view of literary careers," in Hardie and Moore (eds.), 287–99.

Liveley, G. (2011) *Ovid's Metamorphoses: A Reader's Guide*. London and New York.

Lloyd-Jones, H. (ed.) (1996) *Sophocles: Fragments*. Cambridge, Mass., and London.

Lloyd-Jones, H. and N. G. Wilson (eds.) (1990) *Sophoclis Fabulae*. Oxford.

Loraux, N. (1987) *Tragic Ways of Killing a Woman*. Cambridge, Mass.

Luck, G. (ed.) (1967–77) *P. Ovidius Naso: Tristia* (2 vols.). Heidelberg.

(1967) Vol. I. *Text und Übersetzung*.

(1977) Vol. II. *Kommentar*.

Luschnig, C. A. E. (1988) *Tragic Aporia: A Study of Euripides' Iphigenia at Aulis*. Berwick, Victoria.

Lyne, R. O. A. M. (ed.) (1978) *Ciris: A Poem Attributed to Vergil*. Cambridge.

McKeown, J. C. (ed.) (1987–) *Ovid: Amores: Text, Prolegomena, and Commentary in Four Volumes*. Liverpool.

(1987) Vol. I. *Text and Prolegomena*.

(1989) Vol. II. *A Commentary on Book One*.

(1998) Vol. III. *A Commentary on Book Two*.

Mader, G. (1993) "*Annibas hubristes*: traces of a 'tragic' pattern in Livy's Hannibal portrait in book XXI," *AncSoc* 24: 205–24.

Maggiulli, G. (2007) *Per alta nemora: la poesia del mondo vegetale in Seneca tragico*. Pisa and Rome.

Malcovati, H. (ed.) (1967) *Oratorum Romanorum Fragmenta*. 4th edn. Turin.

(1970): See *M. Tulli Ciceronis Scripta Quae Manserunt Omnia*, vol. IV.

Manuwald, G. (2000) "Pacuvius' *Iliona*: Eine römische Version des Polydorus-Mythos," in Manuwald (ed.), 301–14.

(ed.) (2000) *Identität und Alterität in der frührömischen Tragödie*. Würzburg.

(2003) *Pacuvius. Summus tragicus poeta: Zum dramatischen Profil seiner Tragödien*. Munich and Leipzig.
(2010) *Roman Drama: A Reader*. London.
March, J. R. (1987) *The Creative Poet: Studies on the Treatment of Myths in Greek Poetry*. London.
(2003) "Sophocles' *Tereus* and Euripides' *Medea*," in Sommerstein (ed.), 139–61.
Martin, J. (ed.) (1969). *De Rerum Natura Libri Sex*. Leipzig.
Martindale, C. (ed.) (1988) *Ovid Renewed: Ovidian Influences on Literature and Art from the Middle Ages to the Twentieth Century*. Cambridge.
(1997) *The Cambridge Companion to Virgil*. Cambridge.
Martindale, C. and A. B. Taylor (eds.) (2004) *Shakespeare and the Classics*. Cambridge.
Masselli. G. R. (2009) *Il vecchio e il serpente: Ovidio, Medea e il ringiovanimento di Esone*. Bari.
Mastronarde, D. J. (1979) *Contact and Discontinuity: Some Conventions of Speech and Action on the Greek Tragic Stage*. Classical Studies vol. 21. Berkeley, Calif.
Mattingly, H. B. (1960) "Naevius and the Metelli," *Historia* 9: 414–39.
Michelini, A. N. (1987) *Euripides and the Tragic Tradition*. Madison, Wis.
(1989) "Neophron and Euripides' *Medeia* 1056–80," *TAPhA* 119: 115–35.
Moles, J. L. (1984) "Aristotle and Dido's *hamartia*," *G&R* 31: 48–54.
Monro, D. B. and T. W. Allen (eds.) (1917–20) *Homeri Opera*. 3rd edn. Oxford.
Mossman, J. M. (1995) *Wild Justice: A Study of Euripides' Hecuba*. Oxford.
(1998) "Tragedy and epic in Plutarch's *Alexander*," *JHS* 108: 83–93.
Most, G. W. (2000) "Generating genres: the idea of the tragic," in Depew and Obbink (eds.), 15–35.
Muecke, F. (1983) "Foreshadowing and dramatic irony in the story of Dido," *AJPh* 104: 134–55.
Murray, G. (ed.) (1902–9, 1913) *Euripidis Fabulae*. 3 vols. Oxford.
Mynors, R. A. B. (ed.) (1972) *P. Vergili Maronis Opera*. Oxford.
Nagle, B. R. (1983) "Byblis and Myrrha: two incest narratives in the *Metamorphoses*," *CJ* 78: 301–15.
Nauck, A. (ed.) (1964) *Tragicorum Graecorum Fragmenta*. 2nd edn. Hildesheim.
Newlands, C. (1997) "The metamorphosis of Ovid's Medea," in Clauss and Johnston (eds.), 178–208.
Nikolaidis, A. G. (1985) "Some observations on Ovid's lost Medea," *Latomus* 44: 383–7.
Nugent, G. (2008) "Passion and progress in Ovid's *Metamorphoses*," in *Passions and Moral Progress in Greco-Roman Thought*, ed. J. T. Fitzgerald. London and New York: 153–74.
O'Bryhim, S. (1992) "Hercules' gesture at Ovid, *Met.* 9.210," *RhM* 135: 383–4.
Otis, B. (1970) *Ovid as an Epic Poet*. Cambridge. 2nd edn.
Ovidio, Metamorfosi: a cura di A. Barchiesi. 6 vols. Milan.
Barchiesi, A. (ed.) (2005) Vol. 1. *Libri I–II*.

Barchiesi, A. and G. Rosati (eds.) (2007) Vol. II. *Libri III–IV.*
Rosati, G. P. (ed.) (2009) Vol. III. *Libri V–VI.*
Kenney, E. J. (ed.) (2011) Vol. IV. *Libri VII–IX.*
Padel, R. (1990) "Making space speak," in Winkler and Zeitlin (eds.), 336–65.
Page, D. L. (1934) *Actors' Interpolations in Greek Tragedy.* Oxford.
(ed.) (1938) *Euripides: Medea.* Oxford.
(ed.) (1962) *Poetae Melici Graeci.* Oxford.
Panoussi, V. (2002) "Vergil's Ajax: allusion, tragedy and heroic identity in the *Aeneid*," *CA* 21: 95–134.
(2003) "*Ego maenas*: maenadism, marriage, and the construction of female identity in Catullus 63 and 64," *Helios* 30: 101–26.
(2005) "Polis and empire: Greek tragedy in Rome," in Gregory (ed.), 413–27.
(2009) *Greek Tragedy in Vergil's Aeneid: Ritual, Empire, and Intertext.* Cambridge.
Parker, H. N. (1993) "Sappho schoolmistress," *TAPhA* 123: 309–51.
Pavlock, B. (2009) *The Image of the Poet in Ovid's Metamorphoses.* Madison, Wis.
Pfister, M. (1988). *The Theory and Analysis of Drama.* Cambridge.
Plasberg, O. (ed.) (1922): See *M. Tulli Ciceronis Scripta Quae Manserunt Omnia*, vol. XLII.
Purves, A. C. (2010) *Space and Time in Ancient Greek Narrative.* Cambridge
Quinn, K. (ed.) (1973) *Catullus: The Poems.* 2nd edn. New York.
Rabinowitz, N. S. (1992) "Tragedy and the politics of containment," in *Pornography and Representation in Greece and Rome*, ed. A. Richlin. Oxford: 36–52.
Radt, S. (ed.) (1985): See *Tragicorum Graecorum Fragmenta*, vol. III.
(ed.) (1999): See *Tragicorum Graecorum Fragmenta*, vol. IV.
Raval, S. (2001) "'A Lover's Discourse': Byblis in *Metamorphoses* 9," *Arethusa* 34: 285–311
Rehm, R. (2002) *The Play of Space: Spatial Transformation in Greek Tragedy.* Princeton.
Rhorer, C. C. (1980) "Red and white in Ovid's *Metamorphoses*: the mulberry tree in the tale of Pyramus and Thisbe," *Ramus* 9: 79–88.
Ribbeck, O. (1875) *Die römische Tragödie im Zeitalter der Republik.* Leipzig.
Richardson, L. (1992) *A New Topographical Dictionary of Ancient Rome.* Baltimore, Md.
Rosati, G. (1983) *Narciso e Pigmalione: illusione e spettacolo nelle Metamorfosi di Ovidio.* Florence.
(2005) "Dinamiche temporali nelle *Heroides*," in *La représentation du temps dans la poésie augustéenne = Zur Poetik der Zeit in augusteischer Dichtung*, ed. J. P. Schwindt. Heidelberg: 159–75.
(ed.) (2009): See *Ovidio, Metamorfosi*, vol. III.
Rosenmeyer, P. (1997) "Ovid's *Heroides* and *Tristia*: voices from exile," *Ramus* 26: 29–56.
Ross, D. (1975) *Backgrounds to Augustan Poetry: Gallus, Elegy, and Rome.* Cambridge.

Rudd, N. (ed.) (1989) *Horace: Epistles Book II and Epistle to the Pisones ("Ars Poetica").* Cambridge.

Sabot, A.-F. (1976) *Ovide poète de l'amour dans ses oeuvres de jeunesse.* Paris.

Salzman, M. R. (1998) "Deification in the *Fasti* and the *Metamorphoses*," in *Studies in Latin Literature and Roman History* 9, ed. C. Deroux. Collection Latomus 244. Brussels: 313–46.

Sargent, J. L. (1997) "Ovid's *Heroides:* Libretti for Pantomime." PhD diss. Bryn Mawr.

Scaffai, M. (1999) "Mirra in Ovidio, tra elegia e tragedia (*Met.* 10, 298 sgg.)," *InvLuc* 21: 371–87.

Schadewaldt, W. (1926) *Monolog und Selbstgespräch.* Berlin.

Schiche, Th. (ed.) (1915): See *M. Tulli Ciceronis Scripta Quae Manserunt Omnia,* vol. XLIII.

Schiesaro, A. (2002) "Ovid and the professional discourses of scholarship, religion, rhetoric," in Hardie (ed.), 62–75.

(2003) *The Passions in Play: Thyestes and the Dynamics of Senecan Drama.* Cambridge.

(2005) "Roman tragedy," in Bushnell (ed.), 269–86.

Schlesier, R. (1988) "Die Bakchen des Hades. Dionysische Aspekte von Euripides' *Hekabe,*" *Metis* 3: 111–35.

Scodel, R. (2005) "Tragedy and epic," in Bushnell (ed.), 181–97.

Scripta Quae Manserunt Omnia. 48 vols. Leipzig.

Malcovati, H. (ed.) (1970) Vol. IV. *Brutus.*

Plasberg, O. (ed.) (1922) Vol. XLII. *Academicorum Reliquiae cum Lucullo.*

Schiche, Th. (ed.) (1915) Vol. XLIII. *De Finibus Bonorum et Malorum.*

Seaford, R. (1994) *Reciprocity and Ritual: Homer and Tragedy in the Developing City-State.* Oxford.

Secci, D. A. (2009) "Ovid *Met.* 9.1–97: through the eyes of Achelous," *G&R* 56: 34–54.

Segal, C. P. (1969) *Landscape in Ovid's Metamorphoses: A Study in the Transformations of a Literary Symbol.* Hermes Einzelschrift 23. Wiesbaden.

(1983) "Greek myth as a semiotic and structural system and the problem of tragedy," *Arethusa* 16: 173–98.

(1998) "Ovid's metamorphic bodies: art, gender, and violence in the *Metamorphoses,*" *Arion* 5: 8–41.

(2005) "Il corpo e l'io nelle «Metamorfosi» di Ovidio," in Barchiesi (ed.), xv–ci.

Seng, H. (2007) "Ovids Phaethon-Tragödie (*Met.* 1,747–2,400)," in *Ovid: Werk, Kultur, Wirkung,* ed. M. Janka, U. Schmitzer, and H. Seng. Darmstadt: 163–81.

Shackleton Bailey, D. R. (1956) *Propertiana.* Cambridge.

(ed.) (1977) *Cicero: Epistulae ad Familiares.* 2 vols. Cambridge.

Sharrock, A. (2000) "Intratextuality: texts, parts, and (w)holes in theory," in *Intratextuality: Greek and Roman Textual Relations,* ed. A. Sharrock and H. Morales. Oxford: 1–39.

(2002) "Gender and sexuality," in Hardie (ed.), 95–107.
Showerman, G. and G. P. Goold (eds.) (1977) *Ovid: Heroides, Amores*. 2nd edn. Cambridge, Mass., and London.
Silk, M. S. (1985) "Heracles and Greek tragedy," *G&R* 33: 1–22.
Simon, B. (1988) *Tragic Drama and the Family: Psychoanalytic Studies from Aeschylus to Beckett*. New Haven, CT.
Simpson, J. A. and E. S. C. Weiner (eds.) (1989) *The Oxford English Dictionary*. Oxford.
Skutsch, O. (ed.) (1985) *The Annals of Q. Ennius*. Oxford.
Snell, B. (ed.) (1971): See *Tragicorum Graecorum Fragmenta*, vol. 1.
Solodow, J. B. (1988) *The World of Ovid's Metamorphoses*. Chapel Hill, N.C.
Sommerstein, A. H. (ed.) (2003) *Shards from Kolonos: Studies in Sophoclean Fragments*. Bari.
(2005) "Tragedy and myth," in Bushnell (ed.), 163–80.
Spentzou, E. (2003) *Readers and Writers in Ovid's Heroides: Transgressions of Genre and Gender*. Oxford.
Spoth, F. (1992) *Ovid's Heroides als Elegien*. Munich.
Steiner, H. R. (1952) *Der Traum in der Aeneis*. Noctes Romanae 5. Bern.
Steinmetz, P. (1987) "Der literarische Form der *Epistulae Heroidum* Ovids," *Gymnasium* 94: 128–45.
Suerbaum, W. (2000) "Religiöse Identitäts- und Alteritätsangebote im *Equos Troianus* und im *Lycurgus* des Naevius," in Manuwald (ed.), 185–98.
Syme, R. (1978) *History in Ovid*. Oxford.
Taplin, O. (1977) *The Stagecraft of Aeschylus: The Dramatic Use of Entrances and Exits in Greek Tragedy*. Oxford.
Tarrant, R. J. (1978) "Senecan drama and its antecedents," *HSPh* 82: 213–63.
(ed.) (1985) *Seneca's Thyestes*. Atlanta, Ga.
(2002) "Ovid and ancient literary history," in Hardie (ed.), 13–33.
(ed.) (2004) *P. Ovidi Nasonis Metamorphoses*. Oxford.
(2005) "Roads not taken: untold stories in Ovid's *Metamorphoses*," *MD* 54: 65–89.
Taylor, A. B. (2000) *Shakespeare's Ovid: The Metamorphoses in the Plays and Poems*. Cambridge.
Thalmann, W. G. (1993) "Euripides and Aeschylus: the case of the *Hekabe*," *ClAnt* 12: 126–59.
Theodorakopoulos, E. (1997) "Closure: the book of Virgil," in Martindale (ed.), 155–65.
Thomas, M. D. (1991) "*Sunt lacrimae rerum:* An Analysis of the Tragic Elements of Livy's *Ab urbe condita*." PhD diss. University of Washington, Seattle.
Thomas, R. F. (1982) "Catullus and the polemics of poetic reference (poem 64.1–18)," *AJP* 103: 144–64.
(2004) "Stuck in the middle with you: Virgilian middles," in Kyriakidis and De Martino (eds.), 123–50.
Thomson, D. F. S. (ed.) (1997) *Catullus*. Toronto.
Tissol, G. (1997) *The Face of Nature: Wit, Narrative, and Cosmic Origins in Ovid's Metamorphoses*. Princeton.

Toll, K. (1989) "What's love got to do with it? The invocation to Erato, and patriotism in the *Aeneid*," *QUCC* 33: 107–18.

Tragicorum Graecorum Fragmenta. Göttingen.

Snell, B. (ed.) (1971) Vol. I. *Poetae Minores*.

Kannicht, R. and B. Snell (eds.) (1981) Vol. II. *Adespota*.

Radt, S. (ed.) (1985) Vol. III. *Aeschylus*.

Radt, S. (ed.) (1999) Vol. IV. *Sophocles*. 2nd edn.

Kannicht, R. (ed.) (2004) Vols. V.1 and V.2. *Euripides*.

Treggiari, S. (1991) *Roman Marriage: Iusti Coniuges from the Time of Cicero to the Time of Ulpian*. Oxford.

Trinacty, C. (2007) "Seneca's *Heroides*: elegy in Seneca's *Medea*," *CJ* 103: 63–78.

Vahlen, Johannes. (ed.) (1928) *Ennianae Poesis Reliquiae*. 3rd edn. Leipzig.

Venini, P. (1952) "L'Ecuba di Euripide e Ovidio," *RIL* 85: 364–77.

Verducci, F. (1985) *Ovid's Toyshop of the Heart: Epistulae Heroidum*. Princeton.

Vidal-Naquet, P. (1981) "The black hunter and the origins of the Athenian *ephebeia*," in *Myth, Religion and Society: Structuralist Essays*, ed. R. L. Gordon and M. Detienne. Cambridge: 147–62.

Vogt-Spira, G. (2000) "Ennius' *Medea*: Eine Fremde in Röm," in Manuwald (ed.), 265–75.

Warmington, E. H. (ed.) (1935–40) *The Remains of Old Latin*. 4 vols. Cambridge, Mass., and London.

(1935/1956) Vol. I. *Ennius and Caecilius*. 2nd edn.

(1936) Vol. II. *Livius Andronicus, Naevius, Pacuvius, and Accius*.

West, D. A. and A. J. Woodman (eds.) (1979) *Creative Imitation and Latin Literature*. Cambridge.

West, M. L. (ed.) (1966) *Hesiod: Theogony*. Oxford.

Wheeler, S. (1999) *A Discourse of Wonders: Audience and Performance in Ovid's Metamorphoses*. Philadelphia.

White, P. (2002) "Ovid and the Augustan milieu," in Boyd (ed.), 1–25.

Wigodsky, M. (1972) *Vergil and Early Latin Poetry*. Wiesbaden.

Wilkinson, L. P. (1955) *Ovid Recalled*. Cambridge.

Williams, G. D. (1992) "Ovid's Canace: dramatic irony in *Heroides* 11," *CQ* 42: 201–9.

Williams, G. W. (1968) *Tradition and Originality in Roman Poetry*. Oxford.

(1978) *Change and Decline: Roman Literature in the Early Empire*. Berkeley, Calif., and Los Angeles.

Williams, R. D. (ed.) (1972) *The Aeneid of Virgil: Books 1–6*. London and New York.

Winkler, J. J. (1990) "The ephebes' song: *tragoidia* and *polis*," in Winkler and Zeitlin (eds.), 20–62.

Winkler, J. J. and F. I. Zeitlin (eds.) (1990) *Nothing to Do with Dionysos? Athenian Drama in Its Social Context*. Princeton.

Winterbottom, M. (ed.) (1970) *M. Fabi Quintiliani Institutionis Oratoriae Libri Duodecim*. 2 vols. Oxford.

(1974) *The Elder Seneca: Declamations in Two Volumes*. Cambridge, Mass., and London.

Wise, V. (1982) "Ovid's Medea and the magic of language," *Ramus* 11: 16–25.

Wiseman, T. P. (2002) "Ovid and the stage," in *Ovid's Fasti: Historical Readings at Its Bimillennium*, ed. G. Herbert-Brown. Oxford: 275–99.

Wright, F. W. (1931) *Cicero and the Theater*. Northampton, Mass.

Wyke, M. (1989) "Mistress and metaphor in Augustan elegy," *Helios* 16: 25–47.

Zadorojnyi, A. V. (1997) "Tragedy and epic in Plutarch's *Crassus*," *Hermes* 125: 169–82.

Zaidman, B. L. and P. S. Pantel. (1992) *Religion in the Ancient Greek City*. Cambridge.

Zanker, P. (1988). *The Power of Images in the Age of Augustus*, tr. A. Shapiro. Ann Arbor, Mich.

Zetzel, J. E. G. (1983) "Catullus, Ennius, and the poetics of allusion," *ICS* 8: 251–66.

Zimmermann, B. (2000) "Properz 4, 3 und Ovids *Heroides*," *MH* 57: 130–5.

Index of passages discussed

All tragic fragments are from TrGF or SRF unless otherwise noted

General index